Work, Sex and Power

Work, Sex and Power

The Forces that Shaped Our History

Willie Thompson

PlutoPress
www.plutobooks.com

First published 2015 by Pluto Press
345 Archway Road, London N6 5AA

www.plutobooks.com

British Library Cataloguing in Publication Data
A catalogue record for this book is available from the British Library

ISBN   978 0 7453 3341 0   Hardback
ISBN   978 0 7453 3340 3   Paperback
ISBN   978 1 7837 1272 4   PDF eBook
ISBN   978 1 7837 1274 8   Kindle eBook
ISBN   978 1 7837 1273 1   EPUB eBook

Library of Congress Cataloging in Publication Data applied for

Typeset by Stanford DTP Services, Northampton, England
Text design by Melanie Patrick
Simultaneously printed digitally by CPI Antony Rowe, Chippenham, UK
and Edwards Bros in the United States of America

Contents

'People make their own history, but they do not make it out of whole cloth; they do not make it out of conditions chosen by themselves, but out of such as they find close at hand.'
Marx

'History is not the realm of happiness.'
Hegel

'Every document of civilization is also a document of barbarism.'
Walter Benjamin

'Who, whom?'
Lenin

Preface and Acknowledgements

The structure of this volume is thematic, and consequently historical situations and events which appear in one chapter, such as sex or religion, are on occasion discussed later on from a different angle in another context. Some of the chapters are mostly thematic with examples drawn from a variety of very different historical eras, others have a more chronological slant. My modest intention is to try, in a popular fashion, to examine historical development over an extended period and global scope and make linkages where appropriate to the structures of human interaction in context and situation.

The opening sentence of Michael Mann's four-volume masterpiece, *The Sources of Social Power* is: 'This book is bold and ambitious.' Attempting to discuss similar themes within a single volume feels more like megalomania, and I am particularly conscious of Flaubert's remark (also quoted by Mann) that historical writing is 'like drinking an ocean and pissing a cupful'. Much that could be included has of necessity to be omitted. Nevertheless I think that the project is a worthwhile one and my hope is that it will encourage readers to engage not only with the themes which are addressed here but also the historians referred to in the following pages.

For rendering dates I use the modern forms of Common Era (CE) and Before Common Era (BCE) in place of the older forms still widely used, AD and BC. Occasionally, when relevant in dealing with very long stretches in the past, Before Present (BP) is employed. When quoting from texts written in American English I have for consistency's sake changed the spelling (apart from titles) into British English.

Bibliographical Note – the historiographical area surveyed by this volume is so broad that an appropriate bibliography would be as long as the volume itself – and would then still be inadequate. The texts that have been of most relevance to this sketch are referenced in the endnotes.

Thanks are due to friends and colleagues who have enlightened me greatly in discussion of these themes, particularly Myra Macdonald who has read the text and made many acute and helpful suggestions on both content and style (errors of fact and interpretation are of course my own). Appreciation is also due not least to my ever helpful and endlessly patient editor at Pluto Press, David Castle.

Willie Thompson
May 2014

Historical Timeline

c. 200,000 years before present (BP), Palaeolithic Era
The estimated approximate date for the emergence of *Homo sapiens* in Africa with a stone-using (Palaeolithic) technology, hunter-gatherer economy, and little evidence of representational culture. Other human species (hominins) continued to survive.

c. 60–15 thousand years BP, Palaeolithic Era
H. sapiens by the later date had spread through Africa and Eurasia using more developed stone technology and with significant evidence of representational culture. Other human species, principally Neanderthals, continued to exist in a northern hemisphere dominated by glaciation, and interbreeding has been demonstrated. Modern humans penetrated to Australasia.

c. 15–10 thousand years BP, Mesolithic Era
In this period the ice retreated (with intermissions) in a context of global warming. The Palaeolithic economy shifted its emphasis from hunting to gathering and exploitation, when available, of shoreline marine resources. A more developed stone technology is termed Mesolithic (Middle Stone Age) *H. sapiens* reached the Americas and other human species disappeared.

c. 10,000 years BP, earlier Neolithic Era and agrarian era; first great technological revolution
The ice age ended and the beginnings of agriculture and animal stock rearing made their appearance. The most developed and versatile stone-using (Neolithic) technologies were devised, as were a range of new technologies, especially pottery and weaving. There occurred a big expansion of representational culture and the beginnings of significant social differentiation in more concentrated settlements.

c. 4000 BCE, later Neolithic Era, urbanisation
Urban development commenced in Mesopotamia with local rulers and focused on a local god. The process was accompanied by accelerated social stratification. Technology remained predominantly Neolithic. Written scripts were also developed.

c. 3000–1100 BCE, Bronze Age, beginning of written history
The growing importance of metal tools and weaponry, principally bronze, is apparent, spreading throughout Eurasia. Social stratification and division of labour developed increasingly together with the first empires and divine monarchies, initially in Egypt and Mesopotamia. Similar but Neolithic monarchies developed

in Mesoamerica and the Andean coast. Alphabetic script was devised and spread in western Eurasia.

c. 1000–200 BCE, 'Iron Age'
A shift to iron-using technology occurred throughout Eurasia accompanied by social, political, and cultural disruption, invasion and collapse of empires and dynasties throughout the continent, to be replaced by iron-technology based successors.

c. 600 BCE–500 CE, Hellenistic Era
A succession of agrarian and herding-based empires developed in Eurasia and sub-Saharan Africa with iron-using technology; imperial polities remained the norm. Far-reaching technological and cultural developments advanced, especially in China. 'Salvation religions' spread throughout Eurasia, including monotheist ones. Coined money was invented.

c. 500 CE–1500 CE, final phase of dominance of iron-using territorial empires
The empires and dynasties of the first centuries of the millennium largely collapse, to be replaced by similar successors. States upholding the rival salvation religions of Christianity and Islam were in almost continuous conflict. Technological and scientific advance continued, mostly in China the Arab empire and the Indian subcontinent, supplying part of the foundation for the subsequent technological breakthrough.

c. 1500 CE-present, globalisation era, second great technological revolution
Initial 'globalisation' commenced with European societies' acquisition of the American continents and destruction of native civilisations. Production, communication and technology were all transformed with the shift from natural power sources to ones based on fossil fuels and directed on scientific principles. Western global hegemony was established. These changes were accompanied by unprecedented population growth, global shift from rural to urban predominance, cultural upheavals and greatly enhanced destructiveness of weaponry. New forms of seaborne empires became the norm. In the twentieth century nuclear weaponry threatened universal destruction and environmental dangers were belatedly appreciated.

Introduction: The Fabric of History

The Purpose of this Volume

The 'fabric of history' referred to here is a metaphor for the changing range of activities which constitute the human reality along with the world of material artefacts and social institutions which these activities produce. Within a blink of evolutionary time, the species *Homo sapiens* has transformed the world of inorganic materials, the organic world of plants, animals and other life forms – and especially the world of its own activities and the being of its own existence. It was a development through time within a framework of the three universal, tightly interlocking realities – work, sex and power – with their radiating implications – which constitute the reality of human experience as a social species and provide this volume's title.

It is a perfectly normal and understandable presumption to take for granted that the evolutionary emergence of modern humans and the historical transformations they have brought about were in some sense embedded in the nature of things. As we shall see, that was only very partially the case. *H. sapiens* spread over most of the earth's surface as a foraging hunter-gatherer. It will be argued that in the context of planet-wide climate change around ten millennia ago there was indeed a certain inevitability about the first of the great economic revolutions, the shift towards agricultural production or pastoralism as a dominant lifestyle and also the general form of the resulting social structures which emerged. The second and recent great innovation, to a world of artificially-powered mechanisms, it will be argued however, was a contingency which became a reality only against the odds and was not implicit in the nature of the human species and the world it inhabited. Nor is there reason to presume that this current state of affairs will persist indefinitely; natural or social calamity could knock away its material underpinnings and stop it dead.

The human story is certainly not just one damned thing after another (let alone one damned narrative after another). The argument of this book shares the presumption that although the future is unpredictable (as is true of biological evolution) history in the most general sense, combining economic, social political and cultural activity, has a logic which can be deciphered after the event – but the role of contingency and the potential of paths not taken have to be kept under consideration. History could very often have gone in a quite different direction from the one that was actually realised – the species in its early days for example could easily have been wiped out by natural forces when it was still small in numbers and according to some accounts that was actually the most likely outcome – even bare survival was at that point against the odds.

What is being attempted here therefore is to discuss how and why, within the overall framework of the great transformations, history took the general direction it did and other potential ones proved abortive. Humans are the only species which have a history in that sense; others are the province of natural history or biology. The difference arises from the unique form of consciousness that humans possess, the ability through representation to reflect on the past and evaluate the future, to consciously choose one option or course of action over another, to create and attach importance to symbols. These issues are discussed in subsequent chapters.

The emphasis here is to examine the organic, material, social and cultural forces which underlie these developments throughout the course of human experience, with chronological narrative as a secondary concern – although certainly that has to be taken into account. In 2010 the British Museum produced a well-deserved best seller entitled *A History of the World in 100 Objects*. It is a magnificent piece of work and I thought of supplementing it with *A History of the World in 100 Atrocities*, but decided that would be too horrific to cope with. Walter Benjamin's aphorism, quoted at the beginning of this volume, comes forcefully to mind.

What motivated me to write this book was an intense appreciation of his remark combined with an acute consciousness of the improvements in social relations that have been achieved in certain parts of the world and the fragility of these advances in the face both of malign social forces and environmental deterioration. In this context I continue to regard Marx's perspective, loosely defined as historical materialism, as being the most appropriate for human history and human affairs, though also conscious of its insufficiencies.

Regrettably the conclusion seems inescapable: that the human story up to the present, despite all the remarkable material, intellectual and artistic cultural accomplishments over the millennia, has been overall a pretty bleak and grisly one and that the great majority of human beings who have lived and died over its course have been victims, rather than beneficiaries, of the historical process. The fabric of this volume, if not the fabric of history itself, is somewhat grim and dark – though, as will be evident from the record, there is also a contrary weave of resistance, achievement and hope; history need not in the future continue predominantly as a catalogue of calamity, or in Voltaire's phrase, '. . . nothing more than a tableau of crimes and misfortunes'.

I am concerned to examine and to explain so far as possible both the similarities and the differences between social practices widely separated in time and space. The author of *A History of the World in 100 Objects*, the Director of the British Museum, Neil MacGregor, writes that: 'The similarities between the cultures of the old and the new worlds [Eurasia and the Americas] are . . . strong. Both produced pyramids and mummification, temples and priestly rituals, social structures and buildings that function in similar ways . . .'[1] or as Daniel Lord Smail expresses a similar sentiment: 'We celebrate the diversity of human civilizations, but it is the similarities that are the most startling, the thing that continually reminds us of our common humanity.'[2]

Aspects of these processes have been investigated with great depth and sophistication in recent decades by archaeologists, anthropologists, historical sociologists and historians. Just a few names to mention in this context include Perry Anderson, Christopher Boehm, Fernand Braudel, Jared Diamond, Kent Flannery, Ernest Gellner, Jacquetta Hawkes, Michael Mann, Joyce Marcus, Joseph Needham, Chris Stringer and Ellen Wood.

The objective of this volume is to outline and assess in a concise and easily presented form the conclusions which emerge from their and others' work, and to do so within the context and interpretation of historical materialism. This perspective emphasises that human societies are part of an organic world upon which they are ultimately dependent and which they work collectively to transform to their purposes. The notion that nature exists to suit human convenience is not merely fallacious, it is also very dangerous, and yet the human species is the only one to have *also* separated itself from nature. *That separation*, and the manner in which it has developed, is what constitutes history, and is this volume's central concern.

Work

The many terms used in English in relation to work with positive or negative connotations are a reflection of its multiple forms – ranging from 'achievement' at one end of the scale to 'penal servitude' at the other. Work is human activity intended to achieve satisfaction in one form or another for oneself or other persons, but not all activities of that sort count as work. 'Work' implies the expenditure of effort, more often than not against intrinsic difficulty. The boundary however between work and other sorts of activity such as play or entertainment is a very fuzzy one – and even entertainers work at entertaining. Depending on its quality work can be fulfilling and joyful or it can amount to torture. What is indisputable is that socially organised and directed work, both manual and mental, upon natural substances, has been intrinsic to the transformations of the material and social universe that have occurred throughout history, and the changing character of work is the principal element in social development.

As Engels remarked at Marx's graveside, humans first of all have to secure a food supply, tools and facilities for shelter before they can embark on religious speculation, cultural endeavour, law-making or war-making. This is not to say that the latter activities are of lesser importance in the great scheme of things, or that they do not impact upon and give shape to the former ones. Or, as a school textbook of economic history I recall put it in unconscious tribute to the Marxist 'base/superstructure' metaphor; economic activity, of which work is the principal component, is the foundation of everything else, but not necessarily of greater importance, for foundations exist to carry better things.

Following roughly 190,000 years of life working as hunter-gatherers and foragers, humans have in the last 10,000 years carried through the two radical transformations indicated above. The first of these was certainly profound, but the second, with even greater and constantly accelerating consequences, is just over two centuries old and produced the world we are familiar with – which could be designated as the technological era. Its framework was the economic and social structure known as capitalism, which has dominated the era through its protean development, and generated historically momentous endeavours to modify or abolish it while retaining the technological advantages with which it is associated.

Neither of these transformations, despite a certain inevitability about the first, was consciously intended; they followed from innovations and practices intended to fit in with the then pre-existent social order. A key proposition of this volume is that from an indeterminate period following the initial establishment of agricultural production, but probably around 7000 years BP, human history has been principally the history of forced labour in multiple forms, what Michael Mann terms 'compulsory co-operation' – which implies a social class division, based on very different varieties of work, between enforcers and enforced. Basic forms of this relationship include tribute exaction, slavery, serfdom and wage labour, which are discussed in the course of the volume, as is the resistance they have provoked.

Sex

So far as there is any specific purpose in the non-human biosphere that purpose is reproduction – at the micro level genes propagating themselves – and for any land-dwelling vertebrate sex is a necessary precursor to the production of offspring. However it is more than that as, even outside the human context, the existence of non-reproductive sexual activity among numerous species (up to 1,500 of them) indicates.

The discussion of sex in subsequent chapters takes account not merely of acts of copulation among human beings, but also of the very numerous forms it can assume, the consequences which it carries and the associated activities which surround it, far exceeding those engaged in by other species.

In the metaphor of 'the fabric of history' the cultural and social context of sex is the red thread that runs across it. Not only does it result frequently in reproduction, creating family groups in diverse forms and implying all that is associated with child-rearing in such contexts. It permeates every pore of human culture, generating differentiation in occupational roles, modes of clothing and deportment, the social interaction both between and within the genders in particular societies, and is the dominant theme of cultural production – literary, aural and visual – in every one. Endeavours in some cultures to downplay, hide or even deny the importance of sex, such as taboo words, have only served to emphasise it.

Power

According to Michel Foucault power relations constituted by what he would call 'discourse' are crucial to *every* social interaction (and not only work and sex). We need not go quite so far, but even so there is no denying power's centrality. It has in history permeated social relations of almost every sort – though possibly need not do so in the future. Nevertheless, up to the present the voice that has echoed down the millennia has been the voice of command.

Michael Mann's four-volume magnum opus of historical analysis covering developments from the Bronze Age to the contemporary world is entitled *The Sources of Social Power*, and this book is greatly indebted to it, though diverging on crucial aspects. Mann, whose standpoint reflects the influence of Max Weber, identifies three determinant sources, namely economic power, political power and ideological power. He argues that at different times in history one or other of these forms was the dominant one. This necessarily less extensive single volume is concerned to examine how power relations, namely the manner in which a person or persons are in a position to compel another person or persons to do the bidding of the former and how that relationship was resisted. The aim is to examine the complexities of the interweave between such relationships and the other forces which determine the processes of historical development. The concern here is not only with the manner in which these processes work out on a social scale but also to attempt some explanation of the motivations which can be seen or deduced to have inspired individuals, both those who exercise power and those who resist it.

The text embodies the proposition that the most significant of power relations is the means by which elite groups at various levels of society and different phases throughout history forcefully acquire a greater or lesser part of the product of basic producers, the essential foundation of nearly all historical societies to date. Power of course has other dimensions, from the relations within the nuclear family to organisations of varying complexity.

Over the centuries of written history not only has there been a persistent division between elites and basic producers, but they take persistently repeated forms. While relations between the two show multiple variations, they do so within a limited number of basic social structures. Among elites themselves, the parallels in their mode of operation are even more astonishing, whether we are discussing the court of Sargon the Assyrian, that of the Ming dynasty, the Roman and Byzantine emperors, the Muslim caliph, the medieval kingdoms, the Vatican or the

Politbureau. Whether these are polytheist, monotheist or atheist we find the same forms of intrigue, manoeuvre and treachery, flattery and factional alliance. The instances can be multiplied indefinitely and are reflected in organised collectives further down the social scale.

Progress, What Progress?

Unprecedentedly, a creature that was evolved around 200,000 years ago on the African savannah to cope in its ecological niche with the basic objectives of all living organisms, nutrition and reproduction, also, while not neglecting food and sex, ultimately left a representational record of its thought processes and in addition latterly devised technologies covering the globe, so complex in nature that their construction and functioning requires to be carried on by a limited cadre of experts. Moreover, and most remarkably, it has devoted itself to reflection on life, the universe and everything. In the words of the philosopher Raymond Tallis, 'we are cognitive giants'. The phenomenon may be summed up in the fact that the English word 'culture' has two divergent meanings – either the routines of everyday life with the tools which make them possible; or else what we think of as intellectual/artistic achievement.

It was once popular – it is now much less so – to define that course as 'progress'. The concept of 'progress' is a loaded one, and it normally implies approval, as in the phrase, 'We're making progress', but that is not necessarily so; it can be used in the opposite sense, as in Hogarth's title, 'The Rake's Progress'. In this volume it is used neutrally. Certain realities are unquestionable. Since the emergence of the species which has arrogated to itself the arrogant title of *Homo sapiens sapiens* (colloquially, 'very wise guy') its population has expanded from a very small number, possibly only a few dozen at one stage.[3] Peter J Richardson and Robert Boyd argue that 'At the time of the final modernization of the human brain, humans were most likely a rare and, given the nature of the Pleistocene, endangered species',[4] but now six to seven billion in number and still growing, with increasing average longevity. This growth has been accompanied by, and been dependent upon, an unceasing, if irregular, refinement of technique and ability to exercise control over the natural environment, multiplying beyond measure the quantity and character of consumables and material objects available to (some) individuals and communities – I am writing this with a computer keyboard and screen, not with a reed pen on papyrus.

If you like – and with some reason – you can refer to all that as 'progress', but there are few nowadays who would not recognise at the same time its deficiencies and contradictions. As Jacquetta Hawkes once remarked over half a century ago, a man can have equally depraved thoughts whether driving a Cadillac to LA or trotting to Ur on a donkey.

Likewise, the question being addressed is what lies behind or underneath these similarities in social structures and forms of behaviour taking place in radically different circumstances. The 'fabric of history' does not, needless to say, imply any notion of 'human nature', which merely poses the same question in different terms or evades it altogether. No satisfactory answer is pretended here – finding that is a research programme that has been ongoing over many decades past and will be to come. This book tries to bring together a number of considerations – in however introductory a manner – that helps to illuminate the underlying question. It draws on the work of many authors who have contributed to the discussion, as will become apparent. Most of them are of a recent or relatively recent character.

Not by Bread Alone

For all the importance of basic material considerations in relation to long-term historical development, they do not suffice to explain the sphere of social culture both 'high' and 'low' – the whole range from leisure to lawmaking, drinking to drama – nor of ideologies, ethics or attitudes to the imagined invisible world which have at all times, positively or negatively, permeated the waking lives of every human being from cradle to cremation (or alternative means of disposal).

With that in mind, it is scarcely to be disputed that history's course of development is largely determined by the nature of the interaction between productive technique and the hugely varied range of activities, embodied in every collective, from family units to governments, which depend upon it. For example Mao Zedong's aphorism that 'power grows out of the barrel of a gun' implies both a theoretical knowledge and a technology of firearms and explosives. If we can argue that there is a consistency in the socio-economic weave of human societies, nevertheless the patterns of colour incorporated in that weave – in literal terms the range of cultural practices – are as enormously varied and complex as the multiplicity of languages, dialects and argots spoken and written by the bearers of culture. One cultural feature that has had a particularly far-reaching global impact over the past 3,000 and especially the past 2,000 years, has been the emergence, expansion and fragmentation of monotheist religion, originating in a small Levantine community, then spreading and frequently dominating, firstly through Eurasia and part of Australasia, then eventually the remainder of the globe. Its social, cultural and even economic significance has been enormous, and appropriate space is devoted to it in this text, as demonstrating both the consistency and the variation in human practices.

Finally this volume considers contradictions, in the shape of the adverse consequences that have been produced by the course of historical development or progress and the attempts made to overcome them – from the biological consequences of human settlement, increase and agriculture to institutions such as slavery and wage labour or the increasingly destructive powers of improving technology – and eventually to the growing menace of environmental catastrophe which threatens at the present time. To attempt in short compass a general perspective on the course of human development, is no doubt a foolishly ambitious project, but may, hopefully, represent a modest input into the discussion of how humans can cope with a very uncertain future.

To briefly outline the pages that follow, Chapter One is concerned with the place of *Homo sapiens*, humans, in the cosmos, in their planet's biosphere – and that very specific feature of their biology, the consciousness which makes humans what they are. Chapter Two considers the initial millennia of human development, the different species of humans, their migrations, their technologies and what can be known about their lifestyles. Chapter Three deals with the initial agricultural transformation of c.10,000 years BP, its causes and consequences and its continuing heritage. Chapter Four addresses what has been the central reality of human life in all times and places – sex, reproduction and kinship. Chapter Five focuses upon the emergence of two other major realities, domination and hierarchy, the contexts of economic and social exploitation. Chapter Six, dealing with exploitation and violence, examines the praxis of domination and hierarchy. Chapters Seven to Ten examine dimensions of social practice which are intrinsic to the nature of human existence – ethics, religion and identity. Chapter Eleven is concerned with the lead-up to the second great socio-technological transformation, focusing on the centuries prior to the intrusion of European power into the Americas, Eurasia, sub-Saharan Africa and Australasia. Chapters Twelve and Thirteen deal with that transformation itself, in the shape of European-enforced globalisation and the 'Industrial Revolution'. Chapter Fourteen considers the general theme of opportunity costs and unintended consequences throughout history. Chapters Fifteen and Sixteen discuss attempts which have been undertaken throughout history to overturn the structures of domination and exploitation that have characterised historical development; including the most recent and global, namely socialism. Finally, Chapter Seventeen summarises considerations on the significance of humans in the global environment, the central characteristics of their history and prospects for the future.

1

Cosmos, Creatures and Consciousness

Our Place in the Cosmos

In the English language the term 'history' has two distinct though connected meanings. In one sense it can mean a record of human doings, embodied in a written narrative or analysis, sometimes referred to as historiography, and in another the actuality of what occurred in the past. In the narrower sense of the first, the reconstruction of the events involved depends on written records (sometimes supplemented by artwork) – the general form in which the science of historiography is understood, and has a timespan of roughly 5,000 years.

The approximately 2.6 million years of hominin[1] existence on the planet prior to that are reconstructed by archaeologists through material remains of artefacts or preserved body parts. The drawing together of evidence from the millennia of written history and from the longer stretch of archaeological investigation is sometimes referred to as 'Deep History'. The much lengthier span of organic life, extends to around 3.6 billion years, and is studied through biology and evolutionary history. An even greater timespan which saw the formation of the stars, including our own with its planets, and eventually the Big Bang which generated the universe and where it all started, is the province of cosmology. This in its entirety has lately been referred to by some as 'Big History' and all of it is relevant to the present situation of human beings.

We read from time to time, in discussions of the possible universes that might have emerged from the Big Bang, approximately 13.7 billion years ago, assertions that it was fortunate for us that the one which happened to be actualised[2] was also one that happens to be 'favourable to life'. That is a basic error; our universe is for the most part totally inimical to life, which could not conceivably exist either in the cold of interstellar space or in the interior of a star. Its only possible location is as a thin skin on a planet receiving energy inputs from its parent star, along with other conditions which permit the complex chemistry of life to function; and from what is known of our own solar system or the exoplanets identified so far in other systems, few, if any of these, are anywhere like suitable.

Certain conclusions however strongly suggest themselves. The number of exoplanets so far identified is around 5,000 and rising, and these are all comparatively near us by cosmic standards. It is therefore a virtual certainty that there exist many billions of planets throughout our own galaxy. Another near certainty is that the process of evolution that has taken place on our own world was an enormously unlikely outcome. Among the billions of these exoplanets some must be suitably constituted and placed to harbour life forms. The likelihood therefore is that life is actually quite prevalent in the universe. The probability is also that it is mainly if not overwhelmingly unicellular, as it was for most of earth's history and that any multicellular organisms that happen to arise are likely to be primitive and simple.

So far as our own sun's family is concerned, on no other of its planets could multicellular organisms survive for more than a few seconds. Extremophile bacteria could perhaps just possibly cope with Mars, some of the Jovian moons or Saturn's moon Titan, but even that is extremely doubtful, and in any case hardly counts. In this particular region of our galaxy, at any rate, we are utterly alone. A further consideration applies to the galaxy as a whole.

It seems that our own galaxy is untypical compared to its neighbours, especially the nearest one, the Andromeda galaxy (with which we are on eventual collision course). The big black hole at the centre of our galaxy, though millions of times larger than the sun, is relatively small as such entities go, and unusually quiescent.[3] The one in Andromeda is much larger and much more active, blasting out deadly radiation in every direction as it consumes interstellar gas and stars caught in its gravitational field and probably making life impossible on any of the planets that galaxy contains. As long ago as 1930, Olaf Stapledon's science-fiction novel *First and Last Men* envisaged an end to human life due to the radiation of a nearby supernova – which is by no means an impossible scenario.

What applies to cosmic space also applies to cosmic time. Although the earth has existed for around a third of the universe's age, that span constitutes the merest blink on its scale – recent calculations show a future of 100 trillion years before the last stars are extinguished and an inconceivable 10^{100} years before all matter disintegrates and what was the universe consists of nothing but radiation. In what we think of as the present, 'the train of cosmic time has barely left the station'. Needless to say, humans will be long gone well before the universe looks any different from how it does at the moment, even considerably before the sun expands to vaporise the inner planets, as it inevitably will in another five billion years or so.

The Biological Reality – Our Place in the Organic World

The sponge is not, as you suppose,
A funny kind of weed;
He lives below the deep blue sea,
An animal, like you and me,
Though not so good a breed.

This rhyme[4] prefaced a popular textbook of biology from which I learned a great deal as a teenager. However the last line is open to challenge. Sponges are as much evolved as any other life form, including humans, and are adapted to fit into their environmental niche as much as ourselves. To be sure, they are much less structured or complex than any vertebrate creature, or indeed most other invertebrates, but the sponges, if they had the capacity to reflect on these matters, might not necessarily consider that to be a disadvantage, for while structure and complexity has its advantages and privileges it also has its downsides – which apply to societies as well as to individual organisms; and sentience all too often equals suffering.

Humans, members of the biological domain (or superkingdom) of eukaryotes,[5] and the animal kingdom,[6] share the planet with a multitude of other species in that kingdom, not to speak of the kingdoms of plants and fungi, and the two domains of the prokaryotes (less complex unicellular organisms), archaea and bacteria. Any adequate appreciation of the human story has to take account of these absolutely fundamental relationships.[7]

To get a sense of perspective of where modern humans stand in earth's history, famously, if the whole of that history were compressed into one year, the first clearly fossilised multicellular animals, most famously the trilobites, began to flourish in the seas only in late November, the dinosaurs were extinguished around Christmas, *Homo sapiens* appeared about 20 minutes before the end of the year, with the building of the Egyptian pyramids and everything else that has followed in the last two minutes.

At first glance there appears to have been a continuous drift towards greater complexity throughout life history – prokaryotes to eukaryotes, eukaryotes to multicellular life forms, evolution of these towards continually more complex forms until that process resulted in the human brain, the most complex object in the known universe. This appearance however is almost certainly illusory. For about two thirds of life history, originating approximately 3.5 billion years BP (before present) the prokaryotes were the only life forms, and for at least 80 per cent of the time life has existed on earth the only organisms were unicellular ones. It is an open question whether the initial appearance of living organisms was accidental or possibly predetermined by the chemistry and environment of the era in which they first evolved, but the much later development to eukaryotes and then multicellular organisms was more likely accidental.

The late Stephen Jay Gould argued that if the film of life could be rerun from its beginnings, there is no likelihood that the second showing would produce the same or even similar outcomes. His contention is disputed, opponents pointing to the convergent evolution of life forms to suggest that similar evolutionary pressures would bring about similar if not identical results – the eye for example has evolved several times in slightly different ways, and growing brain power does seem to be an overall feature of life's story to date. Nonetheless Gould's contention appears to be the more convincing. The ancestors of the vertebrates were merely one of many competing phyla[8] in the Cambrian seas, with no more likelihood of survival than several others which failed to make it beyond that era. Jumping forward to the Pleistocene, the era in which *H. sapiens* evolved, if matters had gone slightly differently it would have been the Neanderthals who survived and modern humans who suffered extinction. Whether the former, given time, could have replicated the achievements of the latter is an open question.[9]

The Evolutionary Record

Early life most likely evolved in the seas and so certainly did the original multicellular organisms, of which the ancestors of the fish, the earliest of the vertebrate phylum, were one. Between 400 and 350 million years ago one lineage of lobe-finned fish evolved lungs and colonised the land (arthropods – 'jointed legs' – in various genera including insects and arachnids were there before them). These pioneering vertebrates were confined to watery landscapes both on account of their skins and the necessity of laying their eggs in water, as amphibians do. The development of amniote reproduction by means of shell-enclosed eggs enabled opportunities for wider colonisation and was taken advantage of by two lineages, one of which led to reptiles and their bird relatives, and the other, the synapsids (one of the latter, though it was not ancestral, being the famous sail-backed dimetrodon), to mammals. Early reptiles and synapsids, both descended from amphibians, looked externally very similar.[10]

The emergence of the earliest dinosaurs and the earliest mammals was roughly contemporaneous, but for tens of millions of years the former dominated the macro zoology of the planet. The antiquity of the primate lineage, to which humans belong, is uncertain, though it could extend as far back as 85 million years when the dinosaurs were still flourishing. The ancestors of the primates lived in the trees of tropical forests and evolved characteristics suited to that way of life, including advanced colour vision. Most mammals lack significant colour vision as their ancestors were nocturnal and depended primarily on smell. Primates however possess it, for a tree-dwelling lifestyle necessitates the ability to recognise the ripeness or otherwise of fruit. Arboreal life also resulted in the development of forelimbs which were evolutionarily designed for grasping rather than walking, especially the thumb-like character of the fifth digit.

Most primates are even now primarily arboreal (gorillas and baboons are exceptions) and none apart from the ancestral human lineage, extending back between five and nine million years, are bipeds who walk upright, freeing their forelimbs, no longer principally devoted to climbing, for all manner of other purposes. Modern humans are the only existing mammalian true biped – indeed such ability is the distinguishing anatomical feature of the *Homo* lineage.[11] Donald V Kurtz notes that 'Bipedalism and erect posture required morphological changes in the hominins from head to toe and complementary physiological and metabolic changes that affected females in particular . . . Bipedalism is the key factor that defines early humans'.[12]

Palaeontology indicates that around 15 million years ago a large number of ape species flourished in the tropical and subtropical regions of Africa and Eurasia (none existed in the Americas). Only half a dozen or so now remain, including that hyper-predator with a grossly overdeveloped brain, *H. sapiens*. Humans as well as being social animals are also conscious ones – which is not to say that other animals are necessarily without this attribute, but the complexity of the human form is without parallel in the animal kingdom and is fundamental to history. The question of how much longer human life on earth is likely to persist is one which has increasingly come to the fore. Even if we avoid self-extermination or self-created environmental catastrophe, our own species' lifespan is nonetheless limited as much as is the span of an individual life – or that of any particular species, none of which is forever.

Nevertheless, life on planet earth is extraordinarily tenacious overall and has come through unimaginably catastrophic episodes, including the snowball earth which preceded the Cambrian era, the name attached to the emergence of complex life forms around 550 million years ago with a variety of body plans that are still with us today. Later, enough of life survived the worst era of extinction at the end of the Permian 250 million years ago to evolve the enormous complexity which has characterised the following aeons.

All the life forms visible to the human eye, from the titchiest near-microscopic mite to the mightiest redwood and everything in between, are structured assemblages of eukaryotic cells and in the 'wild', are either looking for another one to eat or liable to being eaten. Among animal species this also applies to each other, apart from a few exceptions such as herbivores so big and powerful (elephants and gorillas for example) as to have no natural predators. These were the grim and brutal realities which confronted the earliest humans.

A Social Animal

Human beings are social animals, a characteristic we share with many other species, both vertebrate and invertebrate, but we occupy a unique position on the planet in two critical respects. Recent research has demonstrated that many species of non-human animals – from birds to primates especially[13] – exhibit cultural differences, characteristic social patterns of behaviour varying between different groups; but humans, by means of their unique attribute[14] of language, do so on a scale wholly beyond comparison with any other animal. Secondly humans, also equipped with hands bearing opposable thumbs, beggar all comparisons in their ability to consciously alter and manipulate the surrounding environment to their convenience. The limited use of tools by non-human species are natural phenomena; culture as it is understood by humans is something very different – and it was not invented by the presently existing species of human.

The distinctive feature of later hominin behaviour, beside the use of language, is the control of fire, something that every other animal avoids. It is this ability above everything else that can be said to mark the transition from nature to culture. The first unambiguous evidence of control and use of fire goes back around 400,000 years but was almost certainly practised from around 1.5 million years BP – it was, like the knapping of stones for greater convenience, first undertaken by earlier species of hominin, from whom *Homo sapiens* undoubtedly inherited it as the first critical step in cultural evolution, marking an existential separation from nature.

The entire span of human history can be reasonably interpreted as a sustained endeavour to increase the separation from nature, to control and eliminate as far as possible the natural constraints that the flesh is heir to and must have afflicted severely the earliest members of the species – attacks by predators, failure of food supply, constant discomfort, constant assault from internal and external parasites[15] and dangerous microbes, early death. Most readers of this volume live in societies and cultures where that project has succeeded spectacularly – too spectacularly indeed for the good of the species. However it required a very long time – around 150–170 thousand years as far as can be ascertained – before *H. sapiens'* culture took a dramatic leap forward both in the material sense of made objects and the abstract one of symbolic expression.

In the course of organic history this last represented another dramatic novelty. While the neurological processes of the trilobite or the triceratops (at least 150 million years apart) are not open to investigation, we can take it for granted that neither they nor coexisting animals gave any thought to the meaning of their lives or reflected upon the origins of the world they lived in. Rather, like every other creature, they simply got on with their invertebrate or reptilian thing – namely feeding and breeding, the dominant concern of every animal apart from *Homo sapiens*. Humans though are different; they possess a unique form of consciousness and through that consciousness they are situated in history *as well as* nature.

Consciousness

Human consciousness remains a phenomenally mysterious phenomenon. Understanding of its relationship to that physical object, the brain, has advanced substantially in recent years in the sense of determining which areas of the brain are associated with which forms of mental activity, but understanding consciousness and its central activity, choice, from the inside as it were, has scarcely improved in the course of the past seven decades.[16]

Based on laboratory experiments (rather than Freudian speculation) it has been suggested that the role of consciousness is a very minor one[17] and that most mental activity indeed takes place at an unconscious level. Certainly most of the physical brain is devoted to controlling unconscious bodily processes and only a minor part of it is concerned with conscious activity, and much conscious activity, to be sure, is combined with an unconscious reflex. It is necessary to think only of activities like driving a car, riding a bicycle or playing tennis.[18] Nevertheless it seems rather improbable that our cities are built and our aircraft flown, let alone our quarks or our cosmos investigated, by individuals who, it has been suggested, remain only 10 per cent conscious (though if applied to warfare or financial speculation the idea might be rather more convincing). This volume is written on the presumption that consciousness is a reality, and since it is basic to the history of our species, the immediate concern in this chapter is to discuss how it might have evolved. In the words of Colin Renfrew, '. . . the notion of mind encompasses intelligent action in the world, not merely cognition within the brain'.[19]

In terms of the human metabolism's energy budget consciousness is a very expensive item indeed and could scarcely have evolved unless it fulfilled some very strong evolutionary purpose. Nevertheless it might give us pause to consider that while there are some individuals with such powers of concentration that they can play several chess games simultaneously while blindfolded, and Stephen Hawking can advance our understanding of the cosmos from inside a totally helpless body, for most of us it is surprising how little control we have over our conscious thought processes if resting and not focusing on a specific activity. Our minds skitter all over time and space with streams of different associations all competing for attention.

Consciousness is a process rather than an entity, swirls of electrochemical activity in the brain. The notion that it could exist apart from its physical basis is nonsense, as absurd as imagining that digestion could exist without bowels or circulation without veins and arteries. Disembodied spirits are a contradiction in terms. Nothing in biology makes sense except in the light of evolution, though evolution, being a hit-and-miss affair, may well produce organs or functions which lack any immediate survival value. However the advantages of cognition, even at primitive levels and not necessarily involving what humans would recognise as consciousness let alone *self*-consciousness, are not difficult to perceive.

Basically, cognition enables an organism to take advantage of alternative possibilities. Filter feeders like sponges, which are loosely articulated assemblages of cells without much differentiation, or the tentacled, more developed, sea anemones and corals, which are anchored in place, have to take whatever comes along in the way of food or danger. There is no need for such organisms to have any conscious awareness of the environment, let alone the self, whereas a mobile organism with a nervous system can 'choose' between flight or fight; if a predator it can select its potential victim, and if fleeing estimate the best available place of refuge.

However Derek Denton (*The Primordial Emotions: The Dawning of Consciousness*)[20] has a rather different interpretation of consciousness' origins. He argues for its emergence as an evolutionary consequence of air-breathing vertebrates – initially amphibians then the early reptiles and the related reptile-like ancestors of mammals – moving into parts of the landscape where amphibian skins would be liable to dry out (frogs for example will let themselves die of dehydration rather than actively seek for water).

Awareness

These creatures therefore had to develop a form of cognition enabling them to monitor the level of their bodily fluids so as to take appropriate action in terms of regulating them, including air, '. . . masterpieces of evolutionary invention emerged with the colonisation of dry land. They reflect the genesis of intentional behaviour'.[21] Denton writes that, 'The theory I wish to propose is that primary consciousness arose from the primal or primordial emotions . . . The creature could then begin to exercise options'[22] He goes on to quote Christopher Higgins, 'The idea of a goal is an integral part of the concept of mind, and so is the idea of intention. An organism which can have intentions, I think, is one which can be said to possess a mind'.[23]

Evidently consciousness is not applicable as a concept to unicellular organisms, though some of those, particularly those concerned with the immune system, give a tolerable imitation. There are multicellular organisms, which nobody would dispute fall into the same category – most evidently plants and fungi – but it applies also to certain animals – a worm cannot be aware in any sense when it is being eaten alive by a bird, or a jellyfish by a turtle – neither has any semblance of a brain, nor do sponges, sea anemones, corals and comb jellies, though some of these have nervous systems.

Organs of cognition at the front of the organism, and an expansion of nervous tissue to coordinate its cognition and its activities, namely a brain, has however been throughout evolutionary history a characteristic of most mobile animals whether invertebrate or vertebrate. It is however to be doubted whether any invertebrate possesses consciousness at any level (though claims have been made for octopuses, connected with their ability in captivity to run mazes, and the bees' honey dance is very impressive): they can probably best be regarded as organic robots. On the other hand the larger-brained non-human mammals at least, and possibly even birds, probably do have some rudimentary form of awareness at a pre-reflective level – domestic pets like dogs and cats, for example, can and do demand food and attention from their owners.

It is indisputable that the brain is the physical basis for consciousness – adequately demonstrated by the fact that brain lesions or chemical influences have more or less dramatic effects upon its operation. It is equally clear that human consciousness, and whatever forms of the same are sustained by other species, have a similar physical basis. How that translates into the subjective experience that we know as consciousness is a so far unanswered conundrum. The fact that conscious activities of particular sorts can be identified as occurring in particular regions of the brain does not get us any nearer to a solution.

The likelihood however is that most species of mammals, while possessing an immediate consciousness inhabit a continuous present – specific memory would be an unnecessary and expensive add-on (some unfortunate humans due to brain damage find themselves in a similar situation). It is also probable that most, though not all, non-human learning operates at an unconscious and reflex level without specific conscious memory. However human consciousness operates at an enormously more complex level which involves not merely awareness but *the awareness of being aware and consequently some sense of personal identity*.

It requires a considerable effort of imagination, but it is not altogether impossible, since no doubt it underlies our own more developed one, to envisage what a non-conceptual consciousness might feel like, one which was simply a focus for sensory stimuli without any terms to name them. It is necessarily speculation, but that may well be the sort of consciousness to be found in nonhuman mammals – and very possibly other classes as well, birds, reptiles, amphibians. A consciousness at that level would permit its owner to have subjective experience of suffering and satisfaction. Scarcely less intriguing and exasperating is the question of *at what point on the evolutionary scale* an organism can be said to experience conscious processes. It has practical implications as well, since on the answer depends one's idea of which experiences it is permissible for humans to subject a non-human organism to – whether experimental animals in laboratories, targets of hunts, farm animals or pets.

The development of brain power in the primate order exceeds anything in previous evolutionary history and is almost certainly related to the fact that with a few exceptions primates are predominantly social animals – cooperation, signalling, status and rank, competitive display and alliances are all very much in evidence and even inter-species cooperation has been observed among monkeys hunted by chimpanzees. The reasoning abilities revealed by chimpanzees through experiments are startlingly impressive and chimpanzees both in the wild and in captivity, recognise themselves as individuals. It has even been suggested that humans should be considered the third chimpanzee species along with the common chimp and the bonobo.

Advanced Cognition

As primates exceed all other orders of animals in cognitive ability, so humans exceed all other primates. Verbal language may possibly not be the only factor in this differentiation (brain size presumably has a lot to do with it) but it is certainly one of the most important. What linguistic abilities were possessed by pre-modern humans is impossible to guess, but the likelihood is that, at least among the later species, it was not wholly absent – Neanderthals certainly had the necessary anatomical structures for speech formation (as chimpanzees do not): '. . . human language and intelligence evolved not to make us better at foraging but to make us better at social networking'.[24]

It can be generally agreed that language is not *absolutely* necessary to consciousness. Given memory, it is possible to think in mental images even if one does not have a word for the object of cognition. However consciousness combined with language is an extraordinarily powerful piece of cognitive equipment; it makes us indeed 'cognitive giants'. It enormously increases the scope for the cooperation seen among other primates such as the chimpanzees who hunt monkeys and the monkeys who aim to avoid capture, and of equal or even greater importance we think ahead and evaluate consequences: 'our hypotheses die in our place', according to the saying. We can as a consequence formulate *and discuss* plans and projects and foresee the consequences of alternative lines of action. The importance of that for survival among forager bands is immeasurable.

Two closely connected further cognitive inheritances from our evolutionary past deserve mention in relation to our mental equipment. Firstly, the fact that humans are pattern-seeking creatures, liable to find meaningful patterns in all manner of unlikely contexts, and secondly, the attraction of false positives. The first of these is ambiguous in effect, but has evident advantages. Observation of patterned regularities can reveal facts about the natural or the social environment that would not otherwise be apparent[25] (and in a modern context this disposition is intrinsic to scientific observation). The second, also perfectly understandable in evolutionary terms, is likewise very useful in a Palaeolithic environment – for the liability to mistakenly identify a threat, i.e. a 'false positive', even though erroneous, is certainly not without its survival advantages. To suspect that a rustle in the undergrowth might be a sabre-tooth, or the night-time shadow on the cave wall could be a leopard, suggests swift evasive action. If you are wrong no harm is done, but if you ignore the danger you may well become the carnivore's dinner.

Like all other animals adult humans are, and with good reason, inherently lazy (energy must be conserved as much as possible); greedy (food should be consumed while the opportunity exists); and cautious. Injury reduces prospects of survival; animals of the same species in the wild do not fight with each other unless territory or mates are in question, and when they do such conflicts are seldom or never pushed to the extent of serious injury. The excitement of the hunt is a contrary impulse if the prey is capable of inflicting significant damage, but few predators apart from humans face that problem.

In humans these first two tendencies can, and have to be, countered because they conflict with social functioning and cohesion, and that is what various forms of socialisation are essentially about. At the same time, like certain other foraging animals, humans are also curious and adventurous, and consequently as individuals pursue personal projects, usually culturally determined or influenced ones. Our concern is with the reality that humans are simultaneously biological organisms focused on feeding and breeding, and social entities operating in the matrix of cultural forms. The contradiction between innate evolutionary impulses and the no less evolutionary demands of socialisation is a foundational part of the human reality. That contradiction applies especially to human sexuality, to be discussed in due course, and while paralleled by that of the chimpanzees and their close cousins the bonobos, is quite unlike that of most other animals, even among the primates.

Consider in this context 'the seven deadly sins'. A moment's thought will demonstrate that as usually codified these are dispositions to 'sin', rather than actual sinful deeds. But gluttony, pride, lust, anger etc., in themselves have a clear survival value – gluttony, greed and sloth for the reasons cited above, pride and envy to inspire dominant behaviour, anger to motivate defence or successful aggression, lust for reproductive success. However if they were to enjoy universal, constant and uncontrolled expression social cohesion would be impossible, the basic requirements of living incapable of functioning. These dispositions are inescapable and even necessary but they have to be appropriately channelled, and in all known instances they are channelled in one form or another.

2

Cooperation, Stone, Bone and Dispersal

Human Beginnings

The Palaeolithic (literally 'Old stone age') or prehistoric origin of human society was no mere preliminary to the historical societies but accounted for by far the majority of the human timespan – no less than 95 per cent of it. The reader has to be advised that this is an intensely contentious area with major divisions among experts regarding interpretation and new discoveries making substantial alterations to the picture almost on a monthly basis. Chris Stringer in his *The Origin of our Species*, 2011, remarks that his volume is likely to be out of date even before publication. What follows is therefore an outline dealing with the broad picture connecting the least disputed developments. The first migration of humans from Africa was that of *Homo erectus*, which spread onwards from what is now the Middle East throughout a large swathe of Asia, including the north of China and Indonesia as well. How these humans reached Java is unclear, since it is unlikely they had boats, but they were certainly there.

Modern humans likewise evolved in Africa, probably from an *erectus* line through *Homo ergaster*, *Homo antecessor* and *Homo heidelbergensis* (which also left Africa and whose European component may have been the Neanderthals' ancestor, though there are other possibilities).[1] There is strong evidence that all of these human species, including *sapiens*, or at least some of their communities, practised cannibalism. After all, if you don't recognise strangers to be as mentally real as yourselves there is no reason in principle why you shouldn't eat them. As Christopher Boehm has remarked, 'There seems to be a special, pejorative, moral "discount" applied to cultural strangers – who are not even considered to be fully human and therefore may be killed with little compunction.'[2]

Migrations – the Palaeolithic and After

The period in which some modern humans first left Africa is highly contentious. The tentative majority view (Recent African Origin hypothesis) is that the definitive migration occurred around 70,000–65,000 years BP and that an earlier exodus, possibly as early as 125,000 years BP, was abortive. Whatever the timing, Palaeolithic modern humans spread much more widely than their predecessors, though that of course took time. They reached every corner of Eurasia and all the surrounding nearby islands, arriving on the Australian continent around 50,000 years BP, and eventually the then peninsula of Tasmania. Paradoxically, in view of later developments, the most distant leading edge of the expansion might have been the most technologically sophisticated. Jared Diamond comments,

[A]s of 40,000 years ago, Native Australian societies enjoyed a big head start over societies of Europe and the other continents. Native Australians developed some of the earliest known stone tools with ground edges, the earliest hafted stone tools (that is, stone axe heads mounted on handles), and by far the earliest watercraft, in the world. Some of the oldest known painting on rock surfaces comes from Australia. Anatomically modern humans may have settled Australia before they settled western Europe.[3]

The continental Australian population of eventually 300,000 failed, due to isolation and their relatively small numbers relative to other continents, to develop further their technology of stone, bone and wood. The even more isolated population of Tasmania (c.4,000 in number), cut off by rising sea levels from the remainder of the continent, suffered significant technological regression, becoming by modern times, 'a uniquely simplified material culture', a circumstance which suggests that population size and diversity was indeed important.[4]

The native Tasmanians, exterminated by colonisers in the nineteenth century (though their genes live on due to some interbreeding) actually lost many of the cultural advances that their ancestors had brought with them, such as bone tools and the capture and consumption of scaly fish. 'The stone technology of the Tasmanians, when first encountered by European explorers in A.D. 1642, was simpler than that prevalent in parts of Upper Palaeolithic Europe tens of thousands of years earlier.'[5] They may even possibly have lost the ability to generate fire, having to rely instead on preserving the source or waiting for fire started by a lightning strike, though this is uncertain. Evidently, however, genetic heritage alone did not suffice to ensure cultural advance, environmental (and possibly cultural) pressures were enormously important.

Somewhat later between 15,000 and 12,000 years BP, three migrations across the Bering land bridge connecting eastern Asia and what is now Alaska, or possibly by coastal travel south along the continental coast brought Palaeolithic modern humans to the Americas, filling every part of the continent from Alaska to Patagonia, eventually developing Neolithic cultures based on maize or potatoes and even the only known examples of Neolithic civilisations.

Humans have always been a migratory species, not surprisingly as the earliest bands of *H. sapiens* had to be constantly on the move in pursuit of food sources, whether animal or vegetable. Nor should simple human curiosity (which can be dangerous, but is on the whole a survival advantage) be altogether neglected. However the migrations of this species, filling every habitable niche on the planet, was totally unprecedented, nor has it ever ceased. Striking instances, some of which will be discussed more extensively later on, include the migration of Indo-European speakers westwards and southwards from their point of origin in the region of modern Iran, bringing iron-using technology into Europe and destroying the Bronze Age Minoan and Mycenaean civilisations of the Aegean, while establishing the cultural foundations of the Indian subcontinent.

Also, probably in the first millennium BCE, the Bantu language group spread southwards in sub-Saharan Africa. Greeks subsequently founded nearly a thousand overseas colony city states between 750 and 550 BCE – even prior to the high point of classical Greece. Contemporaneously the iron-using speakers of the Celtic language group covered much of the European peninsula and beyond from Ireland to modern Turkey, to be followed by Germanic speakers during the first millennium CE, to be followed by Slavonic-speaking peoples during the same era, and behind them steppe nomads from further east, who brought their language to the Carpathian plain.[6] In a rather earlier historical period migrants whom generic evidence links with the island of Taiwan were settling the uninhabited islands of the east Pacific archipelagos.[7]

In the first millennium CE there occurred the Arab migrations from their Arabian homeland across North Africa and up the Nile, as well as south along the Red Sea African coastline. In the following millennium Polynesian settlers colonised the uninhabited New Zealand islands and even reached a location as unlikely as Easter Island. During the past five centuries the extent of migration far from declining, increased phenomenally, consisting of voluntary or semi-voluntary migration from Europe to all the climatically temperate areas of the planet (and in North America across the continent from east to west) as well as wholly coerced migration in the form of the slave trade from Africa to the Americas. World migration continues unabated, though now largely in the opposite direction.

If Palaeolithic humans were anything like their descendants of historical times the most important pull behind their long-range migratory behaviour – outside the customary bounds of their necessarily nomad lifestyle – was more than anything else the hope of improving their life prospects. Since the advancing edge of the expansion into uninhabited territories could have no way of knowing what it was likely to encounter since there were no humans to report back, it is reasonable to conclude that these people moved because their existing territories were unsatisfactory for one reason or another, endangerment or failure of food supply being the most obvious.

Life must have been very precarious, under constant menace from drought which decimated plant and food animal populations and affected sources of drinking water; its opposite, flooding, having the same effect. Other climatic disadvantages would have included dust storms; volcanic eruption; intrusion of predatory animals also being forced to migrate and endangering the animal food supply if not humans directly. Another possibility however that cannot be altogether excluded is the exact contrary – growing population putting pressure upon resources, or even interpersonal conflict within the hunter-gatherer society.

Primitive Revolution?

Flint was the material of choice for the manufacture of Palaeolithic artefacts – at least those which survive for the attention of archaeologists. It is a quartz stone found mostly in the form of nodules originally solidified in chalk strata, but often eroded out, as on beaches. It has a somewhat glassy appearance, superficially resembling the chemically very different and scarcer obsidian or volcanic glass. Its principal virtues are its hardness and the fact that it can be chipped to produce a very sharp edge that, when it becomes worn, can be sharpened again by further chipping (though not as much as obsidian which can take an edge sharper than the sharpest steel).

Flint can therefore be used to form all manner of tools, especially hand axes made from the core of the nodule and cutting knives, spear points or arrowheads from the flakes chipped off. To produce these effects the nodule had to be flaked and trimmed in a precise fashion, which must have required a very high degree of skill and practice. At some point around 50,000 years BP it was discovered that by heating the flint in an appropriate fashion it could be made more malleable for working. When flint was unavailable, inferior sorts of stone or other materials had to serve. Wooden artefacts, of which there must have been many, seldom survive, though those made from bone, such as needles, or antler, including ornaments,[8] often do. Objects made from animal skin or sinew are least durable of all, but occasionally leave behind traces of their existence. Shells too might be used as cutting or scraping instruments or worn as jewellery, as they appear to have been by some Neanderthals. Ochre, a pigment derived from grinding a yellow or reddish pigmented clay and mixed with a suitable binding agent such as fat, for body decoration or marking surfaces such as cave walls, appears to have been used by all communities of modern humans and probably Neanderthals as well.

At some point between 77,000 and 69,000 years BP what has been described as a 'mega-colossal' volcanic eruption occurred on the island of Sumatra, leaving behind Lake Toba, the largest volcanic lake anywhere in the world, and constituting possibly the most massive eruption of the last 25 million years. The effect on the biosphere must have been calamitous (several metres of ash were deposited as far away as India) and it is not unlikely, though not entirely certain, that the human population was significantly reduced, so that an 'evolutionary bottleneck' was created with no more than a few thousand breeding pairs left alive. If the Recent African Origin hypothesis is justified, the eruption may have indeed been connected with the beginning of the migration throughout Eurasia and further afield.[9]

If there is argument about the consequences of the Toba eruption there is none that the event actually occurred. Similarly there is no question about the reality of another development in the region of 50,000–40,000 years BP referred to at times as the Upper Palaeolithic Revolution, but intense disagreement regarding its significance. One hypothesis is that it resulted from a population surge which may have occurred once the presumed bottleneck consequent on the Toba eruption had been passed. It signified in long-term perspective a dramatic enhancement of human capacities in both technology and abstract culture.

A far more diverse kit of stone tools appears in the archaeological record from this point on, especially the flint blade, which must have required an especially high degree of skill to produce. Composite bone and flint tools such as harpoons also make their appearance. For the first time in the record symbolic representations also appear, 'an artistic tradition of astonishing competency',[10] represented at its most accomplished level by the famous cave paintings, mostly of game animals.

How is this to be interpreted? One school of thought holds that genetic development, possibly resulting from the previous 'evolutionary bottleneck', reprogrammed the human cognitive and conceptual apparatus so that intellectual accomplishment previously impossible was now on the agenda, and laid the foundation for the remainder of human history to date. The most far-reaching interpretation of these advances is that proposed by Alan Walker, namely that language, as distinct from a much more primitive form of vocal signalling, also had its origin at that point.

The alternative interpretation, which is also the majority view, is that while the Upper Palaeolithic Revolution was real enough, it was less of a sudden novelty but more of a breakthrough (not necessarily unconnected with human dispersal, population growth and climatic variation) based on a long previous accumulation of technique and experience which eventually assumed much more advanced characteristics. The idea that language may have originated from no earlier than 50,000 years BP does appear very improbable; however the hypothesis that the present existing linguistic groups may have originated in that era has rather more traction.

Clans and Initiation Rituals

Undoubtedly the earliest human collectives (as again is the case with other apes) were limited family groups. Clans, which necessitate the use of conscious conceptualisation, and constitute a wider form of association where the presumed genetic relationship is as often as not a mythical one, are a subsequent development. There is of course no record of when they made their first appearance, but 'The Netsilik data suggest that foragers without clans sometimes created extensive networks of cooperating nonrelatives'.[11]

Clans are an association of supposedly related but separate family groups situated in different locations. Their material advantage is that when a particular familial group falls upon hard times – suffering deprivation or threatened with attack – other members of the clan in better provided circumstances elsewhere are under a social obligation to help them out and entitled to reciprocation when the circumstances are reversed. To justify the arrangement a 'blood relationship', real or imagined, is invoked since kinship is of central conceptual importance in such societies. All the clan members are supposedly descended from the same real or imagined ancestor, human or mythic, reinforced usually by supernatural underpinning. Kent Flannery and Joyce Marcus suggest that,

[Forager] societies with clans enjoy advantages over those without them. They have created large groups of people, claimed as relatives, on whom they can rely for defence from enemies, for amassing the foodstuffs needed for major rituals . . . . The advantages of clan-based society may even tell us something about the disappearance of the Neanderthals. Neanderthals displayed low population densities and show no archaeological evidence for social units larger than the extended family . . . . The Neanderthals may simply have gone the way of most foragers who had no social units larger than the extended family.[12]

In spite of the importance of birth relationships Flannery and Marcus note that while one is born into a family one has to be initiated into a clan, and initiation rituals are of central importance in all forager communities; they continue into the early agrarian ones and persist even in places which develop into urban concentrations. It has been suggested that Greek drama had its origin in initiation rituals associated with the god Dionysius.[13] Initiation rituals continue into the present, most notoriously in US student fraternities, but also in schools, military establishments, workplaces and suchlike institutions. They used to be an almost invariable feature at the conclusion of an apprenticeship in the skilled trades of British industry. These latter examples are essentially rather vicious games, but in prehistory and among existing clan societies they were and are a very serious business. While extending also to women, initiation rites mostly applied to males and normally, though not invariably, involved interference with their genitals in one way or another (as tends still to be the case).

Initiation usually proceeded according to the following pattern. Groups of young males on the verge of manhood were taken away from their normal surroundings by designated practitioners, and subjected to painful ordeals, circumcision being a very common one, with the aim both of requiring them to endure painful experience and to fix the experience in their memory, as well as creating a feeling of companionship from having suffered the ordeal together. Following this they were then initiated into the secrets of the clan and the universe as understood by the clan elders. They were next returned to their normal surroundings where celebrations were held to mark their emergence into adulthood and then full membership of the clan. For elites, royalty and particularly monarchs, special initiation rituals were often prescribed. Among one West African tribe, for example, the king was 'recircumcised' – i.e. his entire penis was skinned. Presumably in this case there were not too many applicants for the post – which may have been the idea.

3

The Neolithic Transformation and its Consequences: Settlement, Wealth and Social Differentiation

The hand of history's course at 8000 B.C. lies heavily on us.
—Jared Diamond

This chapter aims to identify and examine briefly a cluster of events which, sometime around 10,000 years ago following the retreat of the last glaciation to date, were to set the stage for all future historical developments. The basic social and cultural structures that have prevailed down to the present day, examined at greater length throughout this volume, were initiated in this period as an inevitable consequence of a fundamental shift in lifestyles. That they were a natural consequence is underlined by the fact that similar developments occurred quite independently within the space of a few millennia in widely separated parts of the globe.

According to Colin Renfrew, quoting Robert M Adams, 'the independent emergence of stratified, politically organised societies based upon a new and more complex division of labour is clearly one of those great transformations which have punctuated the human career only rarely, at long intervals.'[1] The first five millennia or so of these developments can be interpreted only through archaeological remains, while from around 5,000 years BP written documents provide evidence of an entirely novel sort.

The First Agricultural (Neolithic) Revolution

Some signs of incipient agricultural practices are noted as long ago as 70,000 years BP, but these did not lead anywhere, only demonstrating the ingenuity of early *H. sapiens*. It took until the end of the last glaciation, around 10,000 years BP, for the principle to be revived. At that time a Mesolithic[2] hunter-gatherer community or communities in the region which is now termed the Fertile Crescent in the Middle East adopted a new lifestyle,[3] and consequently according to Jared Diamond, '. . . geographic variation in whether, or when, the peoples of different continents became farmers and herders explains to a large extent their subsequent contrasting fates.'[4]

The Mesolithic era was characterised by the disappearance of the tundra big game of the late Palaeolithic and involved instead greater emphasis on the gathering side of the equation and, where possible, the adoption of a seafood diet. The emerging Neolithic[5] economy, in contrast to the nomadism which had defined earlier eras, depended principally on settled habitation, especially at this period in the area of alluvial rivers. It focused on domesticated food crops, in the case of the Fertile Crescent emmer wheat,[6] to be followed rapidly by the domestication of beasts which had previously been hunted as prey, usually cattle, sheep, pigs and equids (principally asses; horses came later) allowing them to be used as a source of meat and skin and in some cases as draught animals. No doubt rising carbon dioxide levels 10,000 BP proved favourable for agriculture. One consequence was that these pioneers had to adjust genetically to a diet containing gluten and milk, which previously had been rejected by human immune systems.[7] They also needed, as historian/philosopher Ernest Gellner remarks, 'a sense of long-term obligation and permanent relations'.[8]

The agricultural revolution did not stop with food crops; other plant species were involved, and the domestication of plant life was followed and accompanied by that of animals. Dogs, all descended from wolves, are almost certainly the first domesticated species, and probably as early as the Palaeolithic, though the earliest definite skeletal evidence is no older than 15,000 years BP. Domesticated dogs are effective companions and assistants for Palaeolithic hunters – domesticated cattle, sheep, llamas, goats or pigs evidently are not. (Horses might be in principle, but never were in reality; they were a hunted meat source and among the last large animals to be domesticated, camels being the last of all.) The domestication of animals was followed by that of birds (pigeons were probably the first) and even of insects – the semi-domesticated honey bee and the wholly domesticated silkworm, the latter being dependent upon humans for survival, the adult breeding form unable even to fly. The Amerindian Neolithic societies however lacked large draught animals.

Overall the consequences, even the relatively immediate ones, were enormous. The shift to agriculture set in motion a cycle of development which transformed the human planet, at first comparatively slowly and eventually with ever-accelerating speed. How it came to be initiated is far from evident and archaeology can only reveal its consequences, doing no more than hint at what might have been the motivations behind its introduction. Latterly the concept of an original Neolithic Revolution, propounded by V Gordon Childe in the 1930s has been challenged on the grounds that the process was replicated elsewhere from the Nile to the Yangtze river valley to the Americas, and settlement prior to agricultural activity certainly occurred, and in different parts of the world. Even so, in global terms the concepts appears to be valid enough. Pre-Neolithic settlements of considerable size have been unearthed, most famously at Göbekli Tepe on the Turkish-Syrian border – though the precise sort of activity which went on in these settlements remains disputed among archaeologists. Michael Mann, the renowned historical sociologist, suggests that pre-Neolithic settlements of flint miners or fishermen were likely developments.

As with revolutions of any sort, whether political, industrial, social or Neolithic, the details always complicate and qualify the main outlines of the concept. The Neolithic was a series of revolutions widely separated in time and place rather than a single event. But the transformation in human lives which they initiated, eventually covering most of the globe, was real enough.

In societies governed by tradition as hunter-gatherers must be, sudden dramatic changes in lifestyle voluntarily arrived at are rare. It has been calculated that agricultural methods depending on vegetable products of the sort practised by the Neolithic farmers have a lower nutritional yield than Mesolithic subsistence practices would have done, not to mention a much less congenial lifestyle for both sexes. As Jared Diamond points out,

> There was often not even a conscious choice between food production and hunting-gathering. . . . in each area of the globe the first people who adopted food production could obviously not have been making a conscious choice or consciously striving toward farming as a goal, because they had never seen farming and had no way of knowing what it would be like.[9]

Anyone who has performed agricultural work (particularly of the arable sort) without machinery will be aware what tedious, laborious and backbreaking toil is involved. Even when the crop has been brought in, tedium and toil continues – mostly for women – in grinding the grains in primitive querns; not to mention the work of processing animal or vegetable fibres into cloth. The adoption of such an economy can be surmised to have been compelled, most likely by changing climatic conditions, to gain access to a more secure source of food supply, if a still highly unreliable one. In one rare instance, namely the coast of the Northeast Pacific Ocean, where seafood was unusually plentiful and easily accessed, a Mesolithic economy could become a settled rather than a nomadic one and no transition to agricultural production took place. Such possibilities do not appear to have obtained anywhere else, and certainly not in the Fertile Crescent where systematic agricultural production originated.[10] Jared Diamond in his account of why agriculture evolved differently in different locations writes that

> [O]ne cannot decide at present whether the origins of Chinese food production were contemporaneous with those in the Fertile Crescent, slightly earlier, or slightly later. At the least, we can say that China was one of the world's first centres of plant and animal domestication. China may actually have encompassed two or more independent centres of origins of food production.[11]

Other Examples

There is some evidence, though no certainty, that Neolithic agricultural practice may have spread from the Fertile Crescent to the Indus valley and laid the foundation for the civilisation which flourished there around the same period as the Egyptian, which was most likely initiated quite independently of the Fertile Crescent. Both the latter and the Indus valley civilisation were dependent on wheat crops, as was the more developed irrigated cultivation which first emerged in Mesopotamia in the sixth millennium BCE.[12] It is unlikely however that the later adoption of rice-based agriculture in the Yangtze valley came about via cultural diffusion. It too is most likely to have been an entirely independent development, and indeed in this case the archaeological evidence demonstrates fairly clearly the transition from a gathering to a cultivating economy. Wherever agriculture developed, Mann notes, 'the overall trend was towards greater social and territorial fixity . . . agricultural success was inseparable from constraint'.[13]

Although full understanding of the Neolithic revolutions remains to be established, what is unquestionable is that the adoption of agriculture in Mesoamerica and the Andean region, the former based on maize and the latter on potato tubers, were entirely isolated developments, independent of each other and evidently of Eurasian ones. Sub-Saharan African agricultural cultures may also have developed independently, though this cannot be known with certainty, and several independent instances in New Guinea also probably did. There is even evidence of its beginnings among the Australian Aboriginals of the temperate eastern zone, where the economic basis prior to European colonisation nevertheless remained a foraging one.

The likelihood is that if the post-Mesolithic agricultural revolutions had not occurred when and where they did, they would have happened at some other times and places, or in other words, once *Homo sapiens* had covered the terrestrial globe this form of living was virtually certain to emerge sooner or later once climatic conditions permitted the production of food crops, even if initially as a supplement to a predominantly gathering economy. The fact that the major instances occur within very roughly the same time period, relatively speaking, all over the world, suggests with near certainty that the impact of the global warming which accompanied the end of the glaciations approximately 10,000 years BP, was a causative factor planet-wide, both putting pressure on the existing resources of a hunting and foraging economy and presenting the possibility of alternative food sources.

Jared Diamond's ground-breaking work, *Guns, Germs and Steel*, includes a very plausible hypothesis, backed up with detailed empirical evidence, of why Eurasian (and Egyptian) developments occurred much earlier and developed much further than those in Mesoamerica, northwestern South America, Australia or sub-Saharan Africa. Basically he contends that geography and biology were intrinsic to the respective outcomes. 'Food production spread much more rapidly to some areas than to others. A major factor contributing to those differing rates of spread turns out to have been the orientation of the continents' axes: predominantly west-east for Eurasia, predominantly north-south for the Americas and Africa.'[14]

Consequently the principal regions of agricultural settlement in Eurasia were located where food crops, particularly those derived from grasses, ripened at approximately similar times, encouraging their spread by imitation. Also, and more importantly, there were far more potential candidates to become food crops, in the shape of seeds, fruits and tubers, than was the case in other parts of the globe. 'Virtually all of [the most suitable grasses] are native to Mediterranean zones or other seasonally dry environments. Furthermore, they are overwhelmingly concentrated in the Fertile Crescent or other parts of western Eurasia's Mediterranean zone, which offered a huge selection to incipient farmers.'[15] They were also easier to domesticate – in the Americas for instance the domestication of maize proved both very difficult, and regionally restricted. It took centuries to accomplish. 'A next stage of crop development [in the Fertile Crescent] included the first fruit and nut trees, domesticated around 4000 B.C. They comprised olives, figs, dates, pomegranates, and grapes.'[16]

The difference in availability of animal candidates for domestication was of equal or perhaps even greater importance. Sheep, pigs, goats and cattle were not only food sources, but in the case of the latter of energy as well, particularly in the use of oxen for transport and ploughing. Likewise with horses, somewhat later, and finally camels. Both of these were sources of milk (rather specialised ones), but much more generally transport and, in the case of horses, agricultural energy as well.

A massive range of innovations accompanied these advances, ones which were central to all succeeding pre-industrial cultures and remain still at the forefront of our own. Among the most important are woven fabrics from either animal or vegetable sources (wool, silk, cotton) and pottery. Although pottery figurines are known from the late Palaeolithic, functional use of this substance, with one known exception, appeared only in the Neolithic. The pottery objects in question are mostly containers, and may well have originated from the practice of lining with clay the baskets or skins used for transporting liquids. In Japan, pottery even *preceded* agriculture. For cutting tools or weaponry however, stone, or occasionally obsidian, remained universal; metal technology still lay millennia in the future.

Even with stone technology, however, an innovation took place; one which has given its name to the era, Palaeolithic (Old Stone Age), replaced by Neolithic (New Stone Age). Alteration occurs in the appearance of the stone instruments. Frequently made by grinding rather than chipping they become more polished and more sophisticated – their often beautiful appearance can still amaze. In some very fertile Mesopotamian areas where any suitable stone was lacking, sickle blades were made of overfired clay, which could be as sharp as glass, but just as fragile.

Economy and Inequality in Eurasia

This section deals with the material basis of inequality in its earlier forms; other dimensions are considered in Chapter 5. Archaeology prior to the appearance of the written word can only reveal to a limited degree the social structures and relationships of the cultures in question, though even that limited degree can be substantial. The remains of buildings can suggest, if not with complete certainty, what kind of activity occurred within them, and if residential, clues to the relative status of the occupant. Indications are even stronger if burial remains of the deceased are found within.

The great Egyptian pyramids and Tutankhamen tomb, albeit from a literate culture, demonstrate beyond any possibility of doubt the mechanical sophistication and expertise not to mention the riches, of the Bronze Age society which created them. Individuals of maximum wealth and prestige, especially rulers, liked to take a lot stuff with them into the afterlife, even though not having future archaeologists in mind. The Sutton Hoo treasure accompanying the burial of an East Anglian king is an example from a very different and possibly illiterate culture. Very few archaeological sites speak so clearly and unmistakably as these spectacular examples, and the degree of social inference which can be drawn from lesser ones is less revealing, though it can still be considerable.[17]

Certain conclusions, from the tentative to the well-established, can usually be arrived at. A settled lifestyle means that stuff can be stored. With the multiplication of stuff, beyond what an individual can eat, wear or carry around (both of non-perishable agricultural produce and manufactured objects of use or decoration) social differentiation inevitably follows. It is speeded up if the well-endowed families (rather than individuals at this stage) help out their less privileged neighbours in times of shortage, for this then sets up an obligation that sooner or later has to be repaid, possibly in labour (or sometimes sexual) services of some kind, and the economic screw is tightened. Moreover, accumulated stuff has to be protected from other covetous fingers and that too has social implications. The early Jericho possessed fortifications (the oldest known) around 8000 BCE, long before the emergence of the first cities in southern Mesopotamia.

The Americas

Thanks to archaeology, for a variety of reasons the origins of agriculture in the Americas is better understood. It emerged in two separate and almost entirely unconnected centres, namely Mesoamerica and coastal Peru, at considerably later dates, 4,000 to 5,000 years behind its Eurasian equivalent. A very informative commentary is to be found in Marcus and Flannery's *The Creation of Inequality*.

In Mesoamerica the foundation plant was maize, developed, with considerable difficulty from its teosinte wild ancestor. Its use spread slowly northwards into the North American southwest, eventually as far north as the Missouri valley. Other food crops included squashes and beans. On what is now the Peruvian coast, this time with the foundation food being the potato, a series of sedentary agricultural communities developed in the valleys of what is now northern Peru.

As was to occur in Eurasia and Africa these communities in due course became part of empires ruled by god-kings and the lineage-based elites around them. The Moche of coastal Peru were to be eventually succeeded by the Inca empire based in the Peruvian highlands. The dominant empire in Mesoamerica following a series of others, most famously the Maya in the Yucatan and adjacent areas, was to be the Mexica or Aztecs. In both these cases this followed a pattern familiar in Eurasia – the ruler of an outlying region of the empire or on its borders, as in Mesopotamia, would take over the empire using military force recruited from kinsmen and dependants.

If the Eurasian equivalents are to be regarded as civilisations, these were certainly civilisations on any account; remarkable that they were based upon Neolithic technology – flint and obsidian were the materials of choice for tools and weaponry, although precious metals were used for decorative purposes and bronze tools were starting to be manufactured in the Inca empire shortly before the Spanish conquest.[18] It is interesting to speculate what might have been the outcome if that civilisation had continued to develop undisturbed.

Social Differentiation

The archaeology of Neolithic agricultural communities makes it evident that they could not have been self-sufficient, but had to engage in trade relations with other communities when necessities such as salt, or indeed luxuries, could not be locally obtained – there were undoubtedly some exchange relations even in the Palaeolithic era.[19] In exogamous clan society trade relations may even have involved trade in sexual partners (and in the case of men or women, depending on culture, accompanied with a dowry of whatever stuff the local community was well supplied with).

Another consequence of agricultural settlement deserves to be mentioned. Since hunter-gatherer times humans[20] have formed close relationships with consciousness-altering substances.[21] Naturally, prior to agriculture these had to be derived from suitable wild plants of the magic mushroom sort. Agriculture opened up a set of wonderful new possibilities – the deliberate manufacture of intoxicating substances out of cultivated products, including honey and fruit – and practically any carbohydrate would do once the technique of fermentation had been developed. The use of barley to make beer was probably the first development; wine followed later.

The domestication of animals did not remain confined to settled agricultural communities. In addition it permitted the emergence of a different kind of society – that of pastoral nomads. One suggestion is that this lifestyle made its appearance around 6000 BCE. Evidently not all domesticated animals were equally fit for a population of nomads, no nomadic society, for example, is known to have concentrated on pigs. Cattle too, in many places, fit awkwardly with this form of social order in view of their rather specialised feeding patterns and nomadic societies dependent on cattle are largely confined to Africa. The preferred animal types for most pastoralist herders are the (geographically very specialised) reindeer and the less specialised sheep, goats, camels and horses. The legendary ancestors of the Hebrew peoples were sheep herders, and, although 'the only pure nomad is a poor nomad' according to one saying, a nomadic lifestyle on occasion could provide opportunities for aggression or the extraction of wealth from settled communities.

The latter point highlights a frequent relationship between pastoralist nomads and settled agricultural populations – one of hostility and frequent hostilities. In some instances the pastoralists, whenever they aspired to take over a settled domain, proceeded to conquer rather than merely levy tribute upon it (especially when, as in the case of the Huns and Mongols, they were dominated by warrior elites and in possession of superior mobility). They then tended to become absorbed into and adopt the ways of the more advanced cultures they had taken over – setting up cycle which would be repeated again in due course. The great medieval Arabic scholar Ibn Khaldun made this kind of cycle the centrepiece of his historical theory.

Settlement and food production from the soil, accompanied with social differentiation, were central themes of the human species' first great transformation. A further central theme however was that in certain geographically suitable parts, steppe land and savannah for the most part, stock raising and herding were adopted as the social norm. As a result in Eurasia and Africa an interaction between agriculturalists and pastoralists was set up which was to dominate significant stretches of pre-modern history. Key aspects of this will be dealt with in subsequent chapters.

4

Gender Differentiation, Sex and Kindred

It is a remarkable feat of nature to weave powerful sexual feelings and desire in the fabric of the brain without revealing the reproductive purpose of those feelings to the eager participants.
—Jaak Panskepp

The basic evolutionary function of the human species, as of all life, is to reproduce itself, with all other activities being directed to that central purpose. As in that of their closest biological relatives, the chimpanzees and bonobos, as well as the slightly more distant other great apes and gibbons (though not monkeys) human reproduction is untypical of most animals both vertebrate and invertebrate. It is not seasonal,[1] but can occur at any time of the year. Humans, while less unique than used to be thought within the animal kingdom[2] in terms of their sexual practice, are certainly more inventive and versatile; their anatomy enables them to assume a multiplicity of copulatory positions far beyond the scope of any other animal, and certainly no other creature has access to the enjoyments of pornography. Sadistic and masochistic behaviours in the sexual sense also appear to be confined to humans. Humans are also the only animals which take pains to conceal their genitals in public, though there are many variant forms within this all but universal practice.

As noted in the previous chapter humans – or rather hominins, for the point relates not only to *H. sapiens* and Neanderthals, but to *H. erectus* and its evolutionary predecessors as well – are the sole mammalian true bipeds. This anatomical peculiarity has enormous consequences not only in the obvious senses of locomotion and the freeing up of the forelimbs for all manner of activities including toolmaking, but socio-sexual implications of the most profound sort, especially when conjoined with the evolutionary hypertrophy of brain and skull. It all represented a very marked difference in hominin social behaviour compared with that of other apes. 'With their hands free, females were able to carry their infants, hold and tend them more intimately, and provide for their needs better, perhaps, than nonhuman primates to whom infants must cling as their mothers move about quadrupedally.'[3]

The pelvises of non-human apes, basically arboreal creatures, are relatively long and narrow and adapted for quadrupedal locomotion on the ground. The hominin pelvis is shaped very differently, and in females is particularly broad and shallow in accordance with the necessities of bipedal pregnancy, and in addition the uterus and vagina are placed more forward in the abdomen. Compared with apes the bipedal hominin female genitalia are more concealed between the legs – whatever significance that may have had for gender and sexual relations in hominin society prior to the adoption of coverings. These changes also make face-to-face copulation possible and usually the preferred position, something very unfeasible for quadrupedal mammals, and this may well have had implications for pair bonding, though of course it is impossible to know.

The Importance of Grandmothers

Of cardinal importance for hominin social relations, however, is the relevance of the hominin (as far as we are concerned, human) female sexual apparatus for childbirth to produce an infant with a relatively huge skull. Evolution has assisted by making the infant's skull plates capable of movement to narrow the head during passage through the birth canal, but that is only a partial solution. Evolution must have favoured the females best adapted to survive the 'obstetrical dilemma' of giving birth to infants with skull formations of exceptional difficulty compared with those of other primates. To cope with that problem, as the species evolved infants were born increasingly immature and therefore requiring longer stretches of nursing and dependency.[4]

Moreover the human vagina is ill-placed to permit unassisted birth, which other ape mothers can do quite easily. It is possible with humans, but extremely difficult and very dangerous – assisted birth is overwhelmingly the norm. And who better to provide the assistance than the mother's own mother, aunts or other experienced older relatives? Hence the importance of grandmothers to human evolution and social evolution, and this consideration is not the only one.

Human infants, toddlers and children, even in forager societies, partly because of their physical constitution, partly on account of the amount of social learning they have to undertake, have an exceptionally long period of dependency compared to any other animal, and yet population sustainability requires mothers to undertake subsequent pregnancies and childbirths while their earlier children remain in a dependent state. Here again grandmothers and great-aunts provide the biological-social solution. Female apes die soon after their menopause; human females do not. Kurtz argues that 'The grandmother hypothesis suggests that postmenopausal women played an unheralded role in the evolution from an ape-like life-history to one more like that characteristic of the genus *Homo* and their associated social organizations, especially the family'.[5]

Sex, Fertility and their Policing

An idea prevalent in the nineteenth century that early humans lived together in a 'primitive horde' practising totally unregulated sexual relations is almost certainly mythical.[6] All social primates sustain a rank order system in their groups (even bonobos, where it is least emphatic) and such ranking almost invariably implies differential access to sexual partners. The almost complete promiscuity of the bonobos (mother–son unions however seem to be avoided) is very much the exception. Differences in rank as a means of restricting and regulating sexual activity is one thing; the need to control population growth in an environment of scarce resources is another; encouraging it when the problem is scarcity rather than surplus of population is something else again. In every known human society in time or space where evidence exists, sexual activity has been hedged around with rules and qualifications and often enough with cultural motivations reaching far beyond those of simple population control.

Noting first of all social restrictions whose rationale is relatively transparent; populations of hunter-gatherer societies and those dependent on unsophisticated forms of agriculture always have very complex systems of family relationship and incest prohibitions which extend far beyond the circle of immediate relatives.[7] The number of permissible potential sexual partners is therefore restricted and those eventually selected (usually by relatives) more often than not confined to persons outside the local community. Thus the intake of new members into the community and the immediate family can be controlled, and possibly advantageous bargaining over territorial rights or dowry (depending on resources available) can be undertaken.

In such societies, especially where there is strong and permanent environmental pressure and a need to restrict population growth, obstacles to enjoyable intercourse may be enjoined by the elders; or even drastic forms of male genital mutilation, usually carried out as part of an initiation ritual, such as crushing one testicle, may be performed to reduce fertility without destroying it altogether; a practice in some Australian Aboriginal societies. On the other hand, when increased fertility is at a premium, one response is to forbid any sort of sexual behaviour which avoids or lowers the likelihood of conception. The injunctions in the Mosaic law against either *coitus interruptus*, or sex with a menstruating woman (liable to the death penalty in Hebrew society) are examples of such social control.

Generally speaking, it is the increase rather than the restriction of fertility which is most commonly favoured, for in prescientific societies death rates from natal mortality, injury, disease or aggression are always in danger of outstripping live birth rates, though agricultural societies had the advantage over nomadic as their mothers could attend simultaneously to larger numbers of infants. Moreover, a population with large numbers of healthy males is more likely to prevail in warfare over one with fewer. From the point of view of parents in agrarian societies numerous offspring to work in the fields are an advantage, and they also provide an insurance for old age – provided the parents are not living in a society which practises compulsory euthanasia upon its members incapacitated by age or infirmity, mainly nomadic ones such as Arctic hunters, but sometimes also agricultural ones, as formerly with Japanese peasants.

Sexuality dominates, overtly or covertly, the overwhelmingly greater part of cultural practice in any society. Garments, as well as giving practical protection against the elements, are designed with few exceptions to either emphasise or hide sexual features, depending on gender or culture; cosmetics to emphasise them.[8] Throughout all recorded history genders have been distinguished by dress codes, often emphatically so – contemporary examples include regimes like the Gulf states and Afghanistan. On the other hand, the contemporary style of androgynous clothing, originating in the twentieth century, symbolised by blue jeans and now very widely favoured in Western and East Asian societies, is historically unprecedented and is still disapproved of in formal contexts even in those countries where its wearing is everyday routine.

Few narratives, from folk tales to television dramas fail to be concerned with gender relations or more explicitly sexual ones, either immediately or at one or two removes. In modern popular songs these dominate overwhelmingly. Gender and sexual relations, frequently linked to property considerations, occupy a large part of legal prescription and practice. In modern times scientific research has many other concerns but remains affected by unequal gender relations that demean the roles played by women.

Sex and Power

The degree of gender inequality varies between cultures, but to a greater or lesser extent it appears to be historically a human universal, or very nearly so, accepted as the natural order of things and challenged only in very recent times. Its origins, it may be safely assumed, lie far beyond recorded history. Mythological justifications were advanced – in Hebrew legend the deity had created man first, the first woman had been formed from his rib and moreover had been the first to taste the calamitous fruit and then tempt her man to do likewise. In Greek legend a woman had been responsible for releasing all the inflictions that humanity had to suffer. In Chinese legend by contrast a goddess creates humanity – not that it much improved the position of Chinese women.

Writing in the late nineteenth century, Friedrich Engels, in *The Origins of the Family, Private Property and the State*, drawing his evidence from the work of anthropologist Lewis Morgan, attributed masculine dominance, succeeding in his view an earlier era of gender equality or possibly matriarchy, to the development of intensive agriculture and stock rearing Dealing with large animals, in this interpretation, required men to take the leading role on account of their larger muscles. Domination and patriarchy followed naturally, 'the great historical defeat of the female sex', according to Simone de Beauvoir in the historical section of *The Second Sex*. She criticises Engels for a degree of superficiality in not accounting for the subjective motivations behind the developments, ' . . . the most important problems are slurred over . . . it is impossible to *deduce* [original italics] the oppression of women from the institution of private property'.[9] Nevertheless she is in accord with his anthropological outlook, which though innovative in its own day must now be regarded as dated.

However there can be little doubt that gender differentiation and subsequently sexual inequality and oppression is rooted in the sexual division of labour, partly based on biological difference, more significantly on custom and usage driven by self-interest accruing to the emergent dominant sex. Once social habits become seriously embedded, especially with the force of self-interest behind them they are extraordinarily difficult to uproot, and when the self-interest relates to something as fundamental and consciousness-dominating as sexual activity, then immeasurably more so.

The driving force of sexuality in the course of history combined with gender differentiation was to have grim consequences. As noted above, precedence in the social hierarchy tends to give males access to larger numbers of sexual partners, and with the accumulation of wealth made possible by the agricultural revolution of ten or eleven thousand years ago, then with the institution of slavery and directed aggression, one of the accumulation possibilities open to dominant males, was that of harems[10] of captive women, evident in the earliest written records and not yet wholly extinct in the twenty-first century.

The rulers of Bronze Age and subsequent empires – Egyptian, Assyrian, Babylonian, Indian, Chinese, Aztec and Inca – naturally possessed the most extensive harems, generally though not invariably staffed by eunuchs; but subordinate officials and favoured subjects also practised the custom. It was one dramatic aspect of the general and comprehensive subordination and subjection of women which accompanied the advance into agriculture, cities, literacy and metal working. There is no record of the occasional female ruler, even the grim and successful nineteenth-century Ranavalona of Madagascar, having a retinue of male sex slaves; at least I have never heard of one, although Roman and Byzantine matrons were said to entertain themselves sexually with eunuchs and the Empress Catherine of Russia maintained a cohort of lovers. However, prior to the twentieth century, women who could openly please themselves with whom they selected or discarded as sexual partners were rare indeed.

So far as eunuchs were concerned, they first appear in the historical record of the Sumerian cities and later imperial powers multiplied their numbers. Imperial Chinese dynasties from the earliest onwards manufactured them on an industrial scale and other cultures were not much behindhand. Their condition was intended to ensure that they could never challenge the power-holders either politically or sexually. The civil service in Byzantium was staffed largely by eunuchs some of whom rose to high positions in the church and military – generals, admirals, and in one case the highest church office, the Metropolitan of Constantinople. During the seventh-century Arab siege of Constantinople the opposing admirals on both sides were eunuchs. The medieval Roman church, by contrast, though it used in its choirs eunuch songsters termed castrati, forbade any eunuch to become a cleric (as was the case in Judaism) and newly-appointed Popes were allegedly checked to ensure that they remained complete.

Some Examples

Sex and Christianity

The official, as distinct from the actual, morality of Roman culture was fairly sexually restrictive in the first place and the Christian church enhanced this enormously. It disapproved of sex and disapproved of it intensely, regarding it as the badge of mankind's fall from divine grace, initially due to womankind. In such Christian communities for a married person to decide upon total abstinence from sexual relations was highly approved of, and perpetual virginity was even better. Jerome, one of the church fathers remarked that the only excuse for sex was that it produced potential virgins.

Both Jesus's reported statements and Paul's writings favoured celibacy (non-marriage) and chastity (non-sex),[11] probably because both expected the apocalypse to occur very soon, and therefore did not need to consider the future of the community. As Jesus is reported to have advised, 'Take no thought for tomorrow, for tomorrow will take thought for itself'.[12] In addition there was the influence carried into Christianity of sexual restrictions embodied in Jewish tradition and foreign to Roman culture. Considerable numbers of early Christians both male and female adopted these styles. Their choice was believed to confer not only holiness but also freedom, 'the paradise of virginity', and in certain respects undoubtedly it did. It released those who opted for it, both men and women – often against the bitter opposition of their pagan extended families – from compulsory sex and onerous family obligations, and in the case of women multiple and dangerous childbearing. All that, though, was without any particular reference to the creation story.

In the early fourth century the sin of disobedience in the Genesis legend became identified with sexual sin in western Christian tradition (less so in what became the eastern Orthodox and Coptic churches). All those who took the text literally were in accord that Adam and Eve's disobedience had brought disaster on their descendants, but the text itself scarcely hints that their sin itself was sexual, only that eating the forbidden fruit caused them to realise that they were naked. Moreover, baptism and faith in Christ were assumed to relieve believers from their ancestral sin and return them to the freedom Adam and Eve had forfeited by their misdemeanour.

The ideological shift which stood this understanding on its head was due above all to the gruesome twosome of the late fourth century (when the empire was still intact) and the early fifth (when it was collapsing in the west); namely Jerome, the

Bible translator, and Augustine the bishop of Hippo in Roman North Africa. Both were men of ferocious polemic in speech and writing and, according to their own statements, of a ravenous sexuality which they hated in themselves. Sex in their opinion was both the marker of God's displeasure and the punishment for it, 'the proof and penalty'.[13] According to Augustine human nature was irreversibly and incorrigibly corrupt. Redemption was possible through divine grace alone, and that would be extended only to a minority. The more widespread the abstention from sex the better both in the empire – and beyond, as far as Christian missionaries could reach and thereby expand that minority.

Clerics

The church however was presented with a dilemma in this regard (it was presented with many others as well, as are discussed in Chapter 9). Sex and reproduction there must be, however undesirable, if Christian men and women were to be around until the apocalypse (expected shortly) and be present to experience its accompanying horrors. (Those who took the principle to its logical conclusion and argued that the creator of the universe was an evil god were soon sidelined.) The answer arrived at was to separate off the truly holy ones who refrained wholly from sexual contact; first of all as hermits in desert areas, or sitting up on pillars all their days, and then in convents which might be either for men or for women (preferably virgins). Economic forces were not absent either, and fathers could save the expense of dowries by compelling their daughters to become nuns.[14]

These religiously separated individuals therefore remained detached from the remainder of reprobate mankind, to practise their holiness undisturbed as a fulltime occupation. Of course they depended on wealthy members of reprobate mankind to support their sanctity, but these, along with their inferiors, could still enjoy a lesser form of salvation by doing and believing (above all believing) what the clergy told them. The Buddhist monks and Hindu Sadhus (somewhat intermediate between hermits and monks) were and are very similar in conception to their Christian counterparts – withdrawal from worldly concerns in order to concentrate on holy matters and rituals, though the variety of practices between and within each religion (Japanese and Taiwanese Buddhist monks and nuns can even marry) make generalisation difficult, except to note that some orders of Christian monks engaged in manual (usually agricultural) labour as part of their discipline.

What in the Christian church were known as the 'secular clergy', comprising everything from archbishops to parish deacons, who did the spadework of keeping the reprobate up to the mark, occupied an intermediate position between the sanctity of the monks and nuns on the one hand and the sinful laity, from kings to serfs, on the other. In the early Christian church these clergy were normally married, but following the eleventh century separation between the Roman church and the Eastern Orthodox or Byzantine portion the papacy became increasingly insistent on celibacy for all of its clergy. The motivation behind this was to prevent possession of any benefice from parish to archbishopric becoming hereditary, as would otherwise tend to happen. It did not of course stop clergymen (even monks and abbots) from fathering children, but these were stigmatised as bastards and ineligible to inherit. In the Byzantine empire, where the hereditary principle was less embedded, the parish clergy continued to be married, as they still are in the Orthodox church, higher ranks being recruited from the celibate monastic clergy.

The Western church was also from the same period busy tightening up marriage regulations and inheritance principles; Stephanie Coontz refers to, 'the variety – and ambiguity – of marriages in the Middle Ages'.[15] The eighth-to-ninth-century emperor Charlemagne, though regarded as an ornament of Christianity, had several wives and numerous concubines. He prohibited his daughters from marrying but did not object to their lovers. The illegitimacy of the (appropriately named) William the Bastard did not stop him from becoming duke of Normandy and subsequently king of England – in subsequent centuries that kind of thing would have been impossible, and indeed the new rules stopped William's illegitimate grandsons from being considered monarchical candidates.

During these centuries, a bastard if suitably placed could rise very high (the founder of my university was a priest's son and a bishop) but could not anywhere in Europe legitimately aspire to a crown. Those who tried to do so had to pretend they were actually legitimate. The church was also significantly widening the scope of prohibited degrees – the closeness or consanguinity of relationship within which it was forbidden to marry or, as a rule, to conduct sexual relations. The aim was, by restricting the availability of marriage partners, to inhibit concentration of wealth in aristocratic families and encourage its donation to the church instead, for the church was desperate for legacies and in addition all secular households were legally obliged to hand over a tithe amounting a tenth of their income.

Gender Inflictions

The inauguration of agriculture, civilisation, and property beyond modest personal artefacts, was especially bad news for women. With property came inheritance and with inheritance considerations of paternity. Women became virtually a trade commodity, compulsorily assigned to husbands/masters according to family advantage and subject to far-reaching behavioural restrictions and even genital mutilation to ensure their compliance. The degree of restriction varied according to local culture and the rank of their male relatives. If peasant women were treated relatively less severely than aristocratic ones in this respect, it was only because they were less valuable commodities and required enough scope in which to do heavy manual labour – the Chinese custom of foot-binding for example disabled any woman from fieldwork.

In the nineteenth century Engels noted that the initial division of labour was the gender one (although he didn't use that term). This was undoubtedly the case even during the Palaeolithic era. The differences in reproductive responsibilities – the sexual division of labour – no doubt provided the basis for the gender division, as pregnancy, childbirth and lactation (and to a lesser extent menstruation) put women at a physical disadvantage when it came to gender relations – not to speak of sexual dimorphism, the fact that men generally are bigger and stronger. In short, males were favourably placed to load the 'shit-work' onto women, in some instances quite literally. In the rural community in which I partially grew up, with no running water or sanitation, emptying the buckets from the dry lavatories into the sea was the province of women. Women among the elites of course delegated such tasks onto female domestic servants.

Anastasia Banschikova, using surviving advisory literature aimed at the literate classes with reference to ancient Egypt, writes of,

[A] complex picture of a gradual evolution of Egyptian stereotypes of the woman from the Old Kingdom concept of wife as 'the second power' in the married couple the relations with whom are to be mutually balanced and aimed at obtaining psychological harmony between husband and wife as two autonomous friendly persons – through the New Kingdom concept of wife as the 'family co-manager' of her husband, while their relations are aimed mainly at providing 'usefulness for domestic wealth' (at the same moment the motif of adultery emerges in the Teachings for the first time) to the Late Period concept of essentially, at heart bad and corrupted woman who is not regarded as a real personality anymore.[16]

The evidence cited in this article suggests a steady deterioration in the social position of Egyptian women over the two thousand years from the middle of the third millennium BCE to the first millennium.

[T]he only aim of marriage is to acquire posterity; the woman's personality is fully ignored and/or dishonoured as well as any possibility to get psychological contact with her. The only example of family relations which provokes the author's special attention is adultery of a wife which is presented as a constant threat to every husband caused by the common nature of women 'as they are', not by any specific negative situation within this or that family . . . to teach a woman is the same as to try to fill a torn bag with sand.[17]

In classical Athens (custom varied between Greek city states and Spartan women were unusually liberated by the standards of the times) women were especially badly treated, secluded within households, and compelled to marry an available cousin should she be the only heir on her father's death – even if this involved divorcing the husband she was already married to. The heiress had to be kept 'in the family'. '[I]n the heyday of ancient democracy the subjugation of women was [regarded as] not only just, but preferable to the liberty they had formerly enjoyed.'[18] Two millennia later Martin Luther was to assert that he had as much or more reason for concern about who sired his daughters' children as he would have for which stallions impregnated his mares.

Over the entire range of written history women have been subjugated, placed under the patriarchal control of male relatives backed up by male legislators and opinion-formers, treated as commodities or as ornaments. In a few places, such as antique Serbia, it was possible for women who had forsworn sexual activity to be accepted as honorary men, but that was anomalous and still designated men as the superior sex. Walter Benjamin's remark quoted at the beginning of this volume can be extended to note that the history of civilisation is also the history of misogyny – a state of affairs which is far from having been satisfactorily changed, even if some initial steps in some parts of the world have been taken during the past century or so.

Sex – Procreative and Recreative

Sexual activity among humans can be undertaken either for enjoyment or procreation, or both together. Undoubtedly the former is the primary motivation in the overwhelming majority of sexual encounters (or likewise with solitary sex), much though that reality has been fiercely denounced throughout history by assorted moralists. (It is not accidental that the word 'morality' in the English language is taken to refer to sexual morality unless specifically stated to be otherwise.)

It is in the area of sexual interaction surely that gender inequality has been most pronounced. Throughout recorded history and no doubt for millennia before that, men have by force imposed themselves sexually upon women (sometimes of course also on other men, and juveniles of both sexes). It was accepted as simply being the way things were, and until late in the twentieth century men in Britain were legally entitled whenever inclined to rape the woman they were married to. Even where marital rape has been made illegal, the distress occasioned to the victim by having to take a partner to court is a great deterrent to exposure.

Of all the forms of subordination to which women have been subjected, sexual subordination and other forms of violence in the home must through endless ages have been the most intimately and keenly felt – and this is not even taking into account molestation or abuse of children by adults, or – what used to be extremely prevalent in former centuries – of servants, especially girls, by employers or their relatives when domestic servants were a prevalent part of the social landscape. The development of what would in our own time be widely (though far from universally) regarded as the ideal of sexual activity – that it should be voluntarily entered into between fully consenting adult partners on an equal footing without any constraint or coercion on either side – has a long and painful history. How far it still differs from the present actual reality is a measure, notwithstanding power imbalances in homosexual and gender relations, of the personal suffering endured in this dimension by over half the world's population.

Marriage and Divorce

Although its forms have been infinitely variable in all known societies and cultures an institution equivalent to what we call 'marriage' has been a central social fact, with formally monogamous unions generally being the norm. Only elites as a rule could afford the costs of recognised polygamy in the cultures where it was accepted, though of course monogamy, regardless of prohibitions and injunctions, has always been, as someone once expressed it, 'ragged at the edges'. The primary purpose of marriage has likewise always been the procreation, nourishment and social education of the next generation, though accommodating additional other purposes, among them, in all non-forager societies, the question of property regulation, especially inheritance.

Throughout recorded history, and most likely prior to that as well, marriage has been a family arrangement, rather than an agreement between two individuals. In circumstances where children, especially daughters, are regarded as a species of property and no premarital association with potential marriage partners permitted, arranged marriages, i.e. ones arranged by parents and relatives often with property and/or dynastic considerations in mind, follow naturally, and might well apply to widows (less so widowers) as well as to unmarried young women. In cultures where arranged marriages are the norm, marriage brokers play a role equivalent to estate agents dealing with properties in home-owning societies.

The dowry system, which has also prevailed throughout diverse cultures ever since settled agriculture and stock-rearing became the central forms of sustenance and social living, has been the occasion of immeasurable heartbreak. Essentially it was an exchange of stuff between families on the occasion of familial acceptance of an unmarried individual from another family as a marriage partner. In some instances it was the man or his family who had to provide the dowry, as with African cattle herders, but far more frequently the dowry came with the woman. Inability to provide a dowry rendered a woman unmarriageable at all levels of society except the most destitute, and to avoid this disgrace borrowing would be resorted to, more often with very evil consequences (see Chapter Six).

The evils of dowry payments are by no means extinct in the present day. In India, although formally illegal, they are still demanded and the demand accepted. This has led to the scandal of bride burning, episodes in which the groom's family, dissatisfied with the level of the dowry payment, have demanded more and frequently escalated the demands after initially receiving the additions. If still not satisfied the result has been that the bride is murdered, usually by being burned alive with kerosene, since that can be passed off as a domestic accident and the reality is difficult to prove.

Sex and Love

Historically therefore the individuals involved have had minimal or no choice in the selection of their marriage partners, with women, as usual, being the more severely affected gender. Historically, the Catholic church did insist that marriage should be a relationship entered into voluntarily, but this was a rule more honoured in the breach than the observance, for family pressure, again especially on women, would normally produce the appearance of a fictitious consent. In medieval Europe (and not only in these past times, according to Terry Eagleton in his memoir *The Gatekeeper*) surplus daughters would be obliged in the same manner to become 'brides of Christ' and enter convents. The current state of affairs throughout most of Western culture, in which most forms of consenting adult sex are socially acceptable (though not in all of its localities and notwithstanding a reservoir of popular prejudice) is historically unprecedented, and the speed at which it has been accomplished, within less than a century, is dramatic and startling.

Though by no means universal, throughout large areas of the globe in present times the accepted norm is that individuals are mutually free to choose which partners of the opposite sex they prefer, while arranged marriages, though not outlawed, are often frowned upon and forced marriage of the traditional kind, now conducted underhand, is regarded with horror and contempt; and in some countries is a criminal offence. Marriage, as distinct from casual sex, is supposed to be based on mutual attraction with a sexual foundation but embracing a much wider degree of sentiment, designated in English by that ambiguous term 'love'. The notion that this should be the normal form of marriage was abroad in the seventeenth century, particularly strongly in England during the middle decades of that century where revolution enabled it to be expressed freely, and in the same country the newly-invented literary form of novels were full of narratives of 'true love' struggling against parental repression.

It has been seriously argued that romantic love is a modern, possibly even a twentieth-century, concept, but certainly no older than European late medieval times. The evidence is quite otherwise. Hebrew legend includes the story of Jacob and Rachel, which in its current form dates from around the middle of the first millennium BCE, but is certainly based on an earlier folk legend. The central legend of classical Greece is based upon an adulterous love match. Hero and Leander are also part of Greek mythology. The Lancelot-Guinevere story and its Tristan-Iseult counterpart, are medieval in their present form, but are based on much older legends, the latter possibly originating in Persia. More prosaically, Heloise and Abelard were actual people, and though medieval, twelfth century not late medieval. Humans are complex animals and it is entirely to be expected that strong sexual attraction between two individuals should have resonances in consciousness far beyond the immediately physical.

Throughout recorded history marriage has invariably been a most unequal institution – a man at the bottom of the pecking order in every other respect, even a household slave, could if married, act as a domestic tyrant, and the occasional man tyrannised over by his wife was regarded as doubly contemptible. Such inequality extended as well, not surprisingly, to the termination of marriage. The absolute prohibition of divorce by the Christian church[19] (though it could be got around by annulment) was unusual. Most societies made provision for it by civil law (or its equivalent if literacy was lacking).

Needless to say divorce was often a male-only prerogative,[20] in one case only requiring the husband to say 'I divorce thee' three times. The frequency of divorce, even in such situations, however was inhibited by consequences relating to children (it was easier if there were none; indeed 'barrenness' was frequently a justifiable ground for divorce) and often required the repayment of any dowry the wife had brought to the marriage. There were historical instances in which women were legally allowed to initiate divorce proceedings on a variety of grounds, in the Roman state for example, but that was a practical possibility only with family support. If that were lacking the wife had no protection against intimidation – or destitution when no longer supported by her husband.

One acerbic epigram has it that in marriage women sell themselves (or are sold) wholesale, in prostitution by retail. Prostitution, euphemistically termed 'the oldest profession' also appears as a social phenomenon in the earliest written records. In antiquity a very large proportion of the prostitutes both male and female staffing the numerous brothels to be found throughout towns and cities were slaves being hired out by their owners, or if not technically slaves were reduced by destitution into selling their bodies in such a manner. Freelance courtesans and 'street girls' (the term is used in the Egyptian writings cited above) did exist throughout the centuries, but the latter were, and continued to be in all cultures, despised as the lowest of the low, exploited by pimps, or if selling themselves independently, in constant danger of being robbed, injured or murdered by clients or rivals.

Where prostitution has been regulated by law, which has been the case in most societies at least since the Sumerian civilisation, the law was biased in favour of the men paying for sex and against the women/boys selling themselves or being sold – not least because the clients were often enough powerful men or soldiers; situations therefore where work, sex and power were particularly closely interlinked.

Pregnancy and Contraception

Though it is only seldom the immediate purpose of heterosexual intercourse, pregnancy is always a possible outcome, and if not in a socially authorised and condoned relationship, a most unwelcome one. Even in 'respectable' but unequal relationships where sex is effectively coerced and contraception absent repeated pregnancies could result, so that one pregnancy was barely ended before another began, with consequent pressures on family resources and the mother's health.

Many and varied methods of variable effectiveness both of preventing and terminating pregnancy have been in use since ancient times. Some were purely ritualistic and purely ineffective, such as that reported of 1950s Britain, that crossing one's fingers during sex, or assuming that particular positions would inhibit conception. An anonymous webpage notes that some 'were, admittedly, more terrifying than most of the methods in use today'.[21] A particularly lethal one, supposedly advised in China, was drinking hot mercury. *Coitus interruptus* (a very chancy method), anal sex and varied forms of non-penetrative sex, were widely employed, even when, as often, resolutely prohibited by authority – so far as these matters can be documented. Condoms date back at least several centuries and with their rubber manufacture from the late nineteenth century onwards, became easily the most popular method of contraception (and very profitable to manufacturers) before the invention of the contraceptive pill in the 1960s.

There is an interesting and telling light thrown on gender relationships by this last comparison. The use of condoms required men to take the contraceptive responsibility; with the spreading popularity of the pill it was women, even though the use of condoms presented no medical risks and there was no certainty that the continued use of the pill did not – certainly it had fairly extensive hormonal effects. Whether or not the pill liberated women sexually – enormously (as generally believed), partially or not at all, certainly it accompanied the undoubted sexual revolution of the late twentieth century in industrialised Western societies. This was marked by general social acceptance of premarital, and to some extent extramarital, sex and to some degree of accepting homosexuality, as well as to a great broadening of sexual discourse. Condoms continue to be used; in some circumstances their use is emphasised as protective barriers against infection, particularly since the 1980s from the initially untreatable HIV and a small indicator of how far sexual attitudes have moved in those cultures is the ready availability of condom-dispensing machines on all manner of premises.

At any rate, until very recently in all cultures and still surviving in some, conceiving a child outside of the prescribed restrictions (which of course varied according to time and place) was, as the evidence of illicit sexual activity, a source of humiliation, contempt and brutal sanctions. At best it meant censure and loss of honour, at worst murder or execution even if the conception had resulted from rape (which unless committed by an invading army, and even then still meriting dishonour, was supposedly always the woman's fault).

Same-sex Sex

In past ages, at least in Western cultures, any form of sexual activity apart from orthodox vaginal copulation in the 'missionary position' (the term is indicative) has been denounced by authority as 'unnatural'.[22] As noted previously, nothing could be further from the truth, the use of the term in this context is purely ideological in the worst sense and aimed at the assertion of power and control. Among humans, children viewing or playing with their own and their peers' genitals of both their own and the other sex is natural enough, and not necessarily to be categorised as sexual, but very possibly as an exploratory satisfying of curiosity.

Both observation of non-human animals and the history of humans demonstrate that same-sex eroticism is perfectly 'normal', though in human societies where it was tolerated or even approved was usually practised within a framework of conventional rules, and within such cultures no contradiction was imagined between homosexual and heterosexual eroticism. Julius Caesar was famously designated according to Suetonius, as 'every man's woman and each woman's man'. In imperial China sexual relations between a teacher and his male student were regarded as normal. In classical Athens the general and author Xenophon was regarded as 'queer' because he was attracted solely to women in a culture where bisexuality was the norm. Conversely, Tom Driberg, a British MP of the 1950s, whose preferred form of sex was to practise fellatio on any available male, was horrified and appalled at the idea of sexual contact with a woman – including the one he had married for the appearance of respectability. At least since Alfred Kinsey produced his research on sexuality in the 1940s and 50s, it seems likely that most humans are born, or else develop in childhood, as innately bisexual along a spectrum of homosexuality/heterosexuality, but that some occupy one or other of the extreme ends. The sociologist David T Evans, in his 1993 volume *Sexual Citizenship*, particularly Chapter 6, argues a very strong case along these lines.[23]

In the Hebrew and Judaic law and culture, however, homosexual acts, along with other forms of non-procreative sex, were denounced relentlessly, and this anathema was passed on to Christianity and majority Islam. The outcome was a cascade of discrimination, cruelty and death throughout the centuries. Much if not most of it was undoubtedly due to plain malice and fear of the Other. The persecutors satisfied their consciences, though, with the conviction that if they did not expunge such offensive breakers of divine sexual law these outcasts would contaminate the population and provoke divine wrath (the legend of Sodom was always to hand). The Byzantine emperor Justinian asserted that laws against sodomy were essential, as such activity was the cause of earthquakes, and contemporary incidents both in the US and the UK demonstrate that similar convictions are not yet dead, right-wing politicians in both countries having attributed natural disasters to toleration of homosexuality.

Though homosexuality was decriminalised in the Turkish empire in the nineteenth century, in most contemporary Islamic states prohibition is fiercely asserted and in some punished with execution. Not until the 1960s did most Christian-majority countries begin to dismantle legal prohibitions and penalties, a development still fiercely resisted with bigoted passion by right-wing Christians in the United States, who continue to invoke the threat of divine punishment (for example the 9/11 attacks on the World Trade Center) on account of legal tolerance. And everywhere the road from tolerance to acceptance has been a long one.[24]

Kinship

Importance

Throughout the entire course of human history the bonds of kinship have been of cardinal importance, the very foundation stone of social relationships. They remain so, and although partially weakening in some contemporary societies, nevertheless even in the most 'developed' countries of the present century still retain a great deal of importance. You were/are supposed to be able to trust your kin in a fashion greater than with outsiders. In Scotland, for example, at least until the earlier twentieth century, the word 'friends' also meant kinsfolk. Kinship provides a metaphor for all manner of non-biological relationships – fatherland, motherland, 'father of the people', 'kith and kin', and the use of 'Father' as a title in the Roman Catholic priesthood.

Evidently the English word 'kin', which is the root of the words 'kind' and 'kindness', named a primary reality of human culture down the ages. Nor was this kind of connection the case only at the level of intimate personal acquaintance, such as between parents and offspring or siblings brought up together in nuclear families; it extended and extends far more widely, even to persons one has never heard of if a genetic relationship is unexpectedly revealed, such as a child given up for adoption encountering its biological parent as an adult.

The political and administrative structures both of the Greek cities and of Rome were based on presumed (though not actual) clan structures. In hereditary monarchies when the monarch died without an obvious heir the nearest living 'blood' (i.e. genetic) relative was sought for in order to fill the vacancy. It was a situation of this sort which led to the Anglo-Scottish independence wars of the late thirteenth and early fourteenth centuries. Today property disputes are notorious between relatives of the deceased, even those who have scarcely known the late departed, or each other.

The Muslim community of believers divided into Sunni and Shia over events in the seventh century hinging on the issue of blood relationship to Muhammad. The Christian community which emerged at the end of the first century CE was presumably fortunate that its founder, Saul of Tarsus, had no descendants, or similar splits would have been likely (other kinds of split are dealt with in Chapter 9). Among the original Christian community in Jerusalem kinship with Jesus of Nazareth was indeed a qualification for leadership, but that community was wiped out by the Romans in consequence of the Jewish revolt in 70 CE (the later claim that it emigrated and survived is mythical).

Kin Structures

Although we have of course no direct evidence from that era, we can be more than reasonably confident that the kin group formed the nucleus of early human communities and that nomadic bands consisting of a few dozen individuals represented the earliest expansion of such communities. All forager and subsistence agriculture societies that appear in the record are organised on kin principles and down the centuries as communities expanded, as cities were established and states created, matters scarcely changed. Work was organised along kinship lines both in urban and in rural settings.

Agricultural plots of land everywhere were occupied and worked on a family basis with family labour central, though outsiders lacking their own property might be recruited into the household if the family were prosperous peasants, and among pastoralists the animals upon which they depended were family-owned. Largely hereditary aristocracies dominated the settled agricultural population. Landownership or occupancy or rural trade proceeded from father to son (or occasionally daughter or other relative) and in urban settings sons followed their fathers into artisan occupations. In the Indian subcontinent such relationships became rigidified into the caste system, a strictly hereditary culture; another example of how work, sex and power became tightly imbricated, and re-emphasising that kinship structures in agrarian-based societies are based upon and reinforce inequality (including gender inequality) in terms of power.

At the top of the Hindu caste system however were what we might term cultural workers – the priesthood or Brahmins. This was also a closed hereditary occupation, as it was in parallel cases in other parts of Eurasia, but not in the cultures descended from imperial Rome, whether east or west, for there the topmost clergy, and in the West all clergy, were required to give up hereditary succession, though they could still practice nepotism – handing on their office and privileges to male relatives if not offspring. At the summit of the secular order however, the hereditary principle prevailed from the most powerful empires to the most insignificant outlying monarchies such as the Welsh princes (though in Byzantium it was rather looser). The Medici family in republican Florence from the fourteenth to the fifteenth centuries built up their quasi-monarchical power both through their immense wealth and also by means of constructing a network of kin alliances. Their increasing power having brought them into conflict with the popes, they extended the strategy by getting their relatives into the college of cardinals and eventually securing the papacy itself.

In areas not well controlled by central authority – primarily isolated agricultural ones – family or clan feuds, often with serious fatalities, were recurrent phenomena. Avenging a fellow clansperson was a duty and cardinal obligation. Areas of special notoriety in Europe were the Balkans in general and Albania in particular, also Sardinia and Corsica, with the Mafia replicating the phenomenon in the less isolated and more urbanised Sicily. The Scottish highlands were notorious in their time, as were the 'backwoods' of the eastern United States, which were the scene of bitter feuding between biologically related clans of farmers and illicit distillers. Other parts of the world were anything but exempt – Jared Diamond cites an instructive example from the New Guinea highlands: 'My first husband was killed by Elopi raiders. My second husband was killed by a man who wanted me, and who became my third husband. That husband was killed by the brother of my second husband, seeking to avenge his murder.'[25]

Regular succession to the top position in the earlier medieval period as often as not did not pass to an eldest son, but always to a close relative of the deceased ruler (in Scotland the relative who killed him); the principle of primogeniture, the succession of the eldest son followed by nearest male relatives in order of proximity and age, and applied to all title holders, was not established until well into the second millennium CE and never in every place.

Prior to the modern era the family, which could include servants and slaves as well as relatives, was thus in all cultures and societies usually the site of production, of occupational training, of education (depending on social status) and of its close sibling, ideological indoctrination, though the role of religious functionaries in the latter was also conspicuous. The importance of the family was all-pervasive – in imperial China both Daoist and Confucian culture for example, stressed family obligations (including to ancestors as well as living members); it permeates the Jewish scriptures – though the Christian ones of the New Testament can be seen on some readings as anti-family. This reflected the tensions which could be generated if some family members accepted the new religion and others did not and the bonds of kinship came in conflict with those of faith – though when the soon-expected apocalypse failed to occur Christianity soon became as family-centred as any other faith.

The impact of industrialisation from the eighteenth century onwards significantly changed the nature of the family, though neither dramatically nor rapidly. It tended to become more nuclear and less extended, though that was a slow process. Indeed it may have been essential to the industrialisation process, and not only because families were a necessary precondition for there to be another generation of operatives. For the industrial enterprises, both manufacturing and financial which were set up were generally family firms, where sons or close relatives were expected to take over from the founder, and many a dispute and antagonism was generated by these relationships, which time and again were reflected in fiction. Dickens's *Dombey and Son* is a representative case from the nineteenth century.

In French nineteenth-century politics the capitalist elite were referred to by their enemies as the '200 families'. Pétain's Vichy regime of 1940–44 attempted to replace the revolutionary slogans of 'Liberty, Equality, Fraternity' with 'Work, Family, Fatherland', (*Travaille, Famille, Patrie*) satirically translated by the Resistance as 'Forced labour, 200 families, Betrayed fatherland' (*Travaille forcé, 200 familles, Patrie trahie*). Throughout the twentieth century reactionary movements around the globe have made a point of emphasising their dedication to 'the family', while radical movements and trade union organisations frequently refer to their members as 'brothers' and 'sisters'.

In Protestant cultures, there was an emphasis on family worship; fathers, with family prayers and bible readings, being supposed to supplement the endeavours of the clergy. Robert Burns's poem *The Cottar's Saturday Night*, which relates to the late eighteenth century, is a representative example. The cottar was a lowly type of agricultural labourer, and the importance of the family to the economic transformation applied as much to the labouring classes as to the moneyed strata. The family unit was naturally essential to the production and reproduction of the labour force, with parents and extended family members having responsibility for the care and upbringing of the emerging intake of labour units. This continued until late into the nineteenth century without any state intervention, until a literate labour force became necessary with the advance of technology and industrial organisation.

Families of the period were frequently very large and functioned as a collective of all its members, with older children, unless and until they entered the paid labour force, recruited to look after younger ones, with gender roles and gender hierarchies strongly emphasised. In the early years of British industrialisation, with textiles moving into factory production during the initial decades of the nineteenth century, the child labourers employed in the spinning mills (though sometimes recruited from orphanages or workhouses) most often worked under the supervision of their parents, especially mothers, employed in the same mill, with the overlookers supervising the parents.

Families can be very brutal environments, and the historical written record may only reveal the tip of the iceberg. The tyrannical mother-in-law was a standard trope of Chinese literature; wicked stepmothers feature prominently in Western storytelling and the tyrannising of children, including adult children and especially female ones, by parents is recorded all over the globe. With children viewed as a form of property and serving as economic and social assets at all levels of society, this was to be expected, and violence and fear were means ready to hand to enforce the parents' preference. The fifteenth-century Paston letters, a unique documentation of relations in an upwardly mobile, proto-bourgeois English family, record the repeated beating of a daughter to force her into the marriage her parents wanted to arrange for her (they failed).

Indeed, prior to the twentieth century, violence and terror were the recommended strategies for child rearing and education in practically all cultures. In ancient Rome the *paterfamilias* was even entitled to execute his adult children if they offended him too severely – surely the ultimate expression of patriarchy. Though females were and are the principal sufferers from patriarchy, and indeed in contemporary discourse it has come to apply almost exclusively to gender relations, historically males were by no means exempt. A notorious instance is the panic over masturbation of both male and female sorts, which prevailed in Western culture during the nineteenth and early twentieth centuries. Indulgence in masturbation, male or female was supposed to lead to all manner of ailments, most prominently insanity, and a range of ingenious devices were advertised in the public prints to enable parents to stop adolescent boys and girls playing with their genitals. Genital mutilation was even resorted to.

Kin connections have been a central element throughout all history, and necessarily so, as without them a social species could never have survived, let alone have gone on to form wider communities. Religious structures have been built around them, most famously in eastern Asia. Apart from the intense emotional relationships involved, they have served as crucial support mechanisms, both in normal times and more especially during episodes of crisis. Even in the contemporary world, where, outside the nuclear family, their practical significance is much weaker than in previous eras, they remain of enormous importance. It is no accident that such relationships continue to be central to imaginative narratives.

However there is also a downside, and often enough kin relations can also be tyrannical ones in many dimensions – especially when they are imbricated with property relations and the preservation and extension of accumulated family property comes to be considered more important than the welfare of individual kinspersons or indeed of public property. For example, the notorious corruption problems which have plagued newly-independent countries from the mid-twentieth century, are not all down to individual greed and egotism but also to kinship demands upon politicians and government servants who are expected to share their larger incomes through a widely extended kin network and take unethical advantage of their positions. As the discussion above underlines kinship pressures too, have throughout history functioned as a very powerful mechanism for enforcing unequal and inequitable gender relations. Kinship is a universal aspect of human reality but its impact in different cultures has been very differential – both for good and for ill.

5

Status Differentiation, Hierarchy and Hegemony

I like the insight that for more than 90 percent of their existence on earth, human groups sought to prevent the emergence of states.
—Michael Mann (*The Sources of Social Power, Vol. 1*)

The mastery gained by one person or group is at the expense of the loss of power of another person or group.
—Ian Kershaw (*Hitler, 1889–1936*)

This chapter discusses the transition and development from conditions of minimal social hierarchy to one of maximum differentiation in power and privilege, their economic foundation having been outlined in Chapter 3. The aim is to discuss how achievement-based societies became oppressive and class-divided ones, the forms of hierarchy, oppression and inequality which have largely constituted the fabric of history since their initial establishment. It deals with hierarchy in the more general sense; subsequent chapters with its particular manifestations. The development which commences with emergence of agrarian societies around 10,000 years BP intensified with the beginnings of urbanisation around 5,000–6,000 years BP, which saw the establishment of god-kings, unaccountable elites and absolute rulers.

Previous chapters have sketched the framework of human development, so far as can be ascertained, with significant attention to what used to be known as 'prehistory', namely the epochs which preceded the invention of literacy and the appearance of written records. The latter innovation, commencing in Eurasia around 5,000 years ago and coinciding roughly with the beginnings of what we are pleased to term civilisation, opened up an enormous and much clearer new window into the past as well as introducing unprecedented forms of social order for the communities subject to rulers with literacy at their disposal. At a later stage parallel developments, though on a very different technological basis, occurred in the Americas.

Some Theoretical Considerations

Human reality can be expressed in the paradoxical phrase, 'we are not what we are and we are what we are not'. In other words, individuals are constantly projecting themselves towards the future to the achievement of goals which vary according to the individual and the culture in which they are situated. Once achieved these goals lead on to further ones, either in the same direction or others – it is virtually impossible for very long to simply enjoy passively what one has attained.

The fundamental project may be something as simple and basic as perpetuating oneself in one's offspring or either escaping from an intolerable situation or schooling oneself to endure it; or it may be as ambitious and complex as unravelling the secrets of the universe. It is important to understand how basic a part of the human reality this is. It applies as much to the most banal of projects as to the most ambitious, to the most worthy as well as the most discreditable. Our sights are always set on the next target even if that should be no greater than bringing in next year's harvest, marrying off one's daughter to a satisfactory suitor and dodging the baron's latest imposition.

In the days of Christendom the ultimate target for most believers was to get to heaven. In a different time, situation and culture, when we have unlocked the secrets of the atom we have to move on to tackle those of the quark and the Higgs boson. This chapter aims to discuss the manner and social context in which these attributes of the human condition (in phenomenological terms being and being-for-others) are transformed into the drive to dominate, command and control, to stand highly not only in achievement and esteem but likewise in wealth and power, so that the stage is reached when, according to a saying from feudal Hungary, 'Beneath the rank of baron no-one exists'.

In our contemporary society it is no accidental shortcoming that when a squillionaire has accumulated more wealth than anyone could possibly use in a hundred lifetimes they should still want to accumulate more; or, a little more modestly, when a salary runs into the hundreds of thousands of pounds, euros or dollars it should still be insufficient – shock horror, 'his bonus is bigger than mine!'

Politicians who reach very high office regard themselves as failures and are so regarded by history if they fail to become prime minister or president. If they do achieve that pinnacle of ambition the attainment is still not enough, they want to be accounted a great one, and even if, like Winston Churchill, they succeed in the latter ambition they still want to cling to office. Less significantly, it is never enough to be number two on the tennis circuit, it is essential to be at the very top.[1]

Thus, among the most attractive of objectives to strive for is *thymos*, the desire to stand well in the estimate of others. All societies exhibit this phenomenon, but only in complex ones with substantial material production does it turn into the ambition to exceed others, and better still to dominate them. The point is relevant to both genders, though because in the past and still to an extent in the present males are more in the public eye, it appears to apply more prominently to them.

Preserving Equality

Hunter-gatherer societies that survived into the recent past, or occasionally still do, were always, anthropologists report, relatively egalitarian, at least among the males, and such hierarchy as existed was based on little more than esteem. Indeed, a variety of social devices were employed to keep matters that way, extending from mockery and satire directed against individuals tending to 'get above themselves'[2] to the assassination of incorrigibly insufferable ones by 'counterdominant coalitions'. 'My hypothesis has been that the immediate agency that created a shameful conscience was punitive social selection . . . .'[3] Christopher Boehm goes so far as to suggest that '[possibly] antihierarchical feelings are an important and evolved component of human nature. It is notable how hard the !Kung worked to prevent a meritocracy of good hunters from arising',[4] he remarks, although the very fact that these precautions were necessary suggest that hierarchical ambitions were also present, if to a lesser extent than egalitarian principles.

Nevertheless in the few hunter-gatherer societies which still exist and doubtless in those of the past and the deep past, some differences of status are to be found, if only ones of esteem and not very marked – between childhood and adulthood, initiated and uninitiated, between differences of physical strength and energy for example, or number of surviving children, the most capable hunter or gatherer as compared to those less competent – and most importantly the person or persons who communicated with the spirits of the natural world and/or with those of the dead. Boehm advances the interesting hypothesis that in the Palaeolithic and the Mesolithic which succeeded it, the alpha persons of these societies were not humans but ancestral spirits or the supernatural beings invented as explanations of natural phenomena.

Leaders then, such as they were, could be no more than what Boehm calls 'betas'. A degree of leadership though, would probably have been necessary in hunting large game animals. If that was a practical consideration, however, so was the necessary sharing, though not necessarily an equal one, of the carcass following a successful hunt. But, and most importantly, there was necessitated the willing cooperation of a hunting band in dangerous circumstances, for which only voluntary cooperation and willing acceptance of leadership could work. Any attempt to apply coercion would undermine solidarity, reduce efficiency and challenge the need for the group members to be able to rely absolutely on each other. This willingness could only be made possible by preserving a large measure of egalitarianism among the hunters.

Equality Undermined

It was this kind of situation that Marx and Engels characterised as one of 'primitive communism' – rather naively, for reality was much more complicated than that, especially when the status of women is taken into account. Nevertheless they had a point, for what in the Palaeolithic and Mesolithic had been societies unable to sustain much social differentiation and whose division of labour, if any, had been the gender one, was succeeded by collectives with dramatic social divisions, hierarchies and domination. Signs could be seen as early as the clan system outlined in Chapter Two.

With the beginnings of agriculture, clans, being composed of separate units, began to fracture into sections, with some claiming superiority over others. The expectation that a favour by one individual or group to another will be reciprocated at some point appears to be nearly a universal attribute of humans in all places and times, which in agricultural societies develop more complex forms. It has great advantages, but also very marked downsides, for it is a powerful lever of social differentiation,[5] as Kent Flannery and Joyce Marcus suggest:

> Clans have an 'us versus them' mentality that changes the logic of human [interaction]. Societies with clans are much more likely to engage in group violence than clanless societies . . . . Societies with clans also tend to have greater levels of social inequality. . . . The germ of such inequality may have been present already in the late Ice Age.[6]

However the transition to dominance hierarchies was far from immediate, and was for a long time restricted both socially and geographically:

> [V]illage societies with achievement-based leadership were among the most common in the world. They were remarkably stable societies, made up of descent groups that exchanged brides and gifts, honoured their ancestors, considered everyone equal at birth, yet threw their support behind gifted kinsmen who sought to achieve renown. . . Achievement based societies became common as soon as [various regions] had adopted agriculture and village life.[7]

Certainly such societies persisted at local level even under the overall rule of mighty empires, a point made at an earlier period by Marx in his account of Indian society, and repeated with emphasis by Mann, writing of village structures, even when overlaid by hierarchical empires; he notes that '*No general social evolution occurred beyond the rank societies of early, settled, neolithic societies*'[8] The lords of humankind, in order to assume their new roles removed themselves from village life.

Citification: Hierarchy and Subordination Intensified

Agrarian societies in all parts of the world, once they had extended geographically, developed highly stratified forms of hierarchy. In any explanation of this, certain logistical realities have to be kept in mind. As explained above, hierarchy of a sort exists in hunter-gatherer societies, but owing to their economic situation, it has to be based largely, almost entirely, on status – the shaman, the leader thanks to his (always 'his') physical prowess, skill in the hunt, descent from a renowned ancestor. Serious distinction in goods in addition to prestige, requires a settled society producing a large surplus of stuff. It requires more than that however – servants and guards and a network of wider support that enables a high-status individual to emerge as a ruler over a defined territory.[9] The ruler moreover must have sufficient resources from which followers can be rewarded. Ideologically, as the earliest written evidence shows, generosity is a highly acclaimed virtue in any ruler – at its most extreme this could give rise to the potlatch of Native Americans of the Northeast Pacific; ceremonies which were centred on competitive gift-giving or even deliberate destruction of valuable objects.

The outcome of the evolution of Neolithic settlement, both in Eurasia and the Americas was urbanisation, and with that hierarchy reached new levels of intensity and differentiation. On the long view this occurred around approximately the same timescale – 3000–1000 BCE, which in Eurasia and Mesoamerica coincides roughly with the emergence of written script, a highly effective tool of government on this scale, Sumerian cuneiform being the earliest clear example. The coagulation of village communities into urban settlements must certainly have been a complex process, and one requiring to have in place a system in which the urbanised area drew its resources from the surrounding agricultural area and sustained trading relations with more distant ones.

Cities also emerge into history as centres of religious cult – in the ideological narratives which are recorded, the cities were creation of a god or gods. With the appearance of cities we enter the domain of civilisation, which, after all, simply means 'citified'. In Mann's words:

Civilisation is the most problematic term, because so value-laden . . . civilisation combines three social institutions, the ceremonial centre, writing, and the city. Where combined they inaugurate a jump in human collective power over nature and over humans . . . that is the onset of something new. . . . I use the metaphor of a *social cage*.[10]

Regularly, at least in riverine civilisations dependent on alluvial agriculture, this produced the hierarchy to end all hierarchies – the institution of god-kings combining divine attributes with earthly authority. Such dynasties appeared in Sumer, Egypt, Babylonia, Assyria, China, Mesoamerica and the Andes – the situation in the Indus valley civilisation is unknown, due to its script being as yet undecipherable, but archaeology suggests that its society was less stratified than those mentioned. 'The Egyptian monarchy is the first we know of in which the ruler was, in effect, one of the supernatural alphas.'[11] However this kind of institution was by no means confined to such geographies but later on could arise anywhere, such as sub-Saharan Africa and the Pacific islands.

There were variations in the degree of divinity attributed to these rulers. At the most extreme level the king actually was the embodiment of the god in human form, like the Egyptian Pharaoh, who was worshipped as the personification of Horus, who was supposed to inhabit whichever Pharaoh was the reigning one. Alternatively he (always 'he' with very rare exceptions) might not actually be the god itself but physically descended from him or her, like the Japanese emperors, or more modestly, be human but especially selected by the god, such as the Hebrew monarchs – a tradition which continues down to the present and remains inscribed on the British coinage.[12] Most modestly of all, the Roman emperors before Constantine (apart from Caligula who is reported to have claimed to be a god) remained human during their lifetime, but could, if well-regarded, be promoted to divinity following their death.[13] Vespasian on his deathbed is supposed to have complained, 'I think I am becoming a god!'

If we consider in general why hierarchies developed and extended along with advances in urbanisation and technique the answer must be, to use modern terminology, a combination of pragmatic, psychological and ideological considerations. Self evidently, an increasingly complex web of social organisation requires expansion of the corps of organisers, but there seems no reason in principle why this could not have happened on much more egalitarian lines than what everywhere actually became the reality.

However if the alpha male who had emerged from the alpha clan to become the central executive officer and rise into rulership was regarded as the representative of and mediator with the gods, or indeed an actual god himself, and being onside with the gods was viewed as essential to public welfare, then a mechanism, powered by *thymos*, was in place for that individual to demand increasing power of command, deference, acknowledgement of divinity or near divinity, and immoderate material artefacts devoted to his majesty, such as the Egyptian pyramid tombs.

The immediate servants of the god-king, especially those who directly ministered to his divinity, the priesthood, naturally occupied an especially privileged position. Their position was normally strengthened by monopoly possession, if not of basic literacy itself, of control of public narrative, and of other monopolies as well, such as that of sacrifice to the god – the Jewish Bible recounts the strenuous efforts of the Jerusalem priesthood to enforce this monopoly. The god-king's secular servants as well, such as generals and lay administrators, benefited from their proximity to the fount of authority, and the servants of the top servants possessed in their lesser estate lesser privileges, but still privileges.

The most important of these privileges was that of possession, and the cardinal possession was that of the ultimate resource of an agricultural society, namely land, which had been initially communally owned and worked. Ownership, property beyond that of personal effects, now comes into the picture, although not yet necessarily resulting in private property. The landed possession of a royal servant might be revocable at will by the monarch, though in the case of the priesthood that would be unlikely, for their properties were supposed to be that of the god (the existence of rival gods might complicate matters). Though the monarch might be supposed to actually embody the god, that was only for his lifetime, and so the priesthood enjoyed provided pretty secure corporate possession of their lands. 'Clearly, then', as David Graeber expresses it, 'property is not a relation between a person and a thing. It's an understanding or arrangement between people concerning things'.[14]

Of course ownership of land is little use to anybody unless it is utilised for food production or other economic activity, and royal servants certainly would not be doing that with their own hands. A labour force was consequently required, which implied the necessity of coercion, physical or ideological (usually the former), for who would voluntarily toil on behalf of someone else for no reward but purely out of altruism? The consequences are discussed in Chapter 6.

Hierarchy and New Technologies

The process of early urbanisation in Eurasia and Egypt was associated with and accompanied by a cluster of technological and other social developments – the two principal ones being written script and metallurgy. These acted to further divide the division of labour and economic differentiation and therefore a further mechanism for intensifying hierarchical division. The impact of these, like urbanisation itself, was historically monumental.

Writing

The earliest written scripts, particularly the cuneiform of Sumer, which spread throughout the Mesopotamian region, is thought to have originated in the use of symbols to keep accounts of trading and tax relations. They were impressed on clay with a reed stylus, clay being the most convenient medium available in the region. Later they were carved on rock, leaving, other things being equal, records that would last not merely for centuries but for millennia.

These latter texts of course were royal proclamations or records of royal triumphs, frequently boasting of successful battles, massacres, tortures and enslavement. The contemporary Egyptian dynasties also left plenty of monumental carved records, using the Egyptian pictogram or hieroglyphic script, but the Egyptians also made use of another medium, papyrus, made from reeds and which could be regarded as a form of paper – certainly the word is derived from it. It was marked with ink, again using a reed stylus, unlike the Chinese ideogram script, which was done with a brush. Papyrus, made from organic material, is very perishable of course, but in the particular Egyptian conditions of soil and climate, could, if protected, last for centuries. The first alphabetic script, the Phoenician, from which all others are descended was again devised for the purposes of trade – the Phoenicians were a great trading community.

The possession of literacy – which need not necessarily mean that a particular individual was literate, but might instead be that they were in a position to employ scribes who had mastered the technique – provided immense hierarchical advantages. It divided a population between the lettered and unlettered, the command or lack of a symbolic resource which went beyond mere speech and those who commanded it were the possessors of wealth and other privileges. They therefore had the leisure to learn to read if so inclined, or if not to hire literate scribes.

Such advantages permitted rulers to communicate more effectively and at long distance, transmitting orders and receiving reports to and from their governing subordinates. It enabled them to keep records of taxes and services owed and which were paid or remaining unpaid. It preserved records of their achievements and ancestry, both important considerations. It gave concrete form to the law codes. It took on great ideological significance, consolidating the religious beliefs which underpinned social function and validated the rulers' position.

Literacy in those eras (one might see an analogy with software programming in our own) was a craft profession, intended at that time to serve the purposes of elites. Scribes, the masters of the craft, wrote and read for their masters, not for themselves. The possession of this tool, strengthening the grip of rulers and priests, enabled them 'to facilitate the enslavement of other human beings', according to Claude Levi Strauss.[15]

This context repeated itself (one is almost tempted to say 'to the letter') in the Mesoamerican Neolithic civilisation. The Andean Inca society did not have a written script but used a code of knotted cords to convey information. The outcome was a similar one. Social differentiation was particularly emphasised when the script was cuneiform, ideographic or pictographic – to master any of these required long training and practice. The appearance of alphabetic script may well have enabled literacy to spread more widely – it nevertheless remained a possession of elites and gave them enormous social and cultural advantage. It is not surprising that the illiterate should have regarded written documents with awe and imagined that if something, particularly laws, was written down it must certainly possess authority.

Metallurgy

Metals, apart from gold and native copper (difficult to find but relatively easy to work) are difficult to produce and process. You need training in the techniques. They mostly require great heat and an intimate knowledge of how to handle both the raw material and the finished product to give the right result – how to turn the ore into crude metal and that into a useable object. This usually required knowledge of how to combine it with exactly the right quantity and character of alloy. Get it slightly wrong and the finished object – tool, container or weapon – could be useless. The Japanese swordsmiths of the European medieval era were probably the ultimate non-mechanised technicians, but the steel they employed lay millennia in the future.

The first metal to be smelted and formed into a functional or decorative object was copper, naturally enough since it is the easiest. The renowned iceman – the frozen corpse of a Neolithic traveller discovered in the Alps relatively recently, preserved for over five millennia by the frozen environment – had among the possessions found beside him an axe with a copper blade.[16] The disadvantage of pure copper is that as well as not being particularly plentiful it is also relatively soft and therefore, while easy to work, of limited advantage as a tool or weapon. Mixed with tin or zinc[17] however, it gives much harder materials – bronze or brass – and these, particularly the former came to be widely used in various functions, one of them giving its name to a historical era – the Bronze Age.

The early urban civilisations of the Middle East and China, both dating roughly to the third millennium BCE, were cognate with the use of bronze as the metal of choice, but since its raw materials were relatively scarce ones (tin is plentiful but of little use on its own) its products were correspondingly valuable ones and so stone remained in wide usage for less esteemed purposes, such as ploughshares or hammers. In the Chinese context bronze was used almost exclusively for ritual objects.

Iron Age

Iron overcomes these disadvantages – the ore is plentiful and when alloyed produces an object far harder and much cheaper than a bronze one. Its disadvantage is that it is much harder to work and requires a much higher temperature (steel, which is an alloy of iron and carbon, even more so). Nevertheless these disadvantages were overcome and iron came to displace bronze for useful instruments – in parts of East Asia and sub-Saharan Africa, to oversimplify somewhat, the Neolithic passed directly into the Iron Age at an uncertain date but probably during the first millennium BCE. With each of the earlier technological/cultural revolutions, which, it is necessary to bear in mind, were gradual rather than overnight developments, social structures were very significantly affected. The general line of development in the movement from stone to bronze, the urbanisation process and the establishment of written scripts, was to widen and reinforce the gap between elites and the mass of the population over whom they exercised their elite powers. Ownership of bronze weaponry and armour was a mark of high status.

The advent of ironworking technology, which probably began in Anatolia but because of its inherent difficulty took time to develop, redressed the balance somewhat for a time, as iron was both a superior metal and much more widely available once the technology was established. A peasant armed with an iron axe could take on and possess an advantage over a Homeric warrior with his bronze sword. Moreover iron tools, now widely available, meant the possibility of much higher productivity in agriculture and handicrafts. Mann suggests that the Iron Age revolution may have generated a self-conscious subordinate agricultural class. The Greek poet Hesiod (seventh or eighth century BCE) would be an iconic example.[18]

The immediate results of the metallic transition however were chaotic,[19] and involved the overrunning and destruction of Bronze Age empires throughout the Middle East on either side of 1000 BCE. The cheapness and availability of iron shifted the power balance towards rain-watered agriculturalists and nomads on the fringes of the Bronze Age civilisations. Mann suggests that iron put an end to the superiority of the chariot as an instrument of war. Undoubtedly there occurred large-scale violent migrations within the eastern Mediterranean around this time, though their exact character is obscure.

Among those which went down were the Mycenaean kingdoms of mainland Greece, empires and kingdoms in the fertile crescent and the Hittite empire in Anatolia (ironically, it having been a pioneer of iron use) and eventually the Egyptian empire. Having fought off the early attacks from the rather mysterious 'sea peoples' it was successively overrun by its Assyrian, Persian and Macedonian rivals. Possibly it may have been the same socio-political environment of the earlier centuries of the first millennium BCE which enabled the establishment of the Hebrew kingdoms around that period. According to Michael Mann 'The collapse of the Hittites and the Mycenaeans, and the retreat of Egypt to the Nile, left a power vacuum along the eastern shores of the Mediterranean. The whole area became decentralised and petty states abounded'.[20] What is striking is that within a few short centuries, when this 'dark age' ended, the divine monarchies had reasserted themselves, expansionist and tyrannical as ever, even more misogynist than their predecessors and with a growing taste for eunuchs.

Empires

The Middle East empires of the first millennium BCE, once the chaotic conditions of the transition had passed, were what we would term as the earliest Iron Age civilisations, were it not that their written records cause them to be regarded as historical (the archaeological concept of 'Iron Age' is applied to preliterate communities). They copied in a fairly exact or even more strongly emphasised form, the hierarchies and habits of their Bronze Age predecessors.

A succession of these empires dominated the entire region, beginning with the Assyrian, through the Babylonian, succeeded by the Persian, followed by the Hellenistic and eventually the Roman. The associated peasantries, including the Egyptian (along with their rulers)[21] were the victims of them all, though even by the standards of Bronze Age or later monarchies, the Assyrian empire,[22] with its capital at Nineveh in northern Mesopotamia, had a particularly unsavoury reputation. This was not only because of their kings' ruthless aggression, which employed massacre, mass torture, including of children, and deportation as routine methods of government (and boasted about them). Even when a community submitted unresistingly, constantly enhanced demands for tribute would reduce them to penury and drive them to distraction or hopeless revolt. The Phoenicians apparently developed their seagoing culture as a means of escaping the intemperate pressures to which the Assyrian rulers subjected them. Assyria owed its period of dominance to the fact that its original capital, the city of Assur,[23] was strategically placed on trade routes. Later its kings gained control of rain-watered cornlands and iron ore deposits. In the empire the role of peasant farmers/soldiers was similar to that of the much later Romans; free agriculturalists in their youth owing military service to the monarch.

It has been suggested that the Assyrian empire, rather than being uniquely brutal, deliberately exaggerated and emphasised its atrocities as a means of terrorising its subjects and rivals, and that the depiction of horrors in which they delighted need not be taken too seriously, the very fact however that such propaganda methods were favoured speaks for itself. 'A militarily inventive group was capable of . . . holding down terrorised population by the threat and occasional use of ruthless militarism', according to Mann.[24]

Imperial Impacts

The brutal impact of these empires was not confined to their contemporaries. Each handed on to its successors styles of government, cultural practices and ideologies that dominated western Eurasia down to the modern epoch. 'Severe social conflict was endemic to the Roman Empire, as it was to all ancient empires . . . in a sense, banditry was perverted class warfare.'[25] Indeed if we consider that the history, religion and mythologies of Judaism were formed in the crucible of these empires, particularly the Babylonian and the Persian, later, for Christians, the Roman, their resonance is still very much with us in the twenty-first century CE. However, the fact that very similar styles of rulership evolved quite independently in eastern Asia and the Americas does suggest that agrarian civilisations, whether employing stone or metal as the instrument of their production and destruction, have a natural affinity for government by god-emperors or their slightly less pretentious equivalents. They create hierarchies with a divine ruler at the apex, a ruling elite, and made up of landowning gentry and often, though not invariably, religious functionaries as a separate elevated caste.

The Bronze Age god king had three basic functions, the first being to ensure fertility (possibly this may in the beginning have involved his own ritual sacrifice, especially if he failed to deliver, though that is speculative). The second was to administer the law, the third to command his warriors for aggression or defence.

In the ideologies of these cultures it was believed that law was not made (at least not by humans); it pre-existed, and was established by divine fiat. In actuality of course it embodied the custom of the community: the king's remit was to interpret it, resolve ambiguities, declare penalties and, possibly, codify it, as was famously done by the Babylonian monarch Hammurabi in the eighteenth century

BCE (although Mann suggests that Hammurabi's code may well have been more ambition than actuality).[26]

Hammurabi begins by announcing that the gods have commissioned him to codify and publicise the laws they have instituted. Penalties for violation vary from fines of precious metals, through torture, mutilation or enslavement to horrific forms of execution. The Judaic law code, famously, was supposed to have been directly dictated by the deity from Mount Sinai – in actuality it was codified during the Babylonian exile in the sixth century BCE, and lays an unusual emphasis on religious duties. Deprived of a king, the exiled Jews refusing to assimilate to the Babylonian culture were obliged to depend upon their religious representatives for ideological leadership, which meant religious observance and the law, with a marked overlap between them.

What law codes did was regulate behaviour and specify sanctions for breaches of the same regulations. They had a lot to say about sexual relations in cultures where women were regarded as a form of property, belonging either to their menfolk, their husband or their owner if they were slaves. The laws also regulated equity, what would be known later as civil law, whereby disputes usually over property rights, would be settled according to the law code. However losing such a lawsuit could have severe consequences for life and limb as well as one's property.

Caste

Separating off of a ruler and immediate acolytes from the remainder of society is only one of the forms in which hierarchical relationships can be embodied. The separation of the entire community into different orders with differential obligations and privileges based exclusively on descent with regulation (almost invariably prohibition) of intermarriage between them, was an important historical phenomenon.

Best known in its Hindu version, caste differentiation was widely practised throughout Eurasia and Africa into historic and even modern times. It combined three elements – occupational exclusiveness, hereditary descent and domination/ subordination. Those at the bottom of the heap suffered not merely physical maltreatment but also ceaseless humiliation in order to remind them of the inferiority of their place.

At the time of the settlement of the Indian subcontinent (c.1500 BCE) by northern invaders, whose military advantage was provided by the use of chariots, the invaders were apparently divided into three castes – priests, warriors and cultivators. Later as the centuries passed the system developed into an extremely complex and differentiated one with endless subdivisions (more fully discussed in Chapter 8).

No other caste structure ever rivalled it in scope or complexity. More commonly elsewhere caste structure consisted of respectable members of the community, rich or poor, contrasted to a class of outcastes, despised, shunned, regarded as dirty and prone to disgusting practices, discriminated against and frequently persecuted – outcasts indeed. Examples include the Burakumin of Japan, Jews and Roma throughout Europe, the Cagots in parts of western France and the Basque country (whose origin is unknown). Outcaste or low-caste status could be linked to ethnic differences, such as the Ainu of Japan, Native Americans or African Americans in the USA, non-whites in apartheid South Africa – but not necessarily so, as in the cases of the Burakumin or Cagots, or non-Roma travellers in the UK and Ireland. There appears to have been a tendency for outcaste groups to be particularly associated with occupations involving the handling of dead bodies whether human or animal – gravediggers, tanners, butchers – which may have implications of ritual pollution.

Evidently this did not apply to Jews, where in earlier centuries religious prejudice was explanation enough, but here too, occupational categorisation was important, Jews being associated in the Christian popular mind with moneylending and trade in valuable objects – they were forbidden to own land and excluded from the craft guilds. The Roma too not only had a distinct language and culture, but were specially associated with itinerant peddling and disreputable practices involving magic. Their itinerant lifestyle was in itself an offence to the settled populations they moved among, populations themselves living on the edge and all too ready to find objects of blameworthy prejudice particularly when encouraged by religious and secular authority.

Honour

Along with the concept of law, sometimes in association, at others in opposition, is that of honour, with its closely associated though not identical concept of *thymos*, recognition or respect. It is suggested that honour originated in nomadic clan societies where codes of honour substituted for the absence of written law codes. It was dishonourable to disrespect a fellow clansperson or infringe his possessions. Such possessions included sexual partners and offspring, personal equipment or herd animals, depending on the society.

With the evolution and establishment of agrarian hierarchical societies, notions of honour were carried over into them, but altered and modified to fit changing circumstances. The point about honour was that it required the individuals often to exert a disagreeable effort and act against what might well be their own sentiment, in other words to accede to the collective demands of their society rather than to follow their personal inclination. Normally it was closely tied to hereditary status but unlike such status honour could be easily lost by deeds of commission or omission.

Clan structures, nominally based on descent but frequently on adoption, continued into agricultural and citified societies – they existed in classical Greece;

the Roman gentes and the Scottish highland clans are further examples. Indeed clan structures are virtually a cultural universal, dying out in lowland Europe only in the medieval era and, at that time, nowhere else. The especial situation of slaves in general and eunuchs in particular was that they were torn away from their clan societies and therefore made totally dependent on the goodwill of their masters.

Honour required a clan to take care of its members, specifically to take their part against injury or threat coming from outside. The worst of all crimes was to injure or kill a fellow clan member. The honour of the clan (later, with the decline of clan society, of the family) was a cardinal consideration, which in unusually lawless societies such as Sardinia or Albania often resulted in the blood feud: if a clan member was killed revenge had to be exacted against a member of the offending clan (not necessarily the offender in person). In order to diminish blood-feuding, Anglo-Saxon kings instituted the wergild system, whereby a specified money payment could be offered in place of blood vengeance. Clan members forfeited their own honour and were liable to severe punishment if they failed to uphold that of the clan.

Honour was also individual and honour was differential – the higher your social standing the more of it you had, but at the same time the more you could lose and the more you were obliged to insist upon receiving due deference. Among males a slight to your honour, whether from an inferior or an equal, required reprisal, otherwise your own honour was compromised – when women were involved the issue was more complicated. Loss of honour on the part of a Japanese samurai could only be expunged by ritual suicide. If the issue was between equals this frequently resulted in a duel, often lethal, though in European society not necessarily so if honour was satisfied with minor injury on either side. An inferior was not fit to duel with; he had to be humiliated at best or more likely physically punished – thrashed, mutilated or even murdered.

Individual honour however was not confined to the elites. Except for those at the very bottom of the social scale, subjects of the monarch or those on legitimate business within his territories enjoyed a graded measure of honour. When ambassadors or inferior lords were in the presence of a god-king they were required to prostrate themselves, but if the monarch then failed to accord them the lesser honour that they were entitled to expect he was regarded as behaving dishonourably. Likewise a nobleman was supposed to respect his personal servants or even, if he were a feudal baron, his freeholder tenants.

As the frequency of aggressive relationships between communities grew, developing into full-scale warfare in agrarian societies, one particular type of honour received increasing emphasis, particularly when elites consisted of military castes. This was the requirement to show courage in battle – a particularly difficult demand in cases when every natural impulse is to avoid fighting, especially if the odds are unfavourable. For a warrior or soldier, therefore, cowardly behaviour, or even to show fear, was the most disgraceful and shameful of all possible acts, particularly if they were leaders or officers. At a famous naval battle of the late tenth century in a Norwegian fiord, one of the Viking leaders panicked and fled and was consequently disgraced for evermore.

For women in honour/shame societies the equivalent was modesty. This included strictly subordinating themselves to their male relatives, keeping closely to the sexual regulations imposed by misogynistic custom or the law, making themselves as inconspicuous as possible in mixed company, staying indoors or even totally covering their bodies and veiling themselves if venturing abroad. In the law code drawn up by the Babylonian monarch Hammurabi, while respectable women were required to veil themselves, prostitutes,[27] who were accorded no honour or modesty, were strictly forbidden to do so and savagely punished if they disobeyed. In the Confucian culture of imperial China respectable women were subjected to the 'three obediences' – obedience to her father before marriage, to her husband during marriage, and to her son during widowhood. In reality, a frequent trope in Chinese narratives both fictional and otherwise was the manner in which women, tyrannised before and during their marriage, in their widowhood tyrannised in turn over their daughter-in-law.

Once law codes were instituted they naturally tried to incorporate considerations of honour, above all for the upper orders – the wergild system is an example – but not infrequently came into conflict with its demands. A priority for the monarch was to institute peace in his realm, which helped to ensure that the taxes and tributes kept flowing satisfactorily, but for an aristocrat honour required violent private satisfaction for any injury or insult. Nor was that the full extent of the problem, for family honour, as mentioned above, could easily result in the initiation of a blood feud with consequent disruption of the peace and departure from the legal process.

The method of settlement for the upper classes in the form of the formal duel between the offender and the man he had offended was termed 'giving satisfaction'. At least it avoided the spreading of the conflict, and though usually illegal was treated rather as cannabis smoking is at the present time – custom refused to consider it as a crime. In the early nineteenth century two British cabinet ministers engaged in a duel, although it was something of a farce. The great Russian poet Pushkin however died in one around the same time, as did a leading American politician, killed by no less a person than the Vice-President. On occasion however governments seriously tried to outlaw the practice, and in seventeenth-century France Cardinal Richelieu, the effective ruler, made it a capital offence. Two young aristocrats defied his decree by fighting a duel in the middle of Paris – and were executed beneath his window for their presumption, but that did little to suppress duelling in France.

Games of Thrones: The Rules of Ruling

Though I could with barefaced power sweep him from my sight and bid my will avouch it, yet I must not.

—William Shakespeare (*Macbeth*)

The seventeenth-century English political philosopher Thomas Hobbes, in his famous *Leviathan*, argued for a social contract origin to government in which men (women didn't count of course, let alone juveniles) by an original agreement surrendered their natural freedom in lives that were 'nasty, brutish and short' in order to live instead under a sovereign. This would usually be an individual but sometimes a corporate body. This sovereign would see to the protection of their lives, properties and families and in return was thereafter owed virtually absolute obedience. In historic terms of course this contract was mythic, though less nonsensical than his contemporary Sir Robert Filmer's notion that monarchs were justified in their sovereign actions on account of the fact that they were successors of Adam. In conceptual terms however Hobbes had a point – even the most absolute of sovereignties embody an element of consent.

Monarchy has been the default mode of agrarian civilisations and of the nomadic pastoral cultures which from time to time in the course of Eurasian history preyed upon them, but it could only emerge in specific conditions and in these two types of society was a very different business. In the latter case it was a much looser and less institutionalised, arrangement. Mobile groups of herders provided an insufficient basis for absolutist forms of monarchy, particularly if the leading men among the flocks objected strongly to it. Leaders of nomadic horsemen such as Attila or Genghis Khan were indeed able to establish monarchies of formidable power but it is clear from the histories of these conquerors that ability to organise and firmly rule tribal coalitions was only made possible by the prospect of plundering or seizing control of the settled areas.

Tightly organised and entrenched monarchy with quasi-divine rulers necessitates a sufficient growth in numbers and settlement in particular locations. It was no accident that such monarchies emerged alongside citification; that was the essential starting point. Farming, depending on geography, soil and climate, could take place in nucleated villages with peasant plots and communal village lands, whether riverine or rain-watered, or in scattered homesteads, the former being typical in most of Eurasia and the Americas, the latter largely confined to heavily forested northern Europe. Village lifestyle, as noted, brought with it social differentiation growing out of kin networks and frequently imbricated with claimed contact to the spirit world. It has been suggested by anthropologists, for example Kent Flannery and Joyce Marcus that the 'men's house' frequently occurring in such contexts, a taboo-protected building with hierarchical seating arrangements from which uninitiated clan members were excluded, was the embryo of the citified temple dedicated to a particular god, becoming a sacred space due to the cult objects conserved within it. Within such a context, they argue, the dominant lineage of a dominant clan was likely to allow the emergence of a dominant individual.

Such an individual would demand and receive deference and gifts and tribute on a more or less consistent basis – but was also expected to redistribute much of that: the tradition of royal generosity was a universal one which continued down into European early modern times. Stingy monarchs were unpopular ones, and though miserliness might sometimes be efficacious in strengthening their rule, it was more likely to endanger it. The same applied lower down the line as well; the wealthy magnates of cities in the Roman republic and empire who held municipal authority were expected to be lavish with their gifts for civic improvement, and one at least was lynched for failing in this respect.

Monarchical rule appears to have been imposed with relative ease in Egypt, Mesopotamia and China (conflict was principally about who should do the ruling) but was not unresisted in some parts of classical urban civilisation, particularly in the Mediterranean area. The legends of the Jewish scriptures hint at popular reluctance to institute a monarchy, while Athens and Rome expelled their early kings and Sparta and Carthage reduced theirs to nominal status. Oligarchic rule was the default option in the commercial cities of the classical Mediterranean, though some were monarchies and the Athenians experimented lengthily with a democracy of male citizens (excluding women, slaves and resident outsiders) until this was overthrown firstly by the Macedonian monarchy and later even more definitively by republican Rome. Such alternative forms of rule tended to exist either among newly-settled nomadic groups, in areas of logistically difficult terrain or else commercially-orientated settlements, particularly coastal ones.

In pre-Iron Age and Iron Age northern Europe, where settled agriculture was practised and social differentiation had occurred, it is possible that sacralised figures were appointed as representatives of the community or clan before the gods and possibly exercised some wider authority, though it could not have been very much. The disinterred bog bodies from that era are a possible sign of such an outcome. Their remarkable anatomical preservation thanks to the chemical qualities of the bogs suggests that most of them were individuals of some social standing rather than executed criminals, and while they may simply be human sacrifices (some undoubtedly were), it appears rather more likely, from knowledge of climatic conditions in which they lived, that at least some were sacred monarchs who had fallen down on their primary responsibility of keeping the weather gods onside and were sacrificed to appease them.[28] The proliferation of petty kings in Ireland in historic times may hint at a similar conclusion.

Further north, principally in Scandinavia, communities of isolated farmsteads, while possibly owing allegiance of a sort to a local 'big man', were even more resistant to the imposition of kingship. Lawmaking and settlement of disputes were conducted at open-air gatherings known as Things, in which at least all heads of families and an even broader range of adult males participated. The kings who appeared from late in the first millennium CE had enormous difficulty in enforcing their sovereignty over the area of their claimed rule and some of them got killed trying.[29]

The establishment of kingship among the Germanic-speaking peoples of Northern Europe during that millennium, with all its momentous consequences for subsequent world history, was provoked by a particular circumstance, namely warfare. In conflict with nomadic horsemen from the east and the Roman principate to the south, tribal coalitions elected war leaders, who went on to style themselves kings. Success in war greatly expanded their power and their pretension, not to speak of their material wealth, though they were still obliged to pay heed to the armed warriors in the tribal assembly. From the beginning of the fifth century, sometimes in alliance with the emperors and their regional administrators, sometimes fighting them, they established domains inside the crumbling structure of the Roman empire in the west. Once consolidated, these regimes speedily took off in an authoritarian direction. Perry Anderson summarises it in a couple of instances: 'The royal "Book of Constitutions" promulgated by the new Burgundian realm . . . was consecrated by a small group of 31 leading nobles, whose authority had now manifestly eliminated any popular say in the laws of the tribal community. The Vandal State in Africa became the most ruthless autocracy of all . . . .'[30]

The initial core of an embryonic monarchy in agrarian communities may have been established by some form of agreement between leading families, in response either to an internal crisis threatening the community or an external threat requiring a war leader selected as an individual possessing appropriate *mana*,[31] who then became a sacerdotal figure hedged around with exceptional privileges and taboos. However subsequent expansion into a more extensive state was everywhere – from Polynesia, through Eurasia, North Africa and tropical Africa and the Americas – accomplished or accompanied by armed violence, supplemented on occasion by marriage alliance. Raiding and acquisition of stuff and territory strengthened the position and prestige of the successful aggressor and also acted as an insurance against rivals.[32] The details of warfare for government and society are examined below. Here we are concerned with the 'civil' aspect of ruling within the area of the prince's acknowledged control. Once he (and very occasionally she) had established their position, how did they proceed within their domain and what dilemmas did they confront?

As indicated, apart from waging war (which involved more than fighting, but also recruitment, logistics and supply), the monarch's primary responsibilities were religious, usually involving public ritual performances, and issuing, or causing to be issued, judgements interpreting law and custom among his/her subjects, or at least the more important ones. Certain intrinsic issues confronted any monarchy, regardless of time or place, intrinsic indeed to the leading individual in any form of government. What is necessary to understand is that while ruling may be a privileged occupation it is not an easy or secure one.

Monarchical Servants

The monarch required of course a retinue of personal servants reaching from the equivalent of butlers and chamberlains to the domestic who emptied his chamber pot (and frequently in specific cases the eunuchs who administered his harem). Monarchs also needed a council of advisors and an administrative staff to execute their commands, and it was this which could present particular difficulties.

The Chinese empire ran a very complex examination system from which the mandarin bureaucracy was recruited, elsewhere the equivalent function was generally fulfilled by systems of patronage. Administrative and domestic functions might of course overlap – Richard III is said to have taken advice from his 'groom of the stool', the lackey who attended to his excremental functions.[33] The domestics, the advisors and the administrators together made up the monarch's court. The English terms 'chancellor', 'steward', 'constable' and 'marshal', derive from these functionaries in the medieval era.

This setup necessarily generated substantial problems. Even lowly domestics, not to mention concubines, could be suspected of having undue access to the monarchical ear, and on account of their inappropriate influence arouse jealousy among those who felt themselves more entitled to be in his or her counsel. A notable instance was Mary Queen of Scots' private secretary, David Rizzio, who in 1566 was suspected of inappropriate behaviour in the queen's bed and murdered for his pains. When it came to the administrative staff matters were even worse, for these, of necessity, on account of their responsibilities had to act as day-to-day advisers. In the Chinese imperial courts, the Byzantine and its Ottoman successors, eunuchs from time to time achieved enormous influence and acted as virtual prime ministers.

The magnates of the kingdom or empire were likely to find this distasteful and feel they were being excluded from the position of influence which was theirs by right, and resent it bitterly. Of course as they had other affairs to attend to – their country estates or whatever – they could not be constantly in the monarch's presence and only on occasion be summoned to meet together as a grand council. It was simply impracticable, particularly in an era of pre-modern transport, that these magnates could act as the monarch's close advisers. Generally speaking, if the monarchs governed to the satisfaction of their elite constituency, members of the latter were prepared to put up with the situation. On the other hand, if no satisfaction was forthcoming, if the ruler was ineffective or overwhelmed by defeat abroad or natural disaster or social breakdown, they were in big trouble, particularly if the dissatisfied magnates had military power to hand.

Even if problems like that were avoided, the sovereign was by no means out of the woods, for they still had to take into account plotting, factionalism and disloyalty in the court itself. Nor was that the end of the difficulties. The monarchical bureaucrats in such polities were not isolated inside the court. In most cases, unless brought in as slaves from beyond the frontiers, they would have friends and kin outside it. This led to factionalising and lobbying on their behalf, generating jealousy and dissatisfaction and corrupting the business of government – not to mention skimming off the monarchical revenues, which they would be accused of doing even if they weren't.[34]

All that was relatively routine stuff, but a much more serious peril was always waiting in the wings of palace politics. A powerful court official, especially one who was well-connected outside, might reduce the monarch to a figurehead and seize the effective power for himself and his descendants. It was a situation which recurred repeatedly in hereditary monarchical polities.

It happened to the Merovingian kings of Gaul in late antiquity, in the European Middle Ages some centuries later, to the Japanese emperors and the Abbasid caliphs of Baghdad, and in the modern era to the kings of Nepal. There were both advantages and disadvantages if the monarchy was only semi-hereditary or non-hereditary. In that case it was more difficult for a powerful official to establish dominance beyond a single reign, but on the other hand dynastic legitimacy was then weakened, public discontent less restrained and the obstacle conferred by sacerdotal inheritance against an ambitious usurper was missing; one reason why palace coups were so prevalent in the Byzantine empire.

It was not surprising therefore that from the earliest days of monarchy, dynasties of effective rulers did not normally last very long. To the often violent dialectic of interaction between the centre and periphery (roughly speaking the rulers and their magnates) was added the poisonous stew of palace politics, often exacerbated by succession crises when an evident heir was lacking (see Chapter Four).[35] Machiavelli's most renowned text, *The Prince*, is intended as a handbook for rulers to assist them to avoid the sort of traps involved in ruling. It was never intended to be a public document. However it might be suggested that the cardinal piece of advice to any individual about to enter a non-figurehead monarchical role ought to be, 'Watch your back!'

It is quite remarkable how not merely in monarchies but almost invariably in any collective, exercising some sort of governance at however modest a level, the same essential social structures emerge with variations according to circumstance. It applies as much (if not more) to the Vatican as to any secular rulership (the Medici example is noted in Chapter 4) and to absolutist regimes in the modern era (Mussolini once said that he was the most disobeyed man in Italy, and the Third Reich was a quagmire of rival factions competing for the Führer's favour).[36] The Soviet regime, particularly its central Politbureau, whether in its pre-Stalinist, Stalinist or post-Stalinist phases, though less incoherent, nevertheless displayed similar characteristics in a modified form.

The same applies at all levels and is found in the subordinate arms of central government, in democratic cabinets, in local authorities at every level, in capitalist businesses,[37] in university senates and courts of governors, in newspaper offices, in voluntary associations and organisations of every sort. I cannot resist referring to what I observed when I was induced in the late 1970s to take on the editorship of the monthly newspaper of the Scottish Old Age Pensions Association, *Scottish Pensioner*, and consequently had to sit in on the SOAPA executive committee. I used to joke that I was getting my old age over with early, but one of the things which astonished me was the degree of personality conflicts, spite, manoeuvre, infighting and factionalism within this elderly collective. All the historical evidence suggests that this sort of behaviour is a universal in even the most minimally hierarchical of structured organisations.

Personality Cults

The early modern king of France, unlike his English/British counterpart, but comparable to most of his European contemporaries, was an absolute monarch, the fount of law as well as the fount of honour (though in practice an absolute monarch was far from being in a position to do whatever he or she[38] liked). These absolute monarchs, enveloped in the sacerdotal atmosphere claimed also by the non-absolute British one, could be justifiably regarded as the conceptual descendants of the god kings of the early civilisations. The sacred character of the latter was eventually assumed also by the later Roman emperors, who passed it on in turn to their European successor monarchs, who found their mystic (and mythic) justification in the practice of anointing described in the Jewish Bible.[39] The Chinese emperors likewise claimed a 'mandate from Heaven', the Muslim monarchs drew their religious justification from their office of 'Commander of the Faithful'.

It raises a very interesting question of how these notions and practices were ever allowed to take hold.[40] No doubt tradition and imitation played a significant part, but again, as with agriculture the institution was invented separately in several different locations, ending up with very similar results. No doubt also, individuals who had the power to do so were inclined to enjoy a life isolated as far as possible from the rigours of the natural world, taking advantage of the benefits which agrarian-based technology made possible without having to endure the endless toil and uncertainties that afflicted the majority of their subjects. Command over force and violence put into their hands the means to enjoy without restraint the labour of slaves, the expertise of artisans, the comforts of numerous concubines – and only sacerdotal *mana* leading to intensities of devotion could provide sufficient excuse for being awarded such privileges.

What is startling is to see this syndrome still alive and well into the present era, and in some particularly unexpected places. The practices of the gurus of esoteric religious outfits such as the Maharaji or Scientology cults are notorious in that the cult leaders live in magnificence while their deluded followers devote their lives to raising the funding necessary to sustain such self-indulgent lifestyles. But the very last place where any similar devotional cult phenomenon would be expected and no sacerdotal *mana* is at issue, namely the twentieth-century communist movement, is exactly where, until Khrushchev denounced it in 1956, it flourished remarkably.

Khrushchev's target was the cult of Joseph Stalin as Soviet and international communist leader. Stalin's power by the late 1930s was about as absolute as absolute power was possible to be, and while affecting simplicity and necessarily eschewing magnificence, he lived in considerable style, and his affected modesty was surrounded by a personality cult of gargantuan proportions.[41] However it was not only a question of Stalin – most of the leaders of communist parties, regardless of whether or not these were ruling parties, cultivated similar styles of adulation around their personalities.

At the same time they were constrained by what Kevin Morgan has referred to as Stalin's super-cult, required to pay him deference, and if they stepped out of line and opposed his policies, even implicitly, could be subject to sanctions in the name of Stalin.[42] Morgan refers to 'the integrating effect of practices of veneration, providing a point of cohesion and authority for deeply fragmented or unsettled societies'.[43] The cult around Mao Zedong in his latter days between 1966 and 1974 paralleled or even exceeded that of Stalin. Formally, in an attempt to evade the comparison, reference was made to Mao's 'thought' rather than his personality – not that this deceived anyone. Even these cults however were modest in comparison to that which the family dynasty of North Korean leaders created around themselves from the 1950s into the present century.

Nothing like that has, by contrast, occurred with the Cuban communist leaders. No evident reason for this exception is easily available, but the pre-revolutionary culture of the island may have had some significance and also that the Cuban communist leaders did not emerge directly out of the Marxist-Leninist tradition but had separate origins and took over the communist party from outside, so to speak. It can be concluded, tentatively, that humans, when they have the opportunity, do indeed have an intrinsic liability to behave in a dictatorial manner but that each case, whether in the usual sequence or among the exceptions, must be explained in its own terms of external and internal pressures combined with inherited culture, to explain which outcome is the one that is eventually realised.

Culmination

By the commencement of the Iron Age around 800 BCE, although huge tracts of the inhabited world in all the continents, amounting to the greater part of the earth's surface, still belonged to foragers, humans in a limited number of areas had come a very long way from their ancestral lifestyles, and the future belonged to them (or rather to some of them).

Neolithic and Bronze Age artefacts can certainly be very impressive, as anyone visiting a museum display of the ancient or pre-Columbian civilisations can testify. Iron-using technology, however, multiplied enormously the productivity of agrarian techniques. For example reaping with an iron sickle (bronze was too valuable to be wasted on such lowly instruments) is greatly more proficient than doing so with a flint blade let alone one of overfired pottery. The same applies to the difference between stone and iron ploughshares.

The Iron Age which succeeded its bronze-based predecessor was the culmination of a lengthy process. Within Eurasia Bronze Age agrarian rank societies had given rise to civilisation (in the technical sense of city life) though the lead-in had stretched over several millennia. With city life came an efflorescence of hierarchy and social differentiation, reinforced by religion, property rules, written script and metallurgy. Iron-based technology greatly multiplied the force of production and weaponry and with them the opportunities for domination and control by elites. In the last analysis what this social differentiation, intensifying over the centuries, meant was that elites were ever more favourably placed to pump resources out of the labour of basic producers. This process will be developed in Chapter 6.

6

Exploitation and Violence

The gigantic protection racket of political history began: 'Accept my power, for I will protect you from worse violence – of which I can give you a sample if you don't believe me.'
—Michael Mann (*The Sources of Social Power, Volume 1*)

Exploitation and the Extraction of Surplus

The intention of this chapter is to consider the methods and manner through which elites, formed in the hierarchies discussed previously, extract material resources from the populations subject to them, the conflicts generated by this relationship, and the mechanisms through which these elites transfer their extracted wealth between each other in the context of power relations. Certain other forms of violent interaction are referred to in other chapters, principally 5 and 7.

Violence and economic exploitation are closely intertwined (as is resistance to the latter). 'The history of all hitherto existing society', according to *The Communist Manifesto*, 'is the history of class struggles . . . oppressor and oppressed stood in constant opposition to one another'. (Later Engels corrected this to exclude what he termed 'primitive communism' and would now be described as hunter-gatherer communities.)

Social class does indeed remain the most effective and most realistic concept for analysing material exploitation, and this is where Marxist analysis is at its strongest. However, though not entirely useless, class is a very poor predictor of social consciousness, for economic or social classes do not as a rule simply line up against each other like opposing armies, and this is where Marxist analysis has proved to be at its weakest and most fallible.

The four structural forms of coercive exploitation are tribute, serfdom (a more intense form of tribute) chattel slavery, and wage labour, with many variations of detail within each form. Tribute was historically the prevalent form whereby dependent cultivators or craft workers were coercively made to render either part of their product, or their labour services or both, either to a local superior or to central government, whether by a contract they couldn't refuse or by naked terror. Serf society went a step further by binding the toilers and their descendants to a particular lord while leaving them in possession of a minimum of customary rights. Chattel slavery removed even that element – slaves were the rightless property of their masters and totally at their disposal (though exceptionally cruel treatment might earn social disapproval). Even formally free labour is not without a coercive element if the labourer has to take whichever employment is on offer however atrocious the rewards or conditions, or else starve. This is the situation which many workers, particularly female ones, find themselves in during the twenty-first century in countries such as India, Bangladesh, Indonesia, China, in the manufacture of consumer commodities like clothing, computer equipment or sports gear.

Such relationships have throughout history been covered with all manner of ideological[1] justifications, very frequently religious ones in the form of divine ordination, but also, and increasingly in the modern era by secular ones focused on the market instead. These justifications are extremely important – they create the ideological hegemony which makes the social order they relate to take on the masks of obviousness and necessity – at least among the elites.

For the latter reason, class alone cannot explain the prevailing social consciousness in any given society.[2] Subordinated classes from time to time resist and revolt, and it is claimed that there were episodes in Chinese history where the recorded rates of peasant revolt amounted to 1.8 *per hour*.[3] In such contexts class struggle at some level, from passive resistance, through strikes and litigation to insurrection, is always going on – but for most of historical time the members of the subjected class have accepted their lot, however reluctantly, and sought private accommodations.

Beyond such social acceptance however there invariably stands violent coercion either as a threat or as a reality. Such violence has always been the ultimate business of the state throughout recorded history and doubtless earlier, and manifested little less in societies in which state formation was embryonic or non-existent. In 'normal' times those at the sharp end give little thought to the matter. If they do, and express their resentment, the threat of repression usually silences them, but when social tension rises beyond a certain point state violence is invariably deployed to resolve matters and conserve the social structure. If it fails we call that a revolution.

As we have already seen in earlier chapters, class differentiation can only become marked with communities' stabilisation of location (nomadic herding communities having been on the whole more egalitarian) and the ability of an individual producer to produce substantially more than they biologically require for immediate consumption. Consequently the surplus can be drained off, by whichever means, for the use and benefit of an elite stratum directing the society, together with the functionaries whose business it is either to serve them in exerting control, or else to produce the artefacts coveted by the rulers. Invariably the exercise of secular power by lords and monarchs comes along with functionaries whose remit is to justify it ideologically and usually with reference to the spirit world – though they may be tasked with other functions as well, such as, in ancient

Mesopotamia, setting the calendar, observing the stars and purporting to predict the future.

Such a development is one of inherent instability. An interaction is set in motion which very often resulted in the unification of settlements into cities and cities with their dependent rural hinterlands into agriculturally-based empires ruled by divine monarchies. This tended to be especially the case in Eurasia and Egypt where the settlements were based around major river valleys. The development, without the riverine aspect, was repeated in Mesoamerica and the Andes, and in all cases involved much conflict with accompanying bloodshed as rival local rulers gambled with their lives and those of their subjects as they struggled to acquire the supreme position. As Kent Flannery and Joyce Marcus note:

> Colonialism was created neither by anthropologists nor Queen Victoria. It is at least 4,300 years old, the product of kings who sought to add land and tribute to their realms. The Sumerians, Akkadians, Assyrians, Hittites, Greeks, Romans, Moors, Aztec and Inca [and Chinese] did not learn their craft from anthropologists and most of their leaders make Queen Victoria sound like Mother Theresa.[4]

These processes, however much they were bad news for those individuals who toiled in the fields and spilled their blood on the battlefield or the subsequent massacre, propelled an enormous expansion in culture both material and intellectual. Perhaps Walter Benjamin's celebrated remark could possibly be turned round to suggest that many documents of barbarism are also documents of culture. The history of progress is very largely the history of forced labour. That takes many forms, of which the most unvarnished is chattel slavery.

Coercive Labour

Tribute

Michael Mann's view is that 'Significant improvements in surplus acquisition have often come in *historical* societies from increasing the intensity of labour – usually requiring increased physical force'.[5] That defined the essential relationship, while it could at the same time take multiple forms. Slavery might be the most unvarnished, but was not the simplest, which was tribute, equally relying on pure coercion, though the precise nature of that and its knock-on implications, are subjects for considerable analysis. With tribute the producers, without any further obligation or manner of legitimisation, are simply compelled to hand over part of their product to the ruler (who may vary from a robber baron to a god-emperor; in the latter case tribute becomes known as taxation).

Tribute may take the form of labour as well as produce, in which case it is known as corvée – for example the Inca used massive coercive labour gangs to build roads and undertake irrigation projects. Their rule was 'an ideological obsession with centralisation and hierarchy, pushed to the limits of the practicable'.[6] Tribute's operation can also be complicated by a situation where the tribute-payer is a subordinate ruler who in turn extracts it from the producers – and this may proceed through several cycles. Further complexities arise from the necessity to police the exaction process. This requires the tribute-taker to dispose of armed force and to appropriately reward the strong-arm enforcers, as otherwise their arms are likely to be turned against him, as many a Roman emperor discovered.

Slavery

Slavery is both a simpler and a more complex relationship. It is simpler in that the slave is the chattel property of the slave-owner, a 'speaking tool' in the Roman terminology, although, inconveniently slaves brought with them the necessity of having to be fed and, normally, clothed, which represented a further expense after purchase. Medical expenses might also be necessary to protect the investment. On the other hand the results of the slaves' labour are wholly at the owners' disposal, whether these be material objects, or services (including gladiatorial and sexual services) or even intellectual products as in the case of slave educators or scribes. This last consideration relates to one of the complexities in slave relationships – the different grades of slaves, which in some unusual instances could even extend to military slaves, or in classical Athens to ones engaged in police duties.

The relationship of sellers and buyers also come into the equation, and of course disputes between owners (and in the Roman instance it was not unheard of for slaves to own slaves). Finally there was also the question of how the owners were to be protected against slave revolt (gladiators, being armed, were especially dangerous). There is no estimate of the number of slaves within the area ruled by Rome at different times or of their proportion of the population. Even Ste Croix comments that '. . . it would be very wrong to draw any conclusions about the total number of slaves in the respective periods',[7] although he notes that 100,000 slaves are said to have been killed in Spartacus's revolt. We do know that early in the imperial period a proposal was made in the Senate to make slaves wear an identifying mark, but this was rejected because it would reveal to the slaves how many of them there were. The Roman legions were above everything else an insurance against slave revolt, the strap which held its slave society together, and the emperors were the buckle in that strap. Therefore the elites put up with these monarchs though they were often enough psychopathic criminals and the terror of the senators.

In the Greco-Roman civilisation along with the privately-owned slaves there were also public slaves, and among these were the least fortunate of them all. They were compelled to toil and largely worked to death in the very worst of environments at the most humanly destructive of labour, especially the mining of precious metals or in the marble quarries which beautified buildings and monuments. The prosperity of Athens at its height was based upon not only slave labour in general but slave labour in the silver mines at Laurion, in conditions which Ste Croix speculates may have given rise to the Christian image of hell. No account exists of what the Laurion mines were like, but there is one of Egyptian mines in Hellenistic times.

> To these mines the Egyptian king sends condemned criminals, captives in war and those who have fallen victim to false accusations or been imprisoned for incurring the royal displeasure, sometimes with all their kinsfolk – both for the punishment of the guilty and the profits which accrue from their labour. There they throng, all in chains, all kept at work continuously day and night. . . . Where the daylight is shut out by the twists and turns of the quarry, they wear lamps tied to their foreheads, and there, contorting their bodies to fit the contours of the rock . . . [toil] on and on without intermission under the pitiless overseers' lash. Young children descend the shafts into the bowels of the earth . . . No-one could look on the squalor of these wretches, with not even a rag to cover their loins, without feeling compassion for their plight. They may be sick, or maimed, or aged, or weakly women, but there is no indulgence, no respite. All alike are kept at their labour by the lash, until, overcome by hardships, they die in their torments . . . and death is welcomed as a thing more desirable than life.[8]

There is no way of knowing definitively when the institution of slavery was actually first established, though it is suggested that it may have been as early as 8000 BCE, in the earlier stages of the Neolithic revolution. Two main sources of slave labour (apart from unfortunates born to it) existed once it became institutionalised. Neolithic communities, like their direct successors in historic times, indulged in frequent aggression, and war captives, male or female, were a regular source of such personnel. The other major source of supply was debt bondage, whereby enslavement was the penalty for inability to meet a debt and represented a major cause of tension and resentment in pre-classical and classical times. The legendary founder of the Athenian state was said to have neutralised revolt and disorder by outlawing debt bondage; slaves had in future to be supplied from war captives or foreign trading connections. Certainly in Athenian society enslaving a fellow-citizen was prohibited.

Slavery had already become an institution by the time the earliest written documents were produced. It features in the Babylonian law-code of Hammurabi of the eighteenth century BCE. In the ancient world, however, and subsequently except in the Greco-Roman world[9] (admittedly an important exception) chattel slavery was probably not the dominant form of forced labour, which, as indicated above, was the exaction of tribute/taxes from a free peasantry. Ironically, what used to be taken as the illustrative example of slave labour, the Egyptian pyramids, are now thought to have been constructed by free part-time labour, though slavery certainly existed in ancient Egypt.

Finally, slavery came into its own again as an economic category during the early modern era, and indeed the modern world was built on its foundation. Chattel slavery came to be practised in the Americas on an industrial scale from the sixteenth century onwards, firstly for the extraction of precious minerals in the Spanish empire, and next, with imported African slaves, as plantation slavery throughout the Americas for the production of cocoa, coffee, rice, sugar, tobacco and ultimately the cotton on which the British industrial revolution was founded, causing Marx to remark that the most advanced form of production was linked intimately to the most primitive. It was not only in the Americas – Scottish miners and saltworkers endured a form of compulsory attachment to and labour for an employer nearly indistinguishable from slavery, until the 1780s and most Russian peasants were the property of their landlords until 1861. Another form of forced labour, prevailing in the twentieth century, was the labour camp for prisoners, widely employed in the European empires (Sartre commented that 'the colonies are our gulags'), the USA, the Soviet Union, China and most spectacularly the Nazi empire.

Slavery ancient and modern has found its ideological justifiers, though it is unlikely that many slaves, if they were aware of them, found these very convincing; but it is manifestly and unmistakably a relationship based on violence, in the first place with the capture of the slaves and thereafter to retain them in that situation along with any offspring they might produce.

Serfdom

Taking into account the varied problems of slave ownership, another method of exacting surplus from basic producers was a more sophisticated version of the tribute relationship, this time dependent upon property in land. In medieval Europe it was known as serfdom, where it had evolved from Roman agricultural slavery. It can be said to have been the prevalent form of economy and surplus extraction between the passing of clan society and the emergence of capitalism.

It had a great many variations and gradations, but in essence the system worked as follows – when for whatever reason a landowner found it uneconomic or inconvenient to cultivate their estates with slave labour or cultivators hired in a wage relationship, the land was leased, either to a family of cultivators or to a managing farmer (the word 'farmer' actually means 'leaser', as in 'tax-farmer', not necessarily an agricultural entrepreneur) who took responsibility for finding the labour force and had the resources to do so and paid rent – in whatever form – to the landowner. A landowner might indeed keep some land for cultivation by his or her own dependants and lease further acreages to enhance their income.

The rent often took the form of labour services, whereby a certain proportion of their time had to be devoted to working the parts of the estate that the lords reserved directly for themselves, in Western Europe known as the demesne. They might in addition have to pay rents in the form of produce – so many pigs, chickens, sheep and so forth, and when the money economy expanded, money rents as well.

The distinguishing feature of serfdom proper, however, was that the cultivators were unfree. They were tied to the lord's estate, as were their descendants, and could not legally depart, moreover their private affairs, such as marriage, were also at the lord's command and for his or her permission required an additional payment. In medieval Europe (including eastern central Europe and Russia, where serfdom persisted much longer than it did in the West), the landowner need not necessarily be an individual – it might be a corporate body in the shape of the church or an urban corporation. Serfdom differed from slavery proper in that it was to some extent regulated by custom and not altogether at the lord's whim. For example a lord could not sell a serf individually to a different owner – that could only be done along with the serf's family and his holding. As a mode of surplus extraction it therefore could have from the landlord's standpoint a certain disadvantage. Its great advantage was that it provided a tied labour force, and in some circumstances, for example in eastern Europe when grain export was at a premium, that advantage outweighed everything else, though it was not the only or the original one, and slavery continued to exist alongside it, though with diminishing prevalence, at least until the twelfth century CE.

The detailed reasons why, in late antiquity, serfdom came to predominate over slavery within Christendom, is something of a controversial issue among medievalists, with Chris Wickham to the forefront.[10] What appears to have happened is that in the former Roman empire, as central control loosened and coercion became localised in monarchies and fiefdoms with less effective coercive apparatus, former agricultural slaves were elevated to the status of serfs, and former free peasants were reduced to that condition. From the elites' point of view agricultural serfdom's advantages outweighed the forfeiture of absolute arbitrary authority – it was marginally more acceptable to the victims than slavery, more easy to defend theologically and less expensive to police.

The landlord could of course also be extracting surplus from free tenants, the difference being that the tenants in question could legally take themselves elsewhere – they were not tied. A feudal system in terms of aristocratic privilege dominating civil, military and political affairs could coexist with an economy of free tenants, as was the case in eighteenth-century France. The advantage of that from the landowner's viewpoint was that they had no responsibility for their tenants' welfare as they would have incurred with serf tenants. The disadvantage of free tenancy from the cultivators' standpoint was that, unless they had a written lease, and in the early modern period many did not, the payments exacted from them could be raised at will, and they could at any point be expelled from their holding if the landlord discovered a more profitable use for it. In Britain and Ireland this was to happen very extensively.

Monarchs in the agrarian empires around the globe, North Africa, Eurasia, the Americas, saw to the transfer of resources from their subjects to themselves, their functionaries and their followers through the customary forms of extraction which they had inherited from their ancestors. Their military capacity guaranteed the flow of surplus, and of course used up a fair proportion of it. Their combined coercive and ideological hold was undoubtedly impressive – not many peasant revolts succeeded, though it is possible that one may have extinguished the Mayan autocracy. There are hints of similar unrest in the Jewish Bible, and the successful revolt led by Judas Maccabeus in the second century BCE was certainly a peasant as much as a religious insurrection.

Another version of the same relationship was debt bondage (see below). This was short of outright chattel slavery, but compelled the debtor family to labour indefinitely on behalf of the creditor, handing over part of their (usually agricultural) product, a form of serfdom or peonage. It was used extensively in China, in traditional South East Asia, by European colonial administrations and in the form of indebtedness for taxes, in Latin America. It was imposed on miners during the British industrial revolution and on Shetland peasants from the early eighteenth to the late nineteenth century.

Wage Labour

The final manner of extracting a surplus through ownership relations was wage labour (dealt with more extensively in Chapter 13) which was to become universal in the modern era though all the older forms described above, from slavery onwards, have survived in certain cases down to the present day. In the wage contract the employer makes a payment, which, being less than the value of the work undertaken, leaves the employer with a profit which then flows through the financial systems that accompany all economies where wage labour is the prevalent mode of exploitation. If the employee has no independent source of income, they are obliged willy-nilly to enter into a relationship of this kind. Though now largely fallen out of use, in the past the term 'wage slavery' was popular in workers' movements. Overall, the relationships of hierarchy and subordination, though they do not altogether coincide with the techniques of surplus extraction, bear a close correspondence with them.

Debt

As a facilitator of social differentiation and exploitation debt was of immense importance. David Graeber's *Debt: The First 5,000 Years*, is a most informative in-depth analysis. Lying at the root of the debt relationship is the universal human propensity to presume that a favour will be reciprocated: 'Anthropology . . . reveals some remarkable commonalities – fundamental moral principles that appear to exist everywhere and that will always tend to be invoked whenever people transfer objects back and forth or argue about what other people owe them.'[11] He defines the principle of debt, as distinct from reciprocity, as an arrangement whereby formal equals agree to be unequal during the time that the debt lasts.[12]

Thus the crucial addition which makes debt such a significant social driver is the presumption that the favour should be measured and be reciprocated with interest – and if the interest is not forthcoming violence will be employed to enforce it. 'Mutual aid can easily slip into coercive inequality.'[13]

> If history shows anything, it is that there is no better way to justify relations founded on violence than by reframing them in the language of debt . . . Mafiosi understand this. So do the commanders of conquering armies. For thousands of years, violent men have been able to tell their victims that those victims owe them something.[14]

A good example of the interrelationship between economy and ideology, this is a very pertinent observation. Operators of protection rackets do not, as a rule, merely demand money, they also purport to offer 'protection' against rival racketeers – and may well do so in order to preserve their investment. Loan sharks do not simply send out the boys with baseball bats to knock randomly on people's front doors – they first establish a financial relationship with their victim.

Graeber is an anthropologist and he points out – something which comes as a surprise to the layperson – that the economy of barter which the pioneers of economics like Adam Smith, and most economists since, have assumed to have preceded monetary economy, is purely mythical. There is *no* example anywhere, or evidence from any period, of an economy which operated primarily through barter. Among forager or non-commercialised agricultural communities, barter does indeed occur, but it is a highly ritualised and occasional event.

How then were pre-monetised exchange relations carried on within or between societies in previous eras, as they must have been? The answer is debt. Transactions were evaluated and recorded against an agreed standard, which could have been anything from a weight of grain to a measure of silver, as was the case in Hammurabi's Babylon. Mesopotamian tablets containing records of debits and credits survive in plenty. Egypt and Sumer economies operated on systems of credit settled in goods. Even in Sumer, where values were *calculated* in silver, the actual metal remained on the whole in temple or royal treasuries. It was recorded debts which made exchange possible, and it did not occur only in the material world of ancient times. Warnings of reincarnative vengeance against defaulters of debts to the gods as well as humans are to be found in Hindu law codes. Graeber notes, apropos of the supernatural element, that in many Indo-European languages the word for 'debt' is cognate with that for 'sin' or 'fault' – and the same is true for the Inca language.

Coinage followed the use of standardised objects, such as ingots or little imitation bronze knives, to calculate exchange and store value.[15] It appeared later, around the middle of the first millennium BCE. Graeber notes that money is not a material object; rather that the material objects, coins or whatever, including banknotes, are more like the beads on an abacus – a means of calculating debt, acting like IOUs.[16] 'What we call "money" isn't a thing at all; it's a way of comparing things mathematically, as proportions: of saying that, 'one of X is equivalent to six of Y'.[17] The electronic money we use today is a symbol of a symbol of a symbol of a social relationship. Graeber argues that the main original purpose of coined money (usually silver during the Greek and Hellenistic eras) since it was an easily transported store of fixed value guaranteed by a powerful state, such as Lydia or Athens, was to pay armies, especially mercenary ones.

Nowadays failure to keep up debt repayments can result in a variety of adverse consequences from repossession up to bodily injury or even death, depending on the creditor. Classical society had other sanctions. Enslavement for debt which the debtor was unable to repay in goods or money was standard in Greco-Roman society and the source of much social conflict. It was not necessarily the debtor himself who was enslaved (though that happened often enough) but, through his patriarchal power, frequently a member of his family. 'This [selling of children by parents] . . . appears in the great agrarian civilisations from Sumer to Rome to China, right around the time when we also start to see evidence of money, markets and interest-bearing loans . . . .'[18]

Indeed, in the classical era, debt became closely aligned with slavery. It was very difficult for ordinary citizens in the Greco-Roman universe to escape falling into debt when bad harvests or other factors beyond their control compelled them to borrow in order to survive. Paying off or partially paying off a debt could often only be accomplished by selling or pawning a family member into slavery, either directly to the creditor or else a slave-dealer. If even that expedient was blocked the debtor himself (or occasionally herself) was enslaved. It was however not only emergency conditions which could trap a householder in the web of debt. Borrowing, to arrange a marriage or for a daughter's dowry or else ritual purposes, could have similar consequences. Graeber suggests that the notion of absolute property rights, stressed in Roman law and handed down through European history, is derived from the relations of slave and master.[19]

Certainly one of the main if not the main social demand of the lower classes, both rural and urban, in Greco-Roman society was the cancellation of debt. It was the one, next to redistribution of landed property, which was most insistently resisted by elites. Very occasionally the demand was successful, as in the Athenian state (ironically a slave society) where at the initiation of the democracy in the sixth century BCE debt slavery was outlawed and it was made illegal to enslave a citizen. That however was a most unusual outcome and did not last very long. One of Graeber's hypotheses is that Greek city-state expansion along the Mediterranean, founding colonies all over it and on the coast of the Black Sea (nearly a thousand between 750 and 550 BCE), was in order primarily to get quit of people who would otherwise have become debtors and generated social crisis.[20]

It is clear that structures of debt have been intrinsic to agrarian societies and their successors, and, based upon the principle of reciprocity, probably existed to some degree even in foraging ones. Certainly in all its forms it is a very powerful engine of social differentiation. Even in the broadest terms, in the practice of making gifts too generous for the recipient ever to repay, it puts the receiver in the debt of the giver both literally and metaphorically, and establishes relationships of superiority and inferiority. Relations of patronage emanating from an original favour remained intrinsic to the fabric of society everywhere down to modern times and persist both in contemporary democracies and the former communist bloc and its successors.

Debt and Religious Rules

Famously, religious institutions have laid down rules regarding monetary debt and have taken a strong interest in interest. Early Jewish law, even preceding the arrival of coinage, prescribed a debt holiday every seven years, the origin of the term jubilee. The very basis of Christian theology is a blood sacrifice 'redeeming' Christians – the word is significant – from their debt burden of 'original sin' in disobeying the deity. Sharia law bans the unvarnished imposition of interest on loans, but since monetary economic activity is practically impossible without it, a variety of clever devices, so that interest doesn't superficially appear to be interest, have been utilised to get around the prohibition. Generally speaking this takes the form of a fee for use of the money.

The medieval Roman Catholic church likewise forbade Christians to take interest, denounced as usury, on loans to other Christians (or at least other Latin ones), but again the impracticality of the rule soon became all too apparent. It was avoided easily enough by the trading cities of the Mediterranean, especially Venice and Genoa, whose trading partners were mostly not Latin Christians. Elsewhere it was more of a problem, particularly for medieval monarchs, who at least by the beginning of the second millennium CE were finding their traditional sources of income insufficient, even for routine governmental requirements but especially for warfare, and had little alternative but to borrow.

Fortunately – or unfortunately, depending on the viewpoint – a solution was to hand. Jewish merchants, not being Christians of course, were theologically permitted to trade in money and make interest-bearing loans, soon developing expertise in the practice. They were banned from landowning or most other professions. The English king Richard I financed his crusade by means of such loans. Of course debtors tend not to like creditors, especially when the latter are pressing for repayment, and so being a medieval Jewish moneylender was a very high risk occupation, for if the lords to whom you had lent had sufficient social authority and insufficient commitment to repay, it was not too difficult to incite an anti-Jewish pogrom as a means of cancelling their debt. Nevertheless some restraint was advisable or they might otherwise find themselves without any necessary creditors.

As the cultural authority of the Papacy weakened in the fourteenth and fifteenth centuries except where kings, as in Spain, found convenience in upholding it, the usury prohibition eroded and Italian moneylenders increasingly came to replace Jewish ones. Both the main Spanish conquistadors, Cortez in Mexico and Pizarro in Peru, were heavily in debt to Venetian and Genoese bankers. For them plunder of Aztec or Inca riches was not merely an expression of surpassing greed but a matter of urgent and pressing necessity.

By the late medieval and early modern centuries in Europe monarchs throughout the continent had found it virtually impossible to wage war without falling into substantial indebtedness. Even the immense bullion revenues spilling into the Spanish treasury from New World plunder, while they helped, did not suffice. The monarchs of the absolutist or would-be absolutist states tried all manner of expedients and devices to cover their deficits, one of the favourites being the sale of offices and honours, or, if nothing else would do, simple repudiation and default.

Popular Protest

The ground-down and exploited peasantries of the Eurasian landmass, despised and treated as dispensable units of production, surviving as best they might with agricultural techniques which permitted in the most favourable circumstances only a small surplus to be produced above bare subsistence. Even that minimal surplus was liable to be seized, along with their womenfolk, by landlords, the state or invaders. Such peasantries, who were subjected to arbitrary ill-treatment, regularly devastated by flood, famine and disease; nevertheless did not submit quietly to their fate.

There is little evidence during the first centuries of civilisation of popular resistance to the Bronze Age elites of the early states and empires (though there are hints of bread and tax riots and a strike among Egyptian tomb and temple workers is recorded) and on the basis of what is known about peasant revolts across Eurasia from subsequent millennia, the likelihood is that such protest against rent (in labour and in product), tribute and taxation (the same) was not unknown in the earlier period. Most of the time no doubt, peasants, slaves,[21] servants, labourers and craft workers endured rather than resisted, for resistance would have been dangerous and without great prospect of success, but on occasions they must have responded collectively to the feeling that 'we have had enough!'. From time to time they could also invoke religious justifications for their action on the basis that the masters were defying the will of the gods by engaging in unfair treatment of their peasant workforce or their artisan producers, or that they were invading outsiders who had destroyed a previously more just social order.

From the time of the later second millennium BCE the evidence grows from a trickle to a torrent. It is initially evidenced by the Amarna Correspondence, a series of fourteenth-century cuneiform tablet letters to the Pharaoh from the rulers of vassal city states of Canaan, covering a number of topics, one of which can be interpreted, as it is by the author and journalist John Pickard, as an appeal for assistance against rural revolt.

> Abdi-Asista . . . sent a message to the men of Ammiya. 'Kill your lord and join the Apiru.'[22] Accordingly the mayors say, 'He will do the same thing to all of us, and all the lands will be joined to the Apiru . . . just now the men of Ammiya have killed their lord. I am afraid' . . . This is clearly a chronicle of *enormous revolutionary upheaval* [original italics]; not a minor skirmish in one town or another, but a mighty movement reaching from modern-day Lebanon in the north to the Egyptian border in the south, involving perhaps tens of thousands of participants, and stretching over many decades . . . one of the earliest *recorded* examples of a revolutionary movement . . . . [23]

It is his suggestion, though this is disputed, that an element of the *Apiru*, which the Egyptian records define as the *Shasu*, constituted a more coherent rural revolutionary movement and were the originators of the Hebrew state under the banner of their god Yahweh. Later the successful Maccabean revolt of Jews against the Hellenistic Seluccid empire and its local collaborators was certainly a social as well as a religious uprising. The supposed origin of Jesus of Nazareth in Galilee is not without its significance, for that region was notorious at the time for dissidence and low-level forms of resistance to the local rulers and their Roman overlords. The great Jewish revolt of 66–70 CE commenced as an anti-taxation insurrection.

Rural revolt erupted in China towards the end of the first millennium, and the founder of the Han dynasty himself emerged from the peasantry. It is also possible, though uncertain, that the establishment of the Gupta empire on the Indian subcontinent was a result of lower-caste revolt against elite oppression. Most of the city states of classical Greece and their rural hinterlands were the scenes of fierce conflict between a landowning aristocracy and their free peasantry and urban craftsmen. The citizen democracy which, after bitter struggles, characterised Athens between the sixth and second centuries BCE was unique and founded upon slavery, misogyny and, at its height, imperialism.

At about the same period the Roman republic, having grown to imperial proportions, was racked by slave revolts, of which that of Spartacus is only the most renowned, and also dissidence among the lower-class free citizens of Rome itself – the original 'proletariat'. The military empire which was instituted by Augustus in 27 BCE was primarily an insurance against slave revolt.

Institutionalised, Organised Violence

The role of force in providing the framework for human relations is simply more explicit in what we call 'traditional societies . . . '

—David Graeber

Organised violence can constitute anything from the penal sanctions to be discussed in the following chapter to armed invasion with full-scale military apparatus. It could also include the unofficial extermination of aboriginal people by private groups of settlers, supplemented, when required, by the official military.

All forms of surplus extraction and many instances of transfer of resources depend in the last analysis on violence. With the wage relationship that aspect is at its most concealed, but any serious threat to it, whether localised or on wider scale, provokes a violent response by the extractors and the armed formations which guard them either privately or on behalf of the state.[24]

Throughout recorded history organised violence has been overwhelmingly the privilege of elites exercising it either against refractory producers or against each other in contests for the forcible transfer of resources (which may well include each other's producers).

Early Contexts

Central to the issue is the question whether humans, and more specifically human males, have a spontaneous disposition to collective violence against each other, a disposition which has served as the underlay to the forms of organised violence discussed in this chapter. Certainly our closest non-human relatives, the chimpanzees and the closely related bonobos, return an ambiguous answer. The former are very violent, and as well as cooperatively hunting other primates to eat them, will attack any stranger intruding on their territory. The latter, by contrast, though they also hunt monkeys, are otherwise remarkably peaceable, as on the whole, are the other great apes. Similar ambiguity attends early human behaviour. Michael Mann notes that, 'In a quantitative study only four out of fifty primitive peoples did not routinely engage in warfare' – but it was not normally very destructive.[25]

Both Neanderthals and Palaeolithic *H. sapiens sapiens* were probably (though not with complete certainty) cannibalistic, at least on occasion. However there is no way of knowing whether those eaten were hunted to death or had died through natural causes or by accident, and whether the cannibalism was ritual or 'economic' in character. There is also the possibility, though the likelihood appears otherwise, that the modern humans committed a genocidal extermination of the Neanderthals in what is now Europe.

Although it is highly unlikely that there was ever in this case a conscious programme of collective violence let alone an exterminatory project, ethnographic and archaeological evidence shows that it is fairly certain there would have been on occasion lethal territorial conflicts between forager bands, particularly in a context of expanding population and climate-induced dwindling of resources. Ethnographic evidence likewise makes it clear that violence would have been threatened or used, for example, against clan members endangering the clan's collective interests by idiosyncratic behaviour.

It is also reasonable to conclude that cooperative violence against other humans would be, if circumstances suggested it, a natural extension of similar violence against large game animals or dangerously predatory ones. In other words, collective hunting and fighting, predominantly undertaken by young males, are closely linked endeavours.

Military and Public Violence

With the Neolithic revolution, and particularly with the emergence of agrarian civilisation, collective organised violence appears to assume a more sustained and directed character. Technological advance, especially the introduction of bronze, made weaponry more effective and also much more expensive, leading to aggressive weaponry in the shape of chariots manned by warriors carrying bronze weapons and defensive weaponry in the shape of bronze armour. Such armour was something available only to elites – the rank and file had to be content with leather protection. Wooden and hide shields could also be strengthened with bronze bosses and studs, but all-bronze shields were made only for ceremonial purposes, such as the Celtic shields recovered from the river Thames. Their weight made them impractical for use in combat. Mycenaean lords wore helmets made of boars' teeth. The Egyptian armies used very little defensive armour, the Assyrian empire became particularly formidable not least because of their innovations in defensive armour as well as military engineering and organisation.

The principal perils for Bronze Age and earlier monarchs came less from their own subjects than from their equivalent rivals. One way to increase your resource base was to invade a neighbouring territory with your army and either loot it or enforce the payment of tribute, or possibly both. Success in such enterprise also had the convenient outcome of enhancing the monarch's prestige and power among his own people and fear of it among other monarchs farther afield.

There were of course major risks, the most immediate one being defeat, which would not merely diminish one's standing but might in addition motivate a palace coup – there were always jealous relatives in the background. Even success could have its dangers, for if the monarch did not take the field in person but sent out his generals, the victorious general might well get to thinking that he would make a better monarch and have the military force at his command to execute his ambition. Better to execute the general instead, but that too could have its dangers, if the latter was well-connected.

Equally, if the monarch did lead his armies himself and endanger his sacred person, he would not be able to keep a sharp eye on what was happening back in his capital.[26] One solution was to restrict major responsibilities, military and otherwise, to close family members (the kin relationship again) but that could be the most dangerous of responses and close family members the most deadly of rivals – a scenario repeated so often throughout the millennia that it became virtually routine. A number of these monarchs, well aware of that reality, were notorious son-killers, Herod the Great of Judea being the most renowned example.

According to Michael Mann, Sargon the Great of Akkad (not to be confused with his later Assyrian namesakes), who reigned in the later part of the third millennium BCE, was the first really historical individual (although the names of earlier kings in Egypt and Mesopotamia appear in surviving records) – and he illustrates a number of important realities, beginning with those discussed above. Sargon was a member of the royal court in the Sumerian city of Kish, and he made himself its ruler by killing his predecessor. He went on to unite the Sumerian cities into an empire ruled by himself and extended his power northwards to the sources of the Tigris and Euphrates, becoming the founder of the Akkadian dynasty. This was accomplished by aggressive conquest, but that was no simple matter, as the logistics of Bronze Age military expeditions were complex indeed. It was no easy matter to fashion out of the militarily proficient young men of the various cities he had brought under his rule, an organised force that could act in a coherent fashion under the pressure of combat. This minimally required planning and some degree of training.

Once a military force had been created it had to be handled carefully if it was to be used effectively. Discipline, usually enforced by serious punishments, was of course essential, but so was provisioning. At times an army could 'live off the land', taking whatever was needed from the inhabitants of the area it passed through, but precautions were still required if that proved to be impracticable. The armies of the Bronze Age were essentially infantry formations, though supplemented by charioteers and archers. The distance they were capable of marching in a day, taking into account the nature of the terrain, had to be considered when planning any campaign. Provision had to be made too for supporting the wounded; they could not simply be left to take their chances if the leader was to maintain the reputation of an able commander.

The feature of pre-modern warfare most dangerous to its participants was doubtless less the encounter with the enemy than, in conditions even more minimally hygienic than those prevailing in civil life, encounter with unicellular organisms, especially should the army be operating in an unfamiliar climate. Even in modern times tropical and subtropical conditions were particularly deadly to eighteenth- and nineteenth-century British soldiers. The medieval popes were better protected by the malarial swamps around Rome than they were by any military force they could summon, and tropical Africa was similarly protected from deep European invasion until the Europeans discovered the prophylactic use of quinine in the nineteenth century.

Iron-using technology brought with it a revolution in warfare, but it did not upset the dominance of autocratically governed empires, merely changed the autocratic personnel. Indeed it reinforced them in the Middle East, south Asia, China and Japan, and permitted their emergence in Africa. An important innovation in the first millennium BCE was the invention of the horse saddle suitable for the use of cavalry, but the full potential of this development could not be realised until near the middle of the first millennium CE, for the original mounted warrior without stirrups could be readily unhorsed by a determined infantryman, and cavalry were mainly employed for reconnaissance and command and used sparingly in actual combat. Stirrups were a Chinese invention adopted by the steppe warriors who attacked the Roman empire in the fifth century CE and the impact this made on the practice of warfare was monumental. These nomads had the additional advantage that little more was needed for the sustenance of their mounts than adequate grassland and sufficient water, and if necessary or even by preference they themselves could live on the mares' milk (or turn it into an alcoholic beverage, kumis).

The evolution of weaponry largely stabilised at this point for the greater part of a millennium, slow steady improvements being made on the technologies already in existence without any further military revolution. The effectiveness of body armour advanced to its ultimate in the fourteenth and fifteenth centuries, where the noble horseman, totally covered in steel, could only fight on a specially bred strong horse – itself extensively armoured – onto which he had sometimes to be mechanically lifted. Advances were also made to the effectiveness of projectile weapons – bows which dated from prehistoric times, and crossbows, used from the first millennium BCE and later becoming the standard Chinese infantry weapon.

The first recorded use of gunpowder as a weapon dates from as early as the twelfth century, when it was employed as a siege weapon by a Chinese general. During the following century references to the artillery use of gunpowder are relatively sparse, especially in the West, but by the fourteenth century it was used on occasion in Britain and in the fifteenth century it was the weapon of choice for conducting sieges, as by the Turks to batter down the walls of Constantinople in 1453 (though they used Italian cannon). Seven years later the Scottish king James II was killed by the accidental explosion of one of his new toys. Hand-held firearms were also devised in the same century. The term 'handgun' sounds modern, but it was also used in that century, as when Henry VII attempted to ban 'hand-gonnes' in case they distracted his subjects from archery practice.

In fact the early firearm was much inferior to the bow or crossbow, being both less accurate and having a much slower rate of fire. Its great advantage was that it could be used by any soldier after minimal instruction, whereas it took a decade and more to train a skilled archer. The problem of inaccuracy in the early muskets was in the eighteenth century overcome to some extent by rifling the barrel. Repeater firearms were possible in principle as early as the sixteenth century (Henry VIII owned a revolver) but were useless because the deposit from the gunpowder then in use jammed the firing mechanism. An eighteenth-century inventor tried unsuccessfully to devise a machine-gun to fire round bullets at Christians and square ones at Turks. It was not until the nineteenth century that improved explosives and the invention of cartridges made repeating rifles, revolvers and automatic pistols practical weapons. These were soon followed by effective machine-guns, most notoriously the Gatling[27] and the Maxim.

These revolutionary killing devices were accompanied by major technological improvements in heavy weaponry, which principally involved replacing the solid cannon-ball with an explosive shell, enormously more destructive in both land and sea warfare. With the dawn of the twentieth century these were joined and used in conjunction with the aircraft and the rocket in the air, and the submarine beneath the water, a vessel with no purpose other than destruction. The development of atomic weaponry in the 1940s, and its enormously more destructive successor, the thermonuclear bomb, in the following decade, with their promise to annihilate human life on the planet, might well have brought about the impossibility of warfare in any rational perspective – but far from it. Although they have never been militarily used again after the initial experiment in 1945, the permanent possibility remains that a terminally destructive conflict could at any time break out, as up to six states have continued to produce and stockpile them.

Meantime, human ingenuity has contrived to continue killing on a mass scale, with 'conventional' weaponry being continually 'improved' to make it still more deadly and inflict superior all-round destruction – but at the same time the massacre and mutilation of huge numbers with the most primitive of instruments, such as steel blades, are not extinct. Organised violence, recent claims to the contrary notwithstanding, remains as all-pervasive in the twenty-first century CE as it was in the twenty-first century BCE.

This summarises the history of military violence. This was of course never simply a matter of contending military forces, but was equally, if not more significantly, exercised against informal armed formations resisting state control, such as the 'social bandits' analysed by Eric Hobsbawm[28] or against unorganised masses objecting to state behaviour. Modern states in these circumstances tend to hold back the military as a last resort, preferring formations loosely referred to as 'police' (armed in most countries) whose specific remit is to exercise violence in civil circumstances. It is when these are threatened with being overwhelmed that the military with their heavier firepower are called into action. It is unusual, but not unknown, for formations which were initially designated for a policing role to become formal military units. The *Waffen SS* of the Third Reich are the most outstanding example, but a somewhat similar development took place within the Soviet NKVD/KGB[29] which created heavily armed units indistinguishable from military ones.

The centrality of military violence to the state structure both ancient and modern is evident in monarchies, given the special relationship maintained between the monarch and the fighting forces and their commanders. In times when the monarch actually led his forces into battle this was wholly understandable, but it persists still in contemporary states where the monarch is primarily a figurehead – most distinctly in the UK, where the navy and the air force are both prefixed with the epithet 'royal'. Even in Western European states which retain a monarch of much less account, attending military parades remains their central ceremonial function and their armed forces have a crown incorporated in their insignia.

Violence was, and often still is, in some countries also the approved method of maintaining discipline within the armed forces themselves – and these methods when judged to be necessary, could include execution. Indeed, from the seventeenth to the early nineteenth centuries English writers recommended that common soldiers and sailors should be treated as foully as possible so that they wouldn't mind getting killed.

Markets and Territory

Apart from the direct extraction of labour or the product of labour from slaves, serfs or wage labourers, military violence was also used from the earliest times to direct the course of voluntary market transactions, or indeed to restrict their voluntary character. This involved the monopoly control of such things as markets and trade routes, either reserving their use to the possessor of violent means or charging others for permission to use the facilities. At the local level, for example, medieval lordships, whether individuals or corporations, secular or clerical, compelled rural cultivators in the areas under their control, in addition to the dues they exacted, to trade any surplus in the markets controlled by the lordship and to pay for the privilege.[30] The same applied to itinerant peddlers. On a wider scale, this could mean control of trade routes, a frequent bone of contention from the beginning of long-distance trade, and was the source of the Punic Wars which prefigured the rise of the Roman state to its eventual domination of the Mediterranean and its hinterland.

Conflict of this kind was often enough combined, as it had been from the time of Sargon the Great, with straightforward territorial aggression to seize control of resources from a rival polity. In the medieval centuries it was a constant feature of political interaction, with excuses ranging from religion to dynastic rivalry. Constant warfare was conducted on the frontiers of Western Christendom either against the usually more poorly armed and organised Slavonic peoples[31] or the more equally armed polities of the Muslims in Spain and the Middle East, or the 'schismatic' rival Christians of the Byzantine empire. From the end of the fifteenth century the practice of religiously justified conquest was carried across the Atlantic, and in subsequent centuries against the by then less militarily proficient empires of the east. The rulers of Western Christendom however were just as ready to fight and rob each other, as testified by the renowned seizure of the English throne by the Norman duke in 1066 and many more examples.

The relationship between economy and organised violence has a further dimension. Huge military expenditure was a very significant drain on the resources of the Roman empire, with all manner of social consequences following from the taxation burden which was involved. Military expenditure in the medieval and early modern states greatly affected the social and political trajectories of the states involved, and towards the end of that period an important part of the banking system which emerged in the eighteenth century was to underpin military expenditure by enabling governments (primarily the British) to raise the finance needed. In the contemporary world the 'permanent arms economy' is central to both the US and the UK – its sudden cessation would provoke mass unemployment and bankruptcies.

Organised Violence and Questions of Perpetuation

The question remains – why did organised violence in all its dimensions become such a central feature of the historical process?[32] We can speculate on the likelihood of whether forager bands in the Palaeolithic engaged in lethal conflicts with each other – probably they did.

Prior to the emergence of centralised states, settled social life was ruled by custom, and violence was intrinsic to it. Customary rules prescribed severe penalties, including mutilation and death for – even accidental – violation of social custom or taboo, and these specifications were carried over into the earliest law codes. Centuries before the codes' appearance, social differentiation had evolved into well-defined class structures and naturally the rules governing relations between social superiors and inferiors featured prominently. Violence was second nature to the god-kings in their domestic society, and therefore to organise, expand and extend it beyond their territory must have come very naturally. These monarchs at the same time as they were violently enforcing social subordination were also engaging each other in armed conflict. It is no accident that the gods of the Indo-European peoples and their Semitic neighbours were mostly violent deities with conflict as their primary vocation, and when combined into one figure, such as the Jewish YHWH, were hyper-violent, using plague, famine and flood as routine instruments of government and administration.

The principal though by no means the only purpose of what we may term 'social violence', the sort of violence whose monopoly Weber argued was the defining character of the state, was and is to ensure the transfer of resources between socio-economic classes. When that process goes ahead peaceably without violence having to be employed, the social order is said to be stable and the relationship accepted as a law of nature rather than the fiat of rulers. At a still deeper level violence or the threat of it was a necessary tool not only to extract surplus from the basic producers but to protect and preserve the socio-political structure which underpinned the process.

Violence, more so organised violence, especially the violence of interstate armed conflict, has a logic of its own – it is not purely an instrument of utility. For one thing, it is very expensive, and particularly if the technology used in conducting it is very advanced, a gluttonous consumer of resources. Occasionally it can be made to pay for itself if victory produces large gains, but often enough victory is ruinously expensive, and as Dr Johnson pointed out in *The Vanity* of *Human Wishes*,

And mortgaged states their grandsires' wreaths regret,
From age to age in everlasting debt;
Wreaths which at last the dear-bought right convey
To rust on medals, or on stones decay.

7

Ethics, Ambitions, Crime and Punishment

This chapter is intended to examine certain general considerations about human social relations closely related to the themes of coercion and exploitation discussed in the previous subsequent chapter. Alongside questions of ontology (what reality actually is or is not) and epistemology (how do we get to know what we know) the nature of morality or ethics (why ought we do certain things and abstain from others) has been a central concern of philosophers in all literate cultures (and doubtless of questioning individuals in preliterate ones). Mostly this has exercised them in what may be loosely termed a religious framework – involving Brahmin, Daoist, Confucian, Buddhist, Islamic, Christian thinkers and scholars; but also by ones who reject any supernatural dimension to right conduct.

According to David Graeber, 'Anthropology . . . reveals some remarkable commonalities – fundamental moral principles that appear to exist everywhere and that will always tend to be invoked whenever people transfer objects back and forth or argue about what other people owe them'.[1]

In a very important ancient example of this discussion deities do not intrude into the argument, (though the participants take their existence for granted). Plato's *Republic* is a disquisition on how the ideal society should be organised. It takes the form of a dialogue between Socrates and several of his acolytes and begins with an argument on the nature of justice and the justification for social rules. Inventing the origins of morals and the principles of justice is a universal practice among humans; societies cannot simply take these for granted, they feel compelled to justify them.

One of the disputants, Thrasymachus, argues cynically that what is called justice is nothing other than the interest of dominant and stronger individuals dressed up as moral rules. Socrates/Plato dodges this interpretation by clever wordplay, basically by assuming what he has to prove, namely that an objective standard of justice or morality does actually exist, and the bulk of the dialogue is devoted to working out its supposed implications, which are hierarchical and authoritarian, in line with Plato's political standpoint as a reactionary aristocrat.

Critias, a relative of Plato (possibly his uncle), was also an author, and the surviving fragment of one of his plays includes a suggestion which, if not identical to that of Thrasymachus certainly matches it in cynicism:

[A]lthough the laws restrained
Mankind from deeds of open violence
They still did wrong in secret, until some
Shrewd and far-sighted thinker had the wit
To invent gods, that all who did or said
Or even imagined evil might be afraid.

Critias, who was also one of Socrates's acolytes, later became one of the oligarchs known as the Thirty Tyrants who briefly ruled Athens with murderous ferocity.

Justifications

Few ethical systems indeed fail to justify themselves without reference to supernatural claims which are considered to be the wellsprings of the moral precepts that bind society together. These points of reference need not necessarily be gods, as indeed is the case in Eastern cultures,[2] where they are related to more abstract concepts such as *karma* and reincarnation. In the classical Greco-Roman or the Norse cultures the gods were, to say the least, not much concerned with moral issues but rather more preoccupied with power-hungry thuggishness and mutual jealousy, with humans filling the role of disposable playthings.

Nevertheless in these cultures the gods were supposed to reward or punish the due fulfilment or neglect of sacrificial duties and social roles. In addition Greek culture postulated the supernatural figures of the Erinyes or Furies who punished family-connected crime, particularly ones committed against parents. In brief, everywhere throughout the globe, virtually a social universal, violation of social mores was expected to incur supernatural punishment even if a human one was evaded[3] – and this debt could be passed down the generations. In Greek mythology, for example, the house of Atreus was cursed; the ancestors had form, including eating their relatives.

It is in the monotheist (or Abrahamic) religions that the connection between deity and morality is particularly strong. According to this narrative, the basic moral code (and often many details in addition) has been laid down by the deity, via prophets to whom he has revealed it, and is binding upon all believers. That kind of assertion however generates a significant conundrum which interpreters have difficulty in avoiding.

It relates to the question – is an action moral because the deity commands it, or does he/she decree it because it is moral? If it is the first, then the very opposite could equally be right and ethical. If instead of 'Thou shalt not commit adultery' (or cannibalism) the divine law code had stated 'Thou shalt commit adultery' (or cannibalism), as in the famous misprint in a seventeenth-century edition of the bible, accordingly termed 'the wicked bible';[4] then it would have been incumbent on a believer to do these things, God being all-powerful and able to decree whatever he wishes at his will and pleasure. Any such suggestion however evokes horror and disgust among believers – the divinity/divinities of any particular society would never command actions, it is presumed, contrary to that society's dominant ethical principles.

If on the other hand the deity only affirms rules that are inherently moral then that implies that ethical rules are separate from and even prior to him or her, which detracts from God's omnipotence – and what then *is* the origin and justification of moral prescriptions? In fact they are a condensed and abstract expression of the rules governing human relations in particular societies. The Aztec deities, notoriously, commanded human sacrifice on a monstrous scale, and doubtless their priests believed that they were acting impeccably.

For millennia efforts have been made to resolve this conundrum. A start is made with the injunction known as the Golden Rule which runs through a number of religions, 'do unto others as you would have them do unto you' – but that would scarcely be suitable for a masochist. Immanuel Kant's injunction to treat other persons as ends in themselves and not as objects is better, but raises all sorts of begged questions as to what such treatment implies. In fact the dilemma is irresolvable, and all systems of ethics are the condensed social practices of the communities which sustain them. Moreover, though tending to absolutism in principle, e.g. *never* lie, *never* steal, in practice ethical precepts are always situational – if pressing circumstances demand that any particular injunction should be broken or bent, a convincing reason can always be found for the necessity of doing so.[5]

Ethical Origins

Humans' two closest biological relatives, the chimpanzees and the bonobos, while genetically all but identical, exhibit very different forms of behaviours. The former, confined to the north of the Congo river, are very hierarchical; a chimpanzee troop being controlled by a dominant alpha male who gains his position by forming alliances with others in the troop, themselves positioned in a definite hierarchy beneath the superior individual, who is then sometimes challenged by alliances among his subordinates. The Bonobos by contrast, living to the south of the river, are minimally hierarchical and do not form male coalitions, but, famously promiscuous, employ sex as a means of settling disputes and use mothers as allies. Nevertheless apes, however intelligent, appear to lack any specifically *moral* sense – behaviour is controlled only by fear or approval.

These relationships are examined in detail by Christopher Boehm in his *Moral Origins: The Evolution of Virtue, Altruism and Shame*, whose concept of that origin has a lot of plausibility, although the author is rather too inclined to attribute some dispositions to genetic origins when cultural ones would account for them just as effectively. 'We arrived at our moral nature in the great evolutionary nature of chance',[6] he writes. 'Humans are moral because we are genetically set up to be that way . . . more was needed than a preexisting capacity for cultural transmission.'[7] Boehm notes that guilt is not a human universal, but that shame tends to be, and that the latter's behavioural manifestation, blushing, certainly is.[8] No doubt genetics are involved to some extent; a social animal with the cognitive and communicative apparatus of *H. sapiens* must necessarily have a predisposition to conceive social rules as much as it does to speech or else social life would be impossible; but, as with speech, the *sort* of rules that evolve are potentially flexible to an indefinite degree and every society without exception invents a different narrative for the origin of its moral codes.

All the same, as Boehm points out, there is a downside, for the moral 'discount' applied to cultural outsiders.[9] 'Thou shalt not kill' means 'thou shalt not kill a fellow-clansman'.

Cultural Conservatism and Right Order

Historically, cultures or social orders have had an inbuilt tendency towards cultural and moral conservatism, manifest, of course, in a variety of ways. It is only in the last few hundred years that the project of deliberately and fundamentally transforming a culture has been entertained by a significant number of its members. The cultural web, after all, is the necessary source of food supply and other material necessities, also of social order and ideological underpinnings which provide a sense of the meaning of individual lives and their place within the cultural complex. Major alterations, whether willed or accidental, could prove catastrophic as it has been for hunter-gatherer societies forced into contemporary modernisation. It is not therefore surprising that social conservatism is deeply embedded in social consciousness. Two examples of agriculture societies of differing cultures and periods will illustrate the point.

Right Order

In ancient Egypt the concept of *ma'at* – right order or right conduct, including everything from government to funerary rites – set the social structure. It kept the peasantry at their toil of tilling the irrigated fields to feed the community; the artisans creating the magnificent objects which fill our museums; the priests calculating and identifying the signs when the Nile was due to flood; the Pharaoh supplying due reverence to the gods and so ensuring the procession of days, nights and years, or mobilising labour for monumental building projects, conducting diplomacy and when necessary leading his troops to battle. His Aztec equivalent some thousands of years later was doing much the same thing, but in addition was required to organise military expeditions to maintain a supply of captives for the human sacrifice on a prodigious scale that was needed to keep the sun moving in the sky and the maize sprouting in the fields.

Fast forward to mainland Britain of the early eighteenth century where the social consensus (not universally accepted but the common sense of polite male-dominated society) was that the country had attained a state as near to perfection as the deity was likely to permit. The country was Protestant, having definitely escaped from absolutism and Papal slavery. Protestant dissenters from the official versions of the creed were discriminated against but tolerated, and even Catholics were not too severely persecuted. It was also a free country, in that the monarch's subjects enjoyed the 'rights of freeborn Englishmen' (most Scotsmen too after 1707). Publication, apart from in the theatre was not subject to pre-censorship, though the reactionary clergy had fought hard at the beginning of the century to retain the official licencing of publications.

Internal trade and production ran largely according to the laws of the market apart from the unavoidable nuisances of customs impositions on foreign imports and excise on a few products. In this near-idyllic construction of that polity those enduring 'homely toil and destiny obscure' were expected to be content with the station into which it had pleased God to call them, to work industriously for the benefit of their masters and the public good, and to conscientiously attend for indoctrination at the church, preferably the Established one; women to obey their husbands and observe the social conventions.

Legislators were expected to suppress Jacobite conspirators, uphold the Protestant settlement, the Hanoverian succession and the privileges of the Established church and its clergy (especially its clergy). They were also expected to protect property as a priority, to keep the wheels of commerce turning with suitable legislation – and everyone was enjoined ideologically as well as in practice to fetishise the Law and the laws, including the code of ferocious penalties which were regularly extended to further offences as the century proceeded.[10] These societies had only one important thing in common – their agricultural economic base. In all other respects they inhabited different social universes and their dramatically different ethical standards reflected the material and social realities of their circumstances. Equivalent variations would have applied to other agrarian societies differently located in time and space.

Law, State, Crime and Punishment

Law Codes

In preliterate societies and some minimally literate ones, ethical codes tend to be embodied in custom, and in literate societies in the form of written law codes, though always there were kinds of socially disapproved behaviour which were not serious enough to be covered by legislation. In traditional Chinese legal theory an ideological clash between proponents of rules based primarily on custom (though written down) and other scholars advocating precisely codified laws promulgated by authority, resulted in rival schools of thought termed Confucianism and Legalism.

It would be naturally assumed that written law codes, however derived, have to be public documents, but this was by no means always the case. Quite separately in both archaic Athens and Rome, severe social struggles were occasioned over the right of citizens in general to have knowledge of the laws, information hitherto confined to the elites, which naturally offered great advantage to the latter. Nor are secret laws a thing of the remote past – they have been used extensively by dictatorial regimes in the twentieth century, most infamously in the Third Reich, though its worst atrocities were committed without any legal authority whatsoever beyond ambiguous verbal statements by the Führer. Secret legislation continues into the twenty-first century, for example the US laws associated with the Patriot Act allow repressive agencies to do what they like without possibility of legal challenge while at the same time avoiding the adverse publicity that publishing these laws would generate.

In dynastic empires embracing historically distinct communities, especially very geographically diverse ones, such as the early Arab empire, or on a much more minor scale, Athelstan's unified England of the tenth century, it was frequently the case that the separate communities continued to function under their own laws for everyday purposes, while the emperors or kings promulgated a general further layer of legislation to serve their own interests. It was also possible, in Western Christendom for example, for two quite separate legal systems namely secular law and canon law to operate alongside each other, sometimes conflicting if a monarch objected to clerical pretensions. A not too dissimilar system existed in the Ottoman empire, Sharia law being the equivalent of canon law, though with a considerably broader scope.[11] Canon law, as well as being concerned with the behaviour of the clergy and the organisation of the church also included the personal behaviour of the lay public, especially regarding matters of marriage, legitimacy and sexual behaviour.

Civil and Criminal Law

Law falls into two major categories – property issues referred to as civil law, where illegal wrongdoing does not principally feature and a settlement had to be reached, and crimes against persons or property. These are modern distinctions of course, and in history the boundary could be very nebulous – for example in the Germanic *wergild* system of the early Middle Ages, under which murder could be redeemed by paying compensation (graded according to rank) to the victim's family or community. Punishment followed if payment could not be made.

Developed legal systems, whether civil or criminal had to be interpreted. Acting as the supreme interpreter was the monarch's principal responsibility since it was a continuous one and military functions were more intermittent. However such interpretation and argument over interpretation required a corps of experts, whether mostly amateurs of rank, as was the case in imperial China, rhetoricians in classical Athens, or professionals; in which case they are referred to as lawyers.

These first came to prominence in the Roman republic and empire (Cicero the most notable) and were inherited – at a distance in time – by the kingdoms which superseded that empire, though in northern Europe for several centuries legal disputes and accusations were conducted in gatherings of free citizens, usually guided in their deliberations by a man of some prestige (in England, for example, professional secular lawyers appeared only in the twelfth century).

A prevalent myth claims that law in general stands above the messy social realities of crime, conflict and dispute and serves as the impartial arbiter which represses crime and settles disputes, an assertion symbolised in the icon of a blindfolded female figure representing the Roman goddess of justice, holding a sword in one hand and a pair of evenly balanced scales in the other. In reality, as has been well remarked, law is the expression of political relations in any given society and expresses the will and values of whoever is politically in charge, while political relationships in turn express the interests of ruling elites. Property law is a good example, expressing the interests of the well-propertied against the unpropertied or minimally-propertied. Such laws were used in eighteenth-century England to strip agricultural copyholders of their rights. Legal restrictions on workers' right to organise and strike is another example.

The State

There are and have been stateless societies, and for many millennia all humanity got on very adequately without any states. States emerged fully in the form of the city states of southern Mesopotamia, after a lengthy period of evolution towards such a formation by the stateless agricultural communities in that region. The state, initially in the form of monarchy – and for millennia monarchy was the default option though not an invariable one – became the institution responsible for administering the laws over a given territory and setting the terms on which those subject to it could conduct their lives. Its basic functions throughout the centuries have been primarily repressive ones – combating external enemies and repressing disturbers of the peace within the realm, whether political, in which case it is termed sedition, or merely anti-social in the form of violations against person, property or social custom.

The realm however has never consisted of an undifferentiated mass of citizens but of individuals, groupings, networks, rival elites and so forth, all with their own projects, ambitions and lust for power and property. Accordingly the state as an institution, if it was to best serve the interests of the topmost elite (usually embodied in a monarch) had to umpire and arbitrate between these divergent social forces, using concession or repression as appropriate. Instituting public works, such as canals, aqueducts or the Colosseum, might be part of that strategy. Its cardinal remit however was always to preserve and protect the power relations which it was instituted to serve. Often state establishment took the form of aggressive conquest as principalities grew violently into kingdoms, kingdoms into empires; on other occasions they emerged by some sort of consensus between social elites in pre-state societies.

Punishment and Cruelty

The practices considered here could equally well have featured in the previous chapter. They were permeated with immoderate violence. Punishment is the exaction of retribution upon offenders against social norms or persons defying the commands of authority. It consists in the infliction of unwelcome consequences upon the offender, with the purpose either of straightforward retribution (aka vengeance), deterring or preventing the wrongdoer from repeating similar offences or serving as a deterrent example to other potential miscreants.

In contemporary societies everywhere, middle range offenders are punished by imprisonment of varying length and severity, and imprisonment is the penalty for all serious crimes in the states which have abolished executions. Lesser misdemeanours are usually punished by financial penalties. For the most seriously regarded crimes such as murder (and in some states many others, including intellectual offences) execution by varying techniques continues to be employed in just under half the states represented at the United Nations.[12] In a few states physical mutilation continues to be practised, which is regarded with abhorrence in most jurisdictions. Generally speaking imprisonment remains the default option.

Sustained imprisonment as a regular form of punishment covering a large number of offences and individuals, however, is only possible in adequately resourced and highly organised societies such as exist today, regardless of the nature of their regimes. It requires a considerable, extensive and expensive structure, of which suitably designed escape-proof buildings are probably the least part of the problem – after all, no modern prison is more complex than the architecture of the Colosseum in Rome. But the organisation and cost in a significantly large country (or even a small one) of a corps of full-time warders, and of supplying even the minimal essentials of life on a regular basis to large numbers of long-term prisoners, was far beyond the capacity of any pre-industrial society, even the Chinese one.

As recorded by Derk Bodde and Clarence Morris with reference to the Sung Dynasty of the early second millennium CE,

The majority of jails, whether located in the capital Kaifeng or in local districts and associated with the sheriff's office, tended to be small in scale, which led to difficulties in providing facilities for the segregation of offenders. Sung jails were characterized by their inability . . . to provide adequate food or sanitation. Despite state mandates for the provision of food for poor prisoners or those whose families were unable to provide for them, food was a constant concern for all prisoners, with starvation occurring frequently in jails. Health care was

another concern, despite edicts that ordered the establishment of jail hospitals
. . . Prisoners found themselves in jails that were unsanitary and cramped, and
they were lucky if they didn't contract an illness or even die before their release.
Imprisonment functioned to hold suspects awaiting trial or sentencing as well
as ensuring that witnesses for crimes were available to testify. It also functioned
unofficially as a method to deal with specific cases, where they sought an
alternative punishment to those proscribed by law.[13]

In Europe the Tower of London was a renowned prison for very high-status
individuals, and the Bastille in Paris accommodated prisoners of that sort as well
as less important ones, but the standard prisons were nearly all gaols or jails,
essentially short-term holding confinements for accused awaiting trial or criminals
due for punishment. Long-term imprisonment in pre-industrial societies was used
only in the case of high status prisoners whom for one reason or another it was
inexpedient to kill, such as Duke Robert of Normandy in the twelfth century or
the famous Man in the Iron Mask (in reality a velvet one) in the seventeenth.

Consequently, pre-modern punishments all around the globe, whenever a
financial penalty was not available or else appropriate, were overwhelmingly ones
inflicted on the body, with execution very much to the fore; but even when not
lethal generally ferocious and designed specifically to cause pain in varying degrees.
Flogging was simple, easily administered and apportioned according to the gravity
of the offence; capable of being used in quantities and intensities ranging from
a relatively mild sanction to execution by torture. Mutilation was commonly
practised; branding, eye gouging, amputation of various limbs and body parts,
and, a favourite of medieval European rulers from Byzantine emperors to the
princes of northern Europe, blinding accompanied by castration, for the purpose
of degradation as well as intense pain and loss of function. A milder form of
combining pain with degradation was employed in medieval and early modern
Western Europe, namely the pillory where the prisoner had their head and hands
confined in holes in a board placed on top of a pillar so that they could be mocked
and pelted by missiles from passers-by. As a supplement their ears might be cut off
or nailed to the pillory. Occasionally if the missiles were both hard and substantial
the pilloried person might be killed.

Execution and Torture

The lavishly used punishment of execution could be supplemented with all manner
of ingenious improvements to make it as prolonged and agonising as possible.
Torture might be used as a means of extracting information, securing a confession
or as punishment on its own account, but overwhelmingly it was employed as an
accompaniment to the infliction of death.

Legalised torture, either as an adjunct or a preliminary to execution, sprang
from a similar disposition which regarded the sufferers as disposable items (usually

though not invariably members of the lower orders) who deserved what they were getting. The Persian empire had forms of execution that made crucifixion, the Roman version of death by torture, appear almost humane by comparison.

The founding fathers of the new Unites States of America in their Constitution specifically prohibited 'cruel and unusual' methods of punishment. They had in mind the physically mutilating penalties used in England to accompany executions for treason by non-aristocrats; nobles were merely beheaded. These, devised in the time of Edward I, continued into the mid-eighteenth century, being used for example against the rank-and-file Jacobite rebels; and remained on the statute book into the nineteenth century; their practical discontinuance from the 1790s was probably because of their public relations liability by comparison with the guillotine.

The ferocious penal systems of the medieval era were explicitly justified by their defenders as necessary to keep the lower orders in order by means of terror, otherwise their depraved instincts would be liable to bring functioning society to its knees. In Britain by the late seventeenth century these enhancements of death, except in relation to treason, had largely been discontinued, but on the other side of the scale, capital offences between 1688 and the early nineteenth century, were expanded prodigiously, mostly with reference to offences against property. The legislators seemed to imagine that the entire population, or at least its lower strata, was itching to rob their neighbours and restrained only by the threat of ending up on the gallows as a consequence.

In fact the number of executions did not increase proportionately with that of capital crimes, and a large majority of those condemned to hang were reprieved. It was the threat, the possibility if not the probability, of execution, accompanied by all the panoply and theatre of courtroom and scaffold – in other words terror – that was supposed to deter, though its efficacy may be doubted. The French revolutionaries, who had explicitly abolished cruel and unusual punishments and instead substituted the guillotine for all capital crimes, nevertheless found it expedient, when under severe threat, to declare *terror* (the word was explicitly stressed) to be the 'order of the day'. The first people to be called terrorists were not people who opposed the state by murderous means but the Jacobin revolutionaries during their time in power.

It was not only revolutionaries however; the Piedmontese arch-reactionary Joseph de Maistre, writing in the early nineteenth century, was not the only theorist to argue that the hangman was the central pillar of social order: the same sentiments were expressed in the 1820s, with if anything even greater virulence by the English jurist Anthony Hammond, a supposed legal reformer.

Torture naturally could have other purposes than inflicting a painful death. As mentioned, it has been employed very widely for extracting information, or also for confessions in regimes where confession was regarded as essential to a conviction, such as continental heresy trials. In Roman law a slave's evidence was valid only if it followed from torture. Torture for such purposes has been used routinely down the centuries and many museums contain ingenious instruments designed to cause excruciating pain without actually killing the victim. Though victims might survive the experience, the vast majority, when they had confessed or informed, were subsequently executed – very few lived on to die natural deaths.

Torture was used extensively by modern colonial regimes, the French in Algeria and the British in Kenya being only the most notorious. In Europe itself it underwent a major revival in the twentieth century, employed extensively in Stalinist regimes and especially by the Nazis, who were past masters in the art. It continues in vigorous health into the present century, more prevalent now than for some decades even despite the profile of organisations like Amnesty International, increasing public indignation around the world more readily expressed by the use of social media, and official emphasis on 'human rights' and condemnation of their violation. Additionally, for all his inaccuracies and perverse judgements, Foucault probably had a point when he suggested that in modern societies where torture had genuinely been abandoned, it was replaced by more precise, nuanced disciplinary regimes.

Mentalities

To the destructive bodily tortures of past centuries has been added a variety of psychological tortures which are especially useful when a victim has to make a court appearance and physical injuries would be too embarrassing in front of the world's media. The Stalinist regime may be said to have pioneered these techniques. The manner of their application in Koestler's novel *Darkness at Noon* was not too far from the actuality, as described for example by real-life survivors such as Artur London. The accused would be made to convince themselves that they were betrayers and scoundrels and could redeem themselves only by confessing to crimes they knew they were innocent of. If that failed to work, the cruder method of threatening reprisals against their relatives was used, and that usually sufficed.

In other regimes fake execution was a method used to frighten and demoralise the prisoner. More sophisticated techniques include waterboarding, where the victim experiences what feels like drowning, and sensory deprivation, whereby sight and sound are shut out, sense of time and reality is lost. Though principally psychological, these may be accompanied by forms of physical duress, as well as loud, aggressive and intimidatory language.

The mentalities underpinning these refinements of cruelty are difficult in the extreme to comprehend. A famous example is the execution in 1757 of Robert Damiens for making an ineffective knife attack on Louis XV. An account of it opens Foucault's *Surveiller et punir: Naissance de la prison*, translated as *Discipline and Punish: The Birth of the Prison*.[14] Although inaccurate in many details when compared with contemporary accounts, Foucault is probably right in pointing out that the conception behind the execution was that any violation of the royal body, even the most minor, had to be compensated for by the infliction of maximum pain on the body of the offender. However even if the Damiens case was exceptional, execution with extreme cruelty was practised for many lesser offences everywhere throughout the world. These kinds of thing were going on in the very same communities in which great works of knowledge and art were being created.

Human and Inhuman

A frequently-used phrase is 'inhuman cruelty', now more usually applied to conflict situations rather than judicial practices. 'Dehumanisation' in this context is discussed in the journal *New Scientist*: 'Rivals in such conflicts describe each other in ways that deny their shared humanity: they may liken each other to vermin or pests to be exterminated';[15] and 'Hitler did it when he referred to German Jews as viruses, parasites and rats . . . Hutu extremists did it to the Tutsis, calling them cockroaches . . . .'[16]

'Dehumanisation' however is a mistaken explanatory approach. The undoubted use of such descriptive rhetoric (used in everyday speech as well as in genocidal or similar contexts) belies the reality of the relationship between perpetrator and victim. As the same editorial points out, 'The cruelties meted out can be so ingenious as to betray the work of a sophisticated social brain'. Nobody killing rats or cockroaches feels inclined to torture them first, indeed in the case of mammalian pests it would be considered a crime. Cruelty towards animals is a persistent trait in human societies, not generally much disapproved of before recent centuries; the English were notorious for their animal cruelty in the early modern era before they became notorious as animal lovers (except towards foxes). However the infliction of cruelty on animals did not involve an attitude of hatred toward the non-human victims, rather it was functional, as with working animals, or regarded as amusing entertainment in such activities as baiting bulls or bears. Targets of cruelty are never compared to robots; there would be no satisfaction of any sort gained by torturing a robot.

Indeed it is precisely *because* the perpetrator recognises the victim as another human consciousness that they inflict pain and distress because they expect their techniques to produce the outcomes they seek. Laura Spinney in the *New Scientist* article quotes Jeroen Vaes at the University of Padua: 'It's as if we have a little humanness gauge in our heads that twitches whenever we see another person'.[17] That is well put, but it has to be added that it applies as much to ill-will as to goodwill. Perpetrators know that their victim is as real as themselves so far as humanness is concerned – but not that they are of equivalent value. Their brutality (animal metaphor again) is attempting by pain and humiliation to force other absolute subjects to recognise themselves as objects and identify with reduction to that status.

Conclusion

It is a universal characteristic of humans, regardless of their society (and not only of humans, it applies also among non-human primates) that violation of social rules, however established and whatever they may be, provokes offence and some form of sanction, extending from reproof and/or exclusion to the range of penalties outlined above.

However, no society could function adequately if all its members or even a large majority of them stuck to the rules only because they feared the punishments likely to follow if they acted otherwise. In reality most members of a community internalise the rules and norms into which they are socialised and are not normally motivated to break them, and this applies with different degrees of strength not only to the wider society but to subcultures within each one. However, the situation becomes complicated in circumstances where a society is divided by serious class and cultural differences, and all the more so where these are conjoined with coherent oppositional movements claiming ethical principles in defiance of the ruling authority.

Despite the enormous differences which continue to exist between and within different cultures, twentieth-century globalisation, particularly the globalisation of communication, has brought about a greater degree of uniformity in this sphere than has existed in any previous era. Most striking perhaps is the fact that physical torture is not now accepted anywhere as an appropriate judicial penalty. It still of course continues in vigorous depraved health, but no longer as a prescribed sentence or in public except insofar as some forms of public execution still practised, such as stoning, incorporate an element of additional cruelty.

In most regimes nowadays the theory and practice of penology is supposed to be guided by motives of rehabilitation and reformation of offenders (or protection of society if they are dangerous psychopaths). In reality, if the expression of opinion in political statements, newspaper reports and correspondence or the social media are any guide – not to speak of what goes on in penal institutions – the prevailing public sentiments everywhere are ones of reprisal and vengeance. Nearly all of us, no matter how rational and ethical we may be, want to see particularly hateful figures get their just deserts, and if that kind of instinctive reaction is ever to be overcome across society through reason and education it will prove a very long-term and challenging enterprise.

8

The Origins of Belief in the Supernatural and the First Salvation Religions

T'is the eye of childhood that fears a painted devil.

—Lady Macbeth

Magic is a way of making people believe they are going to get what they want, whereas religion is a system for persuading them that they ought to want what they get.

—V G Childe

Religious belief has remained a central characteristic of social life around the globe throughout all recorded history and almost certainly for long beforehand as well – an explanation for the universe and the human place within it, a framework for social order – and during the last ten millennia a justification for hierarchy and inequality and a consolatory practice for those who suffer under them. In all cases religion has been integrated with work practices, greatly exercised about sex, and usually mobilised to justify powerful elites, though on occasion to challenge them.[1] Defining exactly what is meant by 'religion' however is no easy matter. Jared Diamond in his book *The World Until Yesterday* lists sixteen 'different definitions proposed by scholars of religion . . . it will be obvious that we are not even close to agreement on a definition'.[2] There is dispute about whether Daoism, Shinto, Confucianism and even Buddhism should be described as religions rather than philosophies of life. Various Christian sects, especially Jehovah's Witnesses, when canvassing for converts insist, however disingenuously, that they are *not* religions, and Ernest Gellner writes that, 'In Hinduism and Buddhism, *this* world includes a multitude of spirits; the mundane and animistic worlds are *jointly* distinct from the truly *Other*'.[3]

Nevertheless, whatever the precise terminology, what all of these have in common with the undoubted religions, especially the monotheist ones, as well as with all manner of folk beliefs, occultism, astrology and so forth, is acceptance of the existence of supernatural beings and forces. Thus the title of this chapter could as easily have been 'Supernaturalism'.

Supernaturalism, though this definition is not immune from difficulties, is more susceptible than religion to being pinned down. It means belief in conscious agencies (which may or may not take the form of a deity and its supernatural servants) which are not susceptible to evidential rules; that is, they violate Ernest

Gellner's principle that there are no privileged revelations: that any explanation of anything must be capable of being investigated with the possibility of refutation. The existence of supernatural entities however is beyond public demonstration[4] and is based purely on assertion which may or may not seem convincing.

In a prescientific age they might well appear very convincing indeed. Supernaturalism in such an environment is a perfectly natural and rational intellectual response for a pattern-seeking animal where contingent associations between events are mistakenly interpreted in terms of cause and effect (known to logicians as the *post hoc* fallacy). Although there is no way of knowing, it is a fair guess that supernatural belief emerged more or less simultaneously with language, or at least more developed language, for although there are hints that Neanderthals, as evidenced by their burial practices, may have held some ideas of this sort, there is no evidence that *H. erectus* did so – though of course absence of evidence is not evidence of absence.

Likely Origins

As soon as extended social communication becomes possible, supernatural belief would seem to follow almost inevitably. Firstly there is in Palaeolithic circumstances the precariousness and fragility of existence and the near inevitability of early death. As a pattern-seeking species, humans look for explanations, and these circumstances form a pattern which touches them most intimately. An explanation is sought for, and if possible some way of avoiding unwelcome contingencies. It is also important to keep in mind, that though death was ever-present in the Palaeolithic era, it is extremely difficult if not impossible to imaginatively envisage one's own death ('the black sun at which no-one can look', according to Simone de Beauvoir). Curiosity about what had become of the personalities of those who had already died must also have been a driving factor.

One possible answer is that they come to inhabit other bodies. Belief in reincarnation is mostly associated today with Hinduism and Buddhism, but in fact it is quite prevalent in remaining hunter-gatherer communities. The Inuit faith for instance holds to the belief that the spirits of the animals they kill for food proceed to inhabit other animals of the same species, and that if the hunters (or rather the women who cut up the carcass) show respect for them, for example by offering the carcass a drink, the animal's reincarnation will be grateful and more willing to be killed subsequently.[5]

Humans too in this belief system undergo reincarnation, being reborn in a new infant once a person dies. This belief also justifies infanticide when times are hard or the newborn is too weakly or is afflicted with disabilities which will render it incapable of contributing to the community in the challenging circumstances of an Arctic environment. This is not seen as killing a person; merely indicating that the person is not yet ready to be reborn but will be so later on with a subsequent birth.[6]

Secondly there are the natural forces over which humans have no control, extending from seasonal variations in climate and temperature, which has implications for food sources, to unforeseeable disasters like forest fires, earthquakes, floods, volcanic eruptions. It would be natural, indeed most compelling, to attribute conscious agency to natural phenomena – after all, at least a hundred millennia down the line, we still get angry with our mechanical or electronic equipment when it frustrates us, and individuals involved in dangerous occupations such as deep sea fisherman, or addicted to very perilous sports, like racing drivers, are notoriously superstitious.

Thirdly, and of no less importance, there are dreams, still in our own times a mysterious phenomenon, though the current scientific consensus appears to be that they are simply mental garbage with no meaningful significance. Nevertheless they certainly appear subjectively to have some, and unquestionably our ancestors at the dawn of social communication must have discussed their dreams and concluded that they were signals from a world different from the day-to-day one that they inhabited. They must have contributed powerfully to the notion of a human spirit separate from its physical body. By extension, if natural forces were regarded as having conscious agency, the idea that they were in turn inhabited by an immaterial spirit was a perfectly logical conclusion.[7]

Taking religion in its broadest sense to include all manner of supernatural belief, its utility is evident. It represents a veritable intellectual Swiss army knife, adaptable to fulfil an enormous number of purposes – explaining the nature of the natural world and of the human place within it, promoting ethical rules and objectives; reinforcing community cohesion; offering consolation in hard or disastrous times; and not least, by the time rank societies evolved into rulerships, justifying domination, subordination and extreme social inequality – not to mention providing a career path for a corps of experts in religious practice. According to Michael Mann, 'Ideological power derives from the human need to find ultimate meaning in life . . . '[8] and 'Powerful ideologies provide a bridge between reason, morality and emotion'.[9]

Getting Started

The area is very unclear and controversial, but a tentative consensus among experts would suggest that the earliest form of supernatural practice, first described for arctic Siberia but subsequently identified all around the globe, was what is known as shamanism. In this belief system, specially initiated individuals possessing exceptional powers (the earliest confidently recognised archaeological example is a woman),[10] when in a trance state induced in various ways including naturally occurring psychedelic substances, made journeys into the world of the dead and the spirit world more generally and brought back essential knowledge from these realms regarding what was to happen and what to do about it.

So far as religious practice was concerned, shamanism was linked closely to totemism, the mystic association between a community and a particular species of animal (or more rarely plant) which was regarded as being a blood relation of the clan and not to be harmed – biological relationship being regarded as all-important. Totemism seems to be a universal constant for both forager and early agricultural communities. It must be kept in mind that in these societies – and for many centuries thereafter – no categorical distinction was made between the spirit world and the material one; they were assumed to interpenetrate.

It was a natural and perhaps inevitable step in agrarian societies, as totemism declined, to invent powerful supernatural beings who oversaw the natural order and kept it moving, determining human destinies and acting either as protectors of the society or shape-shifters who might behave either benevolently or with mischievously evil intent. Deities were viewed as operating differently depending on cultural differences. Among the Mexica (Aztecs) the gods required prodigies of human sacrifice to maintain the natural world in working order. For the classical Greeks, despite being immortal and all-powerful they shared all the human attributes of lust, jealousy, anger and sadism. Among the Germanic pagans (probably with ultimately the same origins as their Greek/Roman counterparts) they themselves, despite their powers, were mortal and subject to fate, and would all be killed at the end of time.

In fact the notions of the fates among the Greeks on the one hand and Scandinavians on the other, were virtually identical, in both cases envisaged as three old women of whom the first spun the thread of an individual's life destiny, the second wove it and the third snipped it. The Scandinavians knew them as the Norns, the Greeks as the Moirai, and in the Greek pantheon they were explicitly in existence before the Olympian gods and the gods were subject to them. As noted above the Greeks added the conception of the Erinyes or Furies, mythological beings who pursued and punished transgressors of clan custom, especially those who attempted to violate their destiny as prescribed by the Moirai. However not all cultures developed the notion of such superhuman deities whether spirit or material. The great exception was the Chinese, which although it certainly postulated spirit beings, did not have a pantheon of deities in the manner of the Aztec, Egyptian, Indo-European or even the Japanese.

All pre-modern cultures, facing the perils of nature, of social life and of hostile humans, gave a great deal of attention, most understandably, to trying to determine the will of the gods or supernatural forces. Astrology, developing in several different cultures, was a predictable expression of this ambition. If astral phenomena, which are often predictable, are manifestly associated with natural events, it is natural to assume, however erroneously, that they are also associated with human destinies. Different methods were also employed, such as the roll of dice or inspecting the condition of the entrails of sacrificed chickens. Oracles pronounced by specially sanctified figures, often referred to in the Jewish and

Christian bibles, represented another source of divination, and the importance of divinatory procedures in Greek society is suggested by the fact that the location of the Delphi oracle was referred to as the navel of the world.[11] Historically many decisions of extreme importance, such as whether or not to fight battles, notably those in the Greco–Persian wars, have been made on the basis of diviners' predictions.

Sacrifice

Sacrifice does not always necessarily involve violence to humans, and mostly it did not – animals were the principal victims in most cultures. Historically, in all social practices that could be regarded as religions (though not necessarily in every version of supernaturalism) sacrifice, both routine and exceptional has always formed an intrinsic, and in some a central, element. It could cover actions as diverse as spilling beer or wine on the ground to killing a favourite child.

The logic behind sacrifice was simple enough. If something welcome was expected from the deity such as seasonal rainfall, flourishing crops, absence of pestilence, success in warfare, personal good fortune and so on, then something must be given in return – the principle of reciprocity acting in this case on a supernatural plane rather than the merely human one. Public sacrifices were performed at seasonal festivals, with which they were closely integrated – a generalisation which applies to all varieties of what is usually termed paganism, to Daoism, Shinto, Brahmanism and all the monotheist religions. Sacrifices could either be a thank-offering for some favour already shown or intended to procure a later favour or avert the gods' anger.

So far as the monotheist religions are concerned, animal sacrifice continues in Islam as it did in the Yahwist religion prior to the destruction of the Temple cult centre by Roman power in 70 CE. Animal sacrifice, central to the cult, was, after the return of the Yahwist community from Babylon at the end of the exile in the sixth century BCE, concentrated in the new temple in Jerusalem and forbidden anywhere else to pious Jews. (It functioned also in the rival Samaritan temple to the north.) Jewish peasants wishing to slaughter animals for food were obliged to take them to the Temple for the purpose (and of course pay a fee to the priests) if they lived within travelling distance. It was therefore discontinued once the temple no longer existed.

Animal sacrifice was never practised by the Christians, an attitude possibly reinforced by its prevalence among their pagan neighbours. Other forms of sacrifice were prescribed instead; of material wealth, of energy and of time – and so it has continued to the present day. Animal sacrifice was practised ostentatiously in the Vedic religion, the ancestor of modern Brahmanism and Buddhism, of many pagan (and possibly even ultimately of all the monotheist religions), but since abandoned by most, though not all, schools of Brahmanism.

However real adepts in the Hindu, Buddhist, Christian and to a lesser extent Muslim faith sacrifice themselves to lives of ritual, prayer and contemplation, often accompanied by severe ascetic practices, abandoning all prospect of secular satisfaction such as sex, family and material prosperity. Monastic orders exist in Christianity, Hinduism and Buddhism, and the latter two also include freelance holy men (extinct in Christianity) while Islamic Sufi orders exist, although that religion disavows monasticism.

Violation of law or custom was felt likely to provoke the wrath of the gods and endanger the community. Propitiating these violent deities was therefore a prime responsibility of the ruler and his priesthood. That could include the violence of formal human sacrifice (distinct from executions) though by the time of the early civilisations in both the Middle East and China it had become uncommon, and in the former replaced by animal sacrifice. However it was still occasionally practised in an emergency (probably including child sacrifice in the case of the Carthaginians) even by the Romans, who generally disfavoured it, and there are plenty of legendary accounts in both Greek and Jewish narratives. However only among the Mexica does it seem to have been an everyday occasion extensively used at every seasonal festival. Elsewhere it appears to have been reserved for a limited number of victims on special occasions, such as the start of a major enterprise or founding a city, or the funeral of an important ruler, when his attendants would accompany him into the afterlife, as was practised in the other Amerindian cultures, in early Chinese dynasties, in African chiefdoms, in the Pacific islands and possibly in early or pre-dynastic Egypt. Aztec (Mexica) practices, undertaken to propitiate the gods and thereby keep the rain falling, the maize growing and the sun moving in the sky, reportedly shocked the conquistadors, though to be sure they themselves had little enough to boast about in respect of mass slaughter.

If consciousness is attributed to natural forces, it is evident that these may on differing occasions be either benign or malevolent, creative or destructive and similar attitudes will be adopted when spirit beings are regarded as the movers behind the forces. The normal and self-evident thing is therefore to conciliate these beings, pay them due deference and sacrifice, avoid provoking their anger and pray for them to show their smiley face rather than their ferocious one. Moreover severe punishment awaited anyone (and their relatives) who by violating the prescribed rituals was likely to annoy the divine beings, whose wrath would then be visited upon the entire community.[12]

Ethical frameworks based on the custom of the community ultimately derived from the necessities of cooperation and interrelation in clan society with its conceptions of status and honour, economic practices, decision-making, childrearing, and so forth and in some instances developed in a manner which did not give priority to deities whether threatening or benevolent. Both the Confucian and the Buddhist cultures follow this pattern, with gods, if they exist, relegated to minor roles. Gautama, the Buddha, himself insisted that he had little if any comment to make about the gods. Right behaviour however is encouraged by the principle of *karma*, common to both the Brahmin and the Buddhist traditions, by which rewards and punishments in subsequent incarnations of a person are regulated, but *karma* is an abstract principle, not a specific deity. To be sure, the Egyptian gods were concerned with moral behaviour and judged souls in the afterlife, but their mechanism for ensuring moral practice was originally the abstract concept of *ma'at*, though it was later in addition personified as a goddess.

As for the cultures in which the gods figured significantly, these might be regarded as creators of the known universe, as in the Greek/Roman pantheon, or not, as in the Germanic one; they might be protectors and guardians against the hostility of monsters of desert and sea, like Indra in the Sanskrit pantheon or Ba'al in the Canaanite one. The gods of the Bronze Age were generally satisfied with reverence and sacrifices of greater or lesser moment, generally left law-making to the secular power and got on with their godly interests, pausing only to assign benefit or inflict suffering in their arbitrary godly fashion. Hammurabi's code, for example, begins and ends with addresses to the gods who conferred the kingdom upon him, but there is no pretence that the laws he formalises issued directly from the deities (perhaps in a polytheistic society that would have been impossible).

In religions which evolved pantheons of gods these deities were effectively expressions of human sentiments and practices projected onto a supernatural scale. Different ones, as reported by their adherents, had different styles of activity in the world (in the Greek pantheon frequently taking time off from their divine business in order to rape a mortal woman), but tended to be similar in their relations among themselves, which were generally ones of violence, adultery and deceit. Most of them being immortals they could not kill each other, though in Norse mythology they could, but they could certainly hurt, embarrass and make fools of each other, sometimes drawing mortal humans into their games. Both the Norse and the Greek pantheons possessed gods of deceit, Loki in the former and Hermes in the latter. In Homer the Trojan war is represented as being the outcome of a quarrel between three goddesses. In Norse mythology Loki brings about the death of the rival god Baldur (whose spirit nevertheless lives on in an afterlife).

Life and Afterlife

As noted above, acceptance of the reality that death is the end of all things for the individual is one that is very difficult, originally even impossible, to absorb. Virtually all known cultures postulated an afterlife of some sort, either one in which the spirits of the dead continued to share hearths, homes and fields with the living, went through processes of reincarnation, or else removed to a separate realm of the dead. In both the Greco-Roman and Semitic traditions this was a grim and gloomy place, where a miserable existence was passed among the shades, and all the delights of life on earth were absent.

In the *Iliad,* when Hektor is slain by Achilles, as his soul departs his body it laments the joys of the world he is leaving, and in the *Odyssey* when Odysseus pays a visit to the underworld and meets Achilles there, the latter complains that he would prefer the lowliest social position among the living to his existence in the world of the dead. In the *Book of Job* there is no hint that Job, suffering unjustly, can be expected to be compensated in the afterlife for his infliction. The Egyptian afterlife however was different, for following death an individual soul (to simplify several aspects of spiritual existence) passed through terrifying ordeals, but if it had lived a *ma'aHy* existence on earth and was judged worthy by the gods, would thereafter enjoy a glorious (the degree of glory depending upon rank) afterlife in an idealised version of Egypt.

How far these notions may have influenced neighbouring cultures is uncertain, but certainly by the later centuries BCE, and the earlier ones of the Common Era important shifts were occurring. During the Hellenistic era when the region was dominated by Alexander's successors and social tensions resulting from class oppression were on the increase, the Homeric conception of Hades as a horrible place was increasingly called into question. Access to Elysium, previously reserved for the gods and not even all of these, was broadened for the souls of the virtuous in general, with a particularly unpleasant dungeon of Hades, Tartarus, reserved for the particularly wicked. The elite classes of both the Stoic and Epicurean schools of thought, generally thought of as opposites, for all their disagreement, tended to reject altogether the notion of an afterlife. Significant new perspectives on life and afterlife were to appear in the later centuries of the first millennium BCE in the form of what Michael Mann terms the 'salvation religions'.

The Mystery Cults of the Classical World

These proved to be more ephemeral forms of approach to the supernatural world, but of considerable importance on account of their contribution towards preparing the ground for the appearance of the most successful, in spread and numbers, of all the salvation religions. In later classical antiquity in the Greco-Roman world at large, mystery cults flourished, from the traditional ancient Eleusinian Mysteries based near Athens, to the much later ones (of which Orphism was the most significant) and which promised to purify the initiates' souls to their great benefit and possibly to confer immortality and communion with the gods.

Orphism, a religious cult of the mythical musician Orpheus, originating in Thrace, and transplanted into Athens in the wake of trade and industry, was 'an outgrowth of the urban revolution'.[13] It may have reflected the outlook of a dispossessed peasantry. Their account of the origins of the earth and humanity is derived from Hesiod, the eighth-century BCE poet of an independent but hard-pressed and overworked peasantry – he describes his own holding at the foot of Mount Helicon as 'a cursed place, cruel in winter, hard in summer, never pleasant'.

The Orphics treated life as bad news for the living person, a penance which had to be lived through in toil and misery to atone for the sin of the Titans who killed and devoured Dionysus (he was subsequently resurrected), for the human soul is born from the ingested god after Zeus blasted the Titans with his thunderbolt, but the human body from the ashes of the Titans. 'The body is the tomb of the soul . . . All life is a rehearsal for death [through which] the soul can hope to escape from its imprisonment.'[14] However if the individual has been very evil the soul is damned to eternal torment. If it is salvageable it undergoes reincarnation till after three lives of asceticism and following the correct rituals it is allowed to join the blessed in the Elysian fields. ' . . . [M]an is to God and body to soul what the slave is to his master.' It was a doctrine which, turned upside-down, was at the foundation of Plato's aristocratic and virulently anti-democratic metaphysic and the resemblance to Christian mythology is not accidental. Possibly the movement drew its initial inspiration from the sufferings of the peasantry, turned off the land and enslaved or driven into destitution. However it subsequently penetrated into all classes of society, including aristocrats like Plato – and, with modifications, a moderately prosperous Hellenised Jew, Saul of Tarsus.

According to George Thomson,

[The Orphics] could not rest content with what they had because they had nothing, and their hopes were as infinite as their desires. All life was strife and struggle. And if man would only run the race with courage, there was none so humble or debased but he might win the prize of glory and become a god.[15]

Whether this argument will stand up to investigation might be questionable, given the reality that, like Christianity, Orphism soon came to be adopted by all classes in society including the elite, but given the emphasis on suffering and redemption it is not an unreasonable interpretation of its beginnings. The Classical mystery cults too, less concerned with right order than with offering comfort and hope to their initiates, though they proved to be historically ephemeral, reflected the social tensions and distresses which generated the great salvation religions.

The First Salvation Religions and their Competitors

The salvation religions that Mann discusses represented something totally new in the human narrative after around 200,000 years of doing without them. Their continuing importance is testimony enough to that. They supplemented or supplanted the communal religions which had prevailed up to that point. Their attraction was that they offered promises to the individual believer, who by appropriate belief and practices usually, though not invariably, including intense asceticism, would be offered an improved existence either in a future reincarnation or else in the afterlife.

First in the field were Brahmanism, a development of the original Vedic faith, and its later offshoot Buddhism, which, displaced from its original home in the subcontinent, was to become dominant in Ceylon and Tibet and strongly influential in China, Indo-China and Japan, where it rivalled or supplemented the indigenous cultures. Judaism was to develop in a similar manner, to be followed by its offshoot Christianity and six centuries later the last of the great salvation religions, Islam. The remainder of this chapter deals with the earlier versions and their rivals.

While being careful to avoid any suggestion of technological determinism it is highly suggestive that these religions began their emergence in the aftermath of the expanding use of iron in tools and weaponry. The first millennium BCE was an era of increasingly aggressive, disruptive and oppressive empires that shattered the preceding Bronze Age empires and cultures less well equipped technologically for extracting labour and surplus from their subjects. In a new world of oppression and exaction punctuated with social calamity it is scarcely surprising that there should, according to Benedict Anderson, have arisen new 'imaginative response to the overwhelming burden of human suffering – disease, mutilation, grief, age and death'.[16]

Nonetheless it is important to keep in mind that salvation religions however defined did not spring out of nowhere but with the possible exception of Islam, were evolved, with a shifting emphasis, out of the established communal religions, which in parts of Eurasia continued to survive and flourish and influence. One form of religious competitor which did not survive, but nevertheless made its contribution to the emergent Christian faith and left behind a significant inheritance was Classical paganism, returned to at the conclusion of this chapter.

Vedism and Brahmanism

The Vedic religion, the oldest of the 'salvation religion' group, takes its name from the *Rig Veda*,[17] the oldest still operational sacred text, which assumed its written form at some point around the end of the Bronze Age, but evidently had a much longer oral history. The religion associated with it was developed during the second millennium BCE by the speakers of the Indo-Iranian or Indo-European language group living in the region of the Iranian plateau, and is of immense importance in history. Its importance derives from the fact that different communities of its adherents moved west, south and east, and through them it was the fountainhead of the classical pagan religions of Europe including the Celtic, Germanic and Norse ones, of Hinduism and its derivative Buddhism, and, via Zoroastrianism, most likely the monotheist ones as well.

Its most direct descendant today, though much altered, is the Hindu or Brahmanist faith of the Indian subcontinent, which continues to use the *Rig Veda* as a sacred text, so that will be the first to be discussed here. Warrior elites professing this form of religion invaded the subcontinent, initially the Indus valley, from the north in the course of the second millennium BCE. At the time of their arrival and being Bronze Age peoples, their development of chariot warfare gave them the military advantage which enabled their takeover, later supplemented by iron-using technology which furthered their expansion southwards (this summarises a very complex process with numerous rival localised empires and kingdoms based on agricultural exploitation rising and being overwhelmed in their turn).

It is worth quoting at some length the description of Brahmanism given in the *Great Soviet Encyclopaedia* of 1979. According to this,

Brahmanism is characterized by polytheism with the inclusion of various local tribal deities in the pantheon, by the retention of animistic and totemistic views, and by ancestor worship. The supreme deities of Brahmanism are Brahma, the creator and embodiment of the universe, and the beneficent Vishnu and terrible Siva, which embody the productive forces of nature. At the basis of the dogma of Brahmanism are the notions of the animation of nature and the reincarnation of all living beings. Rebirth of the soul in one or another new corporeal form proceeds as requital (karma) for virtuousness or sinfulness in the preceding life: in the first case, a soul is reborn in the body of a human being of higher social standing or even as an inhabitant of heaven; in the second case, the soul is reborn in a person of lower social standing or even in an animal or plant. . . . The accurate execution of the ritual of reading the sacred texts in a language incomprehensible to the people (Sanskrit) required long training; this helped increase the importance of the Brahmins (the priestly class). The notion of ritual purity was extremely persistent; its violation required compulsory purifying rites. Brahmanism developed the notion of man's ability to obtain the favour of the gods and acquire superhuman capacities by means of ascetic feats. In the struggle against Buddhism, and under its influence, Brahmanism was transformed into Hinduism in the first millennium A.D.[18]

Undoubtedly the depiction is crude and oversimplified, but nevertheless not altogether off the point. Brahmanism did constitute, in a particularly emphatic and focused manner, ideological underpinning for a structure of domination and subordination in social relations typical of agrarian civilisations, and was viewed by the historian Norman Cohn as 'a divinely appointed order that was basically timeless and unchanging, yet never wholly tranquil'.[19] The Vedic religion encompassed a range of deities with their roots in the ancestral Indo-Iranian culture, particularly Indra, 'the uncompromising hero of wrath hundredfold, subduer of troops', and cognate with equivalents in both Middle East and European paganism,[20] and the earliest documents of the culture are hymns to these divinities and accounts of their exploits.

The social structure of the people who composed and transmitted (orally for centuries) the *Rig Veda*, and its succeeding sacred writings, maintained a social order which had as its central tenet the doctrine of *varna* (allied to though not identical with caste or *jati*) which prescribed the division of the population into three hereditary orders – priests, warrior cattle herders and tillers of the soil. When the Indo-Iranians first entered the subcontinent all fit men were expected to participate in armed conflicts on behalf of their lords, but settlement and social differentiation had given rise in due course to an order of 'professional' fighters.

The fact that these early texts are concerned so centrally with the doings of warrior gods suggests that at the time they were composed, warriors served as the dominant *varna*. However as oral transmission was the rule and these texts increasingly assumed the status of sacred knowledge, they overtook in importance the deities they celebrated. The guardians and purveyors of that knowledge, the masters of worship and ritual, displaced the warriors, even the warlords, as the leading element in the social structure and themselves assumed sacred attributes. The professional priests, the Brahmins, monopolised sacred knowledge and the correct procedures for carrying out sacrifice, critically important because the health of the gods themselves depended on plentiful sacrifice, and all but the most elementary sacrifices required a Brahmin to officiate and to be paid for his expertise. Natural disasters were attributed to insufficiency of sacrifice and the worst of sins became hostility to, or disregard for, Brahmins.

Caste

The passage of time and interaction, both violent and otherwise, between the newcomers and preceding populations brought change and development. Hinduism develops continuously and has no final form, but the basic framework was constructed around the middle of the first millennium BCE in what is termed the 'Hindu synthesis', with the Vedas as its starting point but incorporating many other religious and social strands, developing, according to Michael Mann, into a system of 'Intense ritual penetration of everyday life, greater than of the other world religions'.[21] The number of castes multiplied greatly until the religion became and remains a very complex phenomenon, with its central principle being degrees of ritual defilement. It can be compared to the terminology of a Japanese ruler dividing the polluted from the unpolluted in the creation of the Burakumin outcaste section of Japanese society; the lowest castes were 'full of filth' while the Brahmins were exempt from it.

Like social class, *jati* was based upon the division of labour but by no means represents an equivalent – it was possible for an individual to change their social class, but never their caste, which is exclusively hereditary. In modern India a low-caste person can become a very important politician or potentially a millionaire, but they remain of lowly caste. No individual could convert to Hinduism, for there is no caste to which they could be assigned – in principle a community could do so, and in the past Brahmanism spread by this means into the Himalayas and in Southeast Asia, but it would require the community in question to form a new caste. For individuals the situation changed somewhat with the establishment in the twentieth century of the Hare Krishna movement with its dynamic proselytism – if that indeed is regarded as an authentic form of Hinduism.

Caste, in the theology of the religion, is an expression of *dharma*, also termed *rita*, a concept rather similar to the ancient Egyptian *ma'at*. The particular caste an individual is born into is an expression of one's *karma*, for the concept of reincarnation is central to the religion, and this abstract form of supernatural justice will reward or punish in a subsequent life how well or badly one has performed in one's assigned station during the present. For example, if one has been very bad one may be reborn as a worm. It is a magnificently effective ideology of social control, a 'moral acceptance of hierarchy' in Mann's phrase, and will also incidentally tend to promote vegetarianism, for if one is carnivorous one may end up eating the corpse of one's reincarnated grandmother.

Reincarnation, as already noted, is a frequent feature of hunter-gatherer belief and penetrated into Daoism. It was taken over by the Buddhist belief system and found also among some of the classical Greek intellectual schools, particularly the Pythagoreans of the sixth century BCE. Whether or not there was any Indian influence remains uncertain, but there may have been for trade and intellectual links certainly existed.

In Brahmanism it was generally held that on reincarnation any memories of one's past life or lives were cancelled, not carried over, in which case reincarnation would seem to be indistinguishable from death, for if all memories are inescapably erased and one can never remember anything from one's previous life, one might as well have never had it. As Sartre remarked, we do not *have* a past; we *are* our past.

Ambiguity

What most forcibly strikes an outside observer about the Hindu religion is the staggering complexity and variation developed within its essential principles. Unlike the monotheist religions its clergy did not try to suppress rival interpretations of these principles – it simply absorbed them all, leaving a believer free to apply them according to inclination. Gods may be regarded as specific entities or alternatively avatars or manifestations of each other or else of the supreme divine principle, Brahma. Brahma can be either the supreme god, or one of a trinity (the Trimurti) concerned respectively with creation, maintenance and destruction, or even as an abstract cosmic principle. Hence Hindus could be either polytheists, monotheists or even, if Brahma is interpreted as a principle without a personality or attributes, atheists so long as traditional precepts are observed. The last, according to some, is a perfectly respectable interpretation of the Vedas. Hinduism is the most syncretic of any religion. Taking one thing with another, however, Perry Anderson's historical verdict on Hinduism and its caste structure is scathing:

Hereditary, hierarchical, occupational, striated through and through with phobias and taboos, Hindu social organisation fissured the population into some five thousand *jatis*, few with any uniform status or definition across the country. No other system of inequality, dividing not simply, as in most cases, noble from commoner, rich from poor, trader from farmer, learned from unlettered, but the clean from the unclean, the seeable from the unseeable, the wretched from the abject, the abject from the subhuman, has ever been so extreme, and so hard-wired with religious force into human expectation.[22]

Buddhism

Though Buddhism is most normally regarded as an offshoot of Brahmanism there is some reason for believing that its original source lay partly within a pre-Vedic or non-Vedic form of religious belief and practice. Its founder, Siddhartha, later known as Gautama or the Buddha (the enlightened one) was reputedly born a prince of a minor principality between the sixth and fifth centuries BCE (the dates are uncertain as there are no contemporary records) in the north of the Indian subcontinent. Certainly his doctrines differed substantially from central elements of Brahmanism, which was at the same time in a state of turmoil and division before consolidating into what was to remain its form during subsequent centuries, partly in response to the Buddhist challenge.

The theology or philosophy of Buddhism took little account of gods. Gautama considered that they had little relevance to his project of enlightenment, which was roughly the understanding which would enable an individual by means of meditation, mental exercises and righteous behaviour to transcend the suffering intrinsic to earthly life and eventually, possibly after a number of reincarnations, reach the state of nirvana, in which all desire was annihilated and the individual spiritually awakened, bringing rebirth to an end. The subsequent state of an individual's consciousness following that annihilation was treated as an illegitimate question.

There are two major breaks with Brahmanism however; rejection of the culture of animal sacrifice that was practised within it, and relative indifference to caste. On the other hand, acceptance of karma and reincarnation was appropriated. For a time, especially when it was patronised by the emperor Asoka who ruled most of the subcontinent in the third century BCE, Buddhism flourished there and spread far beyond it, north and south, beyond the Himalayas into what is now Afghanistan and Tibet, through China and Korea, reaching even Japan; into Southeast Asia and to the island of Ceylon (Sri Lanka), which lay outside Asoka's domains. However in its homeland it withered (though there still remain around seven million Buddhists in India)[23] probably because of the decline of imperial and elite patronage. It was hotly contested by the Brahmins, but its Achilles heel was its rejection of sacrificial rituals, the performance of which was an important source of income to its rivals, and so Buddhism was much more dependent on patronage and donations, a less reliable income stream.

In Ceylon and Tibet it became the overwhelmingly dominant form of supernaturalist faith, and in the other areas mentioned a very important one alongside the already established forms, especially Daoism in China and Shinto in Japan, where Buddhist monks became a very significant social force, even at times in armed conflict with the secular authorities. The secret of its success in these areas outside the subcontinent may have been that in Buddhism, at least the Chinese version, karmic debts from past lives could be cancelled by donating to monasteries, and that the forms it evolved were better adapted to the indigenous forms of supernatural belief in these countries. Accepting them into its praxis Buddhism supplemented rather than tried to supplant them as it did in India. Though sometimes in conflict with the secular authorities, it was normally compatible with them, as it had been with Asoka, teaching values of acceptance and submission.

The Competitors

Daoism

Daoism (or Taoism) takes its name from a legendary founder, Laozi, supposed to have lived in the fourth century BCE. Whatever its origins may have been, it developed out of the ancestral Chinese agricultural folk religion. This postulated all manner of deities and spirits for all manner of situations and occupations, and stressed what is termed in Western cultures 'ancestor worship'. The assumption is that ancestors have survived their demise and as spirits are, if appropriately reverenced, capable of acting on behalf of their descendants (apparently these beliefs are still widely practised even in contemporary China). Daoism shared these presumptions, but incorporated them into a philosophical system of remarkable abstraction and sophistication, developing concepts such as the interpenetration of opposites (familiar in Western cultures through widespread reproduction of the yin–yang symbol).

It was one of a number of philosophical movements emerging in China around that time[24] and initially was seen as a rival to the somewhat earlier Confucian doctrines, which were, according to one commentator, 'used to sugarcoat the harsh Legalist [rigidly authoritarian] ideas that underlay the Imperial system'. Daoism differed in having a more supernatural cast, and was therefore possibly more comforting to lower-order wretchedness, but in essence was not that much unalike the less otherworldly-centred Confucianism[25] in social doctrine, since both stressed harmony, non-resistance and subordination to superiors. Consequently from early in the first millennium CE they could be yoked together with Buddhism as the ideological underpinning of traditional imperial society.

The name Daoism is derived from a root meaning 'pathway' and all three of these religions/philosophies attempted to show their followers a pathway to harmony in their personal lives and social relationships and set them towards the good life – which did not prevent imperial Chinese history, both official and oppositional, from being exceedingly violent. In addition, while these doctrines could embrace large sections of the population, only real adepts were in a position to intensively study and practise their implications – in other words they had to be leisured gentlemen exempt from the manual toil to which the great majority of imperial subjects were destined and who provided the resources that the rulers, priests and philosophers relied on.

Confucianism,[26] Daoism and Chinese Buddhism were all extremely conservative faiths and philosophies of life and social order. They presumed that things ought to be as they were and could not be otherwise. No significant general improvement in material life could be expected (the Daoists were quite explicit about this) and the only recourse for an individual was to pray to the deities, or by means of contemplation and correct behaviour to withdraw mentally from the world (a form of internal exile) into a state of consciousness where material considerations ceased to matter. None of that prevented frequent rebellions and dynastic overthrow.

Shinto

The folk beliefs of the Japanese islands from the very lengthy Jomon period (covering the millennia from the late Palaeolithic to the end of the first millennium BCE)[27] and afterwards were certainly supernaturalist, as would be expected, with multitudes of spirits and gods both minor and major, and a range of practices including, along with worship of particular deities, seasonal and life-course ritual, sacrifices, sorcery, divination, faith healing and so forth. Being rather similar in origin to the pagan traditions found in Europe prior to the appearance of the Olympian gods upon the scene, it has had no particular doctrine even to the extent of Daoist beliefs.

As with Dao, the word means 'pathway', i.e. pathway to a satisfactory life according to prevailing cultural standards, assisted perhaps by the spirits or *kami*. For centuries it remained as diverse and unstructured as any folk religion without central organisation. It did have concepts of ritual impurity, nowhere however as strong as with Brahmanism and capable of being purified by suitable ritual. Different clans and communities practised their own particular varieties of Shinto, while during the historical period, when contacts with the Asian mainland became more prevalent, it assimilated elements and mythologies from both Daoism and Buddhism, which were in turn very much affected in their Japanese form by the indigenous beliefs and practices.

In the seventeenth and eighteenth centuries, however, some writers, such as Motoori Norinaga, began to stress Shinto in nativist terms as distinct from foreign imports such as Dao, Buddhism or, by that time, Christianity (which was later outlawed) and Shinto's position altered dramatically following the forcible Western intrusion into Japan in the mid-nineteenth century, which was reacted against by the Meiji Restoration (or revolution) of 1868. The section of the Japanese ruling class behind this political and social transformation advanced a deliberate and strategically conceived project to 'remain the same by far-reaching alteration'.

In short, they aimed to assert and preserve Japanese elite aristocratic and neo-feudal values by importing and copying Western science, technology, overseas imperialism and organisational methods in order to make Japan an industrial power to stand comparison with the imperial West. To counterbalance this, Japanese traditions at the same time were propagated and emphasised.[28] The previous figurehead emperor, now decreed to be descended from the sun goddess, was increasingly presented as a national icon with great power, real or pretended. Shinto shared in this development, now sponsored by the state as the authentic national and nativist religion. Its most important embodiment was in a multitude of shrines, great and small, where what were supposed to be Shinto rituals were and are officiated over by Shinto priests. Currently there are around eighty thousand such shrines.

Even a fairly superficial survey of the traditions of the faiths discussed so far in this chapter reveal at their heart an essential similarity despite the great variety of concepts and practices found between and within them, implicit in some instances explicit in others. Their similarity lay in their adherence to a concept of a right order in the universe, either laid down by the gods or prevailing as an abstract principle, one which humans must uphold and direct themselves by or else suffer adverse consequences. This was an approach very much in tune with the interests of elites, yet at the same time it offered to the mass of these traditions' adherents practices, techniques, and promises to make life in grim conditions more bearable.

This notion, like the Vedic 'rc, the Chinese Dao or Japanese Shinto, linked the natural world with the supernatural one, so the force that kept the heavenly bodies moving in the sky was the same as those which produced the rain, the growth of vegetation, the reproduction of cattle and, importantly, the lineaments of the social order. These assigned individuals to their appropriate position within it and required them to behave in particular ways towards superiors, inferiors or equals, required a woman to obey her husband (or mother-in-law), a son or daughter, regardless of age, to obey their parents, and all to obey the rulers (though of course reality seldom measured up to the ideal, as rulers often discovered). It is not surprising that the more ambitious of these doctrines, such as the Buddhist one, recommended escape from earthly cares through a discipline of meditation, ritual and mental exercises in order to reach a state of mind where the inflictions did not seem to matter. There are resemblances here to the Stoic philosophy of the Hellenistic era – and there may have been a degree of contact, as Alexander's empire bordered on India.[29] Ernest Gellner is of the opinion that 'Of the great literate civilizations, Hinduism is the one closest to the Platonic blueprint . . .'.[30]

An essential point here is that although Daoism and Shinto were competitors with Buddhism no great hostility developed between the adherents of these faiths. On the contrary, peoples in the areas where they interpenetrated, principally China and Japan, experienced no difficulty in adhering to both Buddhism and either of the other two – they supplemented each other rather than conflicted, quite unlike the monotheist salvation religions further to the west.

These are the subject of the following chapter, and even disregarding the mystery cults discussed above which also possessed the essentials of salvation religion, there is evidence, quoted in Robin Lane Fox's *Pagans and Christians*,[31] that Classical pagan culture in general was heading in a salvationist direction, with increased emphasis on personal communication with whichever god was favoured by the worshipper. The aspiration of an afterlife existence free from the threats of starvation, massacre, torture, plague, enslavement – not to mention the routine torments of toil, illness, ageing, sexual abuse, poverty and parasitic invertebrates – was a very powerful one. The monotheist Christian cult/religion discussed in the next chapter took root comparatively easily because the pagan ground had been well prepared.

9

Monotheism

Monotheist religion was not among the first of Mann's 'salvation religions', but it was something entirely novel, even counter-intuitive, and in spite of its odd novelty was to prove extraordinarily powerful and in time come to dominate for centuries most of the Eurasian landmass – and then spread across the Atlantic and southward into Africa. Of the three great faiths defined as monotheist, none was totally so, as they all postulated other supernatural beings, namely angels and demons in addition to the deity. Neither of the other two however went to the extent of the Christians – at least the mainstream followers of that religion – with their paradoxical doctrine of the Trinity, which, on the basis of contradictions in the scriptures and contorted reconciliation of the Jewish scriptures with pagan Greek philosophy, insisted that their god was both one and three at the same time. One medieval scholastic philosopher, Roscelin, proposed that believers might as well postulate three gods, but his suggestion was not adopted.

In the rise of the monotheist faiths once again the transition that occurred as the Eurasian Bronze Age gave way to the Iron Age at the end of the second and beginning of the first millennium BCE takes on central importance, and what is now the eastern Mediterranean and Middle East was centrally involved.

Zoroastrians

Zoroaster, or Zarathustra, which is now reckoned to be the more likely form, is to some extent a legendary figure, but, as with Jesus of Nazareth, and Muhammad it is probable that an individual of that name did actually exist and the legend contains an essential element of factuality. The religion developed in his name was dualist rather than strictly monotheist, but is included in this section because the two gods were not equal. The good one was superior to the evil. The monotheist religions which exist today probably owe, unacknowledged, a great deal to Zoroastrianism.[1]

By the time of its emergence in the area of the Iranian plateau, as in the Fertile Crescent, the agriculture and stock-raising economy had already predominated for around seven millennia; urban concentrations for around two. Despite its antiquity this was a precarious existence, the more so with the metallurgical transition from bronze to iron; constantly threatened by chaos resulting from flood, desertification, epidemics, famine and – not least – attack from human enemies, whether rival rulers (Zoroaster was reportedly such a victim), seaborne pirates or nomadic herders. Not surprisingly, the dominant religious ideologies reflected such central concerns.

Consequently the chief remit of leaders, who as elsewhere in the Middle East, were soon accorded divine attributes as the representatives of the gods or as subordinate gods themselves, was to preserve stability and repel danger by carrying out the appropriate rituals pleasing to the high gods who decided all things. If the gods were indulgent then the feared chaos would be warded off whenever it threatened, but the dominant reign of insecurity was expected to last forever and traditional hierarchical structures to remain in place for all time. Their pantheon included a mighty warrior hero-god, who subdued and destroyed the chaos monsters which menaced the community.

Zoroaster

An epochal religious change occurred at an uncertain date, but most probably around the beginning of the first millennium BCE, owing to the influence of the Iranian prophet who was trained initially as a priest of a divine cosmogony not unlike the Vedic. From the Vedic religion his followers inherited a particular reverence for fire,[2] a striking feature of their religious practice to the extent that they were sometimes described by Europeans as fire-worshippers. This however was a misperception; fire was not a god but a symbol of purity. For Zoroaster only two gods really counted, 'two primal spirits' in his own words; Ahuru Mazda, the god of creation, light and righteousness and Angra Mainyu (or Ahriman) his evil enemy – other supernatural entities (who were nevertheless important) being merely their servants.

This in itself was a major innovation, but there was more. Zoroaster promised blissful immortality not only to distinguished individuals but to all who followed his ethical precepts and attended to their prescribed ritual duties. More innovative still was the promise of a divine apocalypse, the 'making wonderful' in which there would be a universal resurrection of the dead, the virtuous would be rewarded with immortal bodies in an earthly paradise and the wicked, including Angra Mainyu, utterly destroyed. The parallels with the Christian apocalypse virtually force themselves on the reader.

His teachings reflected contemporary social conflict, and promised that, 'the established order would be abolished, the existing authorities exterminated and [oppressed believers] vindicated and exalted',[3] Norman Cohn writes. Zoroastrianism, when it became the creed of rulers, naturally underwent many modifications, but its essence still remained at the time the Achaemenid Persian empire dominated the Middle East, including Palestine, between the sixth and fourth centuries BCE. This meant that there was plenty of opportunity for the adherents of the then Jewish religion to become acquainted with and be influenced by it.

Judaism

The origin of the ancient Hebrews remains wrapped in obscurity and mythology – certainly the biblical accounts, even when stripped of their supernatural dressing, lack all plausibility. Possibly they were herders from the east who had forced their way into the uplands of that part of the Fertile Crescent then called Canaan, comprising autonomous cities with their agricultural areas and usually dominated by neighbouring empires, initially the Egyptian – or possibly the Hebrews or Israelites were just an indigenous tribal community. John Pickard argues that the Amarna Correspondence (see Chapter Six) of the fourteenth century BCE gives evidence of fierce class struggle in the Levant at the time of its composition and that Hebrew conquest may have been the outcome of a revolutionary struggle, with Yahweh as the rallying symbol for the revolutionaries[4] and their Covenant a political alliance.

At any rate, around the ninth to seventh centuries BCE the Hebrews or Israelites eventually established two minor principalities; Judah based on Jerusalem (King David, if he ever existed, was at most a bandit chieftain) and its northern neighbour, Israel. Moreover they shared with their neighbours the Canaanite religion, including its numerous pantheon and its chief god El, whose name is incorporated into many of their personal names such as Joel or Ezekiel, or even Israel itself.

Yahweh

El had a son and chief subordinate, Ba'al, an equivalent to Indra of the Vedic herders or Marduk of the Mesopotamians, a fierce and powerful storm god who kept chaos monsters at bay. His Israelite equivalent was called YHWH or Yahweh, who shared exactly all the characteristics of Ba'al – indeed may very likely have been the same god under a different name (as with the Greek and Roman deities). Eventually Yahweh was to absorb El (there are clues to their original differentiation still in the Bible) and acquire all his characteristics (including initially his female consort), so that he became both the universal creator, establishing the world and society, and an insanely jealous micro-manager of human affairs in permanent apoplectic fury with his chosen people because of their deviation towards other gods; was amiable and generous as long as his commandments were adhered to, but a raging sadist when they were not.

Yahweh was an innovative deity in many respects – or rather his worshippers were innovators and devised the first religion in which history, real or counterfeit, was a central element. Not initially a monotheistic deity, he nevertheless became the foundation of ethical behaviour in a manner divergent from any of his counterparts. One aspect of this was the close interconnection of ritual and morality, with the first being the more important. As it eventually worked out, the cardinal injunction was to keep him well supplied with animal sacrifices and to offer sacrifices to absolutely no-one else whomsoever. In addition there were an enormous range of ritual injunctions and prohibitions,[5] the intention of which was to separate his worshippers off from any other community and emphasise their otherness, and in subsequent centuries these rather than the sacrifices became, due to contingent historical events, the distinctive markers of the Jewish religion.

As far as the ethical prescriptions were concerned, these formalised the traditional understanding of acceptable clan relations. Not to kill another clansperson, not to seize or aspire to seize his property (including his female subordinates) not to tell lies about him so as to get him into trouble with the clan authorities; and for female clanspersons to observe due deference towards their male relatives and refrain, under grim penalties, from unauthorised sexual relations (the same applied to male ones, but to a lesser extent).

It was of course his priesthood, anxious to institute a profitable monopoly for their own cult, who propagated these notions, against what the Jewish Bible suggests was considerable popular opposition, but paradoxically they achieved success only after the destruction of Jerusalem and its temple by the Babylonian empire in 586 BCE and the deportation of the upper classes, including the priestly one, to Babylonia. There the supposedly historical scriptures were redacted to produce the picture with which we are familiar today, later incorporated into the Jewish Bible. To hold the exile community together, exclusive devotion to Yahweh is presented as their central theme, with apostasy insistently blamed for all disasters and especially the recent catastrophe. Rival gods are abolished or relegated to the status of angels or demons.

The return from Babylonia to Palestine was as important as the exile. Within a few decades the Babylonian empire was overthrown and annexed by its Persian rival, whose ruler, Cyrus, permitted the exiles to return and take over the government of Judea under Persian hegemony. (Not all took advantage of the offer: those who did were of the 'Yahweh only' school). Their gratitude to the Persians was great and presumably reinforced by the Zoroastrians' semi-monotheism, while close contact provided opportunities to learn about their apocalyptic visions.

The first apocalyptic writing in the Jewish Bible or Christian Old Testament (the last book to be composed) is the Book of Daniel. Though purportedly set in Babylonia it was in fact written when the Jews and their religion were under persecution in the second century BCE from the Greek successor to the Middle East part of Alexander the Great's empire, and was designed to encourage their (ultimately successful) resistance. It was followed by the Book of Enoch and the Book of Jubilees, which envisaged an apocalyptic outcome in a manner very similar to the Zoroastrian prophecies.

Among the Jews of the Second Temple, subject to Persian and subsequently Macedonian, followed by Roman hegemony, rival theological schools developed, the best known being the Sadducees, the Pharisees and the Essenes. The Sadducees, generally identified with the ruling elite who collaborated with the

Roman power, rejected belief in any afterlife; the latter two distinguished between the post-mortem fates of the good and the evil. The Christian sect, which in its theological conceptions was nearest to the Essenes, once it became established made a similar distinction even more emphatically. More broadly, the Jesus sect tended in general more to the Pharisees' viewpoint, and the bitter denunciation of the latter in the Christian scriptures are more related to rivalry focused on the person of Jesus of Nazareth than to antagonistic religious conceptions.

Christianity

> *We are the few, the chosen few,*
> *And all the rest are damned.*
> *There's room enough in Hell for you,*
> *We don't want Heaven crammed.*
> —Origin uncertain but possibly US Southern Baptist

The Jesus sect was originally very much a part of the fragmented and internally quarrelsome Judaism which prevailed under the Roman occupation. Though the New Testament gospels are scarcely more historically reliable than the Old Testament narratives, it is clear enough that Jesus of Nazareth, if he existed, which he probably did, was a Jewish prophet preaching an imminent overthrow of Roman power by divine intervention followed by a future of blissful abundance, and targeting initially the Roman collaborators of the Jewish priesthood. The four canonical gospels of the Christian New Testament make a point however of insisting on his alleged pacific intentions. They were written around the time when Jews were under Roman suspicion on account of their great revolts and so their intellectual offspring were naturally keen to emphasise their claimed founder's rejection of insurrection.[6]

Considerable controversy has taken place around the historical status of the person in whose name the sect was founded – one cannot say the 'founder', for although little is accurately known about this individual, such documents as exist make it evident that founding a religion was certainly never his intention. The claim of scholars who dispute his reality is that Jesus of Nazareth is a made-up figure, composed from decontextualised references in the Hebrew Bible and with the characteristics of mythical gods or legendary heroes, attributes such as virgin birth and resurrection from the dead.

A leading proponent of this view early in the twentieth century (he convinced Lenin) was the German historian Arthur Drews and it has been advanced again recently by John Pickard in *Behind the Myths: The Foundations of Judaism, Christianity and Islam*, published in 2013. Pickard deploys an able case, but the weight of evidence appears to be against him, even if that evidence is principally negative.

What the gospel narratives, which diverge in many respects, agree upon is that Jesus preached in Galilee, north of Judea, at the time a peripheral area of the Jewish religion (and also a notorious hotbed of opposition to the Jewish and Roman authorities). Secondly that he was executed as a rebel against Roman rule, though the Gospels do their best to obscure this, which in itself is significant. If a divine or semi-divine or divinely inspired figure was to be invented, it would be unlikely that he would be placed in provincial rural obscurity for most of his career and end up executed as a criminal. More positive is the fact that James the Just, for whom there is fairly unquestionable evidence, was appointed leader of the Jerusalem Christians on the basis of his accepted blood relationship. The probability therefore is that there was a real figure behind the myths and legends, though it scarcely matters so far as history is concerned.

The cardinal event which led to the divergent path of Jesus's Jewish and non-Jewish followers – apart from the activities of the Hellenised Jew, Saul of Tarsus – was the utter destruction by the Romans of the temple and the original Jewish Christian community in Jerusalem during the great Jewish revolt of 66–70 CE. The Book of Revelation with its Zoroastrian parallels, written around 25 years afterwards and most likely by a Jewish Christian, was the culmination of the Jewish apocalyptic tradition and in that text, '. . . *the role that had hitherto been assumed by Jews in general is now assumed by the Christian branch of Judaism*' (emphasis added),[7] in Cohn's words.

Christianity, driven in the catastrophe of 70 CE from its original home as a Judaic sect, found its insertion in the Roman empire. The Christians, initially persecuted, eventually came to regard the empire as a providential dispensation to facilitate the spread of the religion. The imperial world was one of extreme differences of wealth and pauperism, of freedom and slavery, of routine violence and torture, of psychopathic despotism and increasingly crushing taxation, of massacre, plague and famine. For women, apart from a very small and fortunate upper-class stratum, but not even all of them, it was still worse. Women were in effect regarded as the property of their menfolk and wholly subject to their authority, to be married or otherwise disposed of at their pleasure, and with no redress.

It need come as no surprise that populations and individuals – and not only the destitute, at the sharp end of this society, under threat from all the above inflictions with no hope of improvement in the material world – would seek supernatural solace for their woes, more convincing (and less expensive) than the existing mystery cults. The early Christian message could indeed be made to sound very convincing, with the authority of holy written texts behind it; and the Jewish scriptures were rearranged to purportedly predict the appearance of Jesus.

There were material advantages in addition. One of the injunctions to the better-off in the early communities was to practise charity towards less fortunate members of the congregation, who benefited materially as a result, and the donors received for themselves spiritual benefit thereby.[8] Advantages existed too for women, who could now defy their fathers, brothers and husbands (especially in relation to forced marriage and sexual abuse) in the name of intense religious conviction and confidence that they would be rewarded in the afterlife for anything they might suffer in the present one as a result of their intransigence. They might also hope to convert their menfolk.

Internal Conflicts

From its very beginning, Christianity was an inherently contentious and fissiparous movement. There was first of all sharp conflict between the original Jerusalem church and the Christian communities being established throughout the empire in the early decades, to a significant degree by Saul of Tarsus (Saint Paul). It is unclear whether this dispute was ever resolved before the great Jewish revolt and its repression overtook the Jerusalem Christians. That was not all however, for the New Testament writings, both those of Paul and other authors or alleged authors, constantly refer to intra-faith conflicts.

The author of the Book of Revelation starts off his text with a polemic on such matters, and the letters ascribed to Paul issue constant warnings against false teachers purporting to be of the faith but bringing a message divergent in some ways from his own. Evidently he had rivals. In the span of the two millennia during which Christianity has existed literally hundreds of groups of divergent belief have evolved, each regarding all the others as schismatic, heretical, cultic.[9] These have multiplied exponentially since secular governments decreed freedom of religious belief and prohibited any particular Christian orthodoxy from enforcing its monopoly.

That Christianity should have taken this direction was no accident, arising from its theology alone, leaving aside for the moment the material pressures it was subject to. The pre-salvation religions were essentially religions of practice, and to a large extent, apart from the Jesus religion, so were the salvation ones. Some standards of belief were certainly required by the others but they generally tended to be fairly simple ones. Islam for instance requires belief that the Abrahamic god is the only god and that Muhammad is his prophet and that the faithful will enjoy an afterlife – otherwise its demands are largely practical ones, such as pilgrimage, fasting at Ramadan and regular prayer. The Judaic religion too centres around practical requirements on the part of its faithful. As a result, despite variations in belief and practice within these religions, they have not usually had the poisonous character of Christian disagreement – though in recent decades such Christian intolerance and intransigence has increasingly been imported into Islamic societies where rival interpretations of Islam are to be found.[10]

Importance of Belief

The Christian message however, by the standards of other faiths, was extraordinarily complex and it made *belief* central to its message. The apparent simplicity of, 'Believe in the Lord Jesus Christ and thou shalt be saved' hides all manner of unstated assumptions and begged questions. Firstly, who exactly is Jesus, and why is belief in his supernatural character necessary? Secondly, saved from what, and what is meant by salvation in this instance? The Christian believer was required to accept that Jesus of Nazareth was the son of YHWH (whatever 'son' was supposed to mean in this context – certainly not a biological relationship), that his mother was a virgin and he had been sent into the world to redeem individuals from the sin they were supposed to have inherited by descent from the disobedient couple in the Garden of Eden. The manner of this redemption was that he offered himself as a blood sacrifice to his parental deity, taking the place of sinful humanity and thereby appeasing Yahweh's anger. If however, according to Trinitarian belief he was not merely the son of god but *was* god, and since there was only one god, presumably he was a sacrifice of himself to himself – reminiscent of Odin hanging by the neck on the bough of the world tree Yggdrasil, sacrificing himself to himself for the sake of obtaining deep knowledge.

Not even that, however, is the end of the matter. The Christian also had to believe that Jesus was physically resurrected from his tomb and then, after several appearances to his disciples, ascended into heaven. This was taken as proof that at the end of time all humanity would be resurrected from their graves, their bodies reconstituted and their souls reunited with their bodies, after which virtuous believers would be rewarded with eternal bliss in heaven and the reprobate and the infidels tormented for eternity in the underground lake of fire (while the believers established in heaven would enjoy the spectacle).

With a foundation of that sort the range of necessary beliefs multiplied and expanded, and the scope for disagreement was enormous in the range of both belief and practice. Differing interpretations of what exactly was meant by the core beliefs and ambiguities in the sacred texts were a recipe for division, dispute, and hostility, at times resulting in lethal encounters between rival factions. The early Christians were persecuted from time to time by the Roman authorities (and sometimes lynch mobs). This was not directly because of their beliefs but – once they had separated themselves from the Jews, who were tolerated, however grudgingly, in deference to their traditional religion – in consequence of the Christians' refusal to recognise the emperor's quasi-divine status. They were therefore regarded as socially disruptive. At the same time it has been remarked that these Christians suffered more from their own quarrels than they ever did from the attentions of the pagan emperors.

So long as they occupied the position of a persecuted sect and had no power of their own, the differences and antagonisms were relatively manageable and the example and reputation of the martyrs[11] encouraged solidarity across theological divisions – though it could also give rise to them as when dispute burst out over the readmission of weaker brethren who had defected under persecution and wanted back in again. However when the irresistible spread of the cult convinced the emperors[12] that it was ineradicable and if they couldn't beat them they'd better join them, which happened in 312 CE, the Christian cult, now the Christian church under imperial patronage, acquired both power and property. Its leaders, the bishops, particularly those of five great centres, Alexandria, Antioch, Jerusalem, Constantinople and Rome, became very great men, encouraging major rivalries over who was to occupy these episcopal chairs.

With that in mind, the question now became what *was* the church, for theological disputes ballooned, and gave rise to ever more deadly antagonisms. The disputes emerged mostly over the question of the nature of the relation of Jesus to YHWH, or the son to the father as it was usually expressed, and Constantine called a council of bishops at Nicaea to settle the matter. The verdict left the disputants divided, and while imperial power might try to enforce it within the imperial domain, it could not do so among the newly converted Germanic former pagans on the borders of the empire and about to invade it.

Among the orthodox – in other words those sections of the Church which accepted the Council of Nicaea's decision – no less ferocious disputes erupted over the relation of Christ's divinity to his humanity, depending on whether the disputants too closely identified them or incontinently separated them. Orthodoxy propounded a solution which did neither, but orthodoxy was different in Egypt from what it was in Constantinople, Antioch, Georgia or Armenia, or for that matter in what is now Tunisia, or Spain. It all led to the formation of totally separate and hostile congregations even within the empire's bounds. The existing Coptic church of Egypt and Ethiopia among others is a remnant of that era, and its rival, the Nestorians,[13] might well have prevailed throughout central Asia but for the later Muslim impact.[14]

It was something altogether new in world history – that belief or disbelief in undecidable questions, should have become major social issues and indeed matters of life or death. In fact, that expression underrates their importance, for the assumption was that more was at stake than mere life, for on correct belief depended the individual's fate of eternal salvation or damnation, and more, that an individual's heretical notions might infect a community and endanger other people's immortal souls. The destruction of such vectors of pollution was therefore of cardinal urgency.

It cannot be doubted that such rival convictions about the nature of the supernatural universe were sincerely adhered to, but behind them always lay issues of power and property – who would prevail and draw revenues from the believers, who would have the favour and the ear of the ruling authorities. Forcing everyone within reach to become believers was therefore a natural corollary, and in the course of a century within the empire pagan beliefs and practices were suppressed bit by bit until they were entirely outlawed by the end of the fourth century. That could not be done to the Jews, partly because of the belief that their voluntary conversion was a necessary stage in the unfolding of the apocalypse, and of course they refused to convert. Consequently they were subjected to intermittently severe persecution and pogrom which stopped short of their attempted destruction.

The same centuries as saw the great theological uproars were also ones of intense asceticism practised by individuals who as a result won profound public admiration from a population who sought their advice on all manner of issues. Asceticism was likewise and for similar reasons a strong current in both Brahmanism and Buddhism, but the Christian saints of the period excelled in prodigies of the style. These included spending their adult life sitting on the top of pillars in all weathers; extreme fasting, minimal sleeping time, disregarding ulcers and sores, indeed encouraging parasites to breed in them. To be sure, starvation and sleep deprivation would certainly discourage sexual libido and induce states of mind which convinced the ascetic they were getting closer to their objective of divine communion. In time these extremes performances died away and asceticism was institutionalised in monastic communities, though hermits, usually somewhat less exuberant than their predecessors, persisted throughout the medieval centuries.

Power and Schism

The major Christian schism of that period,[15] which occurred in the eleventh century – although it included some theological issues, principally over the correct Latin phraseology for describing the holy ghost – was acknowledged to be mainly about power and authority; whether the bishop of Rome or the patriarch of Constantinople should exercise hegemony within the church. The Latin pope had during most of late antiquity acknowledged himself as subject to the emperor in Constantinople, but at the beginning of the ninth century, having appointed a rival emperor in the person of Charlemagne, who gave him protection,[16] he now began to insist, on the basis of seniority based on Saint Peter's mythical claim to have been the first bishop or Rome, that *he* was the supreme authority in the church; while by the eleventh century all Byzantine power in southern Italy had been expelled by the Normans, who recognised the pope's pretension.

Though there was no possibility of the Byzantine emperor recovering his position in Rome, the pope's assertion was emphatically rejected in the emperor's own territories. In spite of efforts to find a compromise and unite the rival positions, the breach became irreparable in 1054. During the following three centuries growing divergence was punctuated by mutual massacre and destruction, and though a final effort was made in the mid-fifteenth century as Turkish Muslim armies prepared to overrun Constantinople itself, it came to nothing. The catastrophe (from a Christian viewpoint) was certainly expedited by the refusal of any coordinated Latin assistance, whose leaders, apart from a Venetian military unit, left the Eastern schismatics to their fate.

As noted above, issues of salvation or damnation were believed to hang on correct belief (and consequent practice, including due submission) in both matters of principle and matters of detail. The invention of hell, the threat of being dispatched to a divine Auschwitz, only much worse, whereby the sinner was ingeniously tortured in the afterlife, not for any specific length of time or until they submitted to the torturer's demands but through all eternity, was a most effective instrument for ensuring social discipline and religious conformity. Preachers delighted in inventing and dwelling on the refinements of suffering that the damned would undergo. Nonetheless it was not effective enough, for insurrections occurred and religious dissidence continued during the centuries of faith. So severe were the consequences that the dissidents as well as the authorities had to believe passionately that *they* were the saved and their enemies the damned.

On both sides of the great division, East and West, further schisms and heresies emerged during the succeeding centuries, but particularly in the West. The thirteenth century witnessed material destruction, massacre, and torture on an enormous scale in southern France during the uprooting of the Cathar heresy, and lesser persecutions were launched against numerically smaller targets. The sixteenth century saw a further major rupture on the Western side, when papal authority was challenged and rejected, and in states where the dissidents successfully established themselves they soon turned to persecuting each other over finer points of theological controversy.

Of course terror was not the only pillar of the church (or rather churches) although it was the central one.[17] In addition it offered visual, auditory and olfactory spectacle – at least until the Calvinistic sections of the sixteenth- and seventeenth-century reformers denounced such things as distractions from concentration on the Word of God and extirpated them in the regions where they attained political power. The churches however held out the promise of delight as well as torture in the afterlife (if only, in the Calvinist persuasion, for a minority of souls).

The framework of belief provided ceremonial support on important life occasions, principally birth, marriage and death. The congregations were or could be social collectives, not mere assemblies of worshippers, which of course was true for other religions as well. It furnished believers with an understanding of life, the universe and everything, especially the narrative course of their own life. Most of all, perhaps, it brought with it a cloud of powerful imaginary friends in the shape of angels and saints, who assisted the believer in resisting temptation from the malevolent ones in the shape of demons, while also perhaps supporting their material concerns. Often, particularly for evangelical Protestants, the imaginary friend could even be the supreme deity himself – 'What a friend we have in Jesus!'.

Not only Christian individuals or congregations believed they were entitled to divine assistance and support, but also Christian states, even when engaged in conflict with others of the same persuasion. The elites of the Roman empire, Constantine, his successors (apart from the apostate Julian) and their colleagues believed that since they had made the empire Christian, surely divine providence would uphold them. Indeed surviving pagan intellectuals, whenever the empire ran into trouble, as it did with increasing frequency, complained that its woes were a consequence of abandoning the ancient gods.[18] All the successor kingdoms and their monarchs likewise felt that they were, or ought to be, under the special protection of the deity, hence the phrase that Shakespeare gives to Claudius that 'There's such divinity doth hedge a king'.

Gott Mit uns was the slogan of the imperial German military, though going back many centuries, and being used by the medieval Teutonic Knights. The Romanov dynasty in Russia had a similar slogan. Britain of course has its national anthem calling on the deity to make its monarch victorious. At the same time it is certainly important not to overlook the consolatory function which Christianity, along with other forms of religion, exercises as 'the heart of a heartless world'. At times this results in material charity as well as religious consolation. It is also important to acknowledge the reputation of pious believers who do exemplify the values and virtues which Christianity purports to embody but does not.

Islam's Context[19]

Six centuries after Christianity became a significant social force Islam made its appearance in western Arabia, a crossroads of commercial activity, and therefore well acquainted with Judaism, Christianity in its several varieties, and the version of Zoroastrianism (Zurvanism) which was the established religion of the Sassanid Persian empire. Zoroastrianism was recognised by the Muslims as a legitimate faith (though not of course the true one) rather than a form of paganism, a 'people of the book' though it was a dualistic religion rather than a monotheist one.

Much of Islam's monotheist religious belief followed and adapted Jewish traditions, a smaller element came from Christian ones. Jesus for example was recognised as a prophet, though the crucifixion was denied – prophets were not supposed to suffer shameful execution. It has been remarked that medieval Christians would have regarded Islam as a Christian heresy or schism rather than a rival religion – certainly that is the guise under which Muhammad appears in Dante's *Inferno* – disembowelled because he had divided the faith.

As with Jesus, the historicity of the faith's founder has been questioned, including, in 2008 by a German Muslim convert, Professor Muhammad Sven Kalisch.[20] He has pointed out that many scholars are doubtful concerning the ancient sources on Muhammad's life and that the earliest biography, which is no longer extant, dates from a century after the accepted date of the prophet's death in 632 and is known only from references in much later texts. The first coins bearing his name appeared only in the later seventh century. John Pickard makes similar points, also drawing attention to the fact that the inscriptions on the Dome of the Rock in Jerusalem scarcely mention Muhammad, and the one which does may be referring not to an individual but a title – 'one who is worthy of respect'.

Discussing the religion itself, he notes that that the reported early sayings are addressed to Jews and Christians rather than pagans, claiming to be a refinement and true interpretation of their faiths, not something entirely novel. Pickard implies that Islam probably arose in precisely that milieu, among communities of Arab Christians or Jews seeking a purer religion than Byzantium's 'gilded Christianity'.[21] The great significance of Jerusalem to the faith is also held to be a pointer in the same direction. 'The Qur'an assumes familiarity with major narratives recounted in the Jewish and Christian scriptures', he asserts, and possibly some of its content (up to a third in one version) is pre-Islamic, though this is disputed. Following the overthrow of the Sassanid empire and the conquest of Iran local Christians referred to the Arab monotheists as 'New Jews' – for which a modern translation might be neo-Judaism.

Effectively Pickard is arguing that Islam was invented by the ex-Christian and ex-Jewish Arab imperialists to give themselves an ideological underpinning distinct from but compatible with the religious circumstances of the region. He writes,

> Whatever may have been the role of an Arab leader called 'Mohamed' the religion that developed in his name did not exist in the-mid seventh century but arose from the class and ethnic conflicts within the Arab Empire and the stresses and strains of holding together the enormous conquests of the seventh century.[22]

As with the case of Jesus of Nazareth the argument is well developed and effectively presented, but as with that, the probabilities are that a specific individual was the source of the religion whatever the later accretions around his name may have been. Probably these were quite considerable.

Conquest

After becoming hegemonic in Arabia the new faith spread through the regions of Arab conquest, mostly by voluntary conversion. Edward Gibbon devoted a volume of his *History of the Decline and Fall of the Roman Empire* to the impact of Muhammad and Islam. The account is still worth attending to, at least in Gibbon's analysis of the manner in which the practice and rituals of Islam, as well as the unifying ideology, contributed to military discipline and effectiveness thanks to regular prayer, hygiene and well-defined chains of command. The faith had other advantages as well. It was simple and straightforward, avoiding the theological and Christological labyrinths of Christianity – the previously mentioned Sven Kalisch said he converted because it was the most rational form of religion. Unlike the Christian regimes it was tolerant, for although conversion at sword-point occasionally happened, normally unbelievers (at least fellow-monotheists) who did not wish to share the advantages of the new faith were tolerated on fairly mild terms, mostly being required only to pay a special tax – which meant that conversion was initially discouraged. Not surprisingly Islam made rapid progress among populations ground down by Byzantine or Sassanid financial demands and in the former empire persecuted for Christological deviation.

Within a century of the new faith being proclaimed the Persian empire, which included Iraq, was overthrown, the surviving portion of the Roman empire, ruled from Constantinople or Byzantium, was greatly reduced, including Sicily, and the Gothic kingdom in Spain conquered. Even the Frankish kingdom was attacked. By the tenth century Muslim power extended from Spain, along the North African littoral, throughout the Middle East and into central Asia, including part of China, though repelled in Tibet.

Naturally it was impossible for such an extent of territory to continue to be ruled from a single centre, first Damascus and subsequently Baghdad, and it soon enough divided into mutually hostile principalities. Some of that, as in the example of Egypt, was due to religious dispute, not so much over questions of doctrine such as agitated the Christians, though that was not altogether absent, but more over the interpretation of tradition and who should be regarded as the true successor to Muhammad.

In due course Islam spread even further, to Southeast Asia and what is now Indonesia, up the Nile to what is now Sudan, and along the Red Sea coast to what is now Somalia across the Sahara, where Timbuktu became a major cultural centre, and into tropical West Africa, where powerful states were established by Islamic rulers through conversion rather than conquest. That the importance of the religion continues into the twenty-first century needs no demonstration.

Disruptive Implications

The monotheist religions, with their sacred writings which supposedly constitute a revelation direct from the deity via prophets such as Moses or Muhammad, or else the four Christian evangelists, have an attribute which does not apply to their counterparts either in the other salvation religions or others outside that category. This is the fact that sacred writings of that sort contain a disruptive charge, and do so even beyond the most evident sources in the apocalyptic writings in Zoroastrianism, Judaism and Christianity, which threaten damnation and punishment to the high and mighty and paradise for the subjected. These are handmade for rebels, dissidents and religious revolutionaries and were indeed frequently so used, the last notable occasion being the English revolution of 1640–60. Not surprisingly the religious establishments did their best to neuter them; Zoroastrianism was sanitised into Zurvanism, the Jewish apocalypses (apart from Daniel) did not make it into the canon, and the bishops were dubious about the Book of Revelation, only accepting it as canonical after several centuries.

But even without these apocalypses the monotheist sacred writings can still inspire dissidence and revolt. There is only one god (setting aside the reservations concerning Christianity) and his words are sacred. Unfortunately the deity has not spoken unambiguously to all his followers and there are as many potentially different interpretations as there are believers.[23] Despite the disciplinary regimes evolved to institute and preserve an orthodox interpretation – from ecumenical councils to papal infallibility in the case of Christianity – it is always possible to challenge the authorities on the argument that they have misinterpreted, distorted, and debased the holy word. Strangely enough, such challenges have always coincided with and were related to social issues agitating sections of the faithful at the place and time in question.

Taking religion as a whole, although its supernatural postulates have no worthwhile evidential basis, and the multiplicity of varieties which exist round the globe is surely proof enough of that, its foundation is that in any pre-scientific culture supernatural belief follows quite naturally and gets quickly established as a persistent tradition. Whatever may be the percentage of believers that are adherents of the tradition in which they were educated – rather than making a deliberate choice among those available – that proportion must be overwhelming large, probably well over 90 per cent.

Supernatural belief becomes particularly relevant when the issues it addresses are not something to be debated or reflected upon in tranquillity but assume terrifying reality in situations of extreme danger and distress. Superstition and religion then become particular temptations, though such traumas may instead provoke negative reaction when they expose religion's false claims – for example in Europe following the slaughters of the First World War when all the belligerent governments constantly solicited divine aid.

Even when there are no actual real dangers, the conviction that they exist, especially when promoted by skilful publicists, may assist in keeping the faith vigorous and active – for example with 'the paranoid style in American politics'[24] when US citizens were afflicted during the Cold War by the imagined threat of a communist domestic takeover or invasion by godless communists, and now by the equally imaginary one of Islamist ambitions. The widespread conviction in the late 1940s that religion was a dying belief system has only been very partially fulfilled – though matters might well have been different if varied faiths were not being given strenuous and well-funded life support from centres such as Riyadh, Islamabad, Rome and Dallas and been adopted as an answer to life's problems by individuals and nations in mass societies when secular political projects have failed them.[25]

10

Imagined Communities: Signs and Symbols, Identities and Nations

The theme of 'imagined communities' (Benedict Anderson's phrase in respect of national sentiment), is more generally one of enormous scope and purporting to discuss it in one single chapter borders on the preposterous. My objective however is to single out certain aspects which seem to be of particular importance and constantly recurrent in the processes of historical development – symbols and identities that have been intrinsic to the course of history. My focus is also on means used to establish social collectivism and social discrimination whether on the basis of nationality, gender, race, hierarchies or other markers of difference.

Identity and the Other

The conceptual identification of individuals with their social and communal grouping is promoted not only by language, beliefs, ceremonies, cooperative labour and social interaction but by contrast and distinction with non-members and outsiders. In addition to that of course, social cleavages within a community establish further patterns of distinctiveness, linguistic variation, and self-identification *against* other sections of the same community.

Without any doubt the earliest form of community identity was that of the extended family group where all were engaged, within the circumstances enforced by differences of skill, stature and status, in the common business of survival and reproduction and everybody knew everyone else personally. All must have shared the same language, the same rituals, the same concepts of the supernatural and the same accepted precepts for inter-group behaviour, all based upon conceptions of kinship.

With the extension of supposed kin links over a wider area and the creation of a clan structure, there is created, in Benedict Anderson's words, an 'imagined community'. With even wider ranges of association some form of imagined linkage is essential to cement the social order together and make its smooth interaction possible. Almost invariably this tended to take the form of communal religious rites. With the expansion of social groups, regardless of the strength of the symbolic cement, the co-existence of large numbers of separate families and family networks in the tighter settled environment of village or city provided growing scope for social and personal conflicts. Some sort of overall authority, whether communal or personal, was required to mediate or repress these, and that authority was at pains to emphasise its elevated importance.

The god-kings of the early civilisations and their Roman imperial successors understood very well the importance of visual and iconic representation, as did their counterparts throughout Asia. Statues in stone or in bronze were a major component of this, but a much more effective and widespread manner of such propaganda was stamped on coins, once coinage became commonplace. The ruler's head on a coin made his (occasionally her) image, even if it were a stylised one, familiar to the lowliest subject at the outmost bounds of their realm. Muslim rulers were at something of a disadvantage in this respect, since their religion prohibited human imagery, and an early caliph after trying it briefly quickly gave up the attempt and reverted on his coins to a written superscription only.

In forager and early agricultural societies, projecting from what is known about the survivors of such societies into the late modern period, a complex network of interaction between separate clan groupings must have characterised their relationship. Much of it was based on the practices of totem distinction, taboo relationships and exogamy, whereby sexual partners had to be obtained from outside the kin or totem group, who thereafter joined the clan of their residence, while maintaining links with their birth kin group.

Such arrangements have the advantage of spreading and mixing the gene pool – though that could in no way have been their purpose – but also of establishing a network of relationships conducive to peace and cooperation among separate clans, and doubtless it would also facilitate material trade and exchange. On occasion it could also mean hostility and aggression, as among head-hunting communities, but, interestingly, that kind of conflict tended to be ritualistic in nature (which was even the case with Aztec bloodthirstiness) and seldom or never an all or nothing affair.

In the early civilisations the 'we' as against the 'others' referred to the subjects of the god-king – though there was differentiation between his core subjects and his tributaries. The 'others' were the populations outside his sphere of control, with whom hostile postures were frequent and routine, though that did not necessarily exclude exchange relations. Imperial China was the 'Middle Kingdom', regarding itself as the centre of the earth and theoretically entitled to universal hegemony. Its earlier equivalents in Egypt and Mesopotamia advanced similar pretensions. Benedict Anderson makes a pertinent remark when he writes that,

These days it is perhaps difficult to put oneself empathetically into a world in which the dynastic realm appeared for most men as the only imaginable 'political' system . . . borders were porous and indistinct, and sovereignties faded imperceptibly into one another. Hence, paradoxically enough the ease with which pre-modern empires and kingdoms were able to sustain their rule over immensely heterogeneous and often not very contiguous populations for long periods of time.[1]

In the independent Mediterranean city states the identifying distinction was between citizens and non-citizens, both resident aliens and outsiders. The inhabitants of the Phoenician cities thought of themselves as Tyrians, Sidonians or whatever, not as Phoenicians. This applied also to the Greek city states, but beyond that the Greek speakers overall possessed what might be described as a quasi-national identity as Hellenes, with non-Greek speakers being identified as 'barbarians' on account of their different language. They were designated on that account as an appropriate source of slave labour, though again a further distinction was made between civilised barbarians, Persians and Egyptians, and the tribal communities to the north.

The Greek city states were scenes of extreme social tension and conflict, based, quite explicitly, on wealth and property and frequently erupting into massacre and purges, with Athens being the best documented. Sparta, with on the one hand its hyper-militaristic ruling class of citizens where social distinction based on property was restrained as far as possible, and on the other its helot serfs, was very different from anything else found in Greece.

In Athens by contrast, where, as Michael Mann puts it, 'All kinds of social tension were introduced into the polis through the generation of enormous unequally distributed wealth',[2] the landowning wealthy, who hated the citizen democracy but mostly put up with it due to their plentiful supplies of slave labour, explicitly identified themselves, as can be seen in Plato's polemics, against the small property and unpropertied citizen community, the *hoi polloi* – in other words, 'those who are of inferior status'. The modest wealth of peasant proprietors from wine and olives however underpinned the slave-owning misogynist democracy.

The Roman republic, like its Greek equivalents, also maintained the key distinction between citizens and non-citizens, and like them too was severely class-divided, with these divisions frequently exploding into violence. Once again the main opposing sides acquired specific names, in this case the wealthy aristocracy (or patricians), and citizens of moderate property (or plebeians) and further categories below these, apart from the slaves, with the plebeians themselves divided between the not-quite-patrician equestrians and the others. The recurrent brutal conflicts provoked by these class divisions, plus the recurrent threat of slave revolt resulted eventually in the supersession of the republic by the Principate near the end of the first millennium BCE.

A male privilege, citizenship itself, regardless of which class the citizen belonged to, conferred substantial advantages to its possessor. It excused him from torture or crucifixion, and under the Principate entitled him to appeal to Caesar from lower courts, as Saul of Tarsus (Saint Paul) is reported to have done. Saul himself was not a Roman, but an inhabitant of an Anatolian city, for by that time citizenship had become much more widely extended and in subsequent centuries was to be extended still further. In earlier times the notion of Roman citizenship as a binding cement of identity surpassing those of class division, was a favourite trope of senatorial orators contrasting the strong, upright moral Roman citizen with feeble and degenerate easterners and Carthaginians or savage northern barbarians; especially when they wanted to recruit public sentiment to support aggressive enterprises.

During the centuries of Christendom the outsiders were the non-Christians, always despised and regularly persecuted, above all the Jews, but not excluding Muslims and pagans, who were fair game for conquest. In the Islamic kingdoms and empires matters were similar but the outsiders were treated a good deal more tolerantly unless they were pagans; subject certainly to special taxation but not otherwise molested except in crisis situations.

Rationale

The early kin-related hunting and foraging group can be regarded as a rational identity in that its cooperative actions are the necessary condition for the preservation and continuance of the group. The same can also be said about the early village communities, even when social differentiation is beginning to divide them – all the inhabitants would have known each other – but the initial state formations are a different matter altogether. Their necessary social unification is provided not by inescapable conditions of economy and environment, but by the myth, whatever it might be in particular instances, of their god-king and the invisible beings who are associated with him and determine human destinies.

Religion and politics are seamlessly combined, but religion of that kind is a much different beast from what the 'salvation religions' of the first millennium BCE and their seventh-century CE successor were to produce. Pagan religions were enormously variable in their detail but all pretty much alike in their essential belief in multiple deities requiring regular animal sacrifices to keep them well-affected towards the communities of their worshippers. Conquerors, however repressive in other respects, did not regard it as necessary in any manner to abolish or significantly interfere with the religion of their new subjects, though they would of course expect them to respect the new supreme god of the conqueror and his rites, and if the conqueror hoped to be respected as well as feared he might even pay homage in the temple of the conquered community's god, as sometimes did Alexander the Great.

When salvation religion was combined with dynastic rule however, a different social landscape comes into view, though this did not mean that the dynast necessarily set out to persecute, let alone annihilate, the minority faiths in his or her domains – Christianity was exceptional in this respect. What it did mean was that the subjects identified themselves simultaneously as members of a particular faith community and subjects of a particular dynast and faced differently evaluated significant Others. The already noted aim of devising a machine gun to fire round bullets against Christians and square ones, whose shape gave them greater destructive impact, against Turks is telling – it might be necessary to kill fellow-members of the faith if they belonged to a different political monarch, but appropriate to do it in a more civilised fashion.

Once the Roman empire disappeared from history with its breakup into western and eastern sections, the former dissolved into independent kingdoms and the latter slowly but steadily over centuries declined eventually into insignificance. During the subsequent centuries that we dignify as the Middle Ages, that peninsula of peninsulas projecting anomalously out of western Asia, namely Europe, was home to no polity that could equal in significance the great empires of China, the Arab Caliphs and their Ottoman successors (who anyway ruled the Balkans) or even the Muslim Persian empire, or those of Genghis Khan's successors such as Timur the Lame.

Nevertheless Europe's multiple rulers still clung to their pretensions. The Holy Roman Emperor might have no more than local authority, if even that, but he was still an emperor – supposedly – and one of the two pillars of Western Christendom, the other being the Church. Eventually the Habsburg monarchs of southern Germany ensured a monopoly on that title and by means of marriage alliances acquired their own mini-empire along the Danube, though they did not call themselves emperors of that until the nineteenth century.[3] The English monarchs went empire-building in what is now France (as did the Castilian ones in Iberia, Italy and the Low Countries, and the Muscovite ones in what became Russia) and when that failed the British Isles themselves could be regarded as an empire of sorts. During these centuries territorial empires across Eurasia predominated, and their rulers were sacerdotal personages, supposedly appointed by god, and with lesser monarchs attempting to ape them.

By the seventeenth century the sacred patina was beginning to erode. As early as the fifteenth century the Swiss peasants and burghers had bloodily toppled the Burgundian monarchy. The Dutch burghers, religiously inspired, had forcibly seceded from the sacred Spanish monarch, and the Anglo/Scottish king had, in the name of the people, had his head ostentatiously cut off. This was scandalous (the decent form was for unsuitable monarchs to be quietly murdered). Monarchy in Europe, though it continued as the political default option for further centuries, would never be quite the same again. Nationalism would come to replace it as the focus for public loyalty and monarchs, to retain their public credibility, increasingly had to present themselves as the representatives of a nation rather than a dynasty.

Nationality and Nationalism

By the nineteenth century sacerdotal empires, and kingdoms, emperors and kings, were under challenge everywhere, from political and social forces with nationalism as their banner. In that century dynastic states, though retaining the dynasty, were forged into national ones in Italy, Germany and Sweden. Nationalism has proved to be the most pervasive of modern ideologies, generating a sense of identity and loyalty across wide spectra of society, and it has a clear quasi-religious dimension. Anderson writes that,

> It is imagined as *sovereign* because the concept was born in an age in which Enlightenment and Revolution were destroying the legitimacy of the divinely-ordained hierarchical dynastic realm . . . the nation is always conceived as a deep horizontal comradeship. Ultimately it is this fraternity which makes it possible, over the past two centuries, for so many millions of people, not so much to kill, as willingly to die for such limited imaginings.[4]

To underline the strength of these imaginings, he notes the absurdity 'if one tries to imagine, say, a Tomb of the Unknown Marxist or a cenotaph for fallen Liberals'.[5]

From the late eighteenth to the late twentieth century and beyond, the focus of public identity, the imagined community of our days, was to become the nation, whether or not defined by ethnic descent, and the outsiders the citizens of other nationalities, who might always become political enemies. The reasons for this shift are not very mysterious; the nation was a replacement for loyalty focused on a hereditary monarchy, although until after the great wars of the twentieth century every effort was made by ruling elites to combine these sentiments, as in England remains the case. In one case, Japan, the conviction of a special ethnic destiny focused on a god-emperor easily morphed into a hyper-nationalism, with the sense of ethnic superiority rigorously guarded against Japanese nationals of other ethnicities, such as the aboriginal Ainu or even the outcaste community of ethnic Japanese, the Burakumin.

The identification in public discourse of supposed alien groups within a community, whether or not they are citizens of the state in question, who then serve as scapegoats for all manner of economic and social trouble and difficulties, has provided a major historical theme in twentieth- and twenty-first-century politics and social relations. This occurred most notoriously with reference to Jews but has been far from limited to them alone, and with economic breakdown combined with the vast media extension of recent years, it continues as a central discourse around the globe.

Modern Imperialism

As the antique dynastic territorial empires were tending towards decay and disintegration the resurgent European powers were in the process of establishing, from the sixteenth to the nineteenth century, the huge overseas empires (the British one eventually incorporated a quarter of the earth's land surface). These were the precondition for the West's eventual global domination (and hegemony over the old empires even where these formally still existed in China, Turkey and Persia). According to Mann,

> [N]ations also became more passionate and aggressive. Passion derived principally from the tighter links between the state and the intensive, emotional sphere of family and neighbourhood interaction in which state education and physical and moral health infrastructures loomed large. Ideologies saw the nation as mother or father, hearth and home writ large. Aggression resulted because all states continued to crystallise as militarist; all were geopolitically militarist, and some remained domestically so.[6]

The populations of the metropoles were taught a nationalism which embraced 'their' empires as well as their home countries – and which their colonial subjects were expected to share. Such ultra-imperialism naturally provoked reactive counter-nationalisms among their much-abused colonial subjects. Anderson cites a Batavian (Javanese) writer satirising the fact that the Dutch colonists expected their colonial subjects to celebrate the *Dutch* struggle for independence. 'If I were a Dutchman I would not organise an independence celebration in a country where the independence of the people has been stolen'.[7] The same principle applied to Algerian or Vietnamese subjects being expected to sing the Marseillaise and acclaim 1789, or British ones to do the same for 'God Save the King' and Magna Carta. Right up to its end in 1975 the Portuguese quasi-fascist regime tried to insist that its colonial subjects *were* Portuguese under the slogan 'Portugal is not a small country!' counting all the overseas territories as parts of Portugal.

Racism

In what we may define as the modern era – very roughly the last six centuries – racism has been a prominent strand in the fabric of history, glaringly prominent in the era of nineteenth-century imperialism. It has the effect, to adapt a phrase of Anderson's of erasing the victim's cultural quality by 'reduc[ing] the adversary to his biological physiognomy.'[8] Prior to the modern era there was certainly discrimination and persecution aplenty of what were identified as hostile groups or social outcasts. However this was only exceptionally ever justified on the basis of genetic descent, such as with the Burakumin in Japan, the Cagots in France and the Roma, then designated as Gypsies, throughout Europe. The persecution and isolation of Jews, for example was justified on religious not racial grounds.

Dislike of outsiders was of course perfectly traditional and routine, the outsiders could even be the inhabitants of the neighbouring village. In the thirteenth century Scottish people were said to believe that the English had tails, but the idea that entire ethnic categories could be regarded as inferior or vicious on the grounds of descent alone would have everywhere been regarded as preposterous, at least among the literate classes.

The hereditary principle was of course central to social structure and functioning, especially in India, but elsewhere too it crossed language differences and even religious ones; for example the crusader leaders regarded their great enemy Saladin, who had aristocratic forebears, as a very honourable individual, and he appears to have reciprocated. On the whole, again with the above exceptions, a member of a pre-modern outsider group, if they had the requisite qualities and assets, could be accepted as a full member of the community and rise to high office, whether secular or religious.

The first officially sponsored example of discrimination purely on grounds of even distant descent apart from religion or other form of outsidership dates from fifteenth-century Spain, where the key criterion was termed 'purity of blood' (*limpieza de sangre*) and intended to exclude any descendants of Jews or Muslims from official positions.[9]

Undoubtedly the burgeoning of the West African slave trade from the seventeenth century onwards had a lot to do with the growth of racist sentiments as the victims were visually very different from Europeans, as was the very large slave-descended population in the United States. On account of their cultural background they could be regarded as intrinsic inferiors (biblical justifications were also invoked) even if they converted to Christianity,[10] though the very large Arab slave trade in East Africa does not appear to have evoked similar sentiments among Muslim communities. In summary, racism can be defined as a form of stereotyping prejudice based upon the once prevalent dogma that 'bad blood will out'; in other words the belief in hereditary transmission of imagined undesirable traits among identified communities. Blood here is being used in a metaphorical sense to mean heredity, but the metaphor is significant for throughout written history blood, that remnant of the ancient sea in which our remote ancestors swam,[11] has had particularly strong symbolic associations. Across very different pre-modern cultures it was considered bad luck to spill royal blood, and royals were preferably killed by other means.

It was during the course of the late eighteenth and nineteenth centuries that European power, from its footholds on the coasts of the two continents, spread across Africa and Asia in a previously unimaginable fashion, and the settlements on the North American east coast, a number of them heavily dependent on African slave labour, set out on their genocidal progress across the continent, as their counterparts were doing in Australia. In the arrogance of power it was not in the least surprising that their victims came to be viewed as innately inferior in different degrees.

The ones who resisted strenuously as they were being exterminated, such as the Native American 'Plains Indians', the Zulus or the New Zealand Maoris, might gain a grudging measure of respect for their fighting skills, but they were still regarded as savages; others like the Chinese, or most Indians and Africans, were merely contemptible. In the late eighteenth century educated opinion in Europe had been impressed by Indian, Muslim and Chinese cultural, scientific and artistic achievements. In the following century these were downplayed and disregarded in the popular perception of the results of research into these cultures, otherwise known as 'Orientalism'.[12] Learned opinion was divided on whether these 'races' could eventually after a lengthy spell of 'tuition' be brought up to European standards of civilisation, or whether their genetic heritage rendered them incapable of such advancement. It was the latter thesis which generally won out, especially after the 'Indian Mutiny', or 'First War of Indian Independence' in 1857.

Pseudoscience

As science in the nineteenth century began to take an increasing hold on the popular imagination pseudoscientific principles were sought to establish schemes of racial hierarchy, and even those theorists most inimical to imperialism and racial persecution, such as Marx himself, could not escape some degree of contamination. Darwin's principle of natural selection proved a godsend to racists when misapplied to supposed 'races'. It was no accident that the climax of European imperialism in the late nineteenth century coincided with the notion of eugenics and the prophets of 'scientific racism' such as Arthur Gobineau and Houston Stewart Chamberlain.

Antisemitism was a case on its own. Evidently Jews were not physically different from other Europeans, suggestions to the contrary notwithstanding. The arbitrary designation of Jews as a 'race' and a malevolent one at that, was simply a pseudo-scientific add-on to age-old hatreds generated on other grounds.[13] This form of nineteenth- and early-twentieth-century prejudice was at its most vicious in France, the central European Habsburg empire and the eastern portions of the Russian empire, where sections of the petty bourgeoisie, including peasants, regarded Jews as an economic and cultural threat. Never did pseudoscience produce a more virulent outcome.

However it was more than simply pretended science. The most virulent of all racist documents, *The Protocols of the Elders of Zion*, purporting to be the record of a conference in which Jewish leaders plotted to take over the world, was forged by a Russian Orthodox cleric (as part of an intended text on the coming apocalypse).[14]

Language

Language of course as well as conveying major survival advantages to a bipedal primate living upon the African savannah is the beginning of representation. Despite the importance of visual symbols – representations or actions, these have to be explained, interpreted and enveloped in the linguistic narratives attached to them. The significance of language in relation to emerging social distinctions, whether within religious or political realms and to the development of nationalism, forms the focus of the following section.

Language and Status

Words, as is universally recognised, have power and those relating to human identities and status have especial power. This is carried to its ultimate perhaps in certain cultures where personal names are secrets known only to their possessors. Everyone in these circumstances naturally has also a public name by which they are addressed in conversation, but to reveal their secret name would lay them open to hostile magic operations. If this should be thought to be ignorant superstition, it should be kept in mind that in nearly every culture the name of a god is mega-powerful. This is particularly true of the Jewish god, the pronunciation of whose name we do not even know accurately, as it was never spoken in public and the Hebrew alphabet has no vowels. A scribe writing it, YHWH, would afterwards clean his writing instrument, it was so sacred. Nowadays it is given as Yahweh, but that is a guess.

In Anglo-Saxon culture, though there is no legal prohibition, the name Jesus is never used as a personal name, and Christ, Yahweh or Jehovah (the first inaccurate English name for the deity) would be even less acceptable, though Christ (pronounced Creest in these cases) occasionally occurs as a surname.[15]

Lesser variants of the same linguistic phenomenon are also involved when prescribing how a person of superior or lesser status should be addressed.[16] Persons in the militaries of Anglo-Saxon cultures have to address their superior officers as 'Sir' or 'Ma'am' (and salute), and prior to the cultural revolution of the 1960s this applied much more widely. It is still by no means extinct. It might nowadays just be imaginable for an ordinary citizen to address the US president as 'Barack' rather than 'Mr President', but never the English monarch as 'Lizzie' rather than 'Your Majesty'. Her sister, Princess Margaret, was said to be very annoyed with anyone who omitted to use her formal title of 'Your Royal Highness'. Anti-honorific phraseology such as 'your humble servant' is now rare in English but remains prevalent in many languages.

Language does not only discriminate by the use of names or titles. In many cases, though not all, it is also integrated grammatically into the social structure. The 'royal we' is indicative of a presumption of power and authority, and the practice of using the first person plural rather than singular by high-ranking individuals is found in other contexts as well. In many languages these grammatical status indicators are very complex indeed, with numerous honorifics – and grammar changing according to the honorific title being used. Indo-European languages on the whole are simpler in this respect and English possibly the simplest.

The most noticeable marker of this is the withering of the separate second person singular form, with both singular and plural collapsed into the indifferent 'you', although the archaic form still persists in local dialects and among Quakers.

Prior to this the correct form was to address a superior person as 'you', and use for an equal or inferior person 'thou', 'thee', 'thy' 'thine', though, peculiarly, the deity was also addressed in the informal second person. King Charles II was amused when the Quaker William Penn addressed him as 'thou' and omitted to take his hat off. Charles had a sense of humour, he removed his own hat, declaring that only one head should be covered when he was present; any other English king of these times would probably have had Penn executed for *lèse majesté*. Monarchs' subjects were also required to display appropriate body language – by bowing, kneeling, or prostration depending upon the particular culture. This too extended further down the line; you were, if male, supposed to raise your hat or cap to a social superior. It was all an expression of power and subordination.

Language and the State

During the greater part of human history distinctions of language and religion, though markers of identity and social hierarchy, were not divisive ones in the manner which they later became – with one enormously important exception. That exception was of course the post-exilic Judaic religion, which was specifically designed to be divisive and to protect the distinctiveness of the religious community with its highly unusual concept not of a supreme deity but a single one. Pre-modern conquerors did not as a rule regard it as necessary to attack the languages, any more than the religions, of the newly-conquered peoples. It was a multilingual environment and the language of one people was not regarded as in some sense intrinsically better than another – at least until the classical Greeks began to regard non-Greeks as less cultured than themselves, and to identify the distinction linguistically (hence the term 'barbarian'). Ironically, the Greeks' Roman conquerors, apart from some grumpy old reactionaries, actually accepted the Greek definition of cultural reality and identified with the latter's culture, including their language. The language of polite society in Rome in the late republic and early empire was Greek not Latin, except for formal purposes such as Senate orations. The ability to speak Greek, which depended on having an appropriate slave tutor, like literacy itself, further distinguished elite Romans from the others.

In the European medieval centuries, when the degree of communicative inter-connectivity that the Roman Empire had established broke down, communities were much more isolated and embryonic states went their separate ways. Language, to be sure, distinguished, in an even more brutal fashion, conquered populations from their masters of a different speech. England is a good example. Following the eleventh-century conquest by Duke William, English-speakers were specifically identified as an inferior caste and the hitherto flourishing vernacular literature came to an abrupt end. In cases of the unsolved murder of a Norman, the native speakers in the vicinity were subject to a different and more onerous legal practice known to the lawyers as the 'presentment of Englishry'.

For centuries the ruling elite spoke different languages from the remainder of the population, either Norman French or Latin depending on their function in the elite structure. The opening chapter of Walter Scott's *Ivanhoe* has two English peasants discussing their miserable lot. They note that when the farmyard beasts are running around the fields they are Anglo-Saxon and cows, pigs, sheep, chickens, but when they appear on the elite tables they become French-derived beef, pork, mutton and poultry. Ironically, the Viking ancestors of the Normans had themselves spoken a Germanic (or even among some members of William's retinue, a Celtic) language, but within a couple of generations they had become entirely Frenchified.

Had it not been for contingent events between the late fourteenth and early sixteenth centuries the language established in Britain, as education extended and Latin declined, would most likely be a Romance language with its roots in French. Instead, it is argued, what became modern English prevailed as a result of a deliberate policy agenda led by intellectuals both lay and clerical, connected with the court and universities, particularly Geoffrey Chaucer and his circle. This aimed to emphasise English distinctiveness, linguistically as well as politically and ecclesiastically – at a time when France and the Papacy were either regarded as enemy powers or sunk in deep discredit.[17]

It was English itself which became the elite language, a distinguishing mark of superiority, with Latin continuing as the ornament of the intellectual elite well into the seventeenth century. Even from the late medieval era the Celtic languages of the British Isles had come under attack and their speakers subject to discrimination and persecution in England, Scotland, Wales and Ireland, not least because these same speakers, apart from the Manx islanders, were regarded as a political threat.

Language and Nationalism

Nothing quite like the situation in Britain described above was apparent elsewhere in Europe or indeed throughout Eurasia or the Americas. It was the consolidation of nationhood and national sentiment in the nineteenth century, largely in reaction to the Napoleonic empire, that gave linguistic differentiation a social and political charge that it had not previously possessed. Particular languages, rather than language in general, are, in modern conditions the supreme markers of identity, the foundation stone of modern nationalism. It is unusual for hostile nationalisms to arise within the same language,[18] Ireland and former Yugoslavia being exceptions (and even in the Irish case strong efforts have been made to promote a different language, while mainstream Scottish nationalism, as evidenced by the rhetoric of its leaders, cannot be classified as one of hostility to outsiders). Speakers of the same language, such as in Rwanda, tend to kill each other for other reasons, mainly economic, political or religious.

With the rise of nationalism dead languages, such as Hebrew, were revived, and a new one, Indonesian, was even invented, though based upon a variety of

Malay and with much borrowing.[19] Throughout central and eastern Europe mainly, but also in other regions, nationally minded philologists energetically compiled dictionaries and grammars of minority languages and encouraged their official use, and similarly inclined historians compiled celebratory histories of their newly-defined nation's triumphs or victimhood. It is important to emphasise the importance of printing in the dissemination of such texts and the standardisation of linguistic forms.

Not surprisingly these activities were regarded by centralising powers as an irritant at best and a threat at worst, and strenuous efforts made to discourage them. In mainland Britain this amounted to a low-level persecution, with everything short of legal prohibition used to suppress the minority languages (and dialects), especially during schooling. Children were punished severely for using Gaelic or Welsh in the schoolroom, or even in the playground. In Ireland, however, national sentiment was too strong to make attempted suppression a worthwhile endeavour. In France similar repression was applied to Breton, Occitan and Corsican. In the newly-established Italian state of the 1860s onwards, the Florentine dialect was adopted as the official language and imposed throughout the peninsula.[20]

In Spain the official language, Castilian, is the first language of only around 70 per cent of the population (had the Iberian peninsula remained united as it was between 1580 and 1640 Castilian would be in a minority position). Catalan and Basque are its principal rivals. During the twentieth century these minority languages became a major issue when the Catalans and Basques supported the Republic and the regional autonomy it granted, and were consequently identified with communism and separatism in the eyes of the quasi-fascist regime which won the Civil War. Consequently these languages were both ferociously repressed by the regime, which only resulted in more militant resistance, especially in the Basque country. At least until very recently a very similar situation existed in Turkey, with the Kurdish language here forming the target for persecution. In the era of modern nationalism a dominant national group, ruling within a state over linguistically different national minorities who may resent the rulers, seem to have been convinced that their ethnically different subjects would become more obedient and better assimilated if they were made to speak the rulers' language.

Languages, in this case French and Dutch (Flemish) are markers of identity in different parts of Belgium, giving rise to national tensions which threaten to tear the country apart. By contrast, in Norway two different written forms of Norwegian coexist happily, and the spoken language is itself an amalgam. The present situation came about as a result of nationalist agitation in the late nineteenth and early twentieth century, Norway having been lengthily under at first Danish and subsequently Swedish rule (the Norwegian flag, the prime symbol of its nationhood, is the Danish flag with a blue cross superimposed on the white Danish one). The Swiss state, famously, has no difficulty with three different official languages. It is no accident that in recent decades when a territory undergoes a national-political change of regime, the place names of the region or country are changed in accordance. The phenomenon has been at its most marked in central and eastern Europe, when with the Nazi conquest Slavonic place names were Germanified, and following 1945 changed back again, or in the territories taken from Germany into Poland changed from their original German. Thus Terezin became Theresienstadt, and back again; Breslau turns into Wrocław.

Visual Signs and Symbols

Palaeolithic communities certainly used symbolic representations, whose function we can only guess at, as is attested by the famous rock and cave paintings throughout the world. To an even greater extent from the Neolithic era onwards symbolic representations become pervasive in all societies and exist in a great range of media from painting to architecture. Their other common aspect is that to a great extent – though not in every respect – they are associated with social division. It is this aspect that forms the focus of my discussion here. Their frustrating aspect for historians is that in the earlier millennia of the Neolithic, prior to 4000–3000 BCE for Eurasia, there is no written script to assist the interpretation of the symbolic objects and structures. However there can be little doubt that many of them, from the megaliths of western Europe to the Neolithic 'temple' of Orkney were connected with the 'unseen powers' of superstition and religion which are the subjects of the previous chapters.

Garments, Headgear and Power

A form of symbolic representation of a very everyday sort which has been intrinsic to the human story is the differentiation of gender by garments. This has been a feature of nearly all societies as soon as fabric beyond animal skins became available, in other words from the time of the Neolithic revolutions. Violating the associated rules in either direction was often a serious criminal offence (especially so if contradicting male dominance) and invariably, if not illegal, a social scandal. In modern times if a woman was reputed to rule the household and her husband, she was said to be 'wearing the trousers'. Anna Clark's volume is entitled *The Struggle for the Breeches: Gender and the Making of the British Working Class*.[21] Hairstyles too were a very apparent marker of gender differentiation.

As a rule the garments permitted for women were more restrictive than those allowed to men, and the same was true of hairstyles. Modern industrial societies from the second third of the twentieth century were the first, at least since the Palaeolithic, to adopt relatively gender-neutral clothing (and to a lesser extent hairstyles) – though with dress codes this applied only in informal contexts as a rule. A closely allied development has taken place in the matter of what individuals of both genders put on their heads.

In the symbolic display of individuals, headdress has been down the centuries a key component of representation, distinguishing both individuals and social classes (the cloth cap/bowler hat stereotype is indicative). Once again the industrialised cultures of the late twentieth century and afterwards are also the first in history in which it has become normal for individuals of both genders to go around bareheaded[22] – though headgear remains standard for the military and police and in certain formal contexts.

Moving up the social scale, with headgear as symbolic of power; the double crowns of Upper and Lower Egypt worn by the Pharaohs are well known, as is the triple crown, the tiara which represents the office and authority of the Pope.[23] In pictorial illustrations from the early empires of the Middle East, kings are identified by their headdress – as they have continued to be down to the present, though in the case of the Byzantine emperor it was his footgear more than his headgear which signified his imperial dignity. However, in western European monarchies, where the crown was the distinctive mark of royalty from medieval times onwards,[24] there exist distinctions between different sorts of crowns.

The primary difference was between the 'closed' crown, the sort with arches over the wearer's head and a fabric cap beneath them and the 'open' crown, which is shown on illustrations of English and other kings of the medieval centuries. The difference was that the open crown was the one specific to mere kings or queens and the closed crown was reserved for emperors, beginning with Charlemagne – monarchs who stood above other kings and had no earthly superior. The Holy Roman Emperor was recognised as having precedence, if no actual power, over the other monarchs of Western Christendom. It was when the English monarchs, beginning with Henry VIII, insisted on their independence of any superior that they took to using a closed crown. When Henry declared in the 1530s that 'England is an Empire' he meant not that it possessed colonies, but that it was independent of the Pope or any other monarch.

A lesser, but nevertheless distinguishing manner of formal headgear was applied to other aristocrats in England and France, these being known as coronets (little crowns, though other countries did not have that distinguishing terminology). These varied in elaboration depending on the feudal rank, from plain barons at the bottom up to dukes and princes at the top. These types of headdress were only worn on very special state occasions such as a coronation, a parallel to the cardinal's hat or the papal tiara.

The symbolisation of the exclusive headdress is also used in what was to become another distinguishing symbolic mark of social ascendancy in Europe and the monarchical European colonial empires, namely the coat of arms (there is also a Japanese equivalent), which normally included a representation of the appropriate crown or coronet. Coats of arms evolved from the devices used on the shields of early medieval knights and went on to become the – literally ostentatious – exclusive possessions of elite individuals and families. It was the particular heraldic coat of arms that was the exclusive property, the privilege of having one was extended also to towns (provided they had a royal charter) as well as universities and other elite educational establishments. Symbolic power was everywhere.

The coat of arms, which appears to have been adopted in some manner or another well beyond its societies of origin (even the USSR had an emblem very like one) can be viewed as the ancestor of the present-day corporate logo. Many institutions, especially educational ones, use both, with the former for their more formal documents.[25] Heraldic devices employed colours (the use of which in European heraldry was confined by a specific code), objects (usually military ones), plants (the oak tree was a favourite) and animals.

The animals tended to be predatory ones (though horses and mythological unicorns were an exception) with eagles and lions, and their mythological equivalents such as dragons and gryphons, seen as noble beasts, being specially favoured – hyenas were never used, though they would have been equally or more appropriate. Symbolism here above all reflected hierarchy, and this tended to be a constant across cultures – dragons were a Chinese imperial symbol and the Aztec warriors included 'eagle knights' and 'jaguar knights'.

Symbols of status through apparel exist also in hunter-gatherer societies. They frequently use feathers as marks of distinction, such as in Native American headdresses and also, in other cultures, on the bonnets of Scottish highland clansmen. It can be reasonably assumed that something similar applied in Palaeolithic societies, but visual markers of social inequality in regard to entire classes and strata are apparent in the earliest literate societies and have been eroded only in recent centuries. Widely but by no means universally disappeared in the present, in military hierarchies they remain in full flower even if not with quite the degree of ebullience which used to characterise them.

The Roman republic was notable for its sumptuary laws, which prohibited forms of dress and food. These were supposed to prevent excessive luxury but served to distinguish between social classes. During the imperial centuries only the emperor was permitted to have a cloak dyed in the extremely expensive Tyrian purple dye. The rank of the knights or equestrians entitled them to a narrow purple stripe on their togas, the senators to a broad one.

Social stratification marked by aspects of dress operated to facilitate social control. In the European medieval centuries identifying symbols for religious minorities were enforced both in the Christian and the Muslim cultures, which made them easier both to tax and to persecute depending on the state of toleration at the time – and remain an issue in the present century, though now it relates more to the prohibition of certain forms rather than to their enforcement. Socially dif-ferentiating marks were stipulated in both the Chinese and Japanese empires, with the latter being the most comprehensive and tightly regulated of any. In England what one might wear (including the shape of headgear) or display, depending on social level, remained subject to legislation until after the English revolution. As one author phrased it (I am quoting from memory), an individual in Jacobean England would no more think of wearing clothes reserved for persons of higher rank than a contemporary officer would contemplate adding an extra pip to his or her epaulettes.

Standards and Banners

Symbols of collective identity signifying states or military formations date back to the ancient empires. The battle standard was particularly necessary in ancient warfare, identifying the location of the headquarters and the spot which in emergency had to be rallied around for the last stand. Best known of these was the eagle standard of the Roman legions, which was regarded not merely as a symbol but as a sacred emblem, whose loss was a cause of exceptional public distress, as when the Germans in the Teutoburg forest wiped out three Roman legions and captured their standards. The cohorts, individual units of the legion, also had their own standards, though less sacred than the eagle. Throughout pre-modern warfare the capture of the enemy's standard usually signified victory, and this was still the case in naval warfare as late as the eighteenth century, when the lowering of the ship's flag indicated surrender.

Battle standards in the form of cloth flags were universal in medieval Europe (the Byzantines used a form of kite, as did the Chinese) and these were the ancestors of the modern national flag. This has become the key signifier of national identity, in the USA practically worshipped. It is supposed to subsume social (and in many cases minority national) identities into one constructed around the state that the flag symbolises. The flag condenses into one concentrated image the history, the society and the culture of the unit which it represents. Flags are important also to many political movements, and on occasion when these are successful in capturing state power become the national flag; examples include the Irish tricolour and the Nazi flag. The red flag as the symbol of socialist and communist movements is equally famous; trade union banners, though less central to their organisations' identities are also significant.

'All in his uniform . . . '

Although the roughly standardised armour of the Roman legions gave their soldiers a somewhat similar appearance, as did the earlier units of the Chinese emperor, represented in the terracotta army; and while retainers of medieval leaders would display their lord's livery and the Christian clergy had always favoured a uniform of sorts, the military uniform in its modern sense was a seventeenth-century innovation. Military uniform's functional use, namely to distinguish in combat one side from the other and to demonstrate that its wearer was a legitimate combatant (not a *franc tireur* or a spy) and in its later manifestations also to act as camouflage – were all, if anything, subordinate to its major purpose. The central purpose was to promote a sense of collective identity among the wearers, in military terms to strengthen morale. It extended in European armies even to the minor distinguishing marks on the uniforms of different units within the overall army – the regiment, with its specific regimental history and battle honours was a key focus of identification and promoted as such. For the individual soldier or equivalent in other services, the award of medals and decorations signified particular merit. In the British military medals were awarded to all personnel who had taken part in particular campaigns; decorations were more individual and awarded for especially outstanding performance. Even so there were distinctions based on hierarchy. The decorations awarded to officers were superior to those given to their inferiors, with the exception of the highest honour, the Victoria Cross, open equally to all ranks.

The uniform also served as a marker of caste and encouraged its wearers to feel superior to mere civilians – at least once common soldiers ceased to be regarded as the scum of the earth. For the officer corps, a caste within a caste, such assumed superiority was always the case, and particularly within militaristic societies like imperial Germany, uniforms, especially the officers', were deliberately intended to intimidate civilians. The mitre-like hats worn by eighteenth-century grenadier regiments were designed to make the wearers look taller than anybody else, and in Prussia their kings took this a stage further by having these hats worn by units of particularly tall soldiers. In imperial Germany it was a serious offence on the part of an officer to fail to thrash a civilian who had insulted his uniform.

The symbolic impact of uniforms was enormous, and the nineteenth century saw them being adopted in all manner of contexts. Police forces were provided with uniforms (and in England, after top hats were abandoned, the tall helmet modelled on the solar topee favoured by European military and administrators in the tropics). Railway companies put their staff in uniform, as did airlines once passenger flying came on stream, while local authorities instituted uniforms in the municipal transport services. Nursing staff were uniformed and likewise children in elite and even not-so-elite schools. The twentieth century saw the novel phenomenon of paramilitary and political uniforms with the same purpose as military ones – solidarity among the wearers and intimidation of outsiders and opponents; and it was possible to devise one out of items of ordinary clothing, as did the latter-day IRA. The pioneers in this respect were Mussolini's Blackshirts, whose style was deliberately modelled upon that of an elite military unit, the Arditi. Simone de Beauvoir remarks in her memoirs that her and Sartre's friend Jean Genet, though he had absolutely no sympathy with Nazism, compared unfavourably the outfits of the liberating US forces, 'uniformed civilians', with those of the Germans – 'at least the occupiers had style'.

The self-conscious identification of the wearer with his or her (though almost invariably his) uniform is a theme explored from time to time in twentieth-century fiction. Certainly it is a key component of bad faith, generating the conviction that the uniform confers intrinsic privileges, the wearer is absorbed into the meaning of the uniform and enjoys in some metaphysical fashion a dispensation from the rules that govern civil society. Einstein once remarked that the members of marching cohorts absorbed in the metaphysic of their uniforms had no need of a brain – a rudimentary brain stem would prove perfectly adequate. The phenomenon of police forces, given a sense of collectivity by their uniforms, running amok on the streets when confronted by demonstrations is a routine news item. If the SS killers had had to carry out their atrocities while wearing civilian clothes they would almost certainly have found their 'task' more difficult.

Uniforms could also be used as sources of disparagement and denigration, as with the uniforms worn by prisoners in many incarceration regimes. Again the ostensible purpose, easy identification, is subordinate to the main one of institutional humiliation. As military personnel are supposed to take pride in their uniforms, and feel elevated above the common throng, so are the prisoners through their uniform intended to internalise their degradation, worthlessness and exclusion from society – all of which is supposed to promote a reformed lifestyle.

These considerations however only scratch the surface of the issue of social identity and its symbols, matters which have an enormously powerful hold on individual and collective imaginations. 'Workers of the World Unite!', though one of the most famous of nineteenth-century slogans, has also proved to be one of the most futile. The attempt by movements and parties to create a politically resonant social identity based on the rational concept of economic class has always crumbled in the face of appeals to one based upon symbolically-charged 'imagined communities'.

Visual iconography follows the same principles and has done so since the days of the pharaohs, when the monuments of a particular ruler were defaced after his (in one case her) death if his memory was unpopular with his successor; his cartouche chipped off written monumental texts and his face erased from his monuments. Similarly with the statues of detested Roman emperors – and the attitude continues into our own days. Among the first actions of the victors after the fall of communist regimes was to demolish the statues of its iconic figures, and in addition Saint Petersburg, briefly having become Petrograd when Germany was an enemy power in 1914, changed to Leningrad under the Soviet regime and after 1991 resumed its original name.

The auditory and visual markers and symbolism discussed in this chapter – language (in some cases even accent), ritual, dress codes, deportment, bodily decoration, objects of display all serve to produce a sentiment of social identity and common purpose between some individuals – and to exclude others. At the same time they have historically reinforced social differentiation and hierarchical relations and so strengthened structures of inequality.

11

A Broad View – The Rhythm
of Empire

May you live in interesting times.
—Supposed Chinese curse (possibly invented by Ernest Bramah Smith)

Around the middle of the second millennium CE the world's population was about to undergo the second of the great transformations previously referred to. This second transformation, to industrial society in the framework of new forms of empire, was to prove enormously faster and deeper and a great deal more consequential in every dimension of living and dying.

This chapter extends discussion of some of the issues introduced in the previous one in relation to empires, and aims to specifically examine the line of processes which laid the historical foundation for what was to emerge subsequently as the hegemony of European states over the remainder of the globe. On the face of it, this was a most unlikely outcome. The continent's land area, including Russia west of the Urals is less than a quarter of that of Asia and not much greater than Australia, if indeed Europe can be considered to be a continent at all. Its population again has been much smaller than the Asian one throughout historic times.

A pattern of development in Eurasian/North African history is observable from the time of the Pharaohs and Sargon of Akkad onwards; one repeatedly seen throughout Eurasia and North Africa from China westwards. A series of loosely articulated empires was the default political system embracing most of the agriculturally settled populations of this area; and they succeeded each other across the centuries. They were based upon tribute extracted in labour, goods or, latterly, money from the agrarian producers subjected to a hierarchy of lords topped out by divine or semi-divine monarchies. These monarchies were threatened from time to time by nomadic pastoralists beyond their frontiers as well as by popular resistance and inter-elite hostilities. Although the Amerindian example demonstrated that cultures of that kind could be based upon a Neolithic technology, metalworking was central to the evolution of Eurasian and African societies.

Axial Age?

Developments in the course of the first millennium BCE caused the German philosopher Karl Jaspers to postulate an 'Axial Age' of roughly 800 to 200 BCE.

The 'Axial Age' was essentially a religious conception, Jaspers noting that great religious and philosophical systems with their real or assumed founders, evolved during these centuries in China, India, Iran and Greece. Though probably exaggerated, there may be some basis for this in the cultural forms generated through the impact of the social crisis brought on by the iron-using assailants of the Bronze Age empires. Literate thinkers, naturally themselves members of the elites, were seeking explanations of humans' place in the natural order and for the catastrophes being permitted by the gods.

Around or a little later than the turn of millennia from BCE to CE a series of new empires were consolidated across the area; the Roman, the Persian, the Gupta in the subcontinent and the Han in China, the latter two being regarded as then enjoying the respective 'golden ages' of their imperial eras, while Gupta scholars invented the concept of zero in mathematics and postulated a heliocentric explanation of the sun–earth relationship. Like their predecessors, these were hierarchical, iron-using, agrarian, literate empires based upon a tribute-paying peasant underclass. A few centuries later all of them were in deep trouble from internal upheaval and external assault and suffering profound damage or extinction. Others of a similar sort were to succeed them, but their collapse is generally taken to mark the boundary between antiquity and the lead-in to our contemporary world. The circumstances are outlined below.

The Mediterranean

In reaction against the previous Eurocentric overemphasis on the historical importance of the Mediterranean, particularly its two largest peninsulas, the significance of this inland sea (with its eastern extension the Black Sea) has recently been somewhat underplayed. Its historic importance was nevertheless very great.

This particular marine combination is a unique geographical feature on the planet – there is nothing quite like it anywhere else. Just short of three million square kilometres in extent, it could almost be regarded as an enormous saltwater lake, approximately eleven times the combined area of the American Great Lakes, more than twice that of western Europe, and containing both large peninsulas and innumerable islands, some of them significantly large. Moreover, it is bordered by an astonishingly diverse range of geographical features; mountains, deserts, steppes and rich agricultural terrain in which a very diverse pattern of different socio-economic structures and political regimes could evolve. In preindustrial times the sea acted as the principal transport artery between them for both trade and aggression, with uncounted ancient shipwrecks on its seabed.

It therefore bordered the Fertile Crescent and the great empires of the Middle East, and was of critical importance to the three great monotheist religions. Along its shores the great variety of social units which appeared before and during the first three millennia BCE intermingled, spoke to each other and mixed their languages, traded with each other (including slaves), exploited each other's sex workers, learned of each other's cultures, influenced each other and fought each other. Among those best known to history were the Egyptians, the Assyrian vassals on the Levant, the Hittites in what is now Asia Minor, the Persian vassal satrapies, the Minoans, the Greeks with their multitude of outpost colonies around the Mediterranean and Black Sea, the Phoenicians and their colony Carthage, the Etruscans and the Romans. Out of this intermingling emerged the phonetic alphabet, invented by the Phoenicians and adopted by the Greeks (possibly via Crete) and thereafter spread around the great sea.

Something else that emerged was the reality that one of these entities, the oligarchical Roman republic, was by the end of the (supposed) axial age on the verge of rising to dominate the states and peoples around the sea, not to mention ones well inland from it. By the second century CE its rulers were masters of the Mediterranean. Of its imperial rivals only the Parthian empire (formerly Macedonian, formerly Persian) still counted.[1]

In terms of military power, by the installation of the Principate under Augustus it would probably have outclassed even the Chinese empire of that time, then in a state of turmoil; and certainly outranked the warring kingdoms of the subcontinent following Asoka's death and the fall of the Mauryan empire. It took its naval architecture from the Carthaginians, its urban architecture from the Etruscans, its literary culture from the Greeks and eventually in 312 CE its religion from a former Jewish sect. Its cultural influence was enormous on the successor states which took over its western portion and were much later to go on to dominate the globe for a time (and to an extent still do in the shape of the USA). The very words 'empire', 'kaiser' and 'tsar' are Roman-derived.

Sub-Saharan Africa

It is not only during the past five centuries, but long before, that the African continent has been of major importance in Eurasian affairs. Evidently this was the case with the Mediterranean shore of the continent (which in historical terms if not geographical ones, can be regarded as an extension of Eurasia). It applied no less to much more southerly parts of the continent in the course of recorded history. Iron smelting may have developed independently in Africa (as may also have been the case in China) but given the degree of communication links between Asia, Europe and Africa, the possibility of diffusion cannot be ruled out whichever sub-Saharan area first adopted the technique.

The overall pattern in different parts of the continent was not very dissimilar to what prevailed elsewhere; the establishment of more or less widespread empires over agrarian or herding populations, empires which in due course fragmented on account of economic shifts, climate alterations, and internal strains among their elites (which we may guess were accompanied with popular discontent) to be replaced by successors of a similar stamp.

The area between the Nile and the Red Sea was of particular importance due to the marine communication which resulted and the proximity of the Arabian peninsula. The kingdom of Kush, with its capital at Meroe, north of modern Khartoum, supported a highly developed culture derived from Egypt and actually conquered Egypt in the early first millennium BCE establishing a dynasty of Pharaohs. Its successor, Aksum, was of special importance as a trading hub between the Roman empire and India, and sustained commercial links with China as well. In this region, following the Arab seventh century conquest of North Africa, Muslim and Christian rulers contested for control and for their religion. The Christian ones eventually established themselves in the Ethiopian highlands and the Islamic ones everywhere else in the region, as well as further south along the coast to the island of Zanzibar and the coastline opposite it.

The western part of the continent was scarcely less important in the first millennium CE, and embraced both the savannah Sahel region south of the Sahara desert and the rain forest north of the Gulf of Guinea. The vigorous trans-Saharan trade, first with the Carthaginian and Roman polities and subsequently the Arab empire, was its kingdoms' principal form of exchange, the key commodities being gold and slaves, with salt as the most important one coming in the opposite direction. The first of these kingdoms was Ghana (in a very different location from the present state of that name) and one monarch of its successor state, Mali (again not coterminous with the current state of that name) by that time converted to Islam, is said to have astounded the Egyptians with his wealth and train of servants when undertaking a pilgrimage to Mecca. Here too Islam was to make a big impact, converting the rulers of the Sahel and their subjects, but it did not penetrate to the coastal rain forest area, where again independent kingdoms and empires established themselves, such as Dahomey and Ashanti.

What has been described as one of the great migrations in history, occurring in the first millennium BCE and beginning of the Common Era, was the expansion of the agriculturalist speakers of the Bantu languages over the southern continent from their original location in modern Cameroon and western Nigeria. It is analogous to the earlier spreading out of the Indo-European speakers west and south from the Iranian plateau and therefore not a coherent exodus but one proceeding over several centuries and in different southward directions, one in the east and one in the west of the continent south of the western bulge. The forager and pastoralist indigenous societies, now referred to as the Khoisan, who may have retained the physical appearance of the first *H. sapiens*, were driven ahead of these invaders until what remained of them fetched up in the marginal lands and deserts at the southern end of the continent.

The more economically and technologically accomplished Bantu speakers (if they did not have iron artefacts at the beginning of the migration they adopted the technique of its production during its course) like their counterparts in West Africa established agrarian tributary kingdoms and empires wherever they settled, also engaging in trading relations whenever possible and in which once again gold played a prominent role. The course of their development repeated the cycle of breakdown and replacement seen in all similar state structures. The ruins of Great Zimbabwe attest to the power and achievement of the most successful (the final example of which was the Zulu empire of the nineteenth century located in modern Natal).

If Africa was important to the transcontinental society of the pre-modern world outside the Americas, it was to become many times more so when its inhabitants and their descendants played a critical role from the middle of the second millennium in bringing the great economic and social transformation into being. They did so as the personnel of the most basic and brutal of all forms of coercive cooperation, otherwise known as slavery.

From Antiquity to European Feudalism

The great migrations a couple of centuries after the beginning of the first millennium CE which, if they did not bring it about, certainly contributed to the decline of the Roman empire, were a Eurasian-wide phenomenon. The rather mysterious East Asian nomadic herders known to history as the Huns, depended on the horse for their livelihood, for transport, meat, milk and all manner of essentials – an Iron Age people with a quasi-Palaeolithic lifestyle using the horse as their stone age ancestors had used their prey (which also included horses) while at the same time employing it in what was, for the times, almost literally, the cutting edge of contemporary technology. Along with the adoption of the stirrup (and possibly the nailed horseshoe as well) the favourite Hunnic weapon was the cavalry bow, which they also improved.

With this novel technology and the leadership of a capable commander who could unite the related clans into a formidable striking force, the opportunities for invading and plundering both the settled agrarian and citified communities to the south and west were immense and were speedily grasped; but the Huns proved to be more than plundering raiders. In the fifth century CE they briefly established a huge empire stretching from central Europe to western Asia and attacked Italy, Gaul and the Balkans.

The Huns' importance however was less in their own exploits than in their knock-on effects. Their own linguistic group was no more than the core of their empire and was greatly outnumbered by the Germanic-speaking tribes or peoples whom they conquered and incorporated, and who successfully rebelled on the death of the Huns' great leader, Attila. Rather, their significance was in stimulating the armed migration of the Germanic peoples fleeing before the onset of the Hunnic attack who spilled into the Roman empire east and west either by force or reluctant agreement from the Roman authorities, and eventually established their own hegemony on the territory of the western empire – they were the remote origin of some existing west European states.

Interesting Times

The human world would probably look very different today if the empires of the early first millennium had persisted into the second, but they did not. They all disintegrated or were overthrown in one way or another – and replaced by successors of a similar character. A good deal of that was due to short-lived central Asian empires established by the pastoral nomad confederations, especially the Mongols led by Genghis Khan in the thirteenth century. Some of the successor empires, such as that of Timur, whose capital was at Bukhara in south-central Asia – but nevertheless aspired to add China to his many conquests – were also disturbers of the Eurasian peace.

The Roman empire was severely weakened by Attila's incursions and exaction of tribute, and its western portion disintegrated as a coherent polity. Control over its peasantry was seized by tribal aristocracies (who also settled their own rank-and-file followers on confiscated landholdings) The invaders were Germanic-speaking peoples who either entered as Attila's confederates, were fleeing in advance of his forces or simply took advantage of the resulting chaos.[2] The surviving eastern portion, commonly styled the Byzantine empire, revived for a time and subjugated its Persian rival before losing the major part of its territory, including the most valuable, to the Arab Islamic empire, known as the Caliphate, with capitals first at Damascus and subsequently Baghdad.

This empire was itself the major player on the Eurasian/North African scene of the later part of the first millennium CE, before splitting into several mini-empires, including in Egypt and Spain, and finally falling victim first to the Mongol power and its successors and subsequently to the Turks, firstly the Seljuks and eventually the Ottomans, who also disposed in 1453 of the remnants of the Byzantine empire. Penetrating deep into eastern Europe they remained for over three centuries the major world power west of China.

A recurrent pattern, though of course with many specific regional variations, emerges in the life cycle of the Eurasian iron-using empires over two and a half millennia. Such an empire would be established, focused upon the personality usually of a petty prince (who would give his name to the dynasties) who had emerged as its ruler. He would be acknowledged as such by many others of the same category, while his empire incorporated numerous different linguistic groups and local cultures.

The lack of a centralised administrative system and power structure (particularly marked in the nomads' empires), often further complicated by succession disputes between the heirs of the founder, would then result in political disintegration and regional secession until the next empire-builder came along. Some qualification of this picture however applies to China. Here the successful usurpers were either themselves native Chinese, or if conquerors like the Mongol and Manchu, very quickly adapted themselves to Chinese norms, so that it was the dynasty which changed but with continuity of the culture. Further west Islam provided something of the same service, as there the successors of Genghis quickly converted to Islam.

Popular Insurrection

Two other aspects of this cycle should not be overlooked, namely popular resistance and revolt and outbreaks of plague or other pandemic diseases (which were sometimes connected), the most notorious being the bubonic plague or Black Death. This persisted in western Asia and Europe during the first and second millennia CE, with a particularly devastating outbreak in the 1340s, which killed a very high proportion of the European population and had major repercussions upon social structures. Although the responsible bacterium *Yersinia pestis* appears to have originated in the Mongolian region, China and India seem to have escaped this outbreak.[3] The Black Death further west strengthened the bargaining position of the surviving peasants on account of labour shortage, but also the ferocious determination of their masters to continue the pre-existing power relations.

During the first seventeen centuries of the Common Era throughout Eurasia there occurred literally dozens of regime-threatening rural and urban uprisings, with localised ones too numerous to count. The Bagaudae of Gaul and Spain in the late Roman empire took decades to suppress. The An Lushan Rebellion in eighth-century China with millions of casualties, though instigated by an ambitious general of the Tang dynasty, was fuelled by rural and urban discontent.

These popular revolts very seldom achieved a successful outcome, and on the rare occasions in which they did, it was always ambiguous and never long-lasting. They rarely aimed in practice to overturn social structures based upon authoritarian relations of ruling and subordinate classes but only to secure better treatment from more congenial governors. At times however, apocalyptic expectations were in the air, such as Zoroaster's 'making wonderful', or the Jewish apocalypses where through divine agency the social structure would be upturned, 'the poor filled with good things and the rich sent empty away' – but the constituted authority and the classes on whose behalf it ruled, unless themselves in a state of disintegration, normally had much greater resources and far superior military power to crush resistance.

To this was added in many cases bitter quarrels among the participants in the revolt or among their leaders. In the great Jewish revolt for example, the insur-rectionists were split into three factions fighting each other as energetically as they fought the Romans. The best that could be hoped for was that the insurrection's leaders would stick together, succeed in taking over the governing power and follow that by instituting a less brutal regime, as in the early Han or Gupta empires, but one still based on social relations not essentially different from the preceding ones.

Resistance to oppressive class relations however could never be annihilated. No matter how often it was suppressed during these centuries it would sooner or later regenerate and on the eve of 'modern times' became particularly formidable, with revolutionary regimes in power, if temporarily, monarchs publicly executed and the Russian empire swept by peasant revolt across its breadth on two separate occasions. Such contestation would emerge even more emphatically in the following centuries.

The Significance of Europe

The great Belgian historian Henri Pirenne argued in *Mohammed and Charlemagne*, published posthumously in 1937, that the seventh-century Arab conquest of the south Mediterranean coastline plus the Iberian peninsula, was of critical importance. He proposed that turning that sea more into a barrier rather than a highway (except in the Aegean and Adriatic where the Byzantine navy retained a presence) profoundly affected the subsequent development of Europe in several dimensions.[4] Though his thesis has not found universal academic acceptance, nevertheless the main lines if not the details would appear to have relevance. The sudden change from a common culture on both sides of the Great Sea to two antagonistic and incompatible ones professing hostile monotheistic religions, could not have failed to have a major impact. It may well have influenced, if not caused, the peculiar social evolution of post-Classical Europe compared with Asia and North Africa.

That peculiarity lay in the character of Europe's socio-political structure during those centuries. Elsewhere large territorial empires remained the norm. Where one disappeared another soon took its place. (An argument could be made that the Ottoman empire was the legitimate successor to the Roman on the grounds that while Constantine changed it from pagan to Christian, Sultan Mehmed merely changed it from Christian to Muslim.) Whether the earlier Arab Muslim power in eighth-century Spain seriously attempted to conquer Gaul as well is uncertain. Europe west of Kievan Rus was not incorporated in a widespread territorial empire but instead fractured into a number of different sovereign principalities and independent municipalities. This fracturing of Europe was far from being a deliberate piece of political engineering – on the contrary. The Roman empire embracing east and west remained an unforgotten ideal among both the lay and clerical aristocracies, and serious attempts were made to revive it. According to Michael Mann,

[T]he barbarian probably converted to Christianity as a symbol of civilisation in general. . . after the final end of the western empire in 476 Christianity was the monopoly supplier of that civilisation's legacy especially of literacy.[5]
'. . . what replaced central "Romanness" was not barbarism but forms of 'local Romanness'.[6]

The sixth-century Byzantine emperor Justinian's generals successfully reconquered the Germanic Vandal kingdom in North Africa and the isles of the western Mediterranean, then proceeded to try to do the same to the Ostrogoth kingdom in Italy, but although that kingdom was destroyed along with much infrastructure and population and the Byzantines recaptured Sicily and much of the peninsula, nevertheless their resources were inadequate to hold all of it against invasion by the Germanic Lombards.[7]

The next attempt at revival was made by Pope Leo III, who had fallen out with the Byzantine monarchy and renounced previous popes' allegiance to the emperor. In the year 800 he crowned Charlemagne as Roman emperor in rivalry to the actual occupant in Constantinople, the Frankish king's military reputation making him appear a suitable candidate to re-establish a unified empire and possibly even reconquer Muslim Spain and North Africa – but though Charlemagne had certainly established an empire spanning most of west and central Europe east and north of the Pyrenees, any such idea was purely fantasy.

Mini-Empires

Charlemagne's own empire, impressive in extent as it was, disintegrated almost immediately on its founder's death in 814. One further serious attempt to establish a central European empire, formally the continuation of Charlemagne's, was made by the Ottonian dynasty of Saxon dukes (Saxony having been absorbed into Charlemagne's empire). Its leading representative Otto I had the then pope crown him in 962, this time as Holy Roman Emperor in addition to king of Germany and Italy. In little more than a century the title had become a nullity[8] with nothing beyond prestige value, the territory having fallen apart into the domains of various feudatories and commercially orientated cities. Efforts to make it into a reality in the twelfth and thirteenth centuries by Frederick Barbarossa and Frederick II came to nothing. Eventually the title was incorporated into the pretensions of the Habsburg dukes, allowing them to call themselves emperors in addition to whichever lesser titles they possessed in their south-central European domains. Napoleon abolished it.

The later medieval European assortment of states (including city states) of different rankings, populated by speakers of different languages and practitioners of different cultures and economic systems, was unified in no territorial empire but was nonetheless as ferociously aggressive as any. Its rulers fought each other with unrestrained savagery, massacring each other's populations of servile agriculturalists and wrecking each other's infrastructure in order to satisfy their egotistical cravings.

A number of mini-empires were thereby established: by the Anglo-Norman kings of England in France and Ireland (both vigorously contested) but not in Scotland; by the Castilian ones in Spain, by the Habsburgs, already mentioned, by the rival Danish and Swedish monarchs very shakily in Scandinavia; by the

Serbian and Bulgarian monarchs in the Balkans, and by the Polish and Lithuanian ones in eastern Europe. Two commercial empires were added to this mix – in the Mediterranean by the rival maritime city states of Venice and Genoa; in the Baltic and northern waters by the confederation of port cities, the Hanseatic League, controlled by their German-speaking merchant guilds. Similar autonomous mercantile cities were established along the river valleys (principally the Rhine) of the Mediterranean-Baltic trade route.

Nor was this all. The ferocious expansionism displayed by Christendom's elites was not confined to each other's territories but extended to populations and polities unwilling to have the blessings of Christianity enforced upon them. The most notorious series of crusades were directed against the Seljuk Turkish and the Egyptian Mamluk empires from the late eleventh to the late thirteenth centuries. The series was begun by Pope Urban II, bothered about the constant internal wars being conducted by the Christian aristocracies and princes. He was embarrassed by his own quarrel with some of them, and hoped to gain unlimited prestige by bringing about the recapture of Jerusalem, thus underlining reputational superiority over the Patriarch of Constantinople – the Great Schism with the Eastern church having occurred a few decades previously.

Accordingly participants in this enterprise were promised remission of sins and no doubt that was a real motivation for their response – they had a genuine belief in the afterlife and plenty to need remission for – but an equal or stronger one was the prospect of seizing land and property from the infidel, as well as practising the crusaders military and massacring skills. Jerusalem was indeed taken with fearsome slaughter of Muslim and Jewish non-combatants and any Christians who happened to get in the way. Crusader states were set up in the Levant, the last being retaken two centuries later. At the other end of the Mediterranean attacks against the Muslim rulers of Spain were virtually continuous until the latter were finally overwhelmed in 1492.

Another theatre of aggression was along the southern Baltic coastline, where various holy orders of knights, most prominently the Teutonic Order, were in action. The inoffensive Slavonic Prussians[9] were the first victims, but the Lithuanian monarchy, the last pagan state in Europe, proved a more formidable opponent and survived until its monarch made an opportunist conversion, which enabled the Lithuanian nobility to establish their own mini-empire.

The aggressively violent traditions established in Europe during this period certainly helped to provide ideological fuel for the establishment of the overseas empires achieved by several European states in the modern centuries. The conquest by Spaniards of large portions of the Americas was viewed as a continuation of the *Reconquista*; a minor part of Mussolini's excuse for invading Abyssinia was to impose the Catholic faith upon the Copts. Very explicitly the German state in the first part of the twentieth century aimed at an eastern hegemony and to turn Ukraine and Belorussia into vassal states and a little later, famously in *Mein Kampf,*

Hitler was even more explicit: 'And so we National Socialists . . . take up where we broke off six hundred years ago . . . and turn our gaze towards the land in the east . . . and shift to the soil policy of the future.'

The Papacy

Although after Charlemagne the bulk of Europe was never again incorporated into a meaningful secular empire, a substitute of sorts existed in the form of the church governed from Rome, which could perhaps be described as a kind of cultural empire and very largely saw itself as the continuation of the Roman empire. Prior to the eighth century the structure of government in the western church was at a low ebb and the bishop of Rome, a subject of the Byzantine monarch, lacked any particular authority beyond his own city. It was the Frankish rulers of the eighth century who enabled these popes to advance their pretensions and provided them with estates (cultivated by slave and serf labour) to underpin their assets.

The claim to supreme religious authority was made by a number of very dynamic individuals in the subsequent five centuries not least by their insistence that they were authorised to consign any individual to hell. By playing off one set of rulers against another and dispensing spiritual legitimacy upon them, they found acceptance for their claims throughout western and central Europe despite friction from time to time with particular monarchs.

The enterprise was backed up by the church's virtual monopolisation of literacy. Clergymen became indispensable to monarchs for their secretarial functions, and also by the development of canon law, first in the Roman curia, and later extended in the universities which began to function from the twelfth century onwards. This law related not only to the affairs of the church itself but to the personal behaviour of its faithful (which was everyone within its sphere apart from Jews) over such matters as fast days, holy days, marital and sexual practices and suchlike, reinforced with the practice of confession. Until the later medieval centuries it was the only coherent legal code established in western Europe.

The church was economically very important as well. Its monasteries were often agricultural factories in addition to their spiritual purposes. It possessed enormous landholdings which it supplemented with the tithe that every family was obliged to pay along with payments for services such as weddings, baptisms and funerals. Its looting by Henry VIII may have been the beginning of the revolution in landownership which led on to the agrarian capitalism of England in the following century – and so very consequential indeed.

Michael Mann suggests another very important role, namely that its ideological coverage eased the frictions of social life in the areas over which it exercised hegemony and underpinned the efficacy of contracts and oaths, evidently also of great economic importance, and so lubricated the functioning of merchants and markets. If this should be the case (Perry Anderson disputes it) then the Roman

Catholic Church and its supreme authority, the Roman pontiff, fulfilled a role similar to the imperial regimes of China and the Indian subcontinent.

Subsequent chapters will discuss the reasons why the fragmented and mutually quarrelling European states of the medieval and early modern world, unified, after a fashion, only by a degree of common culture and commercial intercourse, later came to overwhelm and dominate the mighty empires of Eurasia. Part of the secret of their predatory 'success' may indeed have lain in their very multiplicity and fragmentation, as aspect discussed extensively in Perry Anderson's two volumes, *Passages from Antiquity to Feudalism* and *Lineages of the Absolutist State*.[10]

Conclusion

From the time of the early Pharaohs onwards the world of agricultural production and natural power sources was a world of empires and would-be empires, accompanied by the usual authoritarian brutality and coerced cooperation of forced labour. This reality did not prevent great material achievements being realised in technique and technology from irrigation to horse collars,[11] and highly impressive intellectual and cultural ones in artefacts, literature and pictorial and sculptural representation.

These developments proceeded at glacial pace against a background of social and gender oppression accompanied by political mayhem, but in the millennium following the collapse of the western Roman empire, in the inconsequential peninsula of Europe underneath the horrors of violence (possibly even exaggerated by the absence of an all-encompassing empire), the basis was forming of an economic and social regime which would transform the planet and with it the fabric of history both in texture and in pattern. Such transformation is the subject of the following chapters.

12

Human Reality in Transformation: Modern Population, Migration and Labour

This chapter deals with some central aspects of the second and previously emphasised most far-reaching transition in human history, the planetary shift from cultures of a basically agrarian character to ones dominated by mechanisms dependent upon artificial power sources, together with all the human consequences which ensued. The direction of events could not be initially recognised and it was of course unplanned. Someone jokingly once remarked that when Henry Tudor killed Richard III in 1485 he didn't then dismount from his horse and say to his officers, 'Right guys, that ties up the Middle Ages, let's get on with Modern Times!' Nevertheless, within not very many years, his European contemporaries, if they hadn't noticed much change in their living conditions, were aware that a huge and previously unknown landmass could be reached by sailing westwards – and certain denizens of that landmass and its associated islands were being forced to realise that hostile strangers bearing the powers of gods were descending upon them with evil intent.[1]

Modern times were indeed about to begin in those years, and not only for the Europeans who gave it that designation, but ultimately for every inhabitant of the globe. World population over the next centuries would grow beyond all imagining, despite the unprecedentedly lethal character of human interactions during those centuries, while towards the beginning of the third millennium urban populations would surpass rural ones in numbers. Methods of gaining livelihood and production of the necessities of life would change beyond all recognition. So would modes of communication and living standards for a significant proportion of the globe's inhabitants, especially those with access to unprecedentedly improved medical techniques. Migrations would occur rendering all previous instances puny by comparison. Age-old political systems would be utterly overturned. Populations would be mixed as never before.

No simple analysis can encompass and explain the forces behind this shattering of the social world which had been the norm for 50 centuries. One point worth stressing, with reference to this and the following chapter, is that short-term aims pursued by individuals and collectives came together to culminate in the world with which readers of this volume are familiar. Some very long-term projects of social reconstruction were indeed initiated in the latter part of the era; these however up to the present have frequently produced outcomes opposite to the intended ones.

Historians, at least western historians, divide these centuries for convenience into Early Modern, running approximately from around 1500 to 1789, Modern from then to the end of the Second World War, and from 1945 to the present, Modern becomes Contemporary History. All such divisions are of course arbitrary, but these ones do at least correspond to significant shifts. Prior to the eighteenth century advances in European technology, though significant, had not been profound, and in social structure, apart from the disappearance of slavery, not very marked. A citizen of the Roman empire such as Constantine, who was originally based at York, if transported into eighteenth-century England would have noted many changes from his own era, but would not overall have sensed a dramatic difference, and in the road system he would have observed significant decline from the civil engineering expertise of his own days.

The mass of the population would still have toiled on the land with equipment not too remarkably different from his own times. They would still have been governed by an oligarchy of wealthy aristocrats exercising a ferocious penal discipline, if not quite so ferocious as that of his own epoch. He might have been puzzled by the non-existence of a chattel slave population, but a voyage across the Atlantic would have reassured him on that point. It is hardly necessary to labour the contrast with the mid-twentieth century. A transformed social universe based on unprecedented technological change came into being during the three succeeding centuries. The foundations of the transformation were population growth, revolution in the nature of mechanisms, reorganisation of the processes of production both rural and urban and the expansion and intensification of market mechanisms.

Population

Population size, in the view of opinion-formers in particular societies throughout history, has never been ideal – there was/is either too little of it or too much. During most of historical time it has been the former that has been the source of concern. The importance of fertility to preliterate societies is a reasonable presumption that is given confirmation by their surviving artefacts. With literacy what seems to have been, not without reason, a near-obsession, becomes explicit. The Mosaic sexual code, as evidenced in the Jewish Bible or Christian Old Testament, was concerned above all to promote fertility by rigorously prohibiting non-procreative sex.

Both then and in succeeding centuries rulers were highly concerned about the size of the populations over whom they ruled, wanting them to be as big as possible both for their taxable capacity and as a reservoir for personnel to use in either aggression or defence. When yoked to personal ambition on the part of these monarchs this was not the least of reasons for expanding their empires, since they had no policy options for naturally increasing the numbers of their existing subjects (other than forbidding non-procreative sex, a command difficult to enforce even when aided by religion).

Worries about the insufficiency of numbers persisted into the earlier years of the twentieth century. In Britain during the eighteenth and nineteenth centuries rapid population growth was generally welcomed, despite Malthus's concerns, as a larger population meant bigger markets and encouraged industry, not least because it generated a 'reserve army of labour' (numerous unemployed job-seekers) and thus kept wages low. For similar reasons US governments until the First World War encouraged immigration – provided it was of European descent (though even so immigrants were popularly unpopular in their earlier generations) as similarly did the British 'Dominions', the parts of the empire where the indigenous populations had been displaced by settlers.

Similarly nineteenth-century French governments, for taxation, military and market reasons, lamented the slow growth of their population – an inheritance of the smallholding peasant culture, reinforced by the Revolution, as a result of which peasant proprietors, aiming to inhibit inheritance disputes, took measures to limit their families in defiance of religious injunctions by engaging in non-procreative sex – those in the south of the country were said to use the more certain technique of anal sex in preference to the less reliable *coitus interruptus* utilised elsewhere. In the twentieth century, when such slow endogenous growth was accompanied by the massive losses of fertile young men in the First World War, what had been a significant concern became a veritable obsession. Pronatalist propaganda was stepped up enormously during the interwar years[2] from all parts of the political spectrum and contraception was not legal in France before 1967.

In spite of the more than impressive British nineteenth-century population expansion by endogenous growth, British journalists and politicians expressed worry in the late century that the country had been outstripped demographically by the new German empire, not to mention the United States. By the early twentieth, both the UK and the US were gripped by fears of the 'yellow peril', given the combination of immense numbers in eastern Asia and the Japanese most effectively displaying their newly-acquired and high-tech military might.

Malthusian Trap?

It is questionable whether populations in the past have ever fallen into the 'Malthusian trap' postulated by the odious clergyman of the early nineteenth century after whom it is named, in which numbers in a given population outrun the ability of available agricultural output to supply sufficient food resources, and famine supervenes. Famine certainly has been a frequent visitor to earth ever since the Neolithic revolution (and very possibly earlier) and even apart from such demographic disasters global population generally has shown a rhythm of growth and decline within an overall upward trend. What is dubious is whether population numbers *per se* have ever been the key responsible factor in famine years. Commonly it has been a sudden and catastrophic failure of a previously adequate food supply, whether due to climatic factors or political action such as scorched-earth policies including massacre of agricultural workers. It is more likely that in the normal times of pre-modern societies the attrition of infant mortality, adult premature exhaustion and also routine disease would have been sufficient to keep numbers below the famine level.

There are a couple of possible exceptions to this generalisation, but in these too we find extraneous factors at work. The first is the population growth in Europe of the thirteenth and very early fourteenth centuries, which, in England at least and most likely elsewhere, was putting pressure on a relatively static grain output, which made its increase possible only by cultivating less fertile land, with diminishing returns. The culmination was a massive population collapse in the mid-fourteenth century, one estimate for the world being a reduction from 450 to 350 million; roughly a fifth to a quarter.

The first two extraneous factors are well known, especially the Black Death (probably bubonic plague) which more than decimated Europe in the middle of the fourteenth century and killed around half of its inhabitants. Less dramatically famous was the 'Little Ice Age', a precipitate temperature drop which began in the early fourteenth century and of course gravely worsened conditions for cultivation. These alone would have been sufficient to account for the demographic collapse, but there was more. In the course of the thirteenth century as population grew landlords were pressing increasing exactions upon the working peasantry and in all likelihood undermining their general health and vitality, making them less able to resist the infection and the deteriorating climate.

The second example (there are plenty more) and even better renowned, was the great Irish famine of the nineteenth century. The Irish population had been growing in the course of the previous century, even faster than the rapid increase in mainland Britain, and the landlords, like their European predecessors eight centuries earlier, were screwing their tenants into the ground, forcing them to feed themselves on smaller and smaller potato patches while the landlords used the remainder of their estates to produce profits. When potato blight struck in the 1840s, mass starvation resulted. Yet as the Irish expression put it, 'God sent the blight but the British sent the famine'. There was plenty of food in Ireland but the government was permitting the export of grain from the island in the middle of the famine. The Tsarist government did the same during the early twentieth century. Once again it was not a simple 'Malthusian trap' and there is no instance of a famine that was not aggravated, or more commonly created, by a combination of climatic and political developments.[3]

None of this is to argue that the Malthusian trap is a complete fiction and nothing more than a device to enable governments to evade responsibility for their crimes against humanity. Even if we have no clear examples of the trap being sprung in the past, it could have been a possibility in Britain itself during the nineteenth century. Such possibility was averted by the ability to import grain and other foodstuffs into the country made possible by the cultivation in the Russian steppes and the American prairies of grain as a cash crop, to be transported to Britain in immense quantities by railway and steamship. World croplands grew by 70 per cent between 1859 and 1920.[4]

Transcontinental Migration

A foundation stone of what we call modernity was the realisation by Europeans around 1500 that there existed a continental landmass (or rather two continents and numerous islands) hitherto unknown to them roughly midway between Europe and eastern Asia. Migration to this 'New World' thereafter took place on an enormous scale stretching over centuries. That, combined with the immigrants' natural increase, was very bad news indeed for the indigenous inhabitants whose remote ancestors had migrated from northeastern Asia probably in several waves, and had themselves migrated southward over the generations, establishing in different regions both foraging and agrarian cultures as well as a series of Neolithic civilisations. Subjugation and/or extermination were to be their common fate.

The feedback effect on Europe itself, environmentally, economically, socially and politically, was to be incalculably enormous. The Spanish conquistadors of Mexico and Peru were initially hunting above all for precious metals. They secured plenty of them, particularly silver from the environmentally deadly Potosí mines located in present-day Bolivia, worked by indigenous and later African slave labour, and bringing fabulous wealth to the Spanish crown (and the English pirates who preyed upon the treasure fleets). The exact role this bullion played in the European economy is disputed, but clearly it at least greatly lubricated trade with Asia and influenced to some degree the economic developments leading eventually to industrialisation.[5]

The precious metals were only the start – a range of domesticated plants and animals arrived from across the Atlantic to transform European culture. A cursory list includes cocoa, tobacco, cane sugar (native to southeastern Asia but enormously expanded in the Americas) maize, potatoes, turkeys and guinea pigs. All except the last were of enormous importance and impact, but if one had to be singled out it would probably be the potato,[6] which may well have underpinned the dramatic European population growth of the eighteenth and nineteenth centuries. Cotton is far from indigenous to the Americas and was domesticated independently there and in Asia, but its production in North America by European colonists proved in due course to be central to the industrialisation process.

Colonists in the Americas extensively cultivated tobacco, cane sugar and cotton in plantations. This was made possible by a different sort of migration, which may be termed forced migration, of slave labour from West Africa – as has been previously discussed in Chapter 6, a major element of seaborne commerce from the seventeenth to the nineteenth century, above all in the eighteenth. The expansion of British cities such as Glasgow, Liverpool, Manchester and Bristol (also Bordeaux in France) depended directly or indirectly upon this trade and the products which resulted. Profits made in this way financed industrial development in cities and towns around Britain, even on the east coast such as Newcastle, and not only the west coast centres themselves which were directly involved.

Indentured Labour

The diminution, if not suppression, of the Atlantic slave trade in the late nineteenth century did not end another form of forced migration. This was known as indentured labour, which in the eighteenth century had been an additional method of securing a labour force on the colonial mainland American tobacco and cotton plantations. It was voluntary insofar as the labourer was offered passage to America in return for agreeing to work unpaid for a given number of years, after which they could hope with reasonable prospects to make a better living there than in Britain.

In the late nineteenth century the practice was used in the South African mines, the main supply being of indentured labourers from China who worked and lived during the period of their indenture as virtual slaves under abominable conditions. The scandal this created in the UK was partly responsible for the landslide defeat in 1906 of the then Conservative government. Although most of these labourers returned eventually to China, a mainly commercially motivated number of Chinese immigrants remained in South Africa, having settled there before racially motivated exclusion policies were adopted in the early twentieth century.[7]

The principal area of indentured labour at the time however was in the sugar cane fields of Australia. The labourers were Pacific Islanders, and their situation was a far from voluntary one. They had either been kidnapped or tricked (known as 'blackbirding') by hired crews of thugs and compelled to undertake such labour under the pretence of a fake contract. Similar tactics were used by South American plantation owners, and were also utilised to acquire the Angolan slave labour employed in the contemporaneous production of cocoa beans on Portuguese-owned African islands.[8]

All the Pacific Islanders working in Australia, whether voluntary or coerced, were unceremoniously expelled at the beginning of the twentieth century. Later on in that century, in postwar western Germany, temporary contract workers from Turkey and Yugoslavia made up a section of the labour force without which the West German economic miracle would have been impossible. Ironically termed 'guest workers' (*Gastarbeiter*), with few social rights during their period of contract, these individuals were on no account allowed to take up permanent German residence.

What was to be cardinally important and to settle the destiny of humanity up to our own times was migration to, and natural increase in, the northern American continent. During the eighteenth and nineteenth centuries it sucked in immigrants on an unprecedented scale from all over Europe and from every state and nation, some more so than others and with Britain and Ireland in the forefront. France, for whatever reason, was unusually underrepresented and most French Americans are descended from previous immigrants to Canada; as most Spanish-Americans in the USA originate from south of the Rio Grande rather than directly from Spain itself.

When in the late eighteenth century the 13 British colonies along the eastern coast revolted and established the independent United States of America the continental ambitions of the new polity were already present in embryo, and within a century had been violently achieved in spite of and through foreign war, internal war against the Native Americans, civil war and massive social and ethnic conflict. Nor did such obstacles and problems prevent it from becoming the world leader in industrial output. In the course of the European war of 1914–18 this enabled it to become the world's dominant economic power, which it continued to be throughout the great depression of the interwar years. After 1945, though challenged, it has additionally been the world's political and military hegemon. From the later nineteenth century it had acted to shut off the Asian immigration which has left a substantial Chinese and Japanese population in the western USA. Following the Great War it also began to restrict and limit immigration from Europe as well.

Meantime, coercive migration has not ceased but continued with mass fatalities in different portions of the globe such as the northern part of the Indian subcontinent after the Partition of British India; in Palestine, in former Yugoslavia and most of all in regions of the African continent. Also since 1945 voluntary migration has taken on a new quality, globalised in a manner not previously imagined. This has principally involved the migration of citizens from what is now termed 'developing countries' into West European states, most prominently but not exclusively West Indians and Pakistanis into Britain, Algerians into France, and forced migrant refugees or asylum seekers,[9] into all of them. The European Economic Community has grown far beyond its originally intended limits. Its transformation into the European Union, with free movement across frontiers of money, commodities and labour, has involved a new pulse of migration – from the more impoverished states of the former Soviet bloc to the much more attractive consumer paradises of the west. It has also stimulated an illegal traffic in sex slaves in the same direction – and more widely, including the former USSR. According to the economic historian Immanuel Wallerstein, 'The capitalist world economy has required for its optimal functioning widespread and continuous migrations of people (both forced and voluntary) in order to fulfil labour-force needs at particular geographical locations.'[10]

Internal Migration

Also significant is one-way internal migration in the sense of population movement within a political unit from rural to urban areas. A current of this sort, albeit a weak one, has been evident throughout history from the earliest eras of urban settlement, though frequently interrupted by major environmental, economic, social and political upheavals, as during the collapse of the western Roman empire, when the trend was reversed and cities decayed.

During the European medieval centuries, while the trend was quite strong in the Chinese and Arab empires, it remained weak and often very weak in Europe, though never altogether ceasing. Towns, such as they were, functioned as a magnet for peasants trying to escape feudal servitude – though generally only unattached young men could take the risk. This circumstance applied even to migrants from the free peasantry who saw little future prospect on their home patch – the Dick Whittington story is a fanciful account of such an episode.

From the sixteenth century onwards the pace of urbanisation in Europe quickened considerably. By the sixteenth century urban concentrations put significant pressure on food and fuel supplies in London and stimulated the substitution of coal-burning for firewood. Established towns and cities grew remarkably and the spread of industrialisation conjured new ones out of what had formerly been rural villages, such as Manchester, among others in the north of England, in the Rhineland and northern France. Naturally, conditions of housing and hygiene were abominable in these growing urban concentrations and diseases were rife. As contemporaries noted, they also became foci for social disruption, generating crime, beggary, alcoholism and prostitution on an expanding scale[11] and presenting a standing challenge to the ordered and hierarchical society of the contemporary ideology – a relationship exemplified in John Gay's *The Beggar's Opera*.

In the twentieth century internal migration became a deluge, creating, in the title used by Mike Davis, a 'planet of slums',[12] as the migrants, with few or no resources, established major areas of makeshift dwellings on the outskirts of cities throughout all the major continents in variously-named concentrations without running water, sanitation, power supply or any basic amenities. Before the end of the century the majority of the world's population had become urban rather than rural.

Motivations

The above outline of world migration patterns to date stimulates the question of what motivates the phenomenon. There are of course many very different answers depending on circumstances. In cultures accustomed to nomadism migration is no big deal and involves no drastic alteration in lifestyle, though there would presumably be reluctance to abandon an attractive hunting-ground – or pasture if domestic animals were the food source – without strong reason if the clan was fortunate enough to possess one. Climatic changes which reacted upon sources of meat, or vegetable food, would probably have provided an incentive, as would the attentions of a larger and more aggressive clan.

For sedentary populations with permanent habitations and agricultural resources including soil, water and domesticated animals, and possibly attachment to a god for whom location was important, such reluctance must have been much greater and migration is likely to have been more coercive. Fear from an aggressor bringing peril of massacre, rape and enslavement would indeed supply a motive if alternative sources of nutrition were potentially available – possibly through aggression against a weaker neighbour. Migration of a satisfactorily settled agrarian population simply in the hope of finding something even more satisfactory 'over the hill' must have been very rare if indeed it ever occurred – except when the food supply was threatened by pestilence (locusts for example) or climatic variation.

In modern times voluntary migration by entire communities has been rare, but forced migration on that scale has certainly not. Leaving aside the African slave trade, which on the whole involved individuals rather than communities, instances of what has been known since the 1990s as 'ethnic cleansing' have occurred with frequency. Early modern times might be said to have opened with the expulsion of the Jews and Muslims from the Spanish kingdom, and later even of the Catholic converts from those religions, 'Conversos', and 'Moriscos'. During the nineteenth century the United Sates government was its leading practitioner, shifting Native American communities around the country at its will and pleasure onto increasing restricted 'reservations'.[13] During the twentieth century in Europe it reached unprecedented levels, the first major instance being between Greece and Turkey at the end of the First World War. It was later applied by Stalin in the 1930s to peasants deemed to be 'kulaks' who were deported to central Asia or Siberia; and during the war to entire national groups suspected of disloyalty, such as the Crimean Tatars and Volga Germans, and even their co-nationals fighting at the front.

The Nazis, in addition to their Jewish extermination project, applied similar techniques to Poles in Poland, in this case a conscious, previously intended programme rather than an unplanned response to emergency circumstances. Following the war the ethnic cleansing went in the opposite direction, when the entire German population living in the Polish territories newly-acquired from Germany, was expelled en masse. There was similar action against the Sudeten German population when the Czechoslovaks recovered that part of their country.[14] Shortly afterwards extensive population transfers occurred between the newly-independent India and its neighbour Pakistan, accompanied by ferocious massacre on both sides of the border. The same, or attempts at the same, was seen in the Yugoslav civil wars in the 1990s, and it was for this occasion that the 'ethnic cleansing' term was first used in English.

On the whole though, the pattern of migration through recorded history has been voluntary or at least quasi-voluntary (in the sense that it might be an offer that could not be refused without dire consequences, or applied to children without any say in the matter). It has generally involved individuals, small groups or families rather than entire populations. Motivation in such cases could vary between dissatisfaction with home life or the lure of preferable circumstances elsewhere, or a combination of both. An illustrative example is the shift in motivation of Irish migrants between the late eighteenth century and the middle of the nineteenth.

In the former case the dominant attraction to fit young men in Ireland, faced with a more competitive labour market owing to population growth, was of work availability across the water. The construction of the canal system in England demanded heavy labour and was highly dangerous, hence it required comparatively high payment levels to maintain the labourers' fitness and attract a workforce which might have found a safer if less remunerative occupation.

The situation in the 1840s during the great famine was completely different. Here the choice was, at best, between migration and starvation; and the USA, with its greater opportunities and anti-Irish prejudice no worse than in Britain, was the destination of choice. Irish migration was not of course the only source that the USA was attracting – plenty came from mainland Britain as well, not to mention all over Europe, either to take advantage of occupational or landowning opportunities, or, at the other end of the scale, to flee persecution from inimical regimes. This especially applied to Jewish populations from eastern Europe. Until the outlet was closed, immigrants in the nineteenth century also arrived in the United States from eastern Asia, both China and Japan.

The South African gold mines came to depend on migrant labour and, following the ending of Chinese immigration, were seriously dependent on an African workforce sourced from the regions north of South Africa – Mozambique, Angola and regions even further afield (there was of course also migrant labour form inside South Africa itself). Conditions for these migrant labourers were always vile, and following the installation of the apartheid regime after 1948, became even viler. The migrant labourers were forbidden to bring their families with them, and at the end of their contract period or working life were peremptorily dismissed and returned to their place of origin. In spite of that, there was always a plentiful supply of potential migrants, so impoverished in their homelands that it was worthwhile for them to put up with the inflictions they suffered on the goldfields as the price of the marginal increase of resources they obtained and could remit in part to their families.

Migration to Australasia, principally from the UK, was a combination of coercive and voluntary factors. There is a joke that the ancestors of the Australian population were selected by some of the best judges in Britain. This refers to the fact that from the 1780s, following American independence, which closed off that avenue, the southern continent was used as a transportation destination for forced labour which was applied to persons convicted of serious crime (which could include the theft of a few shillings) but who had not been consigned to the gallows. The sentences were typically of seven or 14 years (occasionally for life) and the convict could in theory return to Britain at the expiry of their sentence (to do so earlier was a capital offence). Most however did not, either because they could not afford the fare or because they preferred to avoid a further uprooting.

New Zealand was different. The first British settlers were escaped convicts from Australia, but the immigrants thereafter were voluntary ones. They were drawn by the attractiveness of the temperate climate and the impressive fertility of the location – albeit there were greater dangers from volcanism. The indigenous population of warlike agriculturalists was also much better positioned to resist the intrusion than their unfortunate counterparts in Australia.

The global migration which commenced after the Second World War and has expanded continuously since, is motivated mainly by pull rather than push factors – though not invariably. Some of it is stimulated by political instability or war in the migrants' (or would-be migrants) homeland resulting in danger to body and life, particularly from invasions by Western powers and their consequences, such as in Iraq and Afghanistan. Principally though it is stimulated by the attraction of moving to wealthier societies with greater economic and possibly social and cultural opportunities in order to escape a life of impoverishment, even when there is no immediate danger of being murdered, raped or perishing in flood or famine.

13

Inhuman Powers: Capitalism, Industry and their Consequences

Capitalism

Capitalism is first and foremost the art of using money to get more money . . . It is the secret scandal of capitalism that at no point has it been organised around free labour.
—David Graeber

All the developments associated with the great transformation occurred within market societies dominated by property owners whose property was either mobile capital or the possession of assets such as land which enabled them by borrowing to raise such capital, and at least up to the twentieth century these developments could not otherwise have been accomplished. 'The separate interests of the old regime were fused by commercial capitalism', writes Mann. 'Capitalists in land, commerce, and finance fused as a single extensive political class . . . .'[1]

Markets have played a major role in history ever since the institution of settled communities and the practice of agriculture. They are a major force in achieving social cohesion, the more as society becomes increasingly differentiated and complex. They exert an enormous power in driving historical change and development and have increasingly done so throughout the course of time. The modern world could have said to have begun with the creation in the sixteenth century of a global market due to the establishment of communication links between Eurasia, Africa and the Americas – especially the Americas. According to Thomas D Hall writing in the journal *Social Evolution & History*:

Not the least of [the incentives] was a drive to explore and find shorter, or at less contested routes to Asia, to develop new kinds of shipping . . . All these factors helped set western Europe on a trajectory of change that gave rise to colonialism, mercantilism, the rise of capitalist states, and the industrial revolution. Clearly the 'rise of Europe' can not be explained solely by internal factors. Those who claim to do so ignore the Afroeurasian-wide process that created a context within which features in local European social organisation could have the effects they did . . . much of what happened in Europe could only make sense in a larger context . . . .[2]

The bourgeoisie, as Marx expressed it, was a most revolutionary class. However the word 'capitalism' does not appear in the title of any of his writings; his magnum opus is entitled *Capital*, which is not quite the same thing – the subtitle is, *A Critique of Political Economy*. Capital is the social mechanism of economic production and capitalism the social formation in which it is embedded. According to Marx's definition, capitalism represents a society dominated by commodity production in which labour-power itself has mostly become a commodity and throughout society establishes 'conditions that allowed the market to compel people to follow its dictates or perish'.[3] 'The destiny of the bourgeoisie, its champions felt, was to humanise capitalism by bringing the market into every human relation, every facet of social provision, of production, of consumption, of the political process itself.'[4]

Capital and capitalists have existed down the ages, at least since the invention of coined money around the middle of the first millennium BCE. Slave traders, after all, could be regarded as a species of capitalist. However that reference points up a significant difference in the nature of capital – commercial capital in the early modern centuries was accumulated by trading in commodities which had been produced by traditional organisation and technologies and only occasionally by wage labour, whereas the capital characteristic of a capitalist society enters into and modifies the process of production in a manner intended to enhance productivity. This generally means substituting division of labour and/or machine production for the previous modes.

As writers such as Jack Goody and John A Hobson have argued (see below), the Chinese empire and to some extent the Islamic ones, at least until the eighteenth century (they would place it even later), surpassed the European powers in every economic sector – invention, production, output, trade. But these were not capitalist societies, and this proved to be the crucial difference which determined the location of the new industrialisation and the world hegemony which accompanied it.

Globalisation

The most dramatic manifestation of modern times was that (often rival) European powers between them established a part-trading, part-territorial pattern of empires spanning the globe, and from the early seventeenth century they were joined by England. With acknowledgement to Douglas Adams and *The Hitchhiker's Guide to the Galaxy*, the 'Answer to the Ultimate Question of Globalisation, the Planet and Modern Times', could be said to be 1492, for this was the year of the Common Era in which Christopher Columbus (Cristoforo Colombo or Cristóbal Colón) made landfall on Hispaniola (Hobson reminds us that it was also the founding year of the Spanish Inquisition). Although Columbus never accepted that the islands he visited in his four voyages were adjacent to a huge landmass previously unknown to Europeans, his enterprise initiated, within a few decades, the European (initially

Spanish adventurers') plunder of the two continents' choicest bits. It resulted in the eventual takeover of them both, along with the adjacent islands, inaccurately termed West Indies.

Somewhat earlier in the fifteenth century Portuguese adventurers had pioneered a sea route to southern and eastern Asia, where they encountered civilisations who were militarily and economically more than a match for them, but over the course of the following century the Portuguese monarchy gained control over coastal parts of the island later named Ceylon and later still Sri Lanka. Their Spanish counterparts did the same in the Philippines archipelago, as later did the Dutch republic, or rather its trading company the VOC, in Java and other islands of the East Indies archipelago.

High value spices were the principal target. These were already available by overland trade, which depended on camel transport, but the point of the voyages and establishment of outposts was to establish control of the source of supply and also to avoid interruptions to the overland route which might be caused by political upheavals.

Later the VOC allied with the inland king of Kandy in Ceylon resisting the Portuguese in order to help him expel the latter, then cheated him by taking over the island for themselves. Their vessels and their firepower at the time were not greatly superior to what was available to the Son of Heaven, and if they had confronted the sort of fleet captained by Admiral Zheng He in the early fifteenth century they would have had no chance whatever. By the time of the Europeans' arrival however, the empire had abandoned that form of naval power (presumably reckoning that it didn't need it) and the mighty junks which sustained it had been left to rot.

From this initial form of globalisation flowed a torrent of riches, further enhanced when the Caribbean islands and part of the North American coast, with the importation of African slave labour, became mass producers of the then luxury products of tobacco and sugar – and later cotton. Associated industries such as shipbuilding, ironworking, sailmaking, ropemaking and so forth expanded in concert, large enterprises were formed and transport systems expanded and improved. By the last decades of the eighteenth century (possibly taking the abolition of serfdom in the Scottish mining and saltmaking industries as the marker date)[5] Britain was a capitalist society – but a rival interpretation suggests that the world trading system (including the slave trade), which Britain now dominated, though highly important, and identified by Immanuel Wallerstein's 'World systems theory' as centrally important was not the most crucial circumstance in transforming a pre-capitalist society into a capitalist one.

Ellen Meiksins Wood has argued instead that English agricultural economy of the seventeenth and early eighteenth centuries was the starting motor for world capitalism, namely on account of tenant farmers being obliged by economic necessity to 'set in train a new dynamic of self-sustaining growth with no historical precedent.'⁶ This was to spread outwards until it encompassed the entire globe. Robert Brenner has argued along similar lines. The virtual abolition of independent peasant landholdings throughout the UK, a process being completed at the end of the eighteenth century, proletarianised the agricultural workforce, at that time still the largest component of the working population. It thereby generated the pool of potentially available workers in town and country 'who had nothing to sell but their skins' – male, female and of every age from six upwards to decrepitude – and whose unemployed component on the brink of starvation kept the wages of the others at a satisfactorily low level. In this interpretation the world trading system and the wealth it produced for the economies of western Europe was auxiliary to the process, though nonetheless also essential.

Where Did it Begin?

The distinctive characteristic of Marxist interpretations of the birth of capitalism and the industrial revolution is that these were coercive processes. Total reliance on wages was initially regarded as a disgrace by the workforces first subjected to it[7] and only submitted to when all other potential sources of legal income had been closed off. Their successors had no option, and though they constituted 'free labour' and were not subjected to slavery or serfdom for any individual capitalist, they were effectively slaves, wage slaves, to the capitalist class as a whole.

They were ruled in their working lives (in some instances even outside them in 'company towns') by their employers and behind the employers stood the state, designed to forcefully repress any serious opposition to the capitalist structure.[8] Moreover the initial accumulation of mobile capital to set the process in motion was coercively obtained in a process known as 'primitive accumulation', without even the pretence of individual freedom on the labourer's part, by means of dispossession (such as the agricultural enclosure process), robbery, forced labour, colonialism and slave production.

Bourgeois economists and economic historians not surprisingly declined and still decline to recognise these realities, but there is also considerable controversy among Marxist historians as to the relationship of the various coercive aspects of capitalism's establishment, with Wood, Brenner and Immanuel Wallerstein to the forefront. England and lowland Scotland and the North American colonies/USA were market-based societies before they were capitalist ones, and capitalist before they were industrialised. Their market economies (most famously theorised by Adam Smith in the 1770s) were undoubtedly an essential precondition of capitalist development and served as the engine of accumulation which enabled capital to enter and control production increasingly in the second half of the eighteenth century, leading on eventually to mechanisation and growing use of artificial power sources once the technical problems were mastered.

So much is common ground. Where argument, which originated in the 1940s, begins is over the respective contributions to the process from internal developments, principally in Britain, on the one hand, and the global commercial system, with emphasis on foreign trade, upon the other. Neither side to the controversy discounts either of these relationships – the point at issue is the proportionate weight to be given to each.

In 1946 Maurice Dobb, the then unusual phenomenon of an Oxbridge Communist Party academic, published *Studies in the Development of Capitalism*, which combined a deep study of the emergence of capitalism in England with its impact on the world at large. The controversy was kicked off with a review of his volume by the American Marxist Paul Sweezy. It is summarised by one blogger as follows,

> In this debate a main point of contention is between Dobb's attempt to demonstrate that capitalism emerged from contradictions internal to feudalism itself; while Sweezy more takes the position that capitalism developed independently of feudalism and overtook it as an external force because of its dynamism in contrast to feudalism's stagnancy.[9]

A further dimension to be added to this is the claim advanced by Sweezy that Dobb was rather too dismissive and insufficiently appreciative of the impact and importance of long-distance trade to the erosion of feudalism and emergence of a capitalist class; in short that more attention should be given to the structure of world economic systems. Dobb himself made some partial concessions on this point.

Harvey Kaye sums up the argument in the following terms:

> In this exchange we recognise the emergence and divergence of two kinds of Marxist analysis of economic history and development. One is decidedly *economic*, focusing on exchange relations. As in Sweezy's critique. The other is politico-economic, focusing on the *social* relations of production and directing us towards class-struggle analysis, as in Dobb's *Studies* and reply.[10]

This was the starting point of the argument that has been developed further by Wallerstein, Wood and Brenner. A very judicious survey and consideration of the contending positions with all their strengths and weaknesses is to be found in Henry Heller's *The Birth of Capitalism*.[11] This deals with the birth of industrial capitalism. Its expansion and development eventually embraced the entire world. The stage it had reached by the mid-nineteenth century is summarised in vivid prose by Marx and Engels in *The Communist Manifesto*.

What should be noted, however, is the interpretation of capitalism's rise, spanning the eras of commercial and industrial capital, in Giovanni Arrighi's *The Long Twentieth Century: Money, Power, and the Origins of Our Times*. Arrighi contends that the globalised market system of the modern era has always existed in the context of a dominant centre, an economic global hegemony which over the centuries shifted from one state system to another following the economic/ military exhaustion of its predecessor. He notes the states in question as being the Dutch republic (though surely the Spanish kingdom is more entitled to be considered the earlier pioneer) followed by the United Kingdom and afterwards by the United States.

Industrialisation

The form of capitalism described above, sometimes termed, though inaccurately, 'merchant capitalism' supplied the necessary foundation for the industrialisation which produced the modern world, otherwise known as the industrial revolution. Within the past two-and-a-half centuries this revolution has changed dramatically the fabric of history in texture and colour; the second great alteration (and acceleration) following the Neolithic revolution ten millennia earlier. The term 'industrial revolution' was first used in the 1820s on analogy with the French Revolution and was also employed by Engels midway through that century, but was popularised only as late as the 1880s by Arnold Toynbee (not to be confused with his nephew Arnold J Toynbee) when the profundity of the change was fully appreciated.

The validity of the term 'industrial revolution' has been questioned (as have various political revolutions including the French) on the grounds that the changes were not particularly speedy, often instead being incremental and extending over decades and that nobody, or very few at any rate, realised that they were living through a revolution. Suffice to say that if what happened between 1750 and 1850 did not constitute an industrial revolution, what then might one look like?

That said, many aspects of the process remain appropriately the subjects of lively debate. The simplistic popular view has tended to be that it was essentially about technological innovation – which was clearly its most dramatically visible feature. The reality was somewhat more complex. These innovations were made possible not only by the international commercial order but also by the far reaching non-technological developments which underpinned the new technical ones, and by the accumulated experience, stretching over decades or even centuries in older technologies (such as clockwork) which produced the skills necessary for the technological leap with which we are concerned here. Moreover, in several instances, particularly the most centrally vital one of coal mining, there was little or no technological improvement apart from the safety lamp[12] during this century of revolution – traditional techniques sufficed.

Any textbook on the industrial revolution will devote a substantial section to population growth (See Chapter Twelve) and without very substantial expansion of population and migration industrialisation could never have taken place in the manner in which it actually did occur. Rising population numbers had the twin effect of expanding both markets and the labour force for economic growth.

Britain was the first industrial nation (the title of a renowned textbook) in the modern sense and as we have seen population growth on the island was most impressive and additionally supplemented both by migration from Ireland and internal migration to the industrial centres. Probably the most important migration however was the coercive migration of the slave trade to provide the labour force for the production of semi-luxuries on the Caribbean islands and tobacco and cotton production in mainland North America, first as British colonies and later the United States. The most sophisticated technology in Britain in the eighteenth and early nineteenth centuries was in cotton manufacture, and slave-produced raw cotton was central.

Cotton manufacture and marketing, which well into the nineteenth century depended mostly on natural power sources, was enormously profitable. That was the case not only because British cotton had an enormous market available to it on a world scale, but a major wind-powered shipping industry to carry it, along with other profitable commodities, around the globe. These profits, were combined with colonial plunder, with which foreign trade was often indistinguishable, especially in relation to India, and also until 1807 with the slave trade, to provide the mobile capital through which further economic growth was advanced. To take full advantage of this a banking and credit system accompanied by paper currency was also essential, and these were soon devised, though for nearly a century they functioned in a very ramshackle fashion with frequent crashes and bankruptcies.

Without these preconditions the industrial revolution could not have occurred, but they were by no means the only ones. The first industrial nation also enjoyed very favourable natural endowments, particularly its plentiful and phenomenally productive coal seams, producing coal of many different sorts suitable for diverse purposes, from steam coal to consumption in domestic fireplaces. It was likewise provided by geology with extensive supplies of iron ore and other minerals essential for iron and steel manufacture. Its shape also ensured that it had an easily available waterborne internal transport system of natural rivers and artificial canals which served as an essential predecessor and also accompaniment to the nineteenth-century railway network.

Technological Marvels

At the same time, while it is apparent that the technological breakthrough associated with the industrial revolution would have been impossible without the physical and economic context sketched above, which in the end boils down to the availability of markets and workforce, nevertheless the popular image of industrialisation as centred on technology, while certainly inadequate, nevertheless goes to the heart of the matter. Not least in reaction to this popular assumption, economic commentators and historians have tended to underplay technology's central role and overemphasise the other essentials of the industrialisation process. What was cardinally important was not technology *per se*, but the *sort* of technology which came on stream.[13]

Though technology dependent on natural power sources can reach an extremely advanced level, inherently it is limited, given the techniques available at the time.[14] It was only once engineers learned how to effect controlled release of the energy locked up in fossil fuels that the modern world was truly born. I am rather surprised at the degree to which historians seem to underrate the central significance of steam power. Even such an acute analyst as Henry Heller appears not to stress its centrality.

Steam engines had existed since the beginning of the eighteenth century, but they too were initially of limited application – in essence they could only drive a pump, even when they functioned adequately, which was often not the case. Only with such an engine capable of driving a wheel did the sky become the limit, technologically speaking. It is therefore scarcely any exaggeration to suggest that the single most important individual in all history since the Neolithic was James Watt, who devised the first mechanism of this kind – which is not to say that someone else would not have succeeded if he had failed to do so. Even so, the rotary steam engine at first spread slowly in factories since they were expensive to build and maintain – water power was cheaper and not much less reliable, again underlining the importance of the economic context.[15] Only the immensity of the cotton market could make worthwhile the relatively few engines which were adopted in almost three decades. Steam power only really came into its own with the development of the railway and sea transport networks. Both were critically important, the former the most emphatically transformative. Without this development the use of steam power would have probably been confined to a very restricted level.

Railways

Ironically, taking into account the state of the British economy in the early nineteenth century when the first essentially modern railways powered by steam locomotives appeared, the network should never have been built. The existing transport system of rivers, canals and horse traffic was perfectly adequate to the needs of the time. The construction of the new system was driven by the lust for profit, the availability of cheap credit and new instruments of investment. The canal system created in the previous five decades had been extremely profitable both in construction and operation and the rail investors hoped to replicate that success, which in general they failed to do. Though not a black hole, the returns on rail investment were only modest.[16]

Nevertheless the railway system had all manner of spillover effects (economically the principal ones were in demand for coal and iron) and soon radically transformed Britain and its society, industrially, economically, socially, militarily, politically and culturally in ways too numerous to list, soon going on to do the same for the remainder of the globe.[17] Without the railways the general and universal transformation associated with the industrial revolution would have been much retarded. The application of steam power to shipping was only relatively less important, its effects too were momentous, not only in the dramatically increased speed and carrying capacity of sea transport, but in the industrial development it provoked in the manufacture of steamships. In addition it enhanced the appetite for coal and iron and the need for coaling stations to be be established around the globe; a significant factor in European, particularly British, imperial expansion.

Second Industrial Revolution

Economic historians often refer to the developments during the last three decades of the nineteenth century as 'the second industrial revolution'. Though there were substantial and significant developments in existing technologies, such as steelmaking, and to the steam engine was added the steam turbine, particularly useful in shipping, the 'second' designation comes from the introduction and development of three particularly important and novel technologies. These were the use of oil as a fuel source, applications of electricity and new branches of the chemical industry.

The first made possible the petrol and in due course the diesel engine, which would eventually transform the railway and shipping network. However, much more economically, socially, militarily and culturally significantly was the fact that the petrol engine, much lighter than its steam counterpart, was applicable to road transport, and from the early twentieth century to powered flight, with all that these developments implied, not least the sourcing of the necessary fuel.

Electric current had been employed since the 1840s for the purpose of telegraphy. From the 1870s a wide range of fresh applications included telephone communication, the beginnings of radio communication, lighting, the electric motor, which could be made more compact even than the petrol engine, and of course, in the USA, a novel means of execution, first pioneered, unsurprisingly, on an African-American. Electricity in the shape of the sparking plug was also a necessary adjunct to the operation of petrol engines. One aspect of its employment had implications also for imperial policies, for that was the necessity to obtain reliable sources of copper ore for the wiring.

The third of these technologies stretched across a wide range of applications. Artificial dyestuffs and pharmaceuticals were important, as were new types of explosives to add to and supersede the old traditional standby, gunpowder, in military use since the fourteenth century. By far the most important, however, was the adaptation and use of the tropical plant gum, rubber, in an enormous number of different contexts, but above all for the manufacture of vehicle tyres, which made possible the full benefit of the petrol engine in road transport (and also in the new exercise of cycling). Again the sourcing of the raw material, originally a South American plant, was a matter of extreme political importance to the industrial societies of Europe, the USA and eventually Japan, and resulted in horrific atrocities committed against the effectively slave labour forces in South America and central Africa.

Why not China?

An outgrowth of this controversy, which has emerged in the past few decades, is over the question of whether capitalism could have developed and an industrial revolution could have occurred elsewhere in the world. It is a question that has been given especial bite with the theorisations known as 'postcolonialism', which accuses interpretations which focus on European ascendancy of Eurocentric bias. Was it merely certain accidental contingencies, especially its military apparatus, that enabled Britain to get there before any other society that had an equal or better likelihood of prevailing in the race?

In dealing with this question it has to be stressed that there was no race. The individuals and groups who laid the economic foundations for the modern world and a European hegemony over it had no project for transforming the globe in the manner that eventuated – of covering the earth with factories, mines, megacities and railways and the oceans with steamships – and instituting rule over them all by European or European-descended nations. They simply wanted to make money and were not particular about the methods they used to secure it. They devised the world we are familiar with today essentially as a by-product of that ambition. Marx once remarked that every generation only sets itself the tasks it is capable of accomplishing. Every project, no matter how ambitious or how consciously revolutionary, even social transformation, is set within the parameters of the society that the projectors are familiar with – the far future is shrouded in deep darkness. The point applied, as we shall see, to Jacobins and Bolsheviks as much as to industrial entrepreneurs.

It has been demonstrated convincingly[18] that certainly until the eighteenth century and possibly as late as 1800, Asia, and China in particular (it is worth recalling that the Chinese invented not only printing but printed money)[19] was ahead of Europe technologically, economically, and in some respects socially (to be fair, European intellectuals at the time appreciated this fact). Notoriously, at the time the quality of Chinese products far outstripped anything the Europeans could offer – the only European invention which could impress them was the barrel, a strong, efficient, economical and mobile means of storage which they had not themselves devised. Could capitalist industrialisation then not have been first initiated in the Turkish or Persian empires, the Moghul empire or the Chinese, or even Japanese, which, as Perry Anderson has pointed out, had a feudal structure not too different from the English one?

A passionate partisan of such a view is John A Hobson, whose volume *The Eastern Origins of Western Civilisation*, propounds it with extreme vigour. The book provides an interesting read, though unfortunately not a very convincing one. He certainly details at great length the respects in which Chinese and to a lesser extent Islamic, knowledge, organisation and technology were in advance of the west until very late in the day, but these accounts are spread over a theoretical apparatus which cannot be taken seriously.

Confidence is not inspired by the bizarre and manifestly erroneous claim that, 'Crucially, the actual landmass of the southern hemisphere is exactly twice that of the northern hemisphere'.[20] In any case both China and almost all the Islamic world lie inside the northern hemisphere. To this is added Hobson's reference to 'globalisation' during centuries when the Americas were totally isolated from the remainder of the world. What he means are communication links, which certainly existed, between eastern and western Eurasia, with the addition of Africa, nevertheless making 'globalisation' a wholly inappropriate term.

John Hall, reviewing Hobson in the *English Historical Review*,[21] writes that Hobson 'tends to cite only those parts of an author's work that agree with his argument, and misses out whole realms of scholarship', also characterising his particular construct of Eurocentrism as being 'Often a straw man'. Indeed a whole procession of straw men parade through Hobson's pages. The impression is given that Eurocentrism represents some sort of intellectual conspiracy with a definite and focused agenda of doing down Eastern achievements. In fact the unquestionably Eurocentric remarks of nineteenth-century commentators are presented as though they still represented the intellectual consensus. These certainly presented the rise of the West as 'a moral success story'. Marx is written off in the same terms, though his remark, with specific reference to the imperial record, that capital came into the world 'dripping with blood and filth from every pore' is never quoted, nor is the fact acknowledged that Marx presented capitalism's triumph as an *amoral* success story.

The problem with this kind of approach is that it tends to cast discredit on the correction of the historical picture that is necessary if the reality of the Chinese empire's power, influence and achievement up to that time is to be adequately presented. Ethically speaking, East and West were as worse as each other, the question therefore is why the Celestial empire, which had taken an economy based on natural power sources about as far as it was possible to go, with all the advantages at its command, did not become the initiator of what we know as the industrial revolution.

Eric Hobsbawm remarks somewhere that since the First World War was not avoided there is no point in disputing whether it could have been. Avoidance of the conflagration was certainly one of the potential outcomes of the 1914 crisis, but it was not the one that was realised. A similar approach needs to be taken with the question of which society could have initiated the industrialisation process driven by artificial power sources. There can be no doubt that Imperial China had a perfectly adequate preindustrial economic potential and financial instruments to accomplish, had its elites wished, what the western European ones, particularly Great Britain, did in the late eighteenth and early nineteenth century – but they did not. The reasons for this disparity may be in practice now irrelevant, but nevertheless inquiring into it is unavoidable.

Two substantial considerations can be advanced. In the first place, during the era of preindustrial capitalism the empire's power, though covering a very extensive area of eastern Asia, did not reach around the globe in the manner of the European powers with their colonies and depots (known to the British at the time as 'factories'). It therefore did not have the enormous volume of resources thus acquired to risk investing in the doubtful new experimental technologies of steam power and railroads (railways do not appear in Hobson's index). It was western power not Chinese which looted the Americas and subsequently the Indian subcontinent and Indonesian archipelago, and generated enormous revenues by slave labour. The Celestial empire moreover had other calls on its resources.

The second significant obstacle was the empire's social structure, which remained 'feudal' in the broadest sense, founded upon a depressed peasantry in an essentially tributary relationship to local landlords and the state. China certainly had a large cadre of merchants and dealers, indeed what could be appropriately identified as a merchant class. But they were not a capitalist class in the sense that they took command of production, had access to a reserve of proletarianised labourers, and invested in technological devices to drive accumulation forward. The conclusion of the encyclopaedic Joseph Needham,[22] the incomparable western expert on all matters of Chinese science and society, appears to be the most convincing diagnosis. He argues that China's advance to what became the Western mode of production was stalled by the fact that its society and government were in the grip of a Confucian[23] elite of authoritarian bureaucrats who were in a position never to permit the emergence of an authentic capitalist class, particularly in agriculture, which would have been the essential foundation.

Assessment

To be sure, the first industrial revolution, the one which occurred in Britain, was dependent on an assembly of the contingencies listed above – favourable geography, natural endowments, greedy entrepreneurs, an available low-paid workforce, the plundered Atlantic and African resources, a friendly government, etc. Had any of them been absent the industrial revolution would not have happened, though capitalism might, albeit with reduced probability. It is essential to understand that for a take-off of mechanisation, and more especially the use of artificial power, to happen for the first time a very formidable hump has to be surmounted. In brief – such innovations have to be worthwhile to those projecting them, and only in the right conditions can they become so.

If a plentiful supply of low-wage labour is available new-fangled mechanisation may well not be worth the effort and expense. Handicraft employment may be cheaper, particularly if the handicraft workers are employed part-time and feed themselves from subsistence agriculture. The necessary incentive is simply not there. At the same time, factory production *also* requires an adequately numerous workforce plus an unemployed or underemployed reserve army of labour to keep wages satisfactorily low, not to mention market outlets for the product. In other words the balance has to be exactly right, not merely temporarily, but over the long term. A further obstacle is presented by governments eager for taxation revenue making the exercise unprofitable, or even being suspicious on principle, constantly aware of the social disruption likely to result from the new system. My own view is that the first industrial revolution could have occurred only where it did, for only in the British Isles were the conditions quite right for the process to begin. The 'success' was indeed contingent, but nowhere else were the contingencies appropriate.

Once started however, the process has built-in momentum in a number of dimensions. Other regimes, which want the products made available by the new technologies, especially the military ones, have no alternative but to play catch-up, and here the transformation, as occurred in Japan, is imposed by government from above rather than generated by lowly entrepreneurs from below. Internally too, competition between capitalists within and across frontiers forces each economic unit to constantly deepen and cheapen production by improved organisation and more advanced machinery rather than merely expand it through further employment of existing methods and technologies.

A famous text by Peter Laslett is called, with reference to the pre-modern centuries, *The World We Have Lost*. Much, indeed most of it, is well lost, although as Christopher Hill noted, 'we do not need to idealise "merrie England" to realise that much was lost by the disruption of the medieval village'. Such positive communal features as it possessed however were accompanied, as he points out, by grinding poverty and much else intolerable to a contemporary inhabitant of the consumer society. For good or ill, however, it is irrecoverably lost, and can never be reconstructed, at least not in any non-catastrophic manner.

The Twentieth Century

The innovative technologies of the second industrial revolution fitted together in a complex socio-economic structure. It was during the interwar years of the twentieth century when, in spite of the great depression, these technologies, together with spinoffs such as cinema, the beginnings of television and the first plastics, fully came into their own as the foundation of full-blown consumer societies, and were continued with growing intensity and improvement into the industrial societies of the postwar world. In that world they were joined by the spread of electronic technologies, themselves dependent of course in one way or another on the use of electric current, as are virtually all technologies of the contemporary era.

Computers were first used for military purposes during the Second World War for code breaking and in the Manhattan Project for the manufacture of the first atomic bombs. That use, as very large apparatuses, continued into the subsequent decade, as well as for control mechanisms in nuclear power stations; while in the 1960s and 70s they were also applied to industrial purposes (it was known at the time as automation) and to space flight. Their true revolutionary impact began in the 1980s with the introduction of the personal computer, which in the past quarter-century has grown exponentially, alongside a process of continuous min-iaturisation and the creation of the worldwide web. It has happened to the extent that I often feel that I'm living in a science fiction universe,[24] and when I hear the usage statistics of the latest computer equipment and digital media platforms, start thinking I'm a proper Luddite (or at least what the Luddites were reputed to be).

Technologies however, central though they are, form only part of the story. Nor do they have an independent existence, their place in the fabric of history depends upon the manner in which and the purposes for which they are used. Moreover they, like everything else, are subject to the demands of the market economy, of which the dot-com bubble at the turn of the century was an outstanding example but by no means the first.

The destructive force of nineteenth-century military technology had been exhibited properly for the first time in the American Civil War, and subsequently in the employment of the early machine guns against lightly armed colonial populations foolishly unwilling to be 'civilised' by humanitarian western armies or to be drawn into the delights of the capitalist universe. However the next two significant wars, the Franco-German and the South African were not very prolonged, new technologies were denied the opportunity to realise their full destructive potential, and lessons in this respect were forgotten. The ferocious Balkan Wars of 1912–13 gave more of a hint of what was to come.

The Great War of 1914–18 brought it home all too bloodily and the Russian Civil War of 1918–20 underlined it emphatically. The annihilatory power of technology applied to destructive purposes reached further heights during the years 1939–45 after having been well tested throughout the decade of the thirties in China, Ethiopia and Spain. With the creation of nuclear weaponry in 1945 and its expansion thereafter in the possession of mutually hostile regimes, the prospect of planetary destruction was offered and very nearly accomplished.[25]

This particular sequence of events was not an autonomous process. The world-shattering impact of the First World War was not *directly* due to economic and colonial rivalries, a contest for the economic division of the world – although the industrial and landowning elites of Imperial Germany certainly aspired to achieve that on a European scale. It owed its origins to the collision of industrial capitalist powers (including even Imperial Russia for all its economic backwardness) each of which was ready for war if it believed its vital interests, certainly economic ones at root, were seriously threatened.

The responsibility of the war and subsequent political upheavals for the crash which overtook the global economy at their conclusion is a disputed area. Certainly the war, by bankrupting the western powers engaged in it as well as giving the Bolsheviks the opportunity to take power in the Russian empire, disrupted the prewar system based on the pound sterling and so propelled the USA into the position of economic hegemon. There is however an argument that the great depression of the interwar years and the nadir of the collapse between 1929 and 1932 were due to deeper processes of economic development, essentially imbalance between raw material producers and industrialised economies, and that the war was only an ancillary factor.

Be that as it may, the world slump and its impact upon Germany were directly responsible for enabling Hitler's seizure of power in that country, without which there would have been no Second World War, at least in the form it actually took, and without that the world's history in the second half of the century would have been markedly different.

The communist parties of the time were convinced that the depression marked the final crisis of capitalism, and they may not have been so wrong as subsequently it appeared. In spite of a weak and petering out recovery in the late 1930s there was no realistic prospect at that point that the depression was likely to lift. What pulled the US and the capitalist world economy out of depression was the Second World War and the subsequent Cold War, creating an enormous level of demand and government willingness to supply it – military in the first instance but with all manner of knock-on effects. What would have been the social and political outcome had the depression continued indefinitely (as its present-day successor appears to be doing) is anybody's guess.

Central to this development was the power of the US empire and the elites which control it. Their global hegemony, economic, political, military and incidentally cultural, was a deliberate and carefully planned long-term project, as was destruction of their communist rival. According to Perry Anderson, 'All [US geopolitical and other advantages] could be, and were, synthesised into an imperial ideology commanding popular consensus . . . at home and power of attraction . . . abroad'.[26] If necessary military force would be applied, as it had been continuously in Latin America during the nineteenth and earlier twentieth centuries.[27] The notion that US values would come to dominate world society had been voiced from the very earliest years of the republic, so that 'For all its scope and intensity the Cold War was . . . "merely a subplot" within the larger history of global domination', 'the construction of a liberal international order with America at its head'.[28] With the project apparently accomplished, its apparent success was the occasion of Francis Fukuyama's celebration in 1992 of the 'end of history'.[29]

However history in the event has not taken very long to come back to life. To quote Anderson once more:

> The institutions and acquisitions, ideologies and reflexes bequeathed by the battle against communism now constituted a massive historical complex with its own dynamics, no longer needing to be driven by the threat from the Soviet Union. . . . The Cold War was over, but a gendarme's day is never done. More armed expeditions followed than ever before; more advanced weapons were rolled out; more bases were added to the chain; more far-reaching doctrines of intervention developed. There could be no looking back.[30]

14

No Such Thing as a Free Lunch: Trade-Offs, Opportunity Cost and the Dynamic of Unintended Consequences

This chapter, in some respects a summing-up of the discussion so far, is concerned with the reality that in numerous different contexts both in organic nature and more especially in human affairs, scarcities of various sorts and structural limitations force a trade-off between purposes and possibilities, and that unintended consequences are intrinsic to any form of praxis. On occasion these can be beneficial, but in historical experience unwelcome ones have tended to make the greater impact.

The Biological Foundation

The reality of trade-off is something that all of organic life is subject to – partly it is a matter of energy conservation and partly of opportunity cost. Since both body and brain are not so much stable objects but more in reality dynamic systems, evolutionary development in one direction is bought at the expense of its restriction in another. Additionally, the more complex an organism's descendants become the more opportunity exists for their malfunction (as with any mechanism) and the more likely it becomes that malfunction will occur. The simplest of organisms, archaea and bacteria, are already molecularly complex, and the eukaryotic cells which constitute many unicellular and all multicellular organisms, while still microscopic, are many times larger and much more complex still.

When the eukaryotic domain divided between the plant, the fungal and the animal kingdoms a billion or so years ago, the former two, speaking metaphorically, opted to remain in fixed locations (as do some invertebrate animals such as sponges, corals and sea anemones) and let their nutrition come to them. There are of course certain advantages in this feeding strategy – they do not have to go and search for food, and as for sexual reproduction, which has evolved in both plant and animal kingdoms, they let the wind, the water or insects do the job for them. The price of this however is that they have 'sacrificed' the nervous systems and structured sensory apparatuses which distinguish the animal kingdom. Such equipment would be useless, indeed an inconvenience, to an immobile organism such as a plant, while it is essential to a mobile one that has to seek out food sources and sexual partners.

In the animal kingdom such trade-offs are very numerous. The descendants of sighted animals which have adopted a lifestyle in conditions of total darkness, such as certain fish in underground lakes, lose their visual sense. Brains, marvellous organs that they are, nevertheless have limits to their capacity, and evolution, concentrating on the development of senses appropriate to a totally dark environment, will do so at the expense of visual ability. Even in less definite circumstances, bats enjoy proverbially poor vision – their evolutionary development of echolocation has been at its expense. The ancestors of whales and dolphins were land-dwelling animals but in their case evolution has produced a shape (and in the case of large whales, weight) appropriate to an aquatic environment, which does not include legs capable of terrestrial locomotion. A vertebrate which employs its forelimbs for walking can also, depending on its anatomy, use them to a limited extent for other purposes, but if it uses them in order to fly it cannot. Insects which have both legs and wings, are inherently limited in size and weight.

The giant panda is an instructive example of the trade-off of merits and disadvantages in evolutionary development. Its ancestors were carnivores or omnivores, but in the wild its diet consists 99 per cent of bamboo. This has consequences for its digestive apparatus, since that has not kept evolutionary pace and it has to eat enormous quantities of bamboo to gain adequate nutrition (though it is still capable of eating carnivorously) and tends to be afflicted with lassitude, which may go some way to explaining its reluctance to mate. Presumably its ancestors must have taken to the vegetarian diet since that was at the time much easier to obtain than by hunting small animals. The downside is that the species became dependent on a single food source, and with the shrinkage of the lowland bamboo forests through human activity, remains a highly endangered species.

Human Anatomy

The human anatomy is also an instructive example of such evolutionary trade-offs. Evolution has concentrated here on developing the proportionately largest and most magnificent brain in the animal kingdom, with all its amazing capacities, but, as with cetaceans, if less dramatically, this has come at significant physical expense.

As noted earlier, *H. sapiens* is the only habitually bipedal living mammal, and that, especially in combination with its huge and splendid brain, evidently has splendid advantages. For a ground-dwelling species with a short neck it greatly improves the visual range. Even more importantly, it frees up the forelimbs for all the manner of operations made possible by the opposable thumb. There is also a lesser-known and rather surprising advantage – humans are the champion long-distance runners of the mammalian class. Practically any four-legged animal can easily outpace a human over short distances, but suitably experienced humans can run down any of them to exhaustion. Hunter-gatherer societies made use of use this technique to overtake and kill their quarry.

There is however an analogy with the panda's digestive system. Essential parts of the human anatomy, especially the circulatory system, have not kept evolutionary pace with our upright stance. The consequence is not lethal, but it is uncomfortable – often resulting in haemorrhoids and varicose veins. Hernias too are an unfortunate and more dangerous side-effect of bipedalism.

There is another area where evolution certainly has kept pace, but again with very significant trade-off consequences. Of all the great apes humans are by far the most puny. Compared with chimpanzees, orang-utans, or even large monkeys such as baboons, not to speak of gorillas, humans are physically contemptible. Any other ape could rip apart even the strongest of humans, with no problem. Evolution here, by concentrating on brain power, has had to sacrifice physique – the human brain monopolises 20–25 per cent of our metabolism and requires, proportionately, huge energy inputs. Nor is this the end of the matter. To accommodate the magnificent brain the human face has had to shrink and lose the powerful jaw muscles that other apes possess. Along with that have gone the impressive teeth, especially the great canines, the useful defensive equipment that were our remote ancestors' endowment.

Humans are not quite the potentially longest-lived of mammals, but they stand very near the top and outclass any other primate. For any animal, longevity may be considered good fortune, but it is not without its disadvantages. Old age, as the epigram has it, does not come singly. Anatomy and function both deteriorate with the years. If the animal is a predator it will lose its hunting ability and die of starvation, if it belongs to a prey species it will be singled out by the predators. Vegetarian mammals such as elephants and gorillas, which may be so big and powerful as to have no natural enemies – and humans who also, for different reasons – are in the same position: if they avoid death by accident, infection or violence, they nonetheless fall victim to degenerative diseases. For humans that most often means (there are a few exceptional cases) serious deterioration in the brain. Brains do not come cheap; they are metabolically expensive, though their advantages outweigh their shortcomings, otherwise that evolutionary process would not have occurred. Less generally considered is what evolutionary *disadvantage* might there be in possessing a unique consciousness and a self-consciousness, such as humans do?

A number of answers can be suggested. With this kind of consciousness comes the ability to suffer and to be keenly self-aware of suffering, and humankind has certainly done plenty of that throughout the aeons. 'Man was made to mourn as the sparks fly upward.' Here the dialectic is at its harshest and constitutes the greatest of all trade-offs.

Consider also the evolutionary advantage of a disposition to respond to false positives noted in Chapter One. Useful in the Palaeolithic, however in the context of settled living and socially differentiated communities, the night-time shadow becomes a malignant ghost, coincidental incidents lead to the identification of witches or possessors of the evil eye; ill-treatment by the member of a particular ethnicity brings condemnation of all the members of that group. Random visual differences appear to take on a coherent shape – the tendency to see faces when there is no justification to do so, for example the Virgin Mary in the clouds or Jesus Christ in Martian rocks.

Unintended Consequences

These biological realities have in common the fact that they are all involuntary manifestations, necessary consequences of the organisms' natural constitution, including the human one. Human activity, however, resulting from conscious choice (leaving aside implausible theories that no such thing actually exists) in short the dimension of culture, raises this interaction to a new level.

The controlled use of fire, which, as stressed earlier, marks the dividing line between nature and culture, introduced the dialectic of unintended consequences. The fire which warms and makes possible the habitation of previously over-inclement environments, which processes foodstuffs and makes them both more palatable and safer to eat, which repels animal predators, can also kill and injure, and very painfully at that. So can domesticated wolves, otherwise known as dogs. Despite being invaluable assistants to humans in all manner of enterprises from hunting to herding to guarding there is the ever-present possibility that a large one can resume its ancestors' wolfish habits, turn vicious and deadly. At a later stage of development, domesticated cattle, especially but not exclusively uncastrated male ones, may demonstrate lethal hostility.

Human settlement and congregation around eight thousand years BCE raises the stakes still further. As suggested earlier, this crowded new environment provides marvellous opportunities for invertebrate parasites, as well as vertebrate scavengers such as rats, to spread and flourish, bringing with them a range of lethal micro-organisms, while dependence on plant cultivation necessarily involves the danger of crop failure from drought, fungal blight, or swarming locusts delighted to encounter such munificence.

Though organic evolution has no specific direction – its character is better illustrated as a rounded bush rather than as a pyramid-shaped conifer with humans at the top like a Christmas tree angel – one branch of it, no doubt contingently as we have stressed, has been a trend of expanding and intensifying brainpower. Once the process got started one thing led to another.

Ain't Technology Wonderful?

By analogy, human history has been one of growing technological sophistication, with the improvements tending to shift from location to location and from culture to culture. The most significant of these have been covered in previous chapters. As civil organisation and technology advanced, so did military, increasing in destructiveness as the centuries passed. Less sophisticated weaponry could be as lethal and destructive as the most advanced, but required greater manpower to get the same results in terms of generalised slaughter. In economic terms, the former's productivity was lower. The Romans' great success in conquest and imperial control within the Mediterranean basin and beyond, was due above all to their military organisation, the highly developed, virtually industrial supply system to their legions and not least their very advanced and effective siege engines, bridge construction and road building techniques.[1]

The successful dynastic empires of the following centuries everywhere in Eurasia extended their borders by similar methods, and the Chinese ones were masters of the technique. They made only very limited use for military purposes of the explosives invented there as early as the ninth century CE – which provokes further intriguing speculation. Plenty of available manpower may have made it seem scarcely worthwhile to develop a new technological line, and anyway the culture was, except in technology and the economy a very conservative and traditional one. The early Ottoman sultans, less well supplied with population and less constrained by tradition, did resort to widespread use of explosives, especially for siege purposes. And so it has gone on, up to the twentieth century and the appearance of nuclear weapons.

The essential point is that the dialectic of technological advance could as readily be applied to death and annihilation as to Francis Bacon's project to 'improve man's estate' by scientific endeavour. During the Renaissance Leonardo was as ardently devoted to perfecting the instruments of death as he was to civic invention, anatomical and other research or artistic accomplishment. Even civil ingenuity could be turned in lethal directions; the pioneers of nuclear physics certainly did not expect a military application, and a large number of them objected strongly to this. Though centuries earlier the very notion of flying machines had been regarded with horror, later inventors were less reticent.[2]

The visionaries of gravity-defying rocket engines did not think in destructive terms, though rocketry as such had been used for military purposes since the medieval era. Their attention was concentrated on the then seemingly innocuous and unrealistic projects of eventual space flight and orbiting satellites. They could not have anticipated the use of the latter for military observation. Any computing device that could solve mathematical problems might have potential military applications, but the earlier attempts, of which there were many, were not developed with that in mind. The dialectic of unintended consequences was powerfully active in these instances.

Military devices are invented and developed with the deliberate purpose of killing people and obliterating structures – they are intentional not unintended consequences; but most commonly the science, expertise and technology which lies behind them were not first intended to be used in that manner. They could reasonably be said to be the unintended consequence of technological development in general. Many adverse consequences of human praxis however are not at all related to military considerations, or only related at second or third hand.

Perils of Progress

The perils of shift from a foraging to a settled lifestyle are noted above. In these, generally speaking, there is not a great deal of change from the Neolithic, or at least from the emergence of city states, to the eve of modernity – apart from the appearance in history of the supernatural ideologies discussed in a previous chapter. These could certainly make a grim domestic, social and civic life a great deal grimmer for individuals, multiplying restrictions and obligations and making them more onerous and intrusive than had previously been the case, even if the respective faiths suggested that if these rules were observed the believer could hope for a more congenial afterlife.

The economic revolution which accelerated from the seventeenth century CE onwards grievously multiplied the occasions for grief among increasingly numerous and diverse populations. We can in this instance divide the dialectic of unintended consequences into two overlapping categories. The first and smaller category consists of those consequences which genuinely escaped from deliberate human intention and direction but were by-products of the system. The further destitution and possible starvation of populations and their dependants through shifts in the trade cycle when their life-support consisted of wage payments is one instance. Another is the insanitary conditions of urban living at the time in market societies which bred squalor and disease, together with the appearance in the nineteenth century of pandemics of a previously localised new plague, cholera, as well as an array of new industrial diseases.

Overlapping between the intended and the unintended are the ailments caused by the widespread adulteration of commercially provided foodstuffs, and the large-scale dependence in Europe and the USA on the opium-based analgesic, soporific and pacifier, laudanum. The suppliers of these products did not intend their purchasers to die from ingesting them but they often did in any case. Similarly the absentee landowners of Irish estates who forced their tenants onto shrinking plots of land and to a diet based exclusively on potatoes, did not actually intend to kill them (though some, regarding Ireland as overpopulated, welcomed the outcome) but when the potato blight struck that result was inevitable.

Parallel occurrences on a planetary scale characterised the early modern and modern practices of colonialism. In some instances the genocide and extermination of indigenous populations was no unintended consequence but an intentional and deliberate policy – the Native Americans in North America and the aboriginal population of Australia are examples. US presidents such as Andrew Jackson,

Ulysses Grant and Theodore Roosevelt even boasted about it. However in many other cases it resulted from the unforeseen results of colonial practice.

The Spanish and Portuguese conquistadors of Central and South America did not set out with the intention of bringing about the massive death toll of their imperialism – they preferred to convert and/or enslave the indigenous populations, but starvation and disease resulting from their treatment & the infections they brought with them, together with deliberate slaughter of resisters, had that result.

The late Victorian holocausts examined by Mike Davis were, again, not deliberate results of exterminatory policies, but due to the combination of colonial economic and social policies and climatic disturbance resulting in floods and droughts occasioned by shifts in the el Nino and el Nina ocean currents. Contrawise, the pandemic of syphilis in early modern Europe, particularly during the sixteenth century, is generally attributed to a strain of the relevant bacterium brought to Europe by men returning from the Americas, an infection which the indigenous Native Americans were adapted to but to which other ethnicities were entirely vulnerable.[3] If the New World hypothesis is correct (medical consensus supports it) that was certainly an unintended consequence of a particularly dramatic sort.

These are specific examples of this chapter's theme. Any general perspective on how unintended consequences are part of the fabric of history shows that they are indeed a fundamental part of its pattern – what was advantageous in one situation turns into a menace when times change or are changed. So far as it is possible to speak about a fundamental human project across the millennia that project could be defined as the struggle to escape from nature or to substitute culture for nature, to combat the natural afflictions that characterised the existence of our hominin ancestors, *H. sapiens* and its predecessors – cold, wet, unreliable food source, parasites, predators, early death. Every solution led on to further ambitions and every solution brought with it unforeseen problems. Humans are social animals, and all endeavours to escape from the biological consequences of being human had to be conducted in a social and hierarchical context, for even in a forager society hierarchy exists (and almost certainly did so too in the Palaeolithic) albeit to a limited degree.

Settlement brings with it, as I have emphasised, vulnerability to infestations of viruses, bacteria and parasites to a much greater degree than in hunter-gatherer environments. With it too hierarchy evolves into class division, which means the forcible acquisition of the labour of one portion of society by another one. Misogyny becomes entrenched. Expanded population and class division offers the temptation to find victims for human sacrifice (or to capture them from other communities) in order to propitiate the gods invented to control nature in a manner beyond human powers. Urbanisation and its consequences expands and greatly intensifies the character of such relationships. Evidently no such outcomes were intended by the original communities which pioneered sedentary lifestyles, whether in Eurasia, Africa or the Americas.

Very generally, effective techniques were imbricated with superstitious irrelevancies. Study of the stars can have practical uses for direction-finding purposes, and even in some cases to predict natural events such as when the Nile was due to flood. However their movements, especially if the heavenly bodies are regarded as gods, can by extension be assumed to have implication for human destinies and thereby give rise to astrological superstition. Humans are all too readily tempted to look for patterns in nature which they hope might be capable of predicting events in an uncertain and perilous future. In literate, and presumably pre-literate, cultures other methods of fortune-telling even more absurd than astrology quickly proliferated.

Medicine

Disease, injury, and more minor sorts of ailment are an ever-present reality. Folk medicine and herbal remedies had a certain limited efficacy. When they were consolidated as medical science, along with quasi-scientific studies of anatomy and physiology made by such intellects as Hippocrates, Aristotle and Galen, then some degree of relief could be offered to the sufferer – although the placebo effect cannot be overlooked. However the establishment of a medical profession was by no means an unmixed blessing, as sacrifice, devotion and prayer remained part of the treatment and all manner of useless or noxious remedies got included in the prescriptions.[4]

The situation was little improved by the establishment of hospitals for the sick in subsequent centuries, for these institutions themselves became vectors for the further spread of disease. It was remarked that anyone who entered an English hospital as a patient in the eighteenth century was comparatively fortunate to die of the same ailment as they had been admitted with and not one contracted in the hospital. The medical profession, before the late nineteenth century at the earliest, probably killed more people than would have died without treatment. The one great success, though not an unproblematic one, was vaccination against smallpox.

Even in subsequent decades, when thanks to Hunter, Pasteur, Koch, Simpson, Lister, and the developments which put medicine on a fully scientific basis, the dialectic of unintended consequences was at work. Some developments, such as antiseptics and anaesthetics were almost entirely benign (though misapplication of the latter occasionally killed or brain-damaged a patient) and the ability to treat appendicitis with surgery certainly saved many lives. The extension of vaccination beyond smallpox to inoculation against such ailments as diphtheria (formerly a major infantile killer) and polio (formerly a major infantile physical disabler) were almost (though not quite) unqualified successes, for inoculations could go wrong.

Antibiotics however were a different story. When they first began to be used in the 1940s they appeared as practically a magic wand to treat all manner of previously untreatable or very difficult ailments – sexually transmitted diseases, tuberculosis,[5] pneumonia for example. The unintended consequences emerged in the 1960s when the accidental microbial evolution which the antibiotics had generated, resulted in the appearance of superbugs immune to previously effective doses of antibiotics and eventually entirely immune to the antibiotic which had worked so superbly in the first place. Only one major plague, smallpox, has been entirely eradicated. Malaria still continues to flourish and reservoirs still remain of all the other principal killers, tuberculosis, syphilis, influenza, even bubonic plague.

The British Museum has exhibited a display of the different drugs in capsule form produced by the pharmaceutical industry. The viewer could only marvel at the astounding and mind-bending quantity and variety of these drugs, which laid out on a flat surface, roughly a metre broad, extended for several metres down the room. Undoubtedly these chemical agents have many merits and have eased the conditions of life and saved the lives of innumerable individuals but they can also be the agents of catastrophe, most notoriously with the thalidomide episode.[6] The advancement of medical expertise in general also has its dialectic. One consequence is that people can be forcibly kept alive when they no longer want to be on account of age or injury, and in circumstances in which they would naturally have died. Also, it is a sad reality that doctors can perform as very efficient torturers if willing to submit to the demands of tyrannical regimes. Nevertheless, hardly anyone would wish to forego the benefits of medical science in all its dimensions, but the negatives also have to be kept in mind.

Dangerous Innovations

An interaction of a not altogether dissimilar kind relates to agricultural science and practice, and also has a number of dimensions. Deforestation can render large areas infertile by destroying the rainfall retention and windbreak functions that tree cover can provide. The overuse of fertilisers, especially inorganic ones, but even organic ones as well, can seriously damage the soil. Equally notorious is the temptingly excessive application of pesticides and herbicides, which, like antibiotics, provoke evolutionary development in their targets so that the pests and the weeds emerge more resistant and vigorous than ever. Genetically modified crops doubtless have their advantages, and there is no evidence so far that they are unsafe to eat, but these considerations omit the question of the impact they are likely to have on the soil and other forms of plant and insect life.

In the fields of engineering and fuel supply, nuclear energy appeared to be the answer to numerous prayers. Indeed in the 1950s the movement in opposition to nuclear weapons used to stress the slogan of 'atoms for peace'. What was not taken to account then, or among the advocates of nuclear energy today, were the consequences of the inevitable calamities in nuclear power plants and the permanent problem of disposing of accumulations of nuclear waste that remain radioactive for hundreds of thousands or even millions of years. Also in the engineering context, civil aviation had inestimable advantages and is overall a very safe form of transport, but nevertheless has killed a large number of people.

Market Forces

What these forms of dialectic have in common is that they are driven by market forces (though, to be sure, their publicly owned equivalents in the Soviet bloc did little better) and the aim of their producers is to boost sales and profits and dodge regulation so far as possible.

This leads us on to the dialectic of market forces. Marx begins his first volume of *Capital* with an analysis of the commodity form. A commodity in his terminology is an article produced for sale to satisfy the purchaser whether in the brain or in the belly as he expresses it, in other words to bring either material or mental satisfaction to the purchaser. He had no reason to analyse at that point why purchasers should want to obtain commodities beyond the basic needs of bodily existence (which are certainly considerable), but the initial reason is not far to seek. It is, again, to directly or indirectly put as much distance as possible between the natural existence of the individuals involved in the transaction and the one they hope to enjoy by making the purchase.

Markets have of course existed since time immemorial – they probably existed in a rudimentary form even in the Palaeolithic in relations between forager bands – and are a powerful engine of productive growth and development and of social change. In subsequent millennia they have constantly expanded on a global scale and brought within their scope multiplying sectors of the economy in spite of wars, natural catastrophes and all species of disruptions. Of great importance though, and necessary to keep in mind, is that markets until at least the eighteenth century CE were governmentally controlled, as indeed many still are – and it was a universal consensus that they should be controlled, contrary to the ideological propaganda and widespread assumptions of subsequent decades.

The market too is subject to the dialectic, and the vision of the ideological proponents of the market freed from governmental regulation and interference was far different from the reality that emerged from the decoupling of this relationship. The earlier consensual acceptance of market regulation by authority rested upon two foundations, one from the side of the rulers and the other from the feeling of the ruled.

In the first instance it was agreed, most famously by the seventeenth- and eighteenth-century mercantilists, that government intervention was required both to serve the national interest by keeping the various sectors of the economic system in harmonious balance (mainly for the rulers' benefit of course) and to aggressively promote the nation's trade (which at the time included trade in slaves) at the expense of commercial rivals. The Navigation Acts passed by English governments are a good example of this. They aimed to promote English shipping by compelling merchants to trade only in English vessels or those of the immediate trading partner, and so cut out middlemen (especially the Dutch) in the carrying trade. There was however exception taken to domestic monopolies formerly sold by the monarchy to royal favourites for the purpose of raising revenue, and these were abolished by Cromwell's regime and not reinstated after its collapse. However monopolies for certain areas of foreign trade, especially with south and eastern Asia, remained acceptable.

The second foundation was the popular demand that governments should intervene to address food shortages in particular areas, especially of grain, by means of price controls to discourage movements of grain from the affected area and to prevent merchants from taking advantage of shortages by raising prices to the degree of putting foodstuffs out of the reach of the poor. This was what E P Thompson designated as the eighteenth-century moral economy, and it was exemplified by food rioters who expropriated grain stores (usually in transit) but instead of simply stealing them sold the commodity at what was regarded as a fair price.

Ideologists

The ideologists of free trade disputed these assumptions. Adam Smith, who was primarily a philosopher rather than an economist, was no admirer of businessmen, contrary to the twentieth-century ideologists who argued in his name. His presumption was that merchants, traders and owners of manufacturing establishments were swindlers by nature and would cheat the public whenever opportunity offered. The cure for that, however, was not government regulation, but a free competitive market, so that these same merchants, traders and owners of manufacturing establishments would be compelled in their own interest to also serve the public interest with low prices and good quality goods, or risk losing business when their customers went elsewhere.

The argument was extended. Competitive pressure would also promote innovation and much improved organisation of production (Smith did not foresee the industrial revolution, he assumed natural power sources), resulting in greatly enhanced public prosperity from which everyone would benefit. A free market in grain would not result in shortage and starvation but instead induce progressive farmers and landowners to expand their output, and the outcome would be cheaper bread (which would also enable wages to be reduced).

This would particularly be the case if the argument was also applied to foreign trade. Free markets here would result, as the title of his magnum opus implied, in great enhancement of the wealth of nations. Welcome as that would be, the benefits would be even greater. Such a policy would promote universal peace, as nations linked by commerce, where each concentrated on producing the commodities which it was naturally best fitted to produce, known as comparative advantage, would never go to war with each other. In short, the spokespeople for the free market had beneficent, not malevolent intentions and outcomes in mind. In Smith's time government obstruction undoubtedly was an especially relevant obstacle to increasing production. It was not the fault of these theorists that the acceptance of their prescriptions produced results of quite a different sort.

To the distress of some neoliberal fundamentalists, markets totally free of government interference have never existed even at the peak of free trade ideology. Even during the second half of the nineteenth century when free trade was the reigning orthodoxy in the UK, the government not merely reserved to itself control over the coinage, as all governments do, but also strictly regulated paper money though not directly responsible for its issue, which was the province of banks. It also extensively regulated the privately-owned railway system and did not reject the possible option of taking it into public ownership if the railway companies failed to fulfil their purpose.[7]

The economic affairs of British colonies were controlled much more severely – and in India the regime even copied one of the most hated institutions of the French *ancien régime*, prohibiting even private individuals from producing salt (such as by evaporating seawater) so that the Indian government enjoyed a total monopoly.[8] By that time international trade in the UK was mostly open to all competitors with few restrictions and only light customs duties, but other states, particularly the German empire and the US, operated restrictive tariff policies. Moreover, in every manner of enterprise, commercial, financial, agrarian, or industrial, free competition where it existed inevitably evolved into monopolistic or oligopolistic domination of the relevant economic sector as the more successful capitalists swallowed up the less.

Nevertheless, even taking these particulars into account, open markets with free competition became the bread and butter of modern western societies, and the results were spectacular. The industrial revolution was one of them, and far from lightening the burden of backbreaking toil it enhanced it immensely in industrial establishments and subjected infants along with adults to the disciplines of factory production mediated by the market. Pre-industrial cities were also filthy disease-ridden locations, but to that the early industrial ones added massive smoke and chemical pollution and new records in muck creation. In the realm of transport the branch of commerce concerned with insurance gave birth to the coffin ships, so overloaded that they were likely to sink even in less than severe weather, to the unconcern of the owners who collected the insurance on vessel and cargo.

With land transport, the railway certainly gave rise to many casualties through accidents on under-maintained lines when maintenance was scamped for the sake of profit, but that was comparatively minor stuff. The motor vehicle did not require malpractice on the part of manufacturers or salespersons (though there was plenty of that as well) to take on the role of an angel of death – ordinary human carelessness at the wheel or among pedestrians was perfectly adequate to produce massive death tolls across the decades. The market dialectic even fouled up the ostensible purpose of the innovation – speed of travel – above all in towns and cities, though by no means confined to these alone, owing to unmanageable traffic congestion caused by the multiplying number of private vehicles.

The immediate unintended consequences of market-driven, consumer-directed industrialisation are serious enough, but much worse could potentially be waiting to show itself. In brief, it threatens to wreck the planet by destruction of the rainforests, together with their carbon dioxide-absorbing capacity and their biodiversity, and by the release of trillions of tons of carbon dioxide and possibly methane as well, heating the planet precipitously. This causes the destruction of the plankton at the bottom of the oceanic food chain and has a resulting impact on marine life in general. Additional threats to the planet arise from the production of acid rain destroying terrestrial vegetation and from rises in sea levels through polar melting such as to not only drown coastal landscapes but disastrously affect wind and ocean current patterns.

Certainly global warming is proceeding now at a faster rate than at any time in the geologic record over the past quarter-billion years at least.[9] Even so, comparing it with past episodes, it will probably not render the planet uninhabitable in the manner of Venus or Mars, or even necessarily bring on the extermination of human life, but instead it is likely to kill billions and fit the survivors to re-experience all the horrors of pre-modern living.

Debt and Money in Modernity

Chapter Six has examined the role of debt relations in the pre-modern period. It was then of critical importance. In the era of modernity it has become even more so, particularly in the context of 'liquid resources', in other words money. The biblical pronouncement that 'the love of money is the root of all evil' is frequently rendered as 'money is the root of all evil'. The misrepresentation is significant. Both money and debt could be seen in their early days as convenient innovations lubricating social interaction, but soon thereafter and particularly in recent centuries they have assumed the character of alien forces holding struggling populations in their grip.

For some centuries, during what western historians define as the medieval era, coined money, although never unimportant, played a relatively subordinate role, but from the middle of the second millennium CE individuals, societies and states became increasingly, and thereafter wholly, dependent upon the shiny metal, as they remain to the present. Even without the international gold standard to adjust currencies, as used to be the case, the gold stored in Fort Knox is still the ultimate underpinning for the world's monetary system. Coinage also made debt easier to impose and manipulate. It was bad enough when you had to turn over part of your product to the lord or the monarch, it was worse when you first of all had to transform your tribute into coin. If for any reason money was difficult to acquire because of price fluctuation or other causes, you went deeper into debt and might have to hand over your daughter as security to be the superior's plaything or drudge until the debt was paid – if it ever could be.

It was the Anglo-Scottish state of the late seventeenth century[10] which finally devised an excellent solution to the dangers of bankruptcy into which states at that time were inclined to fall. That solution became intrinsic to the military-commercial success of the Anglo-Scottish state in the following century and rendered it the dominant global power, and which has since become standard practice for market-based states everywhere. This was, through the mechanism of a central bank, the institution of a regime of continuous borrowing and continuous debt repayment. The practice was rendered attractive by means of moderately profitable but rigorously guaranteed securities, 'gilt-edged stocks' in British parlance, to draw in the savings of investors all over the state's territory and even beyond. Graeber writes that,

> I have already pointed out that modern money is based on government debt, and that governments borrow money in order to finance wars. . . . The creation of central banks represented a permanent institutionalisation of that marriage between the interests of warriors and financiers that had already begun to merge in Renaissance Italy and that eventually became the foundation of finance capitalism.[11]

In the course of the past century debt has increasingly come to permeate the existence of ordinary citizens in industrialised societies. The main component of that has been, in the US and Britain, the increasing shift from house renting to house purchase ('house' in this instance including apartments of all sorts). That has meant incurring a very large debt to be repaid over a shorter or longer period. During the 'age of affluence' following the Second World War this form of debt was supplemented by the growing purchase of household utilities by means of deferred payment or 'hire-purchase' – or referred colloquially and tellingly as 'the never-never'. Following the onset of depression (politely termed 'recession') from the seventies into the present century, with intensified pressure upon wage-earners and trade unions, personal debt instead of decreasing did the exact opposite. It expanded as a substitute for the slower growth or even contraction in real incomes.

Thus the advantages of debt to governments, to creditors, to business and even sometimes to individual debtors as well, developed over the centuries until the entire structure came crashing down in the first decade of the twenty-first century – as it had in 1929. On the earlier occasion the details were different but the basic underlying reality was similar. Contrary to the expectations of the 1950s and 60s the historical dialectic of unintended consequences had not gone away and was at work once more.

The industrial economy of the contemporary world is founded upon debt as is the property market and even a very large proportion of everyday consumer expenditure. Organised violence is not absent from the equation even when no actual fighting is taking place, for the importance of the arms economy mentioned above though paid for in the long run by the taxes of the countries' citizens, is in the immediate event financed by borrowing, so that an enormous golden cascade flows via the Treasury into the accounts of the lenders, predominantly banks and financial institutions.

Political Developments

The historical dialectic applies not only to the material underpinnings of society and culture but to consciously directed intervention in the government of societies. The Athenians after their victory in the Persian wars established an Aegean commercial empire to benefit themselves, and it did benefit them – the surviving cultural treasures that we know today, from the Parthenon to artworks in different media, were largely financed by that exploitation. However this empire also raised up deep opposition among the subjected cities and led eventually to the Athenians' own ruin. Two thousand years later the English king Henry VIII took a decision to debase the coinage, an act which put rockets under the already embarrassing monetary inflation of his reign. Henry died in good time to escape the consequences of his policies – it was his successor Charles I who experienced them.

To continue on that theme – when the respectable English parliamentarians of 1642 took the reluctant and awesome step to confront their monarch in arms for limited objectives, the last thing they expected was that they themselves would in due course be shoved aside by the army radicals and that the monarch have his head cut off. Charles's son, restored to the throne in 1660, would have been in a position when he died in 1685 to congratulate himself that he had, despite some very bad moments, successfully relaid the foundations of absolute monarchy. He could not know that his very success would be responsible for the overthrow of his dynasty and of absolute monarchy in the British Isles. The execution of the Irish rebel leaders after the Easter Rising in 1916 was intended to ensure that the independence movement would be permanently crushed – instead it was responsible for its ultimate success. Before the aftermath of the Rising independence was not a majority demand – devolution or Home Rule would have sufficed.

These are specific illustrations of how events might be said to have a will of their own and run beyond the intentions of those who set them in motion. Sometimes there are exceptions. The Dutch republic which emerged from the wars with the Spanish crown in the sixteenth/seventeenth centuries largely took the form which its inspirers intended; a bourgeois republic with a monarchical slant based on commerce and manufacturing, where power was safely concentrated in the hands of the wealthy burgher oligarchy. The American republic established in the 1780s after defeating the colonial power followed the Dutch example, and keeping more or less to the intended plan, prospered as a market-based, property-owning polity with the elites easily able to stay in control without any serious challenge from the lower levels of the society. The fact that, unlike the Dutch, they had an enormous continental territory to exploit helped very considerably (and would have done so even if the Spaniards had succeeded in holding on to the west and southwest of what is now the United States).

Any form of warfare is horrible beyond description – quite literally – for no description of a battlefield, whether verbal or visual, can convey what it smells like as dozens, hundreds or thousands of participants lie bathed in their blood with their guts torn out – and, in modern conditions of urban warfare, civilians as well. The American independence war of 1776–83, fought between opposing formal armies and with little non-combatant involvement, was probably as 'civilised' as armed conflict is capable of being (the Americans even showed sympathy for a condemned British spy): the equivalent Dutch war of the sixteenth century was certainly not. It included generalised massacre and execution accompanying the military engagements. What these revolutions had in common was that neither was aiming at the fundamental transformation of existing social structures, and thus could be supported, in both cases even militarily, by elites outside the specific conflict zone, English in the latter, French and Spanish in the former. However when significant challenges to the property basis of society appeared on the agenda, the dialectic of unintended consequences operated even more dramatically.

15

Social Critique

Class Society – Early Critiques

Before any critique of class society could be advanced certain preconditions were necessary. There had to be recognition that such an entity existed, that it contradicted the hopes and expectations of those who experienced their dissatisfaction not purely in personal or family terms but as part of a wider public; and that deficiencies existed in the very structures of social living.

The earliest known critique of this sort appears comparatively late in historical development, and the term 'appears' is stressed – for with literacy confined to the elite levels of society which benefited from the existence of class structures, no such critique, if it had existed, was likely to have left any written record. However the fact that not even elite attacks on such views are found before, at the earliest, the middle of the second millennium BCE suggests that they were unknown in the pioneer literate civilisations. Grievances might generate revolts, even substantial ones, and palace coups, but these left the social foundations untouched. If they succeeded the most they did was to replace one set of rulers with another who continued except in details to rule as before.

When critiques of class relations did emerge, inevitably they were cast in religious terms and looked to divine assistance to achieve their objectives. Zoroaster's 'making wonderful' was the first of which a record has survived (albeit only partially). In these writings the defects of the class society of the day were attributed along with other inflictions to an evil spirit locked in permanent conflict with his opposite number representing the desirable conditions which his followers were expected to inherit.

Later religious critiques of society (which of course would not have for an instant recognised themselves in that description) followed along similar lines, and continued to do so for more than two millennia, while a favourite stratagem of the powers-that-be was to incorporate the oppositional faith into the official pantheon in order to defuse its revolutionary charge. That, as noted above, was to be the fate of Zoroastrianism, in the form of Zurvanism, and later of Christianity as well.

Apocalypses

In the second half of the first millennium BCE the Jewish kingdoms and their inhabitants were subjected to foreign powers – Assyrian, Babylonian, Persian,

Greek and Roman, who had differing styles of rule (the Persian monarchs were particularly indulgent) but each was in every case hegemonic and exercised the final word regarding Jewish affairs. The Greek successors of Alexander the Great went further than the others and actually tried to destroy the religion. They had a measure of success until defeated by the Maccabean revolt, which naturally reinforced the religion's strength but generated its own subsequent contradictions and problems.

Out of these turmoils emerged the Jewish apocalypses, represented by some of the apocryphal texts or pseudepigrapha surviving as footnotes to the Christian bible. These include the Book of Enoch and the Book of Jubilees for example, with visions of a final overthrow and punishment of foreign oppressors and their hirelings, to be followed by a paradisial state of affairs where there would be material plenty for all believers in beautiful surroundings and total absence of oppression and conflict. As noted in Chapter Nine, at some point around 100 CE an adherent of the new faith produced a Christian version of the same, now termed the Book of Revelation, which foresaw apocalypse in even more fearsome terms than the earlier Jewish versions and promised, with gloating dwelling on mass death and catastrophe, the exact opposite to the promise incorporated in another canonical Christian text of 'peace on earth and goodwill towards men'.

In actual fact the contradiction only emerged once the Christian biblical canon (New Testament) was well established, for initially many church leaders distrusted Revelation's implied social message of ferocious punishment for rulers, and so argued against its inclusion. Bishop Eusebius, in Constantine's reign, the first historian of the Christian church, expressed serious doubt about its authenticity. However the rank and file of the movement loved it, for they naturally read into it their own discontents and resentments along with its promise of their ultimate good fortune when the apocalypse or last judgement finally occurred, which it was thought would not be long delayed.

These pressures, along with its claimed authorship by the apostle John (though the styles of the various writings attributed to this individual are very different) resulted in its eventual acceptance, with the advantage of deferring settlement of social issues till the last judgement.[1] Not that the contents of this text were wholly original and altogether spun out of its writer's brain. The earliest Jewish followers of Jesus of Nazareth had certainly expected him, with divine assistance, to lead the overthrow of Roman power and institute a glorious new social order, and there is every reason to conclude that their rival gentile Christians recruited by Saul of Tarsus also foresaw an imminent end to the world. The author of the Revelation horror-story with a happy ending was undoubtedly drawing on these same traditions.

The suspicious bishops certainly had a point, for throughout the centuries thereafter this text was constantly mined for inspiration and morale by social radicals hoping to overthrow the constituted authorities of their day, and finding in the historical developments of their own time substantiation of Revelation's prophesies. This is a process which continues into our own century except that it is seldom or never social radicals who are now responsible but religiously motivated social reactionaries.

Even in past millennia the possibility of social transformation was envisaged not only by radicals speaking on behalf of the masses, but also social and political reactionaries aiming to serve the ends of the elites they spoke for. The most renowned of these was the Athenian aristocrat Plato in his best-known text, *The Republic*, motivated by the intense social struggles then raging within the Athenian community. The landowning elite detested and abhorred the fact that they had to operate within the framework of the Athenian democracy, limited though it was. Plato envisaged a city in which the most able members of his class – ability in this version consisted in understanding philosophical abstractions – would enjoy unlimited authority over everyone else in a three-level system of caste stratification with some flexibility of movement between the castes. Of course the top-level 'guardians' in this concept would be committed to ruling for the public good, not their own personal advantage. Subsequent social reactionaries, most notably the Roman Cicero, picked up on these notions, discussed and developed them, but in the changed circumstances of their times treated them as speculative and admirable ideals rather than as practical recipes for government.

Religious Rebelliousness

When Christianity, from 312 CE onwards ceased to be an oppositional movement in any sense and instead became part of the governmental machinery of the Roman state, the contradiction between its future vision and its present circumstances became particularly acute. Oppositional 'heretical' movements such as Donatists, Circumcellions and Montanists multiplied within the community. They adhered to the older ideology and imminent apocalyptic expectations, seeking martyrdom in order to hurry it up.

In the latter days of the western empire, the bishop of Hippo in North Africa, Augustine, also in his spare time a persecutor of the Donatists, devised a theology intended to resolve the contradictions. Drawing on his earlier Manichean beliefs, which hated and despised the material world, he propounded a doctrine of total human depravity brought on by disobedience in the Garden of Eden, with sexual sin as its consequence and emblem, and only redeemable through divine grace, sparingly doled out. The apocalypse was probably not imminent; it might be delayed for hundreds of thousands of years and until that far time social transformation was off the agenda and Christians duty-bound to obey both secular and religious authorities. Paradise was to bookend human history. It had been lost at its beginning and was to be regained at its conclusion, but between these events there could be no question that individuals' existence in the Christian scheme must be nothing but a vale of tears. The historian Ellen Meiksins Wood remarks that, '[Augustine] succeeded in arguing a brief for absolute obedience to even the most unchristian of worldly rulers'[2]

During the European medieval centuries, both in Europe and the Islamic world, not to mention the Indian subcontinent and China, there were endless religiously inspired or influenced popular rebellions and oppositional movements, but they did not envisage a new heaven and earth but rather a reversion to the imagined 'good old days', even if these good old days were in the far distant past. One such notion was exemplified in the concept of the 'Norman yoke',[3] which remained alive in English radical politics into the eighteenth century. Even more distant good old days might be envisaged, for example in the slogan of the English fourteenth-century rebellious peasants, 'When Adam delved and Eve span, who then was the gentleman?'

However in Europe from the time of the Reformation in the sixteenth century the pursuit of the millennium, to use Norman Cohn's phrase, was once again practical politics, most notably in the case of Thomas Müntzer, a leader in the German Peasant War which followed Luther's Reformation and which had a programme of radical social equality. John of Leiden was able, during the following decade, to take control of the city of Münster and institute a soon-suppressed Anabaptist[4] version of the new Jerusalem.[5] Similar ideas of a divinely-mandated overthrow of existing institutions emerged during the English revolution of 1640–60, its main proponents being the Quakers (a very different breed from their contemporary descendants), the Ranters and Muggletonians and the Fifth Monarchists (from their doctrine of five monarchies of which Christ's, imminently due, would be the final one). The Puritan emigrants to Massachusetts also intended to construct 'a city on a hill' with a drastically different religious regime from what prevailed in England – but did not propose any upset in property relations.

Property was likewise an institution whose basis the Enlightenment thinkers of the eighteenth century exempted from their far-reaching critique of contemporary institutions. The Enlightenment was no coherent programme but a very divided and contradictory climate in the thinking of eighteenth-century western European intelligentsia. By and large these thinkers, from Diderot, Condorcet and Voltaire in France, Hume and Smith in Scotland, Kant in Germany, to name only the most eminent, were devoted to the concept of progress – institutions and practices had, in Marx's words, 'to justify themselves at the bar of reason'. Reason was their guiding light and, though disagreeing on much, they wanted institutions reformed according to its dictates. They saw free commerce as the rational mode for economic affairs, but they did not challenge the institution of property as such, nor, on the whole, did they advocate upsetting existing political structures. They saw these instead, including absolute monarchy, as the instruments through which the reforms they advocated could be realised (for example the Austrian ruler Joseph II).

Jean-Jacques Rousseau was somewhat different, indeed there is disagreement over whether he should even be included among the Enlightenment figures. The foundation of his thinking was not so much reason as his idea of nature. Nor was he wedded to the notion of progress, arguing in an early essay that the triumph of culture over nature had been a disaster rather than a blessing for mankind. He was also intellectually at an angle to the other Enlightenment eminences in being, albeit somewhat ambiguously, a democrat, with his notion of the general will. Certainly he advocated a transformation of political institutions and educational practices, and was of the opinion that riches and poverty were both obstacles to virtue; his vision was of a moderately prosperous community of agriculturalists and artisans, avoiding extremes of wealth.

Challenge to Property

Issues of property and its consequences for the dispossessed became politically explosive in the early modern era in the aftermath of the last and greatest of what Robert Palmer has termed the 'Atlantic revolutions' of the late eighteenth century: the French Revolution of 1789–99, which also provided the most immediately dramatic example up to then of the dialectic of unintended consequences. Of course, as with the Dutch, English (more accurately British Isles) or American revolutions, nobody at the starting point intended that the process should assume widely lethal dimensions let alone become the mother of all subsequent revolutions – quite the contrary.

The process was set off by an inter-elite quarrel whose originators had reactionary aims in view and which Louis XVI tried to finesse by summoning the archaic feudal representative institution, the States General, redundant for almost two centuries, to the royal residence at Versailles. It quickly ran out of his control, as well as that of its upper elite constituents. Accompanied by upheavals in nearby Paris, it fundamentally altered the terms of French politics, bringing to the forefront a new breed of bourgeois politicians who soon sidelined the declassed aristocratic leaders they had initially accepted.

At the beginning all that was intended was the redress of widespread grievances, economic, social and cultural. When that was attempted however it profoundly disturbed the fundamental social structures. The consensual abolition of feudalism literally overnight (serfdom as such was already largely extinct) constituted an attack on property rights and privilege, giving rise to frenzied panic in the mind of the English reactionary Edmund Burke, who had formerly had no difficulty in ideologically supporting the American rebels. The social instability resulted from the fact that the opening scenes of the revolution had generated enormous hopes throughout the populace who had been afflicted for countless centuries by not only the material exactions of the monarchy and aristocratic elites but their arrogance and disdain as well.

Now they had thrown off these burdens (though still with a constitutional monarch and being expected to pay compensation to the nobility for their loss of feudal rights) they were citizens enjoying 'The Rights of Man', so why should there be any further problem? The revolution had succeeded splendidly in a matter of months – but popular aspirations once ignited could not be so readily contained. The bourgeois politicians now in command aspired to remodel French society according to Enlightenment principles, the masses to remodel it still further.

Democracy Militant

Before long what had been achieved was seen to be under threat from various directions: from unreconciled aristocrats plotting armed action with foreign aid to regain their privileges; from disruptions to the urban food supply consequent on the rural upheaval; from the financial straits of the successive revolutionary governments as the outrageously unfair taxation system, already in a thorough mess and requiring profound reform, disintegrated. The king tried unsuccessfully to flee the country to the reactionary rebels across the frontier, and the neighbouring monarchs who sympathised with them later mobilised their forces, thanks to the frivolous overconfidence of the early revolutionary governments in declaring war to distract popular attention. With the army in turmoil the fighting went badly and the country suffered invasion. It was an ideal combination of circumstances to generate intense suspicion, especially when foreign armies did actually invade and advance quite easily, threatening destruction of all the revolutionary gains.

The mess had already been further compounded when the same revolutionary governments attempted to reorganise the Catholic church. It was not the confiscation of church lands to use as a substitute for bullion to underpin the new paper currency they introduced which created the crisis; rather it was their attempt to subject the clergy to civil control and make them swear an acceptance oath to that effect. This provoked intense opposition at all levels of society, and in combination with economic disruption, centralisation of government in Paris and the overriding of local custom and practices, resulted in many of the newly-emancipated citizenry feeling that they were worse off than they had been under the royal and aristocratic regime. Soon enough it provoked boiling discontent both in substantial areas of the French countryside and in major cities such as Lyons.

The crisis which was the outcome of this situation generated its own chain of unintended consequences. The Parisian petty bourgeoisie (the sans-culottes), who had most to gain from the revolution, took the initiative. In response a new breed of radical politician using the Jacobin Club and the Paris city administration of the Commune as their nerve centres, mobilised popular anger and bloodily overthrew the monarchy in August 1792, following this by executing the king and purging their rivals in the newly elected Convention. The foreign enemy continued to advance however, while civil war exploded throughout France.

The Jacobin-dominated Convention centralised authority even more tightly in Paris, intensified the scale of internal repression in the capital and outside, and seized provisions from the surrounding countryside. Earlier they had looked the other way when fear of imminent enemy attack triggered a frightful spontaneous massacre in Paris of suspected counter-revolutionaries (and many others as well). Responding to sans-culotte pressure they instituted an emergency regime, with terror proclaimed 'the order of the day', to be enforced by special courts. They imposed military conscription, police vigilance and economic controls accompanied by ruthless liquidation of alleged counter-revolutionaries. 'Perhaps no other subject makes it quite so difficult to resist the temptation to read first beginnings in terms of subsequent developments and outcomes. . . ',[6] Arno Mayer argues.

Their grim programme was successful. The regional revolts were crushed, the new armies reorganised and supplied, incompetent or traitorous generals guillotined,[7] internal revolt quelled and the invading forces thrust back. The Republic passed over to the offensive. The Jacobin leaders nevertheless soon found themselves caught up in the wheels of the merciless historical dialectic. The Convention, the Jacobins and the leaders of the Paris Commune divided three ways – between the organisers of the regime which aimed to develop it into the Republic of Virtue, resting on the twin supports of virtue and terror; the faction which thought the Terror not severe enough and too inattentive to sans-culotte needs; and the one which deemed it too severe.

The great majority of Conventionnels, not to speak of the minor revolutionary officialdom, belonged to the last of these. They were eager to enjoy what had been accomplished, to cash in for wealth and status the political influence they possessed. By mid-1794 they were free from the desperate unity imposed by invasion threat, irked by the restrictions of Jacobin virtue and terrified of the Revolutionary Tribunal. In July 1794 their alliance of convenience with the surviving ultra-terrorists overthrew the revolutionary administration, executed its leading upholders, and installed a more 'moderate' regime which rigorously repressed the sans-culottes to the accompaniment of an orgy of profiteering. Property was once again in the saddle.

The succeeding regime however could not stabilise itself. The obvious solution would have been to restore the monarchy under conditions, as its counterpart in the British republic had done in 1660, and this was considered, but rejected as too risky. Too many of the rulers were former regicides who stood to be executed with horrible tortures if the Bourbons ever got back on the throne. Various constitutional experiments were tried but none was stable and the regime fluctuated slightly to the left or to the right depending on circumstances, while both Jacobin and royalist revolts and conspiracies in Paris continued to occur. In consequence in 1799 the republic morphed into a lightly disguised military dictatorship, 'beating guillotines into swords' in Arno Mayer's apt phrase.[8] Five years later the monarchy *was* restored after a fashion when the dictator, Napoleon Bonaparte, had himself appointed as Emperor. At his coronation, one veteran revolutionary general in attendance looked around and remarked, 'Everybody is here – apart from the ones who gave their lives to stop this kind of thing ever happening again'.

Rousseau was the prophet of the most advanced Jacobins, who regarded property as so beneficial that everybody ought to have a sufficiency of it, if necessary by redistribution, and in the final months of the Jacobin republic, in early 1794, it attempted to advance some distance along that route by proposing the redistribution among good citizens of the property of traitors and émigrés. That project was aborted with their overthrow, and was probably unrealistic in any case. It was only in the post-Jacobin decade, with Gracchus Babeuf and his abortive Conspiracy of the Equals, that property itself and not merely its maldistribution, was identified as the key social problem.

The Jacobins not only adopted a constitution (which they never implemented) with a universal (male) franchise but decreed the abolition of slavery in the French colonies. They represented what was probably the farthest imaginable degree of social transformation available at the time. Babeuf's intended conspiratorial coup never had a chance of success. Only with their failure and the unplanned transformation of economic life did a different approach become feasible.

Industrial Impact

It was apparent to any observer that the new industrial world of the nineteenth century, located in western Europe and the United States, was riddled with contradictions, and it was no accident that Hegel placed that concept at the centre of his philosophy. New inventions and innovations made possible the creation of commodities which were marketed as lifestyle improvements, or widened availability of ones hitherto confined to the higher income groups. Cotton for example, the centrepiece of early British industrialisation, was the amazing new fabric of its day, combining qualities of lightness, temperature adjustment – cool in hot circumstances, warm in cold ones – easily washed and readily printed. Other innovations expanded the availability of ceramics and glassware, steel cutlery and woollen cloth. Railway systems enabled communication of goods, persons and information to be carried on at hitherto unimaginable speeds. In *Ivanhoe*, referred to earlier, Walter Scott also remarked as an aside how the aristocracy of past centuries lived in circumstances far less comfortable than the average person (i.e. the middle-class one) of his own day.

Yet the urbanisation associated with these developments turned the new population concentrations into perfect hell-holes of filth and squalor and intensified rather than alleviated the nauseous character of preindustrial towns and cities. The universal fossil fuel, coal, which made it all possible, apart from imprisoning growing numbers of adults and children in underground caverns of unspeakable discomfort and extreme danger, deposited its blanket of soot over public and private spaces alike. Appropriately enough Charles Dickens named his representative urban setting Coketown. Where chemical works were in operation a further ingredient was added to the poisonous brew, and where salt was pumped out of the ground in liquid form town dwellers suffered the additional experience of their buildings' foundations being undermined and frequently collapsing.

Socially and culturally things were no better, with Thomas Carlyle complaining of the reduction of all relationships to 'the inhuman cash nexus'. In Europe, apart from France, but not altogether absent from there as well, territorial lords were still very much on the scene and in their attitudes to dwellers on their estates little improvement on their medieval predecessors, indeed in some instances like Ireland worse if anything. To them had been added the magnates of industry, who in some cases aspired to treat their workforces as a medieval baron would have treated his dependants – the Krupp steel firm in Germany being a classic example.

What it added up to was extreme destitution evident in the middle of plenty, squalor in the middle of the potential for its abolition, and the growth of new social classes out of pre-industrial roots. On the one hand that period saw a development of the middle classes which had existed for centuries as traders and affluent peasants, and on the other there emerged a class of labourers who were cut off from virtually any source of livelihood other than the weekly (often intermittent) payment for their labour power and perpetually threatened with the stoppage even of that unreliable source.

Not surprisingly there were strong reactions on both an individual and a collective level, both theoretical and practical. Visionaries of the Romantic movement looked back nostalgically to the imagined simpler, purer, rural, more 'organic' times of the European medieval period in contrast to the soulless 'mechanical' civilisation in which they found themselves embedded. It would be an exaggeration, but not wholly without foundation, to describe them as nature worshippers. It was an intellectual trend which continued throughout the century, to include towards its end William Morris, who combined his medievalism and attachment to an organic vision of society with Marxism.

However it was not only intellectuals who adopted that attitude. The idea of escaping from an intolerable urban environment to one of rural harmony motivated the groups who tried to found utopian colonies in the American wilderness, one being titled, significantly, 'New Harmony'. The notion of retreating to a family farm had, until at least the middle of the century, great appeal to many members of the English working class and was a significant theme within the Chartist movement.

What was to mark a new and portentous departure was the idea that instead of rejecting the new industrial civilisation it could be embraced and turned into one fit for human beings. Not that its satisfied admirers such as J R McCulloch and Nassau Senior thought any differently in that respect. The renowned English economist Alfred Marshall, late in the century, summed it up in the comment that 'I regard all this poverty as a mere passing evil in the progress of man upwards'.[9] Where the new thinkers differed, was that they combined the promise of industrialisation with the critique of property relations begun by the Conspiracy of the Equals in the 1790s. Babeuf is sometimes credited with being the first (revolutionary) socialist, although the 'socialism' term was not minted until the early nineteenth century by Henri de Saint Simon.

16

Socialism: Its Promise and Paradox

The essence of the socialist thesis in all its multiple varieties was that the essential social problem was not one of industrialisation per se, which had on the contrary the potential of putting an end to the millennial blights upon human existence, but the social context in which it was embedded. The problem was identified as the dog-eat-dog one of possessive individualism. This celebrated greed and the cash nexus and correspondingly was driven, whatever the sentiments of the individual employer, to hire labourers at the lowest possible rates and work them for the longest possible hours in the worst possible conditions and to resist improvements in public health and amenities if these had to be financed by taxation and did not have a short-term financial payoff. Cooperative work and living, plus production for need instead of greed, should replace it.

From this basic starting point socialist thinking diverged in a multitude of conflicting directions. Saint Simon, Charles Fourier and Robert Owen were the most eminent of what were in due course to be designated the utopian socialists, for the reason that they thought these essential aims could be realised through the application of reason and example. Saint Simon appealed to the high and mighty to recognise the merits of his views and help him implement them; Fourier, with greater or lesser success, founded utopian colonies in the United States.

Robert Owen, with experience as a humane but successful capitalist employer, believed initially that society could be transformed by such methods. With his propaganda falling on stony ground among the British influential, he also experimented with utopian colonies and finally with an attempt to institute an alternative cooperative economy in Britain, with a labour currency in competition to the capitalist one. By the second half of the century these approaches were marginalised if not dead (though some ideas of their proponents were to live on in other contexts) and three principal currents of socialist thinking, themselves more fragmented than homogenous, dominated the field of cooperativist ideology.[1]

Anarchism

The first of these was what became known as anarchism, which itself took both pacifist and revolutionary forms. Its basic idea sprung from the reality that humans are a social species, though most varieties of anarchists also, in rather contradictory fashion, stressed individualism, and advanced the conception that the ideal social form was one of small communities of individuals living co-operatively. These, it was argued would neutralise oppressive and inhuman practices.

The big enemy was the state, currently dominated by wealthy aristocrats and oligarchs, but just as vicious if it ever came to be employed as a method of control by alleged revolutionaries. The instruments of the state, especially armies, police and religion, were included in this condemnation. The public that anarchism mostly came to attract were those social strata threatened by the advance of industrial capitalism, such as peasants and independent craft workers. It achieved a degree of purchase in Italy, Switzerland, France, the western Russian empire, the United States and above all in Spain and the former Spanish Latin American countries. Round the turn of the century it gave rise to what were for a time powerful trends among industrial workers, those of syndicalism and anarcho-syndicalism, which postulated that independently of politicians, whether reformist or revolutionary, workers' power mobilised in industrial unions could overthrow capitalism and institute a socialist community.

Reformism

The second major current was that of reformist socialism, which again came in a spectrum of differing shades. The fundamental concept here was that the blights of capitalist society could be overcome by a process of action which displaced the ruling classes from their positions of power and wealth by means of popular pressure stopping short of bloody turmoil. These actions would at least compel the capitalist-dominated governments to accept the socialisation of large parts of the economy and a generous welfare system sustaining decent living standards for the working class in sickness and health, in youth and old age – i.e. comprehensive reforms. This was to be achieved through the use of voting power in a democratic franchise, propaganda and agitation and occasionally coercive power in the form of strike action – which in Belgium in the 1890s actually worked to secure a universal (male) franchise.

A lot of emphasis in reformist socialism was placed on evolutionary conceptions, or rather a misunderstanding of them, which envisaged organic evolution as a teleology and then applied similar thinking to social evolution as well. Organic evolution after countless aeons had at last produced humans as the supreme evolutionary achievement, and social evolution was headed in the same direction when it would before many more decades bring into existence a collectivist society employing the wonders of technology and industry in the cause of human welfare rather than capitalist profit. Ruling classes might object and resist, but resistance was futile, for they were a doomed social species, as the dinosaurs had been a doomed organic one. The failure of Bismarck's anti-socialist programme, embodied in his Anti-Socialist Law of the 1870s and 80s, could be viewed as an instructive example.

It is not surprising that such a perspective proved very attractive to many industrial workers and persons of goodwill from other classes as well. Violent revolution is a very risky business for its participants and their dependants, with imprisonment, destitution and death very much on the agenda; and so not likely to be entered into except in very extreme conditions. Socialists, tending on the whole to be historically well-educated even if in these years, self-educated, were aware of the precedents of the French Revolution and the revolutions and attempted revolutions of the nineteenth century with their extensive bloodlettings.[2]

Among its adherents reformist socialism tended to be viewed as being possible to implement within national borders, contrary to the generally prevailing conception that though the socialist parties were organised within state boundaries, essentially it was an international movement. One of the most conservative German socialists, Georg Vollmar, even used the expression 'national socialism' – to be fair, he could not have been expected to have possessed prophetic powers. A revealing characteristic of the reformist socialists was that they tended to take for granted the colonial empires of the European powers while advocating improvements in the treatment their inhabitants received from the colonisers. Again misapplications of evolutionary thinking came into the picture – European civilisations were assumed to stand on the highest level and therefore represented suitable mentors and guides for 'the natives'.

The first major example of a reformist socialist movement was established in Prussia in the 1860s. Though it remained small during his own lifetime, its originator was the charismatic though unstable Ferdinand Lassalle, who tried to establish an alliance with Bismarck.[3] His organisation the ADAV, was one of the two major components of the German Social Democratic Party (SPD) of the subsequent decade.

Communism

The other component represented the third current, that of communism, though that actual name itself disappeared for almost seventy years.[4] Its basic postulates were embodied in *The Communist Manifesto*, the pamphlet authored by Karl Marx and Friedrich Engels in 1847. It shared with the reformist socialists the conception of social evolution leading on to a collectivist society based upon science and modern industry – but an evolutionary process of a very different sort. A sketch of historical development since the foundation of class society portrayed it as a grim affair characterised by perpetual conflict along the route as one class of oppressors replaced another to torment and exploit the basic producers. .

However this process had finally by dialectical necessity produced the bourgeoisie, who had been responsible for the unprecedented wonders of the modern era. They had indeed thereby outlived their usefulness and achieved their own redundancy as they were no longer needed for the collective and beneficial employment of these same wonders. They could not however be expected to quietly concede their peaceful removal, and though the Manifesto itself did not specify how they might be got rid of, Marx and Engels's other writings made clear that it could only be done by violent revolution.

Whom the revolutionaries were to be was also explicitly set out. Not the conspiratorial groups à la Babeuf or his ideological successor Auguste Blanqui, but what they termed the proletariat, by which they meant the class of wage-earners, with the organised factory and equivalent workers as its core. They specifically disavowed providing any prescription for what the successor socialist society would look like or how it would be run, attributing such schemes to the utopian socialists who specified 'street plans of the New Jerusalem'. Marx however was later at pains to write a pamphlet indicating his opinion of what a socialist society would *not* look like.

The title of that pamphlet was *Critique of the Gotha Programme*, which was a response to developments in Germany, where his followers were proposing to unite with those of Lassalle to establish a unified socialist movement. Despite Marx's criticism of their perspectives, which he regarded as unrevolutionary and utopian, they went on to do so with Marx's grudging endorsement, withstood Bismarck's assault of the 1870s and 80s and under the name of the German Social Democratic Party (Sozialdemokratische Partei Deutschlands, the Communist name being dropped as being too provocative), established the flagship example of a successful socialist movement.

Socialist Development

Early in the twentieth century the SPD's leading theorist Karl Kautsky tried to resolve the contradictions by defining it as 'a revolutionary but not a revolution-making party'. It enjoyed the loyalty of the majority of German industrial and associated workers, providing an alternative cultural universe for its adherents in counterposition to the official national one. It sustained an enormous range of publications – dailies, weeklies, monthlies and learned journals – a powerful trade union affiliation and collectives for every imaginable social collective and cultural pursuit – women's organisations, youth organisations, recreational and educational organisations, consumer cooperatives.

So far as it had an ultimate perspective it was that capitalism would reach an impasse and breakdown as a result of its own contradictions, the bourgeoisie would be unable to control the situation or the economy, and then socialists, with a parliamentary majority, would take over (means unspecified). In short, its leaders found themselves in the dilemma that would be repeated in many different contexts during the century ahead – a movement aspiring to social transformation faced with a social structure and political context in which socio-political revolution was most definitely not on the agenda; the situation theorised by the Italian Antonio Gramsci from his prison cell in the twenties and thirties.

In spite of its rather unthreatening posture the SPD was particularly hated and feared by German monarchical officialdom, especially as its voting strength and parliamentary representation continued to grow. It violated their image of united national sentiment happily focused upon loyalty to the Hohenzollern dynasty and in tune with its great power pretensions and imperial ambitions. The SPD's trade union strength was an irritation to the feudally-minded German capitalist dynasties and those entrepreneurs and aspiring middle-class elements eager to join them; its consumer cooperatives a menace to small shopkeepers; its materialist ideology an offence to religious sentiment and to the romantic idealist philosophy favoured by the mainstream intelligentsia and the universities; its anti-militarist stances a provocation to the military elites and their many admirers.

Proposals were advanced for a military takeover with the Kaiser as political figurehead, to be followed by the thorough uprooting of the party through a more effective revival of Bismarck's Anti-socialist Law. Such schemes were by no means confined to Germany, with similar notions being floated in Italy, likewise to combat a strong socialist political challenge. However in neither case prior to 1914 were the times judged by their proponents to be sufficiently auspicious for such an undertaking.

In the early years of the twentieth century, as Perry Anderson has pointed out, thoughts and expectations of cataclysm and revolution were widespread in public consciousness. Very bloody upheavals had erupted in China, Mexico and Russia with varying outcomes. Full-dress war was fought in South Africa and in the Balkans and the UK stood on the verge of civil war over Irish Home Rule while undergoing at the same time an officers' mutiny and massive civil unrest, which resulted in a gunboat deployed to intimidate strikers.

At the same time the formal Socialist International network linking socialist organisations (even accommodating rival groups from the same country though excluding anarchists) was at the height of its standing and confidence and prepared to pass resolutions denouncing war – which, if entered into, would send workers into battle on opposite sides. It also threatened action to stop any European war which might break out on account of the malevolence of bourgeois governments. Naturally these same governments were alarmed and made preparations for mass arrests and repression to neutralise the threat if the socialist leaders tried to implement it.

In August 1914 push came to shove and the dilemma confronted the socialist leaders in the respective belligerent countries of adhering to their formal anti-war positions when to do so could have very serious consequences. The majority failed the test most conclusively and assisted their governments to prosecute the slaughter, or at most adopted a pacifist standpoint. They were motivated by a variety of considerations, not all of which were wholly discreditable. The French ones convinced themselves that they were supporting a principled war of national defence – after all the German government had declared war and the German army invaded.

However the German socialist leadership also thought their country was engaged in a defensive war, this time against Tsarist tyranny and found texts from Marx and Engels to underwrite their position. Here too it was Germany which had declared war, not Russia, but the Kaiserreich's excuse that Russian military mobilisation had left no alternative was all too easily accepted.

Then there was the attitude of the socialist leaders' constituency – the working classes of the engaged countries on the whole did not doubt that war was justified and if an evil then a necessary one, and they might well have repudiated leaders who tried to argue otherwise. Support for the war made them generally popular for the first time in their political careers and accepted into polite society. It could also give them the leverage to influence political decisions, and in some of the belligerents make socialist participation in governments an accepted part of the political scenery. At the trade union level it also gave opportunities to workers, particularly engineering ones, to assert themselves in consequence of their centrality to war production, though also stoking up industrial conflict as employers did their utmost to frustrate that ambition.

The dialectic of unintended consequences was certainly at work between 1914 and 1918. The war was never intended to last over four years, to kill around 30 million people, to accomplish incalculable material destruction and bring about the liquidation of four empires. It had been planned to be short and decisive, reaching a speedy conclusion followed by a peace treaty or treaties in the style of their nineteenth-century equivalents, with national boundaries and international power relations seriously adjusted but existing regimes remaining in place. The reality was very different and the prolonged war both brought on the carnage and wreckage indicated above, but ruined the nineteenth century global economy, though this was not immediately apparent at its end.

Communism in Action

What was apparent was that the bourgeois nightmare of a socialist takeover had in 1917 been realised, and not in any minor nationality but in the Russian empire, one of the great powers, stretching across Eurasia from central Europe to the Pacific. Not only that, but within a year the new rulers of the former empire made it plain that they intended, if they could, to inspire replication of their feat everywhere else. That project included encouraging the populations of the European colonies and semi-colonies to rise against their masters – something the reformist socialists never dreamed of doing.[5] Even after the international war was over the overthrown ruling classes in the former empire and the governments of the victorious powers made strenuous efforts to destroy the new regime. They failed, but succeeded in reducing the country to a state of utter destitution. The result of that was to haunt the new regime during the seventy-four years of its existence, as Isaac Deutscher expresses the reality,

> Socialism cannot be founded on want and poverty. Against these all its aspirations are powerless. Scarcity inexorably breeds inequality. Where there is not enough food, clothing, and housing for all, a minority will grasp what it can; while the rest go hungry, clothed in rags and crowded in slums.[6]

The socialists who had brought about the 1917 overturn, and then gone on to establish an international organisation to further the project of world socialist revolution, belonged to the most intransigently anti-bourgeois wing of the movement and, for purely accidental reasons, had termed themselves Bolsheviks or majority people. Following the revolution they deliberately revived the old Communist name for themselves and their international co-thinkers who organised themselves along similar lines and with similar aims.

Meanwhile the Socialist International of the prewar years had also been destroyed by the conflict, or rather by the reactions to it of its member parties when they were lined up against each other in armed opposition. An attempt to revive it was made after the war in rivalry to the Communist International, but the revived organisation (which still exists after a fashion) was less than a shadow of its former significance and was specifically orientated towards a reformist agenda and acceptance of capitalist hegemony as a permanent reality – though due to conflicting perspectives among its rank and file membership it took decades for this to become explicit.[7]

The Communist International project based itself on Lenin's analysis of the significance of the war and the Socialist International's collapse and capitulation to the demands of bourgeois governments. His argument was that these developments signified that capitalism was in its death throes and that the exposure of the socialist leaders as 'labour lieutenants of capital' urging their followers on to the slaughter meant both that the developed world was ripe, 'rotten-ripe' indeed, for socialist revolution, and the working classes everywhere were ready to perceive this reality. With effective and determined Marxist leadership, the communists imagined, workers were perfectly placed to rise against their masters and traitorous former leaders and to establish socialist regimes immediately throughout Europe and shortly throughout the world.

The Bolshevik revolution itself had been premised on the assumption that it was setting a precedent and example which would soon be followed (to be fair, the signs of the times did point in that direction). It was the condition of the Russian empire, in catastrophic condition amid a lost war which the Tsar's successors after his overthrow refused to terminate, that provided the basis for the October Revolution. However had the Bolshevik leaders not been convinced of their international analysis (some were not, but these were marginalised) they would probably not have acted as they did.

The suffering masses around the globe however did not respond, or at least not in the manner that the Communist International (Comintern) expected, either because they disliked that scenario on principle, did not see it as a viable proposition in their particular circumstances, or were too severely repressed to attempt it – or for a combination of these reasons. The communist rulers of the new state, which ended up being the former empire with some truncations of border territory, and from 1924 renamed the Soviet Union, refused to accept that their basic analysis had been wrong.

They insisted instead on attributing the failure of similar revolutions which had been attempted, as in Germany, or not even attempted, as in the UK, not to insurmountable circumstances and lack of support, but to inadequate leadership. As a result the Soviet Union stood out all the more as the one great success where Marxist revolution had actually been accomplished. As a result the policies and organisational principles of its ruling party soon came, through prestige, to dominate all the others in the Comintern founded in 1919 and eventually to subject them to detailed direction.

Although these parties had initially been founded by strong-minded individuals of independent views like Gramsci, who well understood that the issue was immensely more complex than the Comintern specified, their leaders submitted to Soviet direction. Within the Soviet Union itself (perpetually in fear of renewed military attack from its enemies) the dilemmas and issues resulting from the country's devastation[8] resulted in an iron dictatorship being imposed by the communist party over the rest of society and its institutions, and in due course even over the party membership by its central leadership, itself the scene of bitter faction fights around policy and personalities.

The culture of the most intense phases of the revolutionary struggle and savage civil war which followed was adopted as the standard context of government. Soviet party domination of the Comintern made it possible for whatever 'line' was in favour to be imposed internationally, at least as regards central political issues. At the same time the other CPs, with new leaderships replacing the original ones and strictly subordinated to Moscow, were left free in the main to work out how they should apply the requirements of the 'line' to local conditions – and subjected to regular tongue-lashings for not being more successful in doing so.

Degeneration

Internally in the USSR at large there was a degree of relaxation of social pressure during the middle 1920s, largely as a result of a tightly regulated resort to market exchange, which greatly improved the country's devastated economy. But in the late 20s, this was considered unsatisfactory and a breakneck industrial drive was instituted – accompanied by an agricultural upheaval resulting in near civil war conditions and seriously damaging Soviet agriculture for the remainder of the state's existence. It did however give the government control over the grain supply, which was its objective. In such circumstances, with social control a priority, the full weight of repression was resumed and intensified to surreal proportions.

In 1903, when what was to become the Bolshevik party was first formed, Trotsky, at that time in the opposing faction, made a remark which was to turn out uncannily perceptive and which, as a Bolshevik, he was to come to bitterly regret and repudiate. He declared that following a successful revolution if Lenin's proposed party rules were applied, the party would come to dictate to society at large, the central committee to the party and eventually a single individual to the central committee. The history of the early USSR followed precisely that route.

Social power became concentrated in the person of one man, a not uncommon phenomenon throughout history of civilisation everywhere around the globe (very exceptionally it was one woman). Indeed as we have already noted, civilised *H. sapiens* appears to have had a propensity for that form of government and social control. Usually it was in the form of hereditary monarchy, or quasi-hereditary as in the Roman and Chinese empires.

In these social formations however, once a regime or dynasty had settled down, convention and habit usually imposed constraints on the reach of the ruler's powers (some monarchs still of course tried to act otherwise). When however the society was gripped in a state of semi-permanent emergency and feeling itself under constant threat from enemies within and without it was a very different matter, especially when that was combined with a world-transforming project and driven by intense ideological motivations. These considerations were at the root of the resemblances between the Nazi and Stalinist dictatorships despite their ideological projects being utterly different.

During the 1930s the ordinary citizen who was not being targeted as a public enemy fared even worse under Stalin's tyranny than under Hitler's. The former was, in addition to other problems (such as military conflict with the Japanese in eastern Asia), in charge of trying to construct an industrialised economy and corresponding military capacity at breakneck speed; the latter had one ready to hand. This led to fierce concentration on national objectives, which in the Soviet case clashed with the international project which featured as the basis of the state's legitimacy and could not formally be repudiated. That international project was however very much marginalised, even more than in the previous decade and the foreign communist parties became, in the words of one critic, no more than border guards for the Soviet state, with their members finding in Soviet achievements, or claimed achievements, vicarious compensation for their own failures.

The national emphasis in these circumstances also induced paranoid suspicion of foreign residents, even or indeed especially, those who were sympathetic to the regime – a similar phenomenon had characterised the last phases of Jacobin rule during the French Revolution. Most foreign communists living in the USSR perished during Stalin's purges between 1936 and 1938.

Bureaucracy

It has been stressed in earlier chapters that no monarch or dictator, however powerful, can govern all by themselves, as well as that, not infrequently, their agents in charge of armed formations may well aspire on their own account to fill the ruler's shoes. A strong principle of hereditary succession provides some, though far from complete, security against this sort of thing, but dictators without that kind of legitimacy have to keep their servants (both civil and military) loyal whether by reward or ideological conformity or a combination of both.

Two consequences follow. One is bureaucratisation – a social stratum is created to implement the rules laid down from above and which, either through inclination or fear of a misstep, become rule-bound and structurally fossilised. Bureaucracies function only if the bureaucrats know when to ignore the rules,[9] as anyone who has been part of one, whether service or commercial, will be well aware. When the constraints of public or market accountability (constraints which businesses try to escape) are removed, bureaucracies focus on their own immediate ends and ambitions – effectively they pass out of the control of their ostensible masters.

The second consequence is faction at the ruler's court as intimates and advisers, necessary agents of rule, engage in rivalry to gain the ruler's ear and favour, jockey against each other and construct gangs of followers to assist with their ambitions. This is an invariable feature of virtually any government, even the most democratic in relation to its central figure, prime minister or president; but it flourishes especially within arbitrary or unaccountable government.

Stalin addressed both these problems by a policy of constant terror. His technique was to keep his bureaucrats both civil and military (particularly party members) in a constant state of tension and uncertainty and their noses against the grindstone in case they should be accused of unspeakable political crimes and hurried to either the gulag or their graves. From time to time he also made examples of entirely conscientious ones in order to keep up the pressure on the others.[10]

There were other motivations as well behind the terror, including spite, revenge and paranoia, but these alone could scarcely account for its extent and nature. The very real problems confronting the state served as the excuse and created the atmosphere where such things were possible. It offered plenty of scope for individuals who enjoyed exercising power for its own sake, particularly powers of life and death, or who even got a thrill out of acting as persecutors and gratifying their sadistic impulses.

When necessary though, as in the emergency of the war for survival between 1941 and 1945, the pressure could be eased. Stalin, unlike his Nazi opponent, had the sense to trust his generals and listen to their advice, a not inconsiderable element in the eventual Soviet victory. It was during those years too that the centrally directed economy showed its potential when all resources were concentrated on a single objective. Soon after the war ended though, the permanent state of terror was reimposed, this time under the pretext of the Cold War emergency, and the command economy began to show its weaknesses.

At this point too, the situation had changed profoundly. Thanks to the postwar boom in the capitalist world, which after a shaky start had got going strongly from 1948, capitalism appeared far more able to fulfil public expectations than had ever previously been the case. In Europe and a few other parts of the world reformist social democracy also acquired a new lease of life and appeared to be a serious socialist contender against communism for working-class, and other class, loyalties. Not that communism too was not enormously strengthened.

The victory of 1945 enormously enhanced its prestige and the USSR had acquired hegemony over eastern Europe, hegemony which from 1948 onwards was transformed into complete domination. That too brought with it a raft of fresh problems – Isaac Deutscher was to title one of the chapters in his biography of Stalin 'Dialectics of Victory'. In 1949 the Chinese communist party drove the last remnants of the US-supported and invincibly corrupt bourgeois-feudal regime out of mainland China and established the Chinese People's Republic. That in due course was to bring even greater problems than the extension of Soviet power in Europe had done, both to the USSR and the Chinese people themselves.

Rotten Foundations

Socialism in both its major forms, which had appeared relatively marginalised during the thirties,[11] had after 1945 in different ways acquired a new lease of life. As it turned out, however, the foundations of both were rotten. In the case of social democracy or reformist socialism, its success rested on a world economic boom driven primarily by the flourishing success of US capitalism in the fifties and sixties and the world dominance of the dollar as a reserve currency to which all the others in the capitalist world were linked in one manner or another.

It provided sufficient resources for social redistribution and steadily rising material living standards within the sphere of North America and Western Europe – and Japan, along with island entrepots such as Singapore and Hong Kong. This outcome was achieved however at the expense of the 'underdeveloped' part of the globe or 'Third World' and was an essentially imperialist relation based on the foundation of cheap raw materials and other primary commodities, especially cheap and plentiful oil, which reflected the poverty incomes of these countries' populations. Following the financial crisis beginning in 1973 social democracy's weaknesses became all too apparent. It was helpless in the face of state powers and financial systems dominated by the enemies of redistribution determined to repress its social and trade union influence, and therefore easily blown away in the neoliberal storm rising in the course of the seventies and reaching its full force in the Reagan-Thatcher axis.

The fate of the communist bloc was similar but different. In its Soviet part efforts were made following Stalin's death in 1953 both to improve security for the general public, including the *nomenklatura*, which meant in essence the end of arbitrary arrest for no reason, and to improve levels of consumption within the framework of a command economy. As a result, up until the beginning of the sixties, despite the shocks of Khrushchev's denunciation of the former idol in 1956, followed by political crisis in Poland and insurrection in Hungary, matters looked relatively hopeful.

Nonetheless the USSR and its dependent regimes in Eastern Europe still remained authoritarian police states governed by parties accountable only to themselves, even those, such as the Hungarian, which were most sensitive to popular demand. The attempt made by the Czechoslovak communist party in 1968 to institute more genuine accountability in combination with a less centrally controlled economy was swiftly suppressed by Soviet military force.

Matters were far worse in China, a materially far poorer society, overwhelmingly peasant in character. The regime's attempt in the late fifties and early sixties to industrialise by dogmatic crash measures turned into a human catastrophe of enormous proportions with devastating famine and millions of deaths. Only the country's huge population and the Chinese communist party's tight political control averted complete social collapse.

This episode, styled the 'Great Leap Forward', was soon followed by the almost equally disruptive 'Cultural Revolution' by which the party leader Mao Zedong tried to regain his slackening grip on power and reassert revolutionary virtue by purging the bureaucracy, especially its communist central element, along with artists, intellectuals and suspected dissidents. His method was different from Stalin's and consisted in mobilising millions of dissatisfied youth to engage in mindless attacks upon the bureaucrat objects of their dissatisfaction and terrorise them by means of humiliation, violence, imprisonment and murder. Prior to this episode and continuing during its course and afterwards, a bitter quarrel which even threatened warfare, had erupted between the Chinese and Soviet regimes. This arose from a variety of issues but centred on the Chinese claim that the Soviet regime was too indulgent and compromising towards the capitalist enemy, displayed great-power ambitions at China's expense, and had even itself reintroduced capitalism.

What all this signified to populations in the West enjoying the benefits of liberal democracy and high consumption was that communism meant at best a combination of impoverishment and repression; massacre at worst; and not surprisingly, few citizens wanted anything to do with it. The communist parties in these countries were mostly small and marginal,[12] and governments, while keeping them under supervision by their security services, could afford to tolerate them (though in the USA and West Germany they were persecuted nevertheless).

Those in Europe that were of some significance owed their popularity more to their anti-fascist record earned either during the Second World War or against indigenous fascist dictatorships. In any event, except briefly during the Portuguese revolution of 1974–75 they had no hope of winning sufficient support to aim at taking over the state. Among Third World populations inside the capitalist orbit, which were anyway enduring impoverishment, repression and massacre the record of the existing communist regimes was a much less convincing argument, and in these locations rigorous repression was the rule. Outside of Indo-China none of them achieved success and in Indonesia members and supporters were physically extirpated.

Within the Soviet bloc itself contradictions accumulated, leading to a steady decline in various welfare indicators and growing reliance on capitalist economies to plug some of the gaps. The Soviet Union itself suffered in addition from the West's implacable hostility, expressed in military as well as political terms, and the crushing burden of the armaments race. The Marxist African-American scholar W E B Dubois once remarked of the Reconstruction in the post-Civil War period that what the South Carolina elites dreaded even more than 'bad Negro government' was 'good Negro government'; and the same applied to their twentieth century US counterparts in regard to communist ones. Had Stalin been a Soviet Mandela, his successors likewise, and their regime a communist Sweden, it would have made little difference to US attitudes.

Downfall

Nevertheless that was not the critical factor in bringing about the regimes' downfall everywhere in eastern Europe and the USSR itself. The command economy was simply not viable in a consumer society or one attempting to reach that state. In fact, as analysis has shown, the overall command economy splintered into a collection of mini-command economies, each enterprise fighting to make itself as self-sufficient as possible and competing against the others for raw materials and labour, and equipment and liquid capital from the central authority.

Cheating on targets and quality, and falsification of returns to central planning made the situation even worse, and various forms of tinkering in the latter years did nothing to improve matters. The final far-reaching attempt at political and economic reform brought the system crashing down and the entire communist experience in Europe and the USSR was also blown away on the neoliberal gale. The Chinese regime managed to survive and stabilise itself by a mixture of fierce repression and abandonment of the entire project of its first quarter-century, turning its economy instead into a form of state-regulated capitalism with plenty of scope for individual enrichment and plenty of state-enforced super-exploitation of the workforce. 'Those who had done well out of Communism generally did even better out of restored capitalism',[13] in Marc Mulholland's phrase.

In Britain 'There is no alternative!' had been one of Margret Thatcher's favourite slogans. In the US, Francis Fukuyama wrote in 1992 to assert more or less the same thing – and by the 1990s it looked as though that really was the case. As Arno Mayer observed, 'In this early dawn of the twenty-first century, following one of humanity's darkest seasons, revolution is seen as offering little promise and posing little threat'.[14] Though to a certain extent it depends on what is meant by 'revolution'.

17

Desperately Seeking Significance

I sensed an infinite scream passing through nature.
—Edvard Munch

More than half a century ago, with the development of nuclear weaponry, the human species acquired the ability to exterminate itself along with a large proportion of the planet's biomass. On more than one occasion that potential appeared likely to become a reality and the human adventure might have well ended in a nuclear fireball. With the political collapse of one of the contenders in the superpower rivalry, along with the ideological vision which was its formal justification, that particular peril has diminished, though it certainly has not vanished.

It has been replaced by another, less immediate and spectacular, though ultimately no less threatening. It also derives mainly from the application of technical expertise, and consists in the likelihood that the destruction of species and of biological habitat, currently proceeding on a geologically unprecedented scale, along with the outpouring of pollutants, will render the planet largely uninhabitable, and certainly so to humans. As long ago as 1948 Fairfield Osborn, aware of this potential scenario, published *Our Plundered Planet*, and since then the threatening catastrophe has grown ever more menacing and indeed is well underway, regardless of the bawling of mindlessly complacent deniers of environmental destruction.

In the most likely outcome, however, the global market-driven industrial system which inflicts the gross environmental damage will itself collapse, along with the web of interchange and cooperation which sustains world society, well before environmental destruction totally wrecks the planet. Though billions would die prematurely the human species, which is present everywhere, is highly adaptable and able to eat practically anything, would probably survive, but all the advances in safety, longevity, comfort and freedom, in liberty, equality and fraternity which have been instituted over the past two centuries, partial and fragmentary though they are, would have gone forever, never to be recovered. A bitter irony in that case would be that the collapse of civilisation with uncountable fatalities and intense miseries for the survivors should appear as one of the more optimistic scenarios – but such an appalling prospect need not be the outcome.

Humans remain utterly dependent for their very survival on the non-human biosphere but thanks to their superior brains cover the planet everywhere, exterminate and exploit other species, and their creations visually dominate the landscape. It is easy to believe that we are the dominant species, but far from it. If bacteria had consciousness and vocal organs they would howl with laughter at such pretension. *They* are the dominant organisms, present everywhere, not excepting the depths of the oceans, the ice of the arctic regions and the hot springs of volcanic ones, present in the human body in numbers greatly exceeding our eukaryotic cells – and essential to our bodies' operation. They always have been, and will unquestionably continue to be, the dominant life form so long as the biosphere exists. They were the first to arrive and will be the last to depart – the bugs always win in the end.

One aspect of Jean-Paul Sartre's novels and short stories is to satirise individuals who imagine that, because they have an elevated position in society, they therefore have inborn *rights*, especially the right to dominate other people. Humans are also mistaken in taking up a similar attitude towards other organisms. Biologically we are on the same level as any of the rest, vertebrate or invertebrate, evolved only to survive and reproduce; the universe has not made any special provision for us, and if it were to destroy the species by asteroid strike, volcanism, pandemic or environmental collapse that outcome would have no more intrinsic significance than applies to any other organism which once inhabited the planet and no longer does so.

And yet in one respect humans *are* unique and even special. As they are a pattern-seeking social species they have developed culture both practical and imaginative, and through that have become the only species which can collectively think about itself, conceptually understand how the environment functions and know what, billions of years down the line, the ultimate fate of the planet and its star, the sun, has to be (that of the universe is still under discussion, but the cosmologists are working on it).

The processes of the cosmos, the subatomic world or the evolution of life on earth over the aeons can be examined, understood and explained but not be taken to mean something beyond themselves. While however for the moment we do continue to inhabit the planet, we cannot avoid asking what significance does that have, what can we do about it and what is the prognosis for the future.

Unavoidable Constraints

At the beginning of the first volume of his great history, published in 1776, Edward Gibbon wrote that what ought to be judged the happiest period in world history would be that of the Roman empire under the rule of the 'five good emperors' of the Antonine dynasty of the second century CE.[1] This remark by a humane and enlightened writer is revealing, for he was referring to a slave empire acquired and sustained by ferocious cruelty and aggression. Nevertheless during most of the second century civil peace prevailed within the empire, exceptional rapacity, famine and plague were avoided, production and commerce were enhanced and the legal system functioned smoothly.

In Gibbon's eyes the pinnacle of human achievement he regards as having been achieved in that era – civilisation and literary culture – rested upon the foundations of productive wealth and opulence, from which, of necessity, only a minority could acquire substantial benefit. According to him this must always be the same. His assessment reveals the nugget of reality hidden under the pulp of apologetics, generally accepted among educated thought in his time; that there was no escaping the concentration of wealth among elites, while the very best the masses could hope for was the avoidance of famine through efficient agricultural and transport technique, with arbitrary despotism kept at bay by a constitutionally balanced oligarchy. A Greek philosopher of the Hellenistic era remarked that the most fortunate fate for an individual was never to be born and if born, to die in infancy, so grim were the contemporary conditions of life, even for social elites.[2]

Not that life in pre-agricultural times was by any means all fun and games. Apart from the dangers and sorrows of reproduction, toil was by no means absent, particularly for women, and if life was not nasty and brutish, certainly it was short. As this volume has tried to demonstrate in outline, with the shift to settled agriculture, and more particularly with the appearance of urban concentrations and civilisation, none of these burdens and rigours was alleviated and many more were added to the populations involved.

Throughout the historical span from that era onwards, forced labour in one form or another has been intrinsic to the human situation and the progress of civilisation – as a form of state taxation, as slavery, as a state of personal dependence on a superior, known in Europe as serfdom or vassalage, as 'free' labour compelled by necessity, or as prison labour organised by modern states. Except recently and then only in parts of the globe, humans in general, and not only the repressed and subordinated, have lived out their time in bodies plagued with parasites and minds plagued with superstition. It would appear that, again except in very recent centuries and among very fortunate minorities, the more *H. sapiens* have removed itself from nature the more exquisitely its members have suffered.

Even within that context, one half of the species has endured the greater suffering. Women in the main down the ages have found their allocated place in society to be that of domestic drudges, sexual playthings subject to gross physical mutilations; breeding machines, counters and pawns in family alliances. In the lower levels of the social hierarchy both genders have been subjected to the contempt and disdain of the upper orders, terrorised by the threats of lords, laws and priests, treated as dirt, their lives held cheap and readily ended, often to the accompaniment of indescribably horrible and ingenious tortures.

Kafka's novels and Munch's famous painting 'The Scream' are frequently cited to characterise and represent the twentieth century – but rather they do so also for the entire historical narrative since the Neolithic revolution. It was not that utopian sentiments, usually in a religious context, were not voiced from time to time. They certainly were, as we have seen in previous chapters, but in the circumstances prevailing down the centuries they had not even the potential of being effectively realised.

What Gibbon presumed though, accurately enough for his own era, was that there was a ceiling to output, quickly reached under favourable social and climatic conditions, and a very restricted surplus above subsistence, available only to a few. So it had always been, at least since the emergence of citified societies. While Gibbon deplores immoderate savagery by the power holders, the routine privations of the masses leave him unmoved, and when he compares a certain emperor to Spartacus it is not intended as a compliment.

A century after his volume was published (coincidentally in the same year as the American Declaration of Independence and publication of Adam Smith's *The Wealth of Nations*) Gibbon's presupposition of inherently restricted labour output was largely discredited and the prospect of a 'society of abundance' was on the agenda. There remained in various quarters hankerings after the old ways. These were evident for example among intellectuals like Arthur Schopenhauer and Friedrich Nietzsche, the traditional aristocracies, the Catholic church of the day and the disciples of Thomas Malthus, with their implicit or explicit admiration for antique hierarchy and inequality and 'the brutal display of vigour in the Middle Ages which reactionists so much admire,'[3] but the tide was running against them.

What was above all responsible for that tide was machinery driven by artificial power sources applied to production, transport and communication in a framework of market capitalism. As Marx and Engels put it as early as 1848: 'Conservation of the old modes of production in unaltered form, was . . . the first condition of existence for all earlier industrial classes. Constant revolutionising of production, uninterrupted disturbance of all social conditions, everlasting uncertainty and agitation, distinguish the bourgeois epoch from all earlier ones.'[4]

Rhetorical Revolution

A further hundred years on, following a century filled with indescribable horrors and two world wars, no elite anywhere on the planet, whatever their practice and private thinking, would dare to proclaim openly that the masses existed for *their* benefit. In earlier eras the privileges of wealth and property in the context of scarcity could be accepted and defended, as there was 'no alternative'; in the context of abundance they could not.

All ruling elites were compelled now to insist that their objectives were fundamentally altruistic, aiming to ensure not merely the satisfaction of basic necessities but to enhance consumption availability and general welfare throughout society. Whether the rulers were liberals, conservatives, social democrats, communists, neoliberals or even fascists,[5] that theme at least was similar, the proponents of each ideology postulating that theirs was the preferred manner of achieving such ends. This transition amounted to a world revolution in rhetoric if certainly not in practice.

Limited though that is, it still represents progress in the positive sense. The cruelties and elite arrogance of past centuries which used to be taken for granted are now no longer found to be ideologically acceptable, even though still hypocritically prevalent behind closed doors. Again, among a significant minority of the world population partial steps have been taken along the road of emancipation, in standards of nutrition, dwelling space, effective medical interventions and longevity, education, gender equality, lessening of sexual and social restrictiveness and authoritarian childrearing practices. Not that any of these advances happened smoothly, purely in consequence of the passage of time. They were accomplished only by intense effort and struggle, through resistance to exploiters, obscurantists and their power structures, and at the cost of much sacrifice and many casualties. A working-class inhabitant of an industrial British city of the 1840s, if transported to the 1960s, would indeed on first impressions imagine that they had arrived in Utopia – clean streets, no smoke pall, everyone of all ages adequately fed, clothed and shod, not a beggar to be seen anywhere, nor a rickety child.

All of these advances remain under threat and active efforts to reverse some of them are in hand – for supposedly unavoidable reasons of course. Bankers stuffed with bonuses take off in their private jets to preach austerity to everyone else. Nor are the improvements without their underside. The enhancement of material comfort all too easily slides into the accumulation of stuff; the loosening of social fetters into the pursuit of immediate sensation with consequent growth in such phenomena as pornography, obsessive addiction to computer games, the dangerous levels of drug use and suchlike.

As pointed out in Chapter One, humans have permanently the potential to be other than they are and as a universal attribute are unavoidably projecting themselves mentally towards a future different from the present they occupy, but any such individual project has to occur within a social framework. Very naturally as a rule that framework is taken for granted, and historical change as it occurs happens behind the back of the individuals involved,[6] emerging from the clash of contrary projects, mostly those of elite groupings and individuals – and with unanticipated outcomes thanks to the dialectic of unintended consequences.

The project was envisaged in the nineteenth century of directed social transformation brought about by deliberate intent. This would break the five-thousand-year cycle of ambitious rival social elites expanding their area of authority, overreaching themselves and suffering political collapse, to be succeeded by a new set of rulers of a similar sort, while popular masses lived on the verge of subsistence in a culture saturated with fear and falsehood. The objective of human emancipation, of replacing that cycle with what used to be called the cooperative commonwealth, of annulling deprivation, repression and superstitions which justified social abominations, could indeed only emerge when technology and social reorganisation had transformed the global pattern of production, distribution and consumption, that is, only in the past two centuries or so.

History on Our Side?

The servants of that project (they used to be called revolutionaries but the name is now unfashionable) were necessarily and inevitably a minority, usually a rather small one, in any of the societies they aspired to overturn. The majority of the citizens they wanted to win over very understandably preferred to get on with their own lives involving individual or limited collective projects and avoiding the risks involved in declaring political (or even real) war upon the authorities – unless the times were very critical, in which case the advocates of really serious change might hope to gain a hearing.

The more usual state of affairs has been for revolutionaries or would-be revolutionaries not only to be faced with the hostility of ruling elites but to be met with indifference or antagonism from their intended constituency. Consequently they then tend to fall into fragmentation, accompanied by mutual hostility among the differing groupings as they quarrel over the most effective way to proceed and, supposing that to be found, over what the intended social outcome ought to look like. Such disputes can turn lethal. 'Happiness is a new idea in Europe', declared Saint-Just the Jacobin – in March 1794 at the height of the revolutionary Terror. These failures and furies have proved to be the most powerful weapon in the arsenal of reactionaries committed to social structures of inequality and injustice, enabling them to argue that any serious attempt to improve the public condition by upsetting these structures will result only in its worsening.

One conclusion which can be reached is that the proponents of emancipation have up to now gravely underestimated the timescales involved in their project, not to mention the severity of the obstacles in the way and the setbacks likely to be encountered (although Marx, somewhat contradictory to his own perspectives at other times, was to stress this point as far back as 1852). The social muck of a hundred centuries cannot imaginably be cleared away in a mere two hundred years – it is necessarily a much longer undertaking stretching over many more generations. A historically informed appreciation of the obstacles involved, and the mistakes made previously in attempting to overcome them, are essential to the continuation of the project. In the past, proponents of emancipatory social change were in the habit of consoling themselves for frustrations and setbacks with the slogan that 'History is on our side!' Although it has seemed of late that the very reverse must be true, nonetheless that belief is not wholly without foundation, though its truth is of a very ambiguous sort. The reality is that at terrible suffering and social cost throughout history, which would never have been voluntarily chosen, the preconditions for emancipation have nevertheless been generated – but it will not come spontaneously.

In the past two centuries, roughly every half century, fundamental change has occurred in technology and consequent social organisation, the latest being in the character of electronic communication, which has created linkages on an unprecedented scale over the globe in a manner previously unimaginable and exceeding every previous advance, from sailing ships to radio.[7] The outcome in the recent past has been that although enormous changes in economic and social life continue to happen behind the backs of global populations, political structures lag behind and remain relatively unchanging. In the past several decades indeed they have gone into reverse so that predatory capitalism under the aegis of the hyper-wealthy in all regions of the globe, becomes ever more firmly entrenched and penetrates into every crevice of social and cultural praxis. To quote Graeber once more: '[T]he last thirty years have seen the construction of a vast bureaucratic apparatus for the creation and maintenance of hopelessness, a giant machine designed, first and foremost, to destroy any sense of possible alternative futures. . . those who challenge existing power arrangements can never, under any circumstances be perceived to win.'[8]

All that is bad enough, but the reality, as indicated above, is even worse. The world is faced with an immediate and enormously perilous crisis. The concentration of resources at one social pole with consequent impoverishment and indigence for vast numbers on our 'planet of the slums' in Mike Davis's phrase is happening in the context of what Elizabeth Ermarth describes as 'an over-populated, under-hydrated, lethally warming planet'[9] and she might have added, with dying oceans in which the jellyfish are taking over; the 'direct result of the externalization of costs by capitalist entrepreneurs. . .'.[10]

The accelerating environmental crisis lacks the dramatic character of Hitler's Wehrmacht poised on the frontier, or superpower leaders a few hours away from unleashing nuclear Armageddon, but the reality is no less perilous, merely less immediate and evident. Writing in the 1970s on the nuclear threat, Jonathan Schell, in *The Fate of the Earth*, invited us to imagine how we would feel if we knew that we and our existing relatives would live out our lives comfortably, but a century after the last of these died, our species would be extinct. We would be desolated and demoralised – evidently our concerns, whatever our status of wealth or education, extend far beyond our own lifetimes.

Still on the Agenda

The overriding issue for the centuries ahead and the present century in particular – far surpassing the murderous regime conflicts of the current decades, important though these are – is whether the ultimate results of the second great human transformation are to be positive or negative. A favourable outcome is imaginable only with clear and realistic appreciation of how threatening the situation has become. That has to be combined with imagination and vision beyond our own lifespan in order to guide the means of addressing the crisis, balancing of environmental necessities against lifestyle aspirations, and all the effort and inevitable sacrifices required to do so.[11] It can be done, but the effort will have to be prodigious, especially considering the billions currently living in deprivation and anxious to win their share of the potentialities of industrial growth.

The reality to be confronted has been forcibly emphasised by the 2014 reports of the International Panel on Climate Change. These reports likewise point to the initiatives necessary to deal with the central feature of the environmental crisis, human generated global warming, which is also a significant contributor to the second main issue, species destruction both animal and vegetable. Accepting the inevitability of environmental cataclysm (with the despairing hope that something might be saved from the wreckage) is neither necessary nor appropriate. In the words of the editorial title in *New Scientist*, commenting on the IPCC report, 'Resistance is not futile'.[12] International cooperation is unquestionably essential, and that of course will not come about of its own accord but only under determined and relentless pressure from all manner of environmentally conscious organisations around the world.

That has to be the immediate human priority, but no less importantly the emancipatory agenda of the nineteenth and twentieth centuries remains on the table, and the effort to save the human world can still be made to morph into a determination to improve it. A challenging project to be sure, but not an impossible one. As the great seventeenth-century philosopher Spinoza once remarked, 'All good things are difficult'.

Notes

Introduction

1. Neil MacGregor, *A History of the World in 100 Objects*, Allen Lane, London, 2010, p.186.
2. Daniel Lord Smail, *On Deep History and the Brain*, University of California Press, 2008, p.199.
3. See Curtis W Marean, 'When the Sea Saved Humanity', *Scientific American*, August 2010, pp.41–7.
4. Peter J Richardson and Robert Boyd, 'The Pleistocene and the Origins of Human Culture: Built for Speed', www.des.ucdavis.edu/faculty/Richerson/Speed.htm.

Chapter One

1. Hominins include both modern and extinct humans, along with those species of proto-humans which evolved subsequent to the species which was ancestral to both modern chimpanzees and modern humans.
2. One theoretical perspective holds that there may have been multiple universes generated at that point or previous to it.
3. It appears likely that around two million years ago 'our' galaxy's central black hole went through an unusual burst of energetic activity. The earth however was too distant to be affected.
4. The verse, by A P Herbert, appeared in *Punch* on 3 November 1920. The complete poem can be found at www.gutenberg.org/files/17994/17994–h/17994–h.htm.
5. Eukaryotes, such as the amoeba, are the complex cells with a nucleus controlling their behaviour and other characteristics (such as the mitochondria which generate their energy) and are the basic building blocks of multicellular animals, plants and fungi. Though mostly microscopic, they are much larger than the simpler bacteria and archaea, which are without any nucleus.
6. 'Kingdom' and 'domain' in this sense are simply classification terms.
7. There is even a suggestion that viruses may have been a necessary organic catalyst for the evolution of structured multicellular organisms. Ken Steadman, 'The forgotten extraterrestrials', *New Scientist* 21–28 December 2013, pp.42–3.
8. Again, phylum is a biological classification. It is based on body plan and comprises all vertebrates; other phyla are, for example, molluscs, worms and arthropods.
9. Neanderthal brains were actually equivalent to or even larger than those of modern humans.
10. Mammals are the only synapsids surviving today, as birds are the only dinosaurs.
11. Some others like kangaroos and gerbils move on their hind limbs, but these hop rather than walk.
12. Donald V Kurtz, 'Gender, Genes, Enculturation: The Origin of Culture and Becoming Human', *Social Evolution & History*, Vol. 8, No. 2, September 2009. p.58.

13. A bear has been observed to use a stone to scratch itself. Otters frequently employ stones, which they can clutch in their webbed paws, to crack shellfish.

14. Again research has shown that non-human social animals have systems of audible signalling (which may even have 'cultural' variations) but these cannot reasonably be defined as 'language' in any meaningful sense.

15. The evolution of the louse for example, can be used to track alterations in hominins' hairiness.

16. Ingfi Chen, 'Hidden Depths', *New Scientist*, 12 October 2013, pp.33–7.

17. Or even that it is an illusion, but as someone has pointed out, the difference between consciousness and the illusion of consciousness appears illusory.

18. There is a simple experiment that anyone can try to make the point. When crossing a busy road one looks both ways – first to the right if one lives in the UK, to the left in most other countries. Try doing it in the reverse order – it is actually very difficult, reflex pulls one's head in the accustomed direction. In Occupied France a British agent was detected by the Gestapo because she looked the wrong way.

19. Colin Renfrew, *Prehistory: The Making of the Human Mind*, 2007, Phoenix, London, 2008, p.115.

20. Derek Denton, *The Primordial Emotions: The Dawning of Consciousness*, Oxford University Press, 2005.

21. *Ibid.*, p.84.

22. *Ibid.*, pp.107–9.

23. *Ibid.* p.50.

24. Kent Flannery & Joyce Marcus, *The Creation of Inequality: How Our Prehistoric Ancestors Set the Stage for Monarchy, Slavery and Empire*, Harvard University Press, 2012, p.58.

25. Even quite far down the evolutionary scale, as far as invertebrates, animals can, at whatever level of consciousness, recognize patterns. Black and yellow colouring for example, indicates that the animal is undesirable to eat, and imitation versions have evolved as a camouflage.

Chapter Two

1. One of them being the recently–identified Denisovans discovered in Siberia.

2. Christopher Boehm, *Moral Origins: The Evolution of Virtue, Altruism and Shame*, Basic Books, New York, 2012, p.135.

3. Jared Diamond, *Guns, Germs and Steel: The Fates of Human Societies*, W W Norton & Co, New York, 1997, pp.297–8.

4. *Ibid.*, pp.312–3.

5. *Ibid.*, p.16.

6. The Greek, Latin Celtic, Slavonic and Germanic languages all belong to the Indo-European group. The Finnish and Magyar (Hungarian) belong to the Uralic family, though the origins of their respective populations are very different.

7. Thus, Polynesian island societies differed greatly in their economic specialization, social complexity, political organization, and material products, related to differences in population size and density, related in turn to differences in island area, fragmentation, and isolation and in opportunities for subsistence and for intensifying food production. All those differences among Polynesian societies

developed, within a relatively short time and modest fraction of the Earth's surface, as environmentally related variations on a single ancestral society. Those categories of cultural differences within Polynesia are essentially the same categories that emerged everywhere else in the world.

Diamond, *Guns, Germs and Steel*, p.65.

8. Neil MacGregor, *A History of the World in 100 Objects*, Allen Lane, London, 2010, p.19.
9. Volcanic eruption is also suspected of responsibility for the European medieval 'little ice age'.
10. Chris Brown, *New Archaeology*, www.newarchaeology.com/articles/uprevolution.php.
11. Kent Flannery & Joyce Marcus, *The Creation of Inequality: How Our Prehistoric Ancestors Set the Stage for Monarchy, Slavery and Empire*, Harvard University Press, 2012, p.7. The Netsilik are an Inuit people.
12. *Ibid.*, p.18.
13. By George Thomson in *Aeschylus and Athens*, Lawrence & Wishart, London, 1946.

Chapter Three

1. Colin Renfrew, *Prehistory: The Making of the Human Mind*, 2007, Phoenix, London, 2008, p.71.
2. Literally, 'Middle Stone Age' – the (relatively) short era between the glaciation and the origins of agricultural practice.
3. '. . . the sacred was deftly translated into a secular key: the Garden of Eden became the irrigated fields of Mesopotamia, and the creation of man was reconfigured as the rise of civilization', Daniel Lord Smail, *On Deep History and the Brain*, University of California Press, 2008, p.4.
4. Jared Diamond, *Guns, Germs and Steel: The Fates of Human Societies*, W W Norton & Co, New York, 1997, p.86.
5. Literally 'New Stone Age', originally named from the more aesthetic appearance of stone tools; now associated with the original development of agricultural practices.
6. Emmer is still grown, mostly in Italy, but is now a marginal crop.
7. In all mammals and still among some humans, the gene which adapts them to their mother's milk switches off after weaning.
8. Ernest Gellner, *Plough, Sword and Book: The Structure of Human History*, Paladin, London, 1988, p.33.
9. Diamond, *Guns, Germs and Steel*, p.105.
10. There is some evidence of what might be called rudimentary agricultural practice far back in the deep Palaeolithic. Before 50,000 years ago the humans living around the Klasies river mouth in South Africa appear to have learned to burn vegetation in order to procure larger outputs of edible tubers the following year. According to anthropologists Kent Flannery and Joyce Marcus '. . . some early humans had learned not merely how to take food out of the environment but to engineer the environment itself', *The Creation of Inequality*, p.7.
11. Diamond, *Guns, Germs and Steel*, p.329.
12. '. . . in Imperial Egypt water legislation was rudimentary and locally administered, there was no centralised irrigation bureaucracy', Michael Mann, *The Sources of Social Power,*

Volume 1: A History of Power from the Beginning to AD 1760, Cambridge University Press, 2012, p.96.

13. *Ibid.*, p.46.

14. Diamond, *Guns, Germs and Steel*, p.29.

15. *Ibid.*, p.139.

16. *Ibid.*, p.141.

17. If the corpse is well enough preserved then dietary evidence can even be available.

18. Diamond, *Guns, Germs and Steel*, p.14.

19. 'Aboriginal hunter-gatherers of northeastern Australia traded for thousands of years with farmers of the Torres Strait Islands, between Australia and New Guinea. California Native American hunter-gatherers traded with Native American farmers in the Colorado River valley. In addition, Khoi herders west of the Fish River of South Africa traded with Bantu farmers east of the Fish River', Diamond, *Guns, Germs and Steel*, p.105.

20. And not only humans – reindeer have been known to seek out intoxicating plants.

21. Smail, *On Deep History and the Brain*, lays a lot of emphasis on this.

Chapter Four

1. The reproductive season can be very short, as notoriously with pandas, or stretch over many months of the year.

2. Homosexual behaviour for example has been reported in around 1,500 different species.

3. Donald V Kurtz, 'Gender, Genes, Enculturation: The Origin of Culture and Becoming Human', *Social Evolution & History*, Vol. 8 No. 2, September 2009. p.57.

4. *Ibid.*, pp.56–7.

5. *Ibid.*, p.64.

6. For example Engels, in *The Origins of the Family, Private Property and the State* (1884).

7. Even today in certain parts of the USA marriage between cousins remains a criminal offence.

8. This cultural practice applies overwhelmingly to women, but not always or only.

9. Simone de Beauvoir, *The Second Sex*, trans. H M Parshley, Picador, London, 1988, pp.86–8.

10. Terminologically 'harem', an Arabic term, does not necessarily mean a collection of concubines, but it has taken on that meaning in Western culture.

11. Celibacy, which means abstention from marriage, is distinguished from chastity, which is abstention from sex, though the confusion is prevalent nowadays. The issue is further complicated by the fact that chastity could also mean sex within marriage if undertaken strictly for procreational and not recreational purposes.

12. Matthew 6:34.

13. *Ibid.*

14. See Peter Brown, *Through the Eye of a Needle: Wealth, the Fall of Rome and the Making of Christianity in the West 350–550 AD*, Princeton University Press, 2012, p.439.

15. Stephanie Coontz, *London Review of Books*, 26 April 2012, p.12.

16. Anastasia Banschikova, 'Woman in Ancient Egypt: Evolution of Personal and Social Positions', *Social Evolution & History*, Vol. 5, No. 1, 2006, p.109.

17. *Ibid.*, p.123.

18. George Thomson, *Aeschylus and Athens*, Lawrence & Wishart, London, 1946, p.293.

19. In pre-modern Christendom marital issues were the province of church courts.

20. An example was nineteenth-century English divorce law. A husband could divorce his wife for adultery but this was not the case *vice-versa*.

21. http://listverse.com/2010/11/14/10–ancient–methods–of–birth–control/.

22. In many states of the USA a remarkable range of 'unnatural' sex remains legislatively proscribed, though these laws are mostly dead letters.

23. David T Evans *Sexual Citizenship: The Material Construction of Sexualities*, Routledge, London, 1993.

24. It has been suggested that because traditionally marriage was not an option for gay men their unions were of a much more innovative sort in all manner of ways, and that this provided the template for heterosexual sexual liberation in the later twentieth century.

25. Jared Diamond, *Guns, Germs and Steel: The Fates of Human Societies*, W W Norton & Co, New York, 1997, p.277.

Chapter Five

1. Thus for Joe Kennedy it was wholly insufficient to be a very wealthy member of the topmost US elite and ambassador to the UK – one of his sons must become President.

2. And not only in foraging societies. In the egalitarian peasant culture of rural Shetland in which I grew up this technique was widely employed.

3. Christopher Boehm, *Moral Origins: The Evolution of Virtue, Altruism and Shame*, Basic Books, New York, 2012, p.317.

4. *Ibid.* p.327.

5. Kent Flannery & Joyce Marcus, *The Creation of Inequality: How Our Prehistoric Ancestors Set the Stage for Monarchy, Slavery and Empire*, Harvard University Press, 2012, p.33.

6. Flannery and Marcus, *The Creation of Inequality*, pp.17–18.

7. *Ibid.*, p.121.

8. Michael Mann, *The Sources of Social Power, Volume 1: A History of Power from the Beginning to AD 1760*, Cambridge University Press, 2012, p.70 (italics in original).

9. This form of social evolution is examined at length by Flannery and Marcus in relation to the Pacific island groups.

10. Mann, *The Sources of Social Power, Volume 1*, p.38.

11. Flannery & Marcus, *The Creation of Inequality*, p.412.

12. 'Dei Gratia' or simply 'DG'.

13. During their lifetimes sacrifice were made to their genius rather than their persons.

14. David Graeber, *Debt: The First 5000 Years*, Melville House, New York, 2012, p.198.

15. *Ibid.*, pp.235–6.

16. The iceman was murdered, shot in the back with an arrow. Why his killer or companions should have left untouched the very useful equipment he carried with him remains a matter of speculation.

17. It can also be modified by addition of further elements such as arsenic.

18. Hesiod was a literate small landowner, to whom we owe much of our knowledge of Greek mythology. He also complains bitterly about the rigours of agricultural work and management and elite attitudes.

19. The aftermath of the Santorini volcanic eruption may also be implicated here.

20. Mann, *The Sources of Social Power, Volume 1*, p.191.

21. During the Bronze Age epoch Egypt had been the regional superpower.

22. More strictly, neo-Assyrian. The original Assyrian empire was a Bronze Age polity.

23. In the neo-Assyrian period the capital was later moved, eventually to Nineveh, but Assur remained the religious centre of the empire.

24. Mann, *The Sources of Social Power, Volume 1*, p.234.

25. *Ibid.*, pp.262–3. Mann also cites a Spartan tyrant addressing a Roman general (according to the historian Livy), 'Your wish is that a few should excel in wealth, and the common people should be subject to them'. *Ibid.* p.269.

26. *Ibid.*, p.145.

27. How prostitution could function in the absence of a monetary economy is rather puzzling in terms of defining and measuring the medium of exchange.

28. The victims were with one exception all adult males, and their diet, which can be analysed, show them to have been of high social rank. Human sacrifice was a common practice in all historic cultures, but whether that ever involved the actual ruler as victim is less certain.

29. In Iceland the Viking settlers, though they were certainly class divided, prevented a monarchy from emerging.

30. Perry Anderson, *Passages from Antiquity to Feudalism*, NLB, London, 1974, p.116. The Vandal tribal coalition had passed through Gaul to Spain and then across to North Africa where they established their kingdom in what is now Tunisia and northern Algeria.

31. '*Mana* is an incorporeal supernatural force that energizes people and things, conferring efficacy upon them', http://what–when–how.com/social–and–cultural–anthropology/mana–anthropology/.

32. Flannery & Marcus, *The Creation of Inequality*, p.206.

33. This was not unusual. With the following two kings the position became one of high standing.

34. James VI and I, surveying the magnificent residence built by his treasurer out of the profits of his office remarked sardonically that the building was much too grand for a king but might possibly do for a treasurer.

35. The Japanese empire has been unusually fortunate in this respect, with the dynasty continuing for centuries without any break in the succession.

36. Numerous texts, attest to this. See especially Ian Kershaw, *Hitler 1936–1945: Nemesis*, Allen Lane, London, 2000.

37. Amusingly analysed by Anthony Jay in *Management and Machiavelli*, Penguin, Harmondsworth, 1967.

38. Female absolute monarchs in Europe were rare, but not wholly unknown – in the Russian empire the Empresses Elizabeth and Catherine were effective, and in the latter case famous, rulers. Maria Theresa fulfilled a similar role in the Austrian dominions, though with less personal scandal. In China the only female who was formally emperor, Wu Zetian in the seventh century, was disparaged for her attempts at reforming the imperial system.

39. They also claimed a mystic power to cure scrofula by touching the patient.

40. Extensively discussed in Mann, *The Sources of Social Power, Volume 1*.

41. Tributes for his 70th birthday continued to appear in the Soviet newspapers for an entire year.
42. See 'Communism and the Leader Cult', title of *Twentieth Century Communism: A Journal of International History*, No. 1, Lawrence & Wishart, London, 2009. This discusses leader cults in non-ruling communist parties.
43. *Ibid.*, p.10.

Chapter Six

1. Ideology here is understood as 'an interconnected system or structure of basic belief applicable to particular social or cultural collectives – one which incorporates conscious beliefs, assumptions, unthinking modes of perception – through which its adherents view the world around them, the interactions and the life processes in which they are engaged'. W. Thompson, *Ideologies in the Age of Extremes*, 2011, p.1.
2. Lenin's early text *What is to be Done?* is largely concerned with this issue.
3. David Graeber, *Debt: The First 5000 Years*, Melville House, New York, 2012, p.258.
4. Kent Flannery & Joyce Marcus, *The Creation of Inequality: How Our Prehistoric Ancestors Set the Stage for Monarchy, Slavery and Empire*, Harvard University Press, 2012, p.557.
5. Michael Mann, *The Sources of Social Power, Volume 1: A History of Power from the Beginning to AD 1760*, Cambridge University Press, 2012, p.54.
6. *Ibid.*, p.123.
7. G E M de Ste Croix, *The Class Struggle in the Ancient Greek World*, Duckworth, London, 1983, p.230.
8. George Thomson, *Aeschylus and Athens*, Lawrence & Wishart, London, 1946, p.149.
9. The most comprehensive analysis is to be found in Ste. Croix, *The Class Struggle in the Ancient Greek World*.
10. See his *Framing the Early Middle Ages*, Oxford University Press, 2005.
11. Graeber, *Debt*, p.90.
12. *Ibid.*, p.120.
13. *Ibid.*, p.119.
14. *Ibid.* p.5.
15. Slaves, particularly slave girls also served as a currency unit of account, a practice which the Vikings used extensively.
16. In the case of British banknotes explicitly so, where the bank still promises to 'pay the bearer on demand'.
17. Graeber, *Debt*, p.52.
18. *Ibid.*. p.129.
19. *Ibid.*, p.199.
20. *Ibid.*, p.187.
21. A Roman practice was to kill all the slaves of an owner if one of them had killed him.
22. A rural rebellion movement drawing on various elements of the dispossessed and exploited. It may possibly be the origin of the word 'Hebrew'.
23. John Pickard, *Behind the Myths: The Foundations of Judaism, Christianity and Islam*, Author House, Bloomington, Indiana, 2013, pp.22–4.
24. According to Marc Mulholland, *Bourgeois Liberty and the Politics of Fear: From Absolutism to Neo-Conservatism*, Oxford University Press, 2012: ' . . . in Britain and America, bourgeois civil society was expansive, confident, and thus securely liberal . . . Liberal

consumerism, therefore, implied a pact of sorts with organised labour', p.207. Dramatic examples of such violence, both state and private, used by employers in the USA against their workforces are noted in Michael Mann, *Sources, Volume 2* and *Volume 3*. Maurice Dobb writing in the 1940s drew explicit parallels with fascism.

25. Mann, *Sources, Volume 1*, p.48. See also Jared Diamond, *The World until Yesterday*, Penguin, London, 2012, Chapter 3, 'A Short Chapter, About a Tiny War'.

26. Not all monarchs had a fixed capital, the Scottish ones for example did not become established at Edinburgh before the fourteenth century. In areas with a poor supply system it was easier to move the court to the food rather than vice versa.

27. The Gatling was not wholly automatic, as the feed mechanism had to be hand cranked.

28. E J Hobsbawm *Primitive Rebels*, 1959; *Bandits*, 1966.

29. The KGB uniform was indistinguishable from the military, apart from their collar patches.

30. And also forbade them to grind their own corn and bake their own flour but instead to use the lord's mill and oven.

31. The pagan Lithuanian monarchy however possessed the best artillery in fourteenth-century Europe.

32. The Stanford Prison Experiment of 1971 demonstrated vividly the manner in which social pressure and social expectation could generate sadistic attitudes among previously normal individuals. Volunteers acted as guards or as prisoners in a mock prison and quickly and spontaneously developed exaggerated versions of the brutality and traumatisation routine in normal prisons. The experiment had to be discontinued for fear of severe psychological damage. Clearly social context is very important, but can scarcely be the whole story.

Chapter Seven

1. David Graeber, *Debt: The First 5000 Years*, Melville House, New York, 2012, p.90.

2. For example, 'The Tao is infinite, eternal. Why is it eternal? It was never born; thus it can never die. Why is it infinite? It has no desires for itself; thus it is present for all beings' (http://taoism.net/articles/mason/ethics.htm).

3. The Australian Aboriginal 'pointing the bone' is a striking example of this.

4. 'Given the number of the faithful who believe in a literal interpretation of the holy word, this new injunction was likely to cause the odd misunderstanding. "(I am not repentant, my dear, I am merely obeying God's will.)"', Rick Gekoski 'The Wicked Bible: the perfect gift for collectors, but not for William and Kate'. www.theguardian.com/books/booksblog/2010/nov/25/wicked-bible-gift-william-kate.

5. A frequently used example in such discussions is to point out that it is morally imperative to lie in order to mislead a murderer looking for a victim; or killing in war, especially a 'just war'.

6. Christopher Boehm, *Moral Origins: The Evolution of Virtue, Altruism and Shame*, Basic Books, New York, 2012, p.337.

7. *Ibid.*, pp.98–9.

8. *Ibid.*, pp.19–20. The distinction is important, shame being the product of condemnation by others whose opinion is respected, guilt the result of self–condemnation by the person experiencing it.

9. *Ibid.*, p.135.

10. See E P Thompson, *Whigs and Hunters*, and Peter Linebaugh, *The London Hanged*.
11. In some states Sharia courts still co–exist with criminal courts, the former being mainly concerned to resolve family matters.
12. The United States is exceptional in that executions are employed in some parts of the country (individual states) and not others.
13. Derk Bodde and Clarence Morris, *Law in Imperial China*, Harvard University Press, Cambridge, Massachusetts, 1967, pp.30–46.
14. Michel Foucault, *Discipline and Punish: The Birth of the Prison*, Penguin, 1991 ('Supervise' might be more accurate than 'Discipline').
15. Editorial, *New Scientist*, 18 January 2014, p.3
16. Laura Spinney, *New Scientist*, 18 January 2014, p.3.
17. *Ibid.*

Chapter Eight

1. 'Over the past 5000 years, humanity has developed an array of religions, all of which have shared at least one basic feature. They have attempted to give some response to, some solace for the perceived material miseries of the world,' Immanuel Wallerstein, *Historical Capitalism*, Verso, London, 1983, p.117.
2. Jared Diamond, *The World Until Yesterday*, Penguin, London, 2012, p.328.
3. Ernest Gellner, *Plough, Sword and Book, the Framework of Human History*, Paladin, London, p.73.
4. Attempts which used to be popular to make spirits take material form in spiritualist séances proved particularly unconvincing, though spiritualist churches still exist.
5. Kent Flannery & Joyce Marcus, *The Creation of Inequality: How Our Prehistoric Ancestors Set the Stage for Monarchy, Slavery and Empire*, Harvard University Press, 2012, p.25.
6. *Ibid.*
7. For an interesting discussion see Henry Frankfort et al *Before Philosophy, the Intellectual Adventure of Ancient Man*, 1946. The argument is summarised in the form that the religions of Mesopotamia had an 'I–thou' relationship to natural phenomena; the Jews initiated an 'I–it' conception, for example, 'The heavens proclaim the glory of God', whereas for Egyptians and Babylonians the heavens *were* gods, while classical Greek philosophy desacralized and disenchanted the natural world altogether.
8. Michael Mann, *The Sources of Social Power, Volume 2: The Rise of Classes and Nation States 1760–1914*, Cambridge University Press, 2012, p7.
9. Michael Mann, *The Sources of Social Power: Volume 3: Global Empires and Revolution, 1890–1945*, Cambridge University Press, 2012, p.7.
10. Unearthed in the Middle East.
11. See Michael Scott, *Delphi: A History of the Centre of the Ancient World*, Princeton University Press, 2014.
12. A legendary example is of an extended family executed because its head had violated a divine command when Joshua captured Jericho.
13. George Thomson, *Aeschylus and Athens*, Lawrence & Wishart, London, 1946, p.144.
14. *Ibid.*, p.146.
15. *Ibid.*, pp.152–3.
16. Benedict Anderson, *Imagined Communities: Reflections on the Origin and Spread of Nationalism*, Verso, London, 1983, p.18.

17. Published as a Penguin Classic, Penguin, Harmondsworth, 2005.
18. http://encyclopedia2.thefreedictionary.com/Brahmanism. That this approach was not confined to Soviet writers however is suggested by an Indian title published not long afterwards, M Paliwahadana, *The Indra Cult as Ideology: A Clue to Power Struggle in Ancient Society*, 1981, http://dl.sjp.ac.lk/dspace/bitstream/123456789/399/1/The%20Indra%20Cult%20as.pdf.
19. Norman Cohn, *Cosmos, Chaos and the World to Come*, Yale University Press, 1993, p.57.
20. Indra, Ba'al, Yahweh, Zeus and Thor are all storm gods.
21. Michael Mann, *The Sources of Social Power, Volume 1: A History of Power from the Beginning to AD 1760*, Cambridge University Press, 2012, p.353.
22. Perry Anderson, *London Review of Books*, 2 August 2012, p.22.
23. And where the faith is growing again as, like Islam and for comparable reasons, it is embraced by the outcaste or Dalit communities.
24. The coincidental timing with the emergence of Greek philosophy has been noted and commented on but in this instance coincidental may simply mean coincidence.
25. Confucianism is not discussed at length here on account of the weakness of its supernatural element. Mann, *The Sources of Social Power, Volume 1*, p.343, comments that 'Confucianism was a marvellous instrument of imperial/class rule'.
26. According to Richard Baum, in *Social Evolution & History*, Vol. 3, No. 1, March 2004, p.52:

    In the hands of Confucian scholars from the Warring States period (403–221 B.C.) onward, the doctrine was stripped of much of its original spiritual premise of divine intervention in human affairs. Mencius (b. 372 B.C.), for example, argued that the will of heaven was manifested on earth only indirectly, through the will of the people; and he claimed that divine control over temporal affairs began and ended with heaven's act of investing the dynastic founder with political authority. In place of heavenly piety, Zhu Xi substituted his own agnostic conception of reverence, rooted in such this – worldly values as propriety (li) and filialty (xiao).

27. It's earliest, Palaeolithic phase, produced the world's oldest pottery.
28. A parallel can be observed in the action of the Bolshevik regime in 1921 when a loosening of state economic control compelled by critical circumstances was accompanied by a severe tightening up of political supervision and repression.
29. Kandahar in Afghanistan probably has the same meaning as Alexandria.
30. Gellner, *Plough, Sword and Book*, p.121.
31. Robin Lane Fox, *Pagans and Christians*, Penguin, Harmondsworth, 1988.

Chapter Nine

1. Norman Cohn, *Cosmos, Chaos and the World to Come*, Yale University Press, 1993, pp.77–104. (A Zoroastrian community still exists in the shape of the Indian Parsis.)
2. The name of the Vedic fire-god, Agni, is the root of the English word 'ignite'.
3. Cohn, *Cosmos, Chaos and the World to Come*, p.115.
4. *Ibid.*, pp.24–9.
5. Making up the biblical texts of Numbers and Deuteronomy.
6. See Robin Lane Fox, *The Unauthorized Version: Truth and Fiction in the Bible*, Viking, London, 1991.

7.   Cohn, *Cosmos, Chaos and the World to Come*, p.213.
8.   This aspect is discussed very informatively in Peter Brown's lengthy volume, *Through the Eye of a Needle: Wealth, the Fall of Rome and the Making of Christianity in the West: 320–550 AD*, Princeton University Press, 2012.
9.   An *Encyclopaedia of Heresies and Heretics* runs to over 350 pages and by no means gets near to including them all.
10. The current intensity of Sunni/Shia hostility, after the initial disputes, is a modern phenomenon. For centuries their difference was more akin to rival schools of Buddhism.
11. See Joyce E Salisbury, *The Blood of the Martyrs: Unintended Consequences of Ancient Violence*, Routledge, New York & London, 2004.
12. The emperor who initiated the change was Constantine. What tends to be described as his 'conversion' following victory against a rival claimant was less a conversion than the decision to identify the god he worshipped, *Sol Invictus* (the unconquered sun) with the god of the Christians, which is why the Christian holy day is Sunday rather than Saturday.
13. Named after Nestor, a fifth-century patriarch of Constantinople; they made a strong distinction between Christ's divine and human natures.
14. A remnant still continues in India.
15. Another major issue was Iconoclasm, when eighth-century Byzantine emperors tried to suppress the use of images in worship, strongly opposed by the Papacy.
16. See Geoffrey Barraclough, 'The Medieval Empire: Idea and Reality', Chapter 8 of *History in a Changing World*, Blackwell, Oxford, 1957.
17. One section of mainly US fundamentalists, adhering to what is termed Dominion theology, proclaims this openly and justifies it as absolutely necessary.
18. Saint Augustine's principal theological work, *The City of God*, was written in response to these accusations.
19. Regrettably this volume was completed too late to make use of the very interesting discussion by Suleiman Mourad, 'Riddles of the Book' in *New Left Review*, 2/86, March–April 2014, pp.15–52.
20. *Wall Street Journal*, 15 November 2008, http://online.wsj.com/news/articles/.
21. John Pickard, *Behind the Myths: The Foundations of Judaism, Christianity and Islam*, Author House, Bloomington, Indiana, 2013, p.318.
22. *Ibid.*, p.307.
23. The Qur'an, it is claimed, can only be interpreted with reference to the subsequently developed holy traditions, the Hadith.
24. A phrase coined by the commentator Richard J Hofstadter in 1964.
25. See Martin E Marty and R Scott Appleby (eds), *Fundamentalisms Observed*, the first volume of Fundamentalism Project, University of Chicago Press, 1991.

Chapter Ten

1.   Benedict Anderson, *Imagined Communities: Reflections on the Origin and Spread of Nationalism*, Verso, London, 1983, pp.25–6.
2.   Michael Mann, *The Sources of Social Power, Volume 1: A History of Power from the Beginning to AD 1760*, Cambridge University Press, 2012, p.208.
3.   Benedict Anderson gives a list of his titles, running to eleven lines of small print – yet includes by no means all of them.

4. Anderson, *Imagined Communities*, p.16.

5. *Ibid.*, pp.17–18.

6. Michael Mann, *The Sources of Social Power, Volume 2: The Rise of Classes and Nation States 1760–1914*, Cambridge University Press, 2012, p.732.

7. *Ibid.*, p.108.

8. Anderson, *Imagined Communities*, p.135.

9. Ironically, the Grand Inquisitor Tomás de Torquemada, whose principal office was to persecute Moriscos and Conversos, himself had a known element of Jewish descent. Ironically too, these statutes were abolished in the late nineteenth century when racism was flourishing throughout Europe.

10. The sixteenth century was more ambiguous. Shakespeare's plays have a black hero, Othello, and a black villain, Aaron.

11. Almost literally so. The chemical composition of blood throughout the animal kingdom is strikingly similar across all species.

12. Brought to notice particularly by Edward Said in his volume of that name.

13. Antisemites disagreed among themselves. Some argued that Jews were tolerable so long as they adhered to their traditional culture and made no sneaky effort to assimilate; others that the traditional communities were the ones to be hated, and assimilated Jews could fit in; still others that Jews were equally vicious whether assimilated or traditional.

14. See Norman Cohn, *Warrant for Genocide: The Myth of the Jewish World Conspiracy and the Protocols of the Elders of Zion*, Penguin, Harmondsworth, 1966.

15. The psychotic CIA chief James Jesus Angleton was highly embarrassed by his middle name, as it revealed his Spanish ancestry.

16. The French revolutionaries banned the use of the *ancien regime* 'Monsieur' or 'Madame' in formal address; everyone had to be addressed as 'Citoyen' or 'Citoyenne'.

17. See Jeremy Catto, 'Written English: The Making of the Language 1370–1400', *Past and Present*, No. 179, May 2003.

18. Though mutually hostile localisms may do so, as evidenced in the Arab world.

19. Attempts to invent a new universal one were actually based on Indo-European models, particularly Romance ones, and never got off the ground, or at most very haltingly, as with Esperanto.

20. In the Ukranian crisis of 2014, one charge against the parliamentary assembly in Kiev was that it voted to remove Russian from its equal position in the country.

21. University of California Press, 1995.

22. Contrast with the early decades of the twentieth century is striking, as crowd photos from that time reveal.

23. Apparently this is no longer used.

24. A medieval illustration of the twelfth-century Sicilian king William III being blinded and castrated shows him nevertheless wearing his crown.

25. In England these have to be ratified by an archaic institution, the College of Arms (founded by Richard III) and the Lyon Court in Scotland.

Chapter Eleven

1. Other Hellenistic successor empires had fallen apart and were dominated by Roman power.

2. By the time they took over portions of the empire they had been deeply influenced by it – for example they were all Christians.
3. See https://contagions.wordpress.com/2011/11/26/did–india–and–china–escape–the–black–death/.
4. Trade links were certainly influenced – for example papyrus disappeared on the northern shores of the Mediterranean.
5. Michael Mann, *The Sources of Social Power, Volume 1: A History of Power from the Beginning to AD 1760*, Cambridge University Press, 2012, p.292.
6. Michael Mann, *The Sources of Social Power, Volume 2: The Rise of Classes and Nation States 1760–1914*, Cambridge University Press, 2012, p.394.
7. Langobardi or Longbeards.
8. Voltaire's joke was that it was neither holy, nor Roman, nor an empire.
9. Known formerly as the Wends and nowadays the Sorbs.
10. Perry Anderson, *Passages From Antiquity to Feudalism* and *Lineages of the Absolutist State*, NLB, London, 1974.
11. The importance of horse collars was that earlier methods of yoking horses to carts or ploughs practically strangled the animal.

Chapter Twelve

1. Though some of these tried to ally with the newcomers against their own indigenous enemies.
2. Marie–Monique Huss, *Journal of Contemporary History*, Vol. 25, No. 1 (January 1990), pp.39–68.
3. See Mike Davis, *Late Victorian Holocausts: El Niño Famines and the Making of the Third World*, Verso, London, 2001, 'the greatest human tragedy since the Black Death'.
4. Michael Mann, *The Sources of Social Power: Volume 3: Global Empires and Revolution, 1890–1945*, Cambridge University Press, 2012, p.552.
5. The most notable participant in the debate was Earl J Hamilton with his key volume, *American Treasure and the Price Revolution in Spain, 1501–1650* of 1934.
6. See R N Salaman, *The History and Social Influence of the Potato*, Cambridge University Press, 1985 (second edition).
7. Around a third of a million ethnic Chinese currently live in South Africa.
8. See L J Satre, *Chocolate on Trial: Slavery, Politics, and the Ethics of Business*, Ohio University Press, 2005.
9. 'Asylum seeker' was originally a neutral term but has taken on negative connotations thanks to the endeavours of the tabloid press.
10. Immanuel Wallerstein, *Historical Capitalism with Capitalist Civilization*, Verso, London, 1983, pp.121–2.
11. Examined famously in the 1840s by Henry Mayhew in *London Labour and the London Poor* and Friedrich Engels in *The Condition of the Working Class in England*.
12. Mike Davis, *Planet of Slums*, Verso, London, 2006.
13. With reference to the 'Trail of tears' see James Wilson, *The Earth Shall Weep: A History of Native America*, Grove Press, New York, 1998.
14. Beneš, the Czech leader, wanted to make discriminations based on wartime behaviour, but his colleagues insisted on a total expulsion.

Chapter Thirteen

1. Michael Mann, *The Sources of Social Power, Volume 2: The Rise of Classes and Nation States 1760–1914*, Cambridge University Press, 2012, p.128.

2. Thomas D Hall, 'Mongols in World-Systems History, *Social Evolution & History*, Vol. 4, No. 2, September 2005, p.111.

3. Michael Perlman in *Choice: Current Reviews for Academic Libraries*, 1999, reviewing Ellen Meiksins Wood's *The Origins of Capitalism: A Longer View*, Monthly Review Press, New York, 2002.

4. Marc Mulholland, *Bourgeois Liberty and the Politics of Fear. From Absolutism to Neo-Conservatism*, Oxford University Press, 2012, p.303.

5. This serfdom had been imposed early in the seventeenth century to secure a labour force in these vital industries.

6. Ellen Meiksins Wood, *The Pristine Culture of Capitalism: A Historical Essay on Old Regimes and Modern States*, Verso, 1991 p.11.

7. 'Fees' and wages were sharply distinguished; the first was honourable, the second demeaning.

8. The ferocity of this repression in the USA is examined at length by Michael Mann in *The Sources of Social Power, Volume 2*, pp.635–60.

9. http://leftspot.com/blog/?q=node/99.

10. Harvey J Kaye, *The British Marxist Historians: An Introductory Analysis*, Polity Press, Cambridge, 1984, p.46.

11. Henry Heller, *The Birth of Capitalism: A Twenty-First Century Perspective*, Pluto Press, London, 2011.

12. It was not such a safety measure as was claimed, as it provided an incentive for coal owners to try to exploit more dangerous seams.

13. The sewing machine, developed commercially in the 1840s is a good example, being powered by female human muscle in domestic workspaces.

14. Which is not necessarily true for twenty-first century forms.

15. At least one profitable water-powered cotton mill was operating in the early twentieth century.

16. They averaged around 5–10 per cent.

17. A significant incentive was to move troops speedily for repressive purposes, and in other countries also for warlike ones.

18. See especially Jack Goody, *The Theft of History*, Cambridge University Press, 2006.

19. The empire even invented moveable type as well during those centuries, but the complexity of the Chinese script made it impracticable to use. That raises the interesting speculation of whether the world today would look fundamentally different if that script had been an alphabetic one and printing in the modern sense been introduced to the world half a millennium before it happened in reality.

20. John M Hobson, *The Eastern Origins of Western Civilisation*, Cambridge University Press, 2004, p.5.

21. John A Hall, review of *The Eastern Origins of Western Civilization* in *English Historical Review*, Vol. CXIII No. 495, 2007.

22. Studying the multiple volumes of Joseph Needham's (unfinished!) masterpiece *Science and Civilisation in China* is almost a lifetime's project in itself. A handy digest of its most important elements with an introduction by Needham himself is Robert Temple's *The*

Genius of China: 3,000 Years of Science, Discovery and Invention, Inner Traditions, Rochester, Vermont, 2007.

23. Confucian ideology, with its emphasis on tradition and right behaviour, might also have presented an obstacle, but in western Europe the Catholic church was similarly placed, which did not stop capitalism from taking root there.

24. The science fiction writer Isaac Asimov envisaged in the 1950s an electronic library catalogue more or less identical to those now in use, and later on something not too different from Skype. His less renowned contemporary E C Tubb in at the same time imagined an ecologically-threatened world with an environmental movement termed 'The Greens'.

25. On at least two occasions, not counting the 1962 Cuba Crisis, only last-minute decisions by fairly junior controllers on either side saved the world from nuclear catastrophe.

26. Perry Anderson, *Imperium*, a special issue comprising *New Left Review*, second series, No.83, September–October 2013, p.33.

27. And not only during the first four decades. Between 1948 and 1990 the US secured the overthrow of at least 24 governments in Latin America, four by direct military intervention.

28. Anderson, *Imperium*, pp.34, 83.

29. Francis Fukuyama, *The End of History and the Last Man*, Penguin, London, 2012.

30. Anderson, *Imperium*, p.110.

Chapter Fourteen

1. Precedents existed in some of the earlier empires, particularly Assyria.

2. Balloons were used for military observation as early as the 1790s.

3. It has been suggested that an earlier form of syphilis in Europe may have been mistaken for leprosy.

4. The most common of those, as least in Europe, being bleeding.

5. A personal note. I myself would not exist but for appendectomy, which saved my father's life in his youth; while my mother died aged 31 of tuberculosis, just too early for antibiotics.

6. Commercial considerations retarded identification of the responsible drug.

7. Many nineteenth-century continental railways were indeed government-owned, even in market societies.

8. One of Gandhi's first defiances of the colonial power was to deliberately make salt by this method.

9. Lee R Kump, 'The Last Great Global Warming', *Scientific American,* July 2011, pp.40–45.

10. These were united through the crown only until 1707, and even afterwards kept their separate monetary establishments and banknotes, though not coinage.

11. David Graeber, *Debt: The First 5000 Years*, Melville House, New York, 2012, p.364.

Chapter Fifteen

1. One of the elite pagan complaints against Christianity was the lowly origin of some of its proponents.

2. Ellen Meiksins Wood, *Citizens to Lords: A Social History of Western Political Thought from Antiquity to the Middle Ages*, Verso, London, 2008, p.153.

3. This concept imagined that Anglo-Saxon England had been a comparatively egalitarian and humane society and that the Normans after 1066 had imposed a tyrannical one still in existence centuries later.

4. The Anabaptists were a socially radical sect named for their practice of rebaptising as adults already baptised infants.

5. They were alleged by their enemies to engage in all manner of sexual malpractices.

6. Arno Mayer, *The Furies: Violence and Terror in the French and Russian Revolutions*, Princeton University Press, 2000, p.96.

7. The guillotine itself illustrated the dialectic of unintended consequences. Intended as a humane instrument of execution it greatly multiplied the number of victims. If Henri Sanson had had to do his job by hand or the British method of slow strangulation been used, the public would most likely have revolted at the spectacle.

8. Mayer, *The Furies*, p.538.

9. Quoted in F A Hayek, *The Constitution of Liberty*, Routledge and Kegan Paul, London, 1960, p.509, n.1.

Chapter Sixteen

1. There were also idiosyncratic individuals aiming at similar results, such as Henry George.

2. The revolutionary socialist James Connolly, in his *Labour, Nationality and Religion* (1910) noted this point.

3. He was killed in a duel over a romantic, not a political, issue.

4. The term 'Communards' applied to the Parisian revolutionaries of 1871 did not mean 'Communists'.

5. For example the Labour Party in relation to India.

6. Isaac Deutscher 'The Unfinished Revolution' *New Left Review* 1/43, May/June 1967, pp.32–3, p.213.

7. The fact that Hitler's followers called themselves 'National Socialists' was indicative of the widespread popularity of the term.

8. At one point during the worst of the crisis even cannibalism was reported.

9. As a commander in the *Kaiserreich* explained to a junior officer, 'The Emperor made you an officer so that you would know which orders to disobey!'

10. See J Arch Getty and Oleg V Naumov, *The Road to Terror: Stalin and the Self-Destruction of the Bolsheviks, 1932–1939*, Yale University Press, 1939.

11. Edmund Wilson wrote in 1940 that, 'Marxism is in relative eclipse. An era in its history is ended', in *To the Finland Station: A Study in the Writing and Acting of History*.

12. The communist parties in France and, more so, Italy enjoyed much wider support and were correspondingly feared.

13. Marc Mulholland, *Bourgeois Liberty and the Politics of Fear: From Absolutism to Neo-Conservatism*, Oxford University Press, 2012, p.270.

14. Arno Mayer, *The Furies: Violence and Terror in the French and Russian Revolutions*, Princeton University Press, 2000, p.3.

Chapter Seventeen

1. Had he been familiar with Chinese history he might have selected one of their dynasties instead.

2. I have from time to time wondered whether the Garden of Eden legend might not incorporate a folk memory of a time when existence did not have to be secured through relentless toil. Adam's curse after all was to become an arable farmer, while Eve's might have related to an imaginary time when childbirth was safe and easy.

3. Karl Marx and Friedrich Engels, *The Communist Manifesto: A Modern Edition*, Verso, 1998, p.38.

4. *Ibid.*

5. Fascists, Nazis in particular, promised such advantages to their own nation or race at the expense of others.

6. Though not always. The social welfare programmes initiated in much of western Europe following the Second World War can be seen as an exception.

7. For example, international monetary transactions can be carried out in, literally, a fraction of a second.

8. David Graeber, *Debt: The First 5000 Years*, Melville House, New York, 2012, p.382.

9. Elizabeth Deeds Ermarth, *History in the Discursive Condition: Reconsidering the Tools of Thought*, Routledge, Abingdon, 2011, p.xii.

10. Immanuel Wallerstein, *Historical Capitalism with Capitalist Civilization*, Verso, London, 1983, p.130.

11. As I used to explain to my students back in the 1970s, our descendants will have to get used to a simpler lifestyle than the one we enjoy – which *need not* necessarily mean that it has to be a worse one.

12. *New Scientist*, 5 April 2014, p.5.

Index